The Spiritual Design

Wave 4

Books by Christine Kromm Henrie and David Henrie

Published by Access Soul Knowledge

The Spiritual Design, Channeled Teachings, Wave 1

The Spiritual Design, Channeled Teachings, Wave 2

Notes from the Second Dimension, Volume 1

Helig Design, Kanaliserade Budskap, Första Vågen (*Swedish*)

Helig Design, Kanaliserade Budskap, Andra Vågen (*Swedish*)

Notes from the Second Dimension, Volume 2

The Spiritual Design Wave 3

Memoarer Från Andra Dimensionen, Del 1 (*Swedish*)

Memoarer Från Andra Dimensionen, Del 2 (*Swedish*)

The Spiritual Design Wave 4

Books Scheduled for Publication in 2024 - 2025

The Spiritual Design Wave 5

Helig Design Tredje Vågen (*Swedish*)

The Spiritual Design

Wave 4

Christine Kromm Henrie

&

David Henrie, Sp.D.

Access Soul Knowledge
Stockholm, Sweden

Copyright © 2024 by Christine Kromm Henrie, David Henrie.

All rights reserved. No part of this book may be reproduced, stored in or introduced into an information storage or retrieval system, or transmitted in any form, or in any manner, including electronic, photographic, mechanical, recording, or otherwise, without prior written permission of the copyright owner. For information, please contact the author.

The Library of Congress has cataloged the paperback edition as follows
Names: Henrie, Christine Kromm | Henrie, David
Title: The spiritual design wave 4 /
      By Christine Kromm Henrie and David Henrie
Description: 394 pages ; 23 cm. | Access Soul Knowledge, 2024
Identifiers: LCCN 2024918119 | ISBN 9781951879174
Subjects BISAC: 1. BODY, MIND & SPIRIT—Afterlife & Reincarnation. |
        2. BODY, MIND & SPIRIT—Angels & Spirit Guides. |
        3. BODY, MIND & SPIRIT—Channeling & Mediumship
 Classification: •BF1275.D2 H-- 2024 | DDC 133.9'01'35—dc22
LC record available at https://lccn.loc.gov/2024918119
Other Formats Available:
      ISBN 9781951879181 (Kindle E-book Edition)
      ISBN 9781951879198 (EPUB Edition)
      ISBN 9781951879204 (Swedish Language Paperback Edition)
      ISBN 9781951879211 (Swedish Language Kindle E-book Edition)
      ISBN 9781951879228 (Swedish Language EPUB E-book Edition)

Editors: Kari Beckstrand | Susanne Kromm

Cover Art Design: David Henrie

Printed in the United States of America
First Edition
First Printing, September 2024

Access Soul Knowledge (Imprint)
Williamstown, West Virginia, USA & Stockholm, Sweden

DEDICATION

To the many spirits who have contributed to the Spiritual Design books, who patiently share their wisdom and compassion week after week without fail. They are our spiritual family, and we are honored to present their words. Our deepest gratitude is given to the true authors of these books, whom we know as: Ophelia, Bob, Jeshua, Isaac, Zachariah, Ari, Eli, Gergen, Ia, Setalay, the Elahim Council, the Council of Nine, the Tallocks, Ole, Willaby, and the multitude of other entities who are silent partners in this collaboration to make the Earth a better home.

~ Christine and David

CONTENTS

Page	Section
1	**The Sessions before 2020**
4	Bob: A Sacred Key of Creation (May 28, 2017)
9	Bob: Unity in the Councils (Apr 29, 2018)
10	Bob: Gravity is a Function of Light (May 6, 2018)
15	Tallocks, Ophelia: Waves of Transformation (Oct 14, 2018)
23	Tallocks, Ophelia: Qualities of Fish Tanks (Dec 31, 2018)
28	Tallocks, Ophelia: The Creator Disk (April 28, 2019)
36	Ophelia: Linear and Multiple Timelines (Sept 26, 2019)
39	Tallocks, Ophelia: Levels of Existence of Elements (Oct 13, 2019)
45	Teh, Ophelia: The Parallel Realities (Nov 9, 2019)
53	Bob: John 11 and the Bloodline of Yeshua (Nov 17, 2019)
58	Ari, Ophelia, Bob: Cycles and Polarity (Dec 1, 2019)
71	**The Sessions from 2020**
71	Bob: Native Shamans (Jan 1, 2020)
79	Bob: The Sleeping Oracle of Egypt (Jan 16, 2020)
89	Bob: The Zooming Device (Feb 13, 2020)
91	Bob: The AD 2178 Life Project (June 21, 2020)
101	Gergen, Ia, Bob: Earthquakes and Evolution (July 26, 2020)
115	Bob: The Astrology of Incarnation (Sept 2, 2020)
123	Bob: The Physics of Parallel Realities (Nov 1, 2020)
130	Ophelia, Bob: The Cave of Dinosaur Eggs (Nov 20, 2020)
144	Visitors from the Past (Mar 22, 2021)
146	VP, Ophelia, Bob: Mars and other Calamities (Jan 15, 2022)
159	Bob: The Highway of Life (Dec 31, 2020)
165	**The Sessions from 2021**
165	Tallocks: The Changing Ecosystem (Jan 7, 2021)
169	Bob: Sniffer and the Dinosaurs (Jan 7, 2021)
173	Bob: The Creation of the Fish Tanks (Jan 9, 2021)
176	Ophelia, Bob: Celestial Astrology (Jan 27, 2021)
187	Setalay: Finding Joy (Mar 7, 2021)
189	Bob: Helmet Friend at the Store (Mar 7, 2021)
195	Bob: The Creator's Hand (Mar 22, 2021)
203	Ophelia, Bob: The Unwinding and Crystal Energy (May 3, 2021)

Contents

212	Zachariah, Bob: The Grand Play (May 16, 2021)
220	Council of Nine: Highway of Humanity (June 24, 2021)
223	Koh, Bob: Filling the V–Shape (July 7, 2021)
236	The Merkaba and the Coat of Karma (Commentary)
239	Ophelia, Bob: Silence and Door 33 (July 28, 2021)
250	Bob: Sewing the Big Sheet (Aug 15, 2021)
257	Ontorio, Bob: Cosmic Time and Evolution (Aug 29, 2021)
273	Bob: Soul Intention versus Karma (Sept 7, 2021)
275	Bob: Epiphany (Sept 12, 2021)
291	Council of Nine: Falling or Flying? (Sept 23, 2021)
297	Bob: The Layer Cakes in the Wheel (Sept 23, 2021)
306	Ophelia, Bob: Becoming a Different Animal (Oct 4, 2021)
313	Gergen, Bob: Managing Expectations (Oct 20, 2021)
320	Klo: Hints on Free Energy Creation (Oct 31, 2021)
328	Bob: Rearranging Notes (Oct 31, 2021)
332	Eli, Leon, Bob: What are we Looking at? (Nov 29, 2021)
342	Ari, Ophelia, Bob: Blindfolds and Snowflakes (Dec 12, 2021)
348	Bob, Ophelia: Dreaming (Dec 24, 2021)
359	Willaby, Bob: The Library of Life Records (Mar 23, 2022)
378	*Acknowledgements*
379	*About the Authors*

Preface

This book, *The Spiritual Design Wave 4*, is the sixth book we have published, and is based exclusively on the messages delivered by various spiritual entities. The books themselves do not constitute separate waves of knowledge, but are part of a long and continuous exploration of reality that started in 2015 when Christine began trance channeling this project. The project, as our friends in spirit call it, is expected to take the remainder of our lives to finish. It is a retelling of creation from a purely spiritual perspective, uncontaminated and all–encompassing. Once the spirits started talking, the information came in such a torrent that we had to cut back on the frequency of sessions so I could catch up with the transcription, research and publishing. This *Wave 4* includes sessions through 2021, and *Wave 5* will contain sessions from 2022 and 2023. The channeling process and information about the spiritual entities are covered in great detail in our earlier books, so we feel no need to continually repeat that information. For the sake of brevity, we usually abbreviate the earlier books in the *Spiritual Design* series simply as *Wave 1*, *Wave 2*, or *Wave 3*, and the *Notes from the Second Dimension* series as either *Notes, Volume 1* or *Notes, Volume 2*.

Changes to Formatting. The sessions are now chronological for two very basic reasons. First, I took to heart something Bob said in July 2023. He was talking about himself and said it was important "to surrender your sensation of control and transform it into trust." In the same vein, I realized that Ophelia and our other spirit friends can organize the material much better than I can. Second, we are no longer separating some talks out to be published in the *Notes from the Second Dimension* series. Bob has become an integral speaker, and it is not helpful to push certain of his ideas off to the side, even though he is very proud to have his own journals. There may have been some benefit to the reader in the early publications when concepts were being introduced. But now, the long and thoughtful discourses delivered by our friends in spirit build one upon the other, session after session, so there is little reason to shuffle topics around. Before reaching that conclusion, 400 pages of material had been set aside for *Volume 3* of the *Notes* series. Those talks are now merged into this *Wave 4* and the upcoming *Wave 5*. The downside is that some topics, which were in the *Notes series*, have not been covered in any detail in the *Spiritual Design* books. We have tried to compensate for that by adding a little extra detail when those subjects first appear in these following sessions.

With all that being said, welcome to *Wave 4*. We hope you find the words of our spirit friends to be enlightening and uplifting.

David Henrie
Stockholm, Sweden
August 29, 2024

Wheel of Creation. This image is the conceptual structure of the Wheel. All spirits have a home somewhere in the spiritual dimensions, including everyone on Earth. To gain knowledge, they travel out into the universes of form, which are called "fish tanks" in our books. Aliens, for example, are also spiritual entities, but they

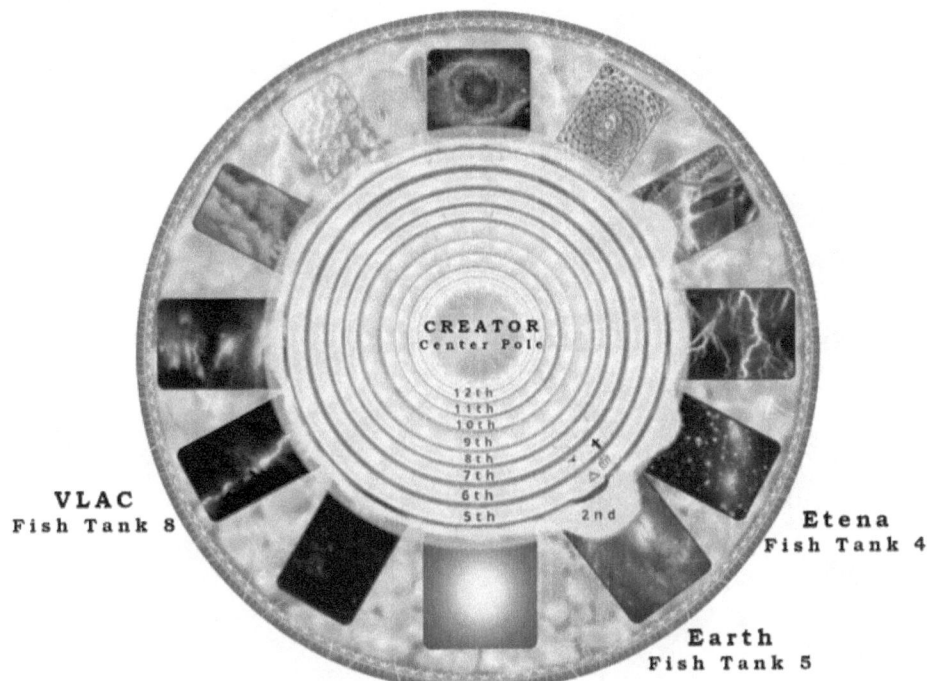

are occupying or manifesting a form on some other planet. Our Universe is contained within fish tank 5. The second dimension is a spiritual reality, but they are more closely associated with the many and varied life forms on Earth and elsewhere. The Creator Disk is part of the Wheel, but is beneath the fish tanks where experiences play out. Hidden from human perception are the parallel planes and lightways. Those are also within and part of the fish tanks. Advanced entities use those bands to travel between planets. The Master Mind and Big Eye form the upper boundary of the sandwich that makes up the Wheel of Creation. The originating intent comes from the Creator Disk. The resulting forms and activities within the fish tanks are then monitored by the Big Eye and influenced by the Master Mind and the spiritual dimensions. The Creator, of course, supplies the energy that makes it all possible.

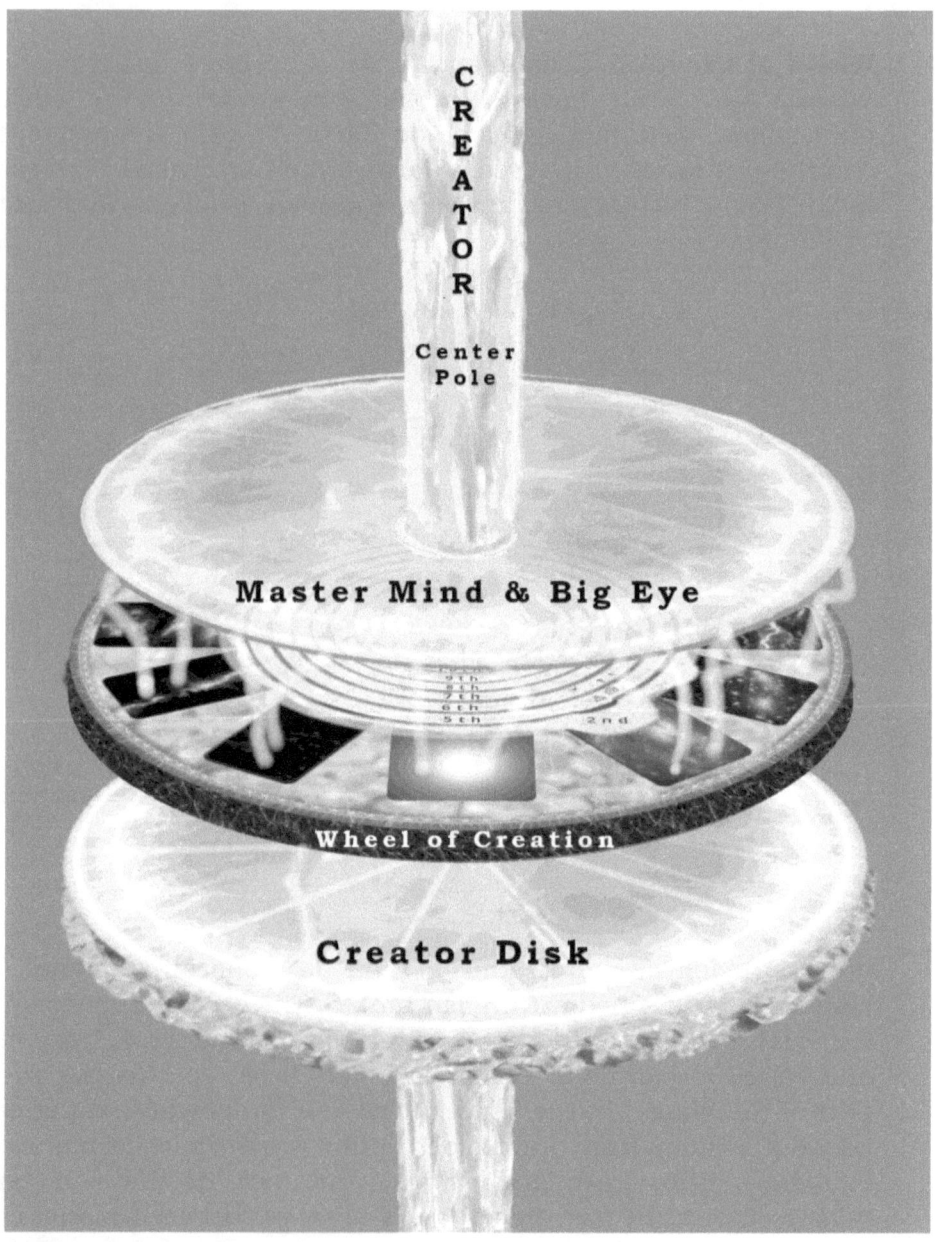

On the following page is a diagram of where the speakers in this *Wave 4* have a home. If they are long–term residents of a planet, like the Tallock, they have both a spiritual home–base on the sixth and ninth dimensions, and also a physical home on the planet Vlac in fish tank 8.

SPIRITUAL DIMENSIONS			FISH TANKS
Individuals		**Councils**	**Planets**
	12th	Highest Councils Healing & Oversight	
	11th	Evolution Group Designers of Universes & Form in Fish Tanks	VLAC
Ari (Elahim) Eli (Elahim)	10th	Elahim Council Astrological Council (Technology, Intentions, Mental)	Fish Tank Eight Storage Pyramids of Celestial Patterns. Center of Learning Home of Tallocks
Jeshua (Elahim) Zachariah Tallocks (Both 6th & 9th)	9th	Council of Form Council of Nine (Galaxies, Energy Webs, Knowledge)	
Isaac	8th	Council of Eight (Atmospheres, Elements, Gravity, DNA, Weather, EM)	ETENA
Ophelia Setalay Josephine	7th	Council of Light (Suns, DNA, Emotional, Healing)	Fish Tank Four Storage of DNA Center of Learning Home of Setalay and Siah (pet)
Seth (Elahim) Lasaray (Elahim) Laslo (Elahim) Nealon (Elahim) Tallocks (Manifested) Zeonians (Manifested)	6th	Council of Six (Celestial Forms, Parallel Realities, Mental)	EARTH
Willaby (Most souls on Earth from 5th)	5th	Circle of Elders (Library, Life Records, Physical Form, Nature & Environment)	Fish Tank Five Greenhouse Planet Souls from 5th, 6th and 7th
Ole Gergen Bob Ia Joel, Sniffer Nature Spirits Taffles (Caretakers)	2nd	Earth Council (DNA, Flora, Fauna, Soil, Water, Earth Energy Grid)	TIDDLE Fish Tank Two Home of Taffles, who work with Colors and Melody

Notes: 5th and 7th closely connected.
6th and 9th closely connected.

The Sessions before 2020

The beginning of a book is normally the first thing an author will write. For us, it is the last, primarily because we are not the ones producing the content. Our friends in spirit dictate the material in the sessions, which we then render into cohesive books. Months after the first draft was done, and still with no introduction, Bob (David's spirit guide) decided to take matters into his own hands, which he often does. He said *Wave 4* should start by addressing the metaphorical questions of, "Are you a dancer or a composer? If you are a dancer, why are you dancing? What music are you listening to?" Most people are dancing, knowingly or unknowingly, to music composed by other people. Bob said the meaning of the idea covers everything that humans believe about themselves, spirituality, the physical world and creation. Bob, with his questions, is asking us to pause and examine the beliefs we hold, since that creates the map we follow to navigate through life. In this and earlier *Spiritual Design* and *Notes from the Second Dimension* books, creation in all its varied forms is immaculately explained by a host of spiritual entities. Many of their teachings are intimately related to the journey of the soul and its human experiences, and it behooves us to compare those philosophies to our own beliefs. As their story of creation unfolds, wave after wave, we are left to ponder how far the sublunary composers have lured the masses of incarnated humans away from a path of pure light. Within many of the teachings in our books, the spirits instruct us to use our free will and choose paths that resonate with our inner composer, the soul.

2   The Sessions

The topics listed in the *Table of Contents* are a limited allusion to all the inspirational stories and omniscient narrations given by our spirit friends in each session. During the hour, there may be five or more different topics that are explored, but are indiscernible from the section title. If we were to categorize the subject matter in the book, it would probably fall into five or six themes: advice on soul awareness and incarnations; Earth history and lifeforms; the fourth dimension and parallel planes; alien visitors and technology; activities in the spiritual dimensions; and creation within the twelve fish tanks. From a higher perspective, the categories merge and blend together as part of the grand spiritual design. Each session is like a little tributary of wisdom in the river of knowledge coming from the spirit realm into the world through Christine. So, we remind the reader that there is gold in the streams, but they have to wade in and pan for it themselves.

Bob's question about composers and dancers is a fruitful area for personal inquiry because it is nearly limitless in scope. He said the majority of people are dancers, but "the strength and the power lie on the side of the composers, because they are the ones orchestrating the music that everyone else are dancing after." He encourages people to question why they are dancing to a particular tune. With free will comes the responsibility to carefully evaluate what we are told by others, especially if it influences how we think or act. People are constantly manipulated and misled by composers whose power requires our consent and cooperation. One of the main leverage points exploited by those who wish to control us is tribalism. Tribalism is intertwined with human nature and survival, but can be in conflict with the ethical urgings of the soul. Tribalism, at its core, is conformity to groupthink. If we examine religion, for example, there are prescriptive beliefs and behaviors that the adherents must follow to prove their loyalty. Some religions, like Judaism, have literally hundreds of dictums that regulate every aspect of life, and Islam even mandates exactly how people must pray. These man–made rules are referred to as 'chains' by the spirits, because they trap the attention on the exaggerated melodrama of ceremonialism. The blind obedience demonstrates submission to the controlling group (the composers), but is void of spiritual meaning. It is interesting that the oldest organized monotheistic religion had no ritualism of worship. Zarathushtra, who lived around 1500 BC, taught people to use the "good mind" (*vohu manah*) to seek truth (*asha*), which was the idealized perfection of existence. Our spirit friends say the same thing in a different way, that we have free will to choose between the soul mind or the lower human impulses. Our higher mind will lead us towards fulfilling our spiritual intent in life. Even though Zarathushtra's ideas were corrupted over the subsequent centuries and lost beneath the centralized trappings of the sacrificial temple cults during biblical times, new teachers always come along and reintroduce freedom of thought. Socrates, Yeshua, Marcion, Copernicus, Descartes and millions of unknown people have chosen to honor the soul's urgings above the tribal impulses of groupthink. We too, have that choice.

Bob's question also applies in the secular world, where the untrustworthy composers are the media, governments, think-tanks, corporations, lobbyists and academia. Sometimes, if enough money is involved, they all join together and try to force everyone to dance to one tune, as they did in 2020-22. Thoughtful observers were rightfully wary of overhyped mandates that were shrouded in deception. When scientific groups abandon open debate and unbiased research, the entire field degenerates into another branch of pernicious propaganda. Those who spoke or sought truthful knowledge were rewarded with ruthless hostility. It has always been difficult to honor your free will when surrounded by petty tyrants. It is a true testament of the spirit to stand firm in your own convictions and not cave-in to groupthink.

The *Spiritual Design* books contain many concepts that, from an orthodox viewpoint, may sound fantastical. Because humans cannot sense or see beyond a narrow band within the spectrum of reality, the hidden realms are dismissed as heresy by the composers of the mainstream belief systems. If we could see the frequency bands above the one we occupy on the third dimension, spirit guides, alien visitors, auras, thought bubbles, and parallel realities in the fourth dimension would be commonplace precepts. Instead, even the verifiable truth that the soul is independent of the body is mocked by mildewed medical minds. Those of us who have glimpsed the mysterious dimensions just beyond the gates of death, or had encounters with alien visitors, know that everything is not as it appears. So, we invite the reader to listen to what our spirit friends have to say and see if it rings true to you.

Before we begin the sessions, it may be helpful to review the Master Mind and how it relates to **The Master Eye** (or the Big Eye). The Master Mind is present throughout the universes of form. It is the energy that animates all living matter, as described in our earlier books. The Master Eye was first shown to Bob during a ceremony on Etena. We described it in the December 25, 2019 session in *Notes*,

Volume 2. In this *Wave 4*, it is mentioned in the November 20, 2020 session when Bob says, "The Eye is an extension of the Creator but it's a mother Eye. So, the Eye is like the Master Mind, but it's a mother energy. The Creator is not a father energy, it's a dual energy, but I would say the Master Mind can shift depending on where the Eye is going. But in general, the Master Mind can transform, being a mental, male observer, or an emotional, female observer." In a later section, Jeshua told Bob, "The Master Mind actually manifests in several different ways. The Big Eye is actually the Master Mind, in one manifested form. […] The Master Mind is like a chameleon, depending on what it is investigating. It's like the Creator transforms into whatever entity it wants to be, in what way it is suitable." And Bob tells us (to be published in *Wave 5*), "Shamans worked with this in ancient times. They knew that if they needed to connect to the Master Eye, they had to work with light and dark in order for them to go back and forth. It's a light and dark realm. When you work with the Master Mind, there are tones and it's connected to gravity. It's heavier."

The concept of the Master Eye is important because it was the vehicle used by our prehistoric ancestors to access knowledge and visually explore the planet. When Bob traveled with the Eye, he said that his sense of self dissolved, and when he saw something, he understood the original intent of why it was created. Ancient shamans were given knowledge about secrets in the natural world by the Master Mind and the Master Eye. We modern humans lack the ability to connect in a similar way, so we are blind to the possibilities that once existed to seek and find hidden knowledge. That makes us extremely fortunate to have these direct communications from entities who know how creation operates.

Bob: A Sacred Key of Creation (May 28, 2017)
After *Wave 3* was published, I went back through 3500 pages of transcripts, searching for messages that had been set aside for various reasons. In this early session, Bob explains that the three components of all creation are the center point, the stabilizer and gravity. Irrespective of size or scale, those forces are what give rise to matter throughout the Universe. Ophelia then told him, "That is one of the sacred keys—that one is the stabilizer, and one is the engine. That is one of the mathematical first keys," she said, "to ALL foundations."

It is significant that Ophelia said it is a mathematical key. She is asserting a hidden relationship exists between the engine and the stabilizer, and within ALL matter and form. Perhaps it is geometric, or it may imply certain relationships within the physical fields, be it electrical, magnetic, or gravitational densities coupled with certain frequencies of vibration. On a macro scale, the mathematical key relates to the web or cosmic grid that is sometimes mentioned. In our Solar System, the Sun is the center point and Uranus is the receiver, and those two maintain the balance within the system. Uranus is a strange planet in several ways. For one, its axis of rotation is sideways at 97 degrees, making the equator perpendicular to its orbit. It also has a bizarre magnetic behavior that is not found on other planets. Its magnetosphere switches on and off every day (which is 17 Earth hours). When its magnetic shield goes off, solar plasma flows directly into its atmosphere, filling it with charged particles. In addition, the magnetic field is tilted so that for parts of its 84 Earth-year journey around the Sun, its north magnetic pole points directly at the Sun. This allows a significant amount of solar wind (i.e., plasma of electrons, ions and charged particles) to enter the atmosphere for years at a time. So, in that sense, Uranus is a receiver. While that is probably not the relationship the spirits are describing, it is an unusual feature between the two.

D. (*Bob came in and tried to not be noticed, but was making facial movements I knew were his.*) If there is someone here by the name of Bob that wishes to speak, please do so now.

B. Hehehehe! Found me! Oh, I feel pushed. I don't know if the other ones are gonna come, but I got a little push. Ophelia says, "You go first today." I don't know if the other ones are gonna talk, but they're all here. Everyone is here, even Isaac is here. But they're laughing and said it's my turn, my turn!

D. You know why they did that, don't you?

B. Uh?

D. It's because you've gotten so good at this! This is your reward, to go first.

B. Ah, might be! Ophelia is just like showing me her hand, like when you leave the floor, so to speak. So, I guess I can talk about anything I want to. No, she said, "Not!" No, no, not everything. She still supervises. She laughs. Even Zachariah is present.

D. Well, hello to everybody.

B. Hello to everybody. Everybody's with. So, I go first. I don't know if they are gonna talk at all today. Ophelia says they will answer depending on what questions you have, so that is why we are all gonna be participating, and depending on what questions you fire off, it would be answered by someone in the group. That is what she said. So we'll see how that's gonna play out. It seems like a game of sorts. I set the pace, she said. I will, indeed. So, I have been given books.

D. What were they about?

B. Uranus.

D. Ah, so you finally got the books on Uranus?

B. Yes, but again, it is only that, a book. Nothing more than a book. Because we did talk about that a lot, and I felt like it was due, really, to introduce the knowledge of the stabilizer. So, we haven't discussed it, but you gave me the book. I think it's also because, you know, I can't read it. So, in some way, you humor me—but then again, not, because you know I can't read it. Every step of the way is covered in a certain manual in a certain book. So, I got the book of Uranus, which was somewhat a little shady because you know I couldn't read it. Huhuhuh.

D. Is it in an odd language?

B. I will explain it to you. It has less dots. (*Bob calls the language of the Elahim the "dot language".*) In the end, there are dots. In the beginning of the book, there are merely images in certain different modalities of how you can use the stabilizer. But then again, I don't know which applies to my solar system because this is the general book, I would assume, of stabilizers.

D. That's what I was going to ask you, if it was specific to Uranus, or if it covered all systems?

B. It's a book about the stabilizer. THE stabilizer. Because regardless of what you have made, it exists. I don't know... let's say, in the big one (*galaxy*) that you did with your friends, there is more than one stabilizer, because a big galaxy contains several baby solar systems. So, the baby solar systems in the galaxy each have a stabilizer. BUT does it (*the galaxy*) also carry its own stabilizer? Everything has a star, so to speak, a core, a center point that is the so-called engine and radiator of heat and light, the conductor of the whole thing, if you like. And it doesn't really matter if it is a solar system, if it is down to molecules and DNA components, or at the other far end, a galaxy, it all carries this center point. Also, it carries a stabilizer. And you should know that it also exists within those spaghetti strings, the DNA strings, as well. So, it exists, this specific... Oh. (*He looks to the left, listening to Ophelia.*) Ophelia says, "Yes, indeed. That is one of the sacred keys, that one is the stabilizer, and one is the engine. That is one of the mathematical first keys," she said, "to ALL foundations." Oh, maybe she wanted to say that? No, she didn't mind. Okay.

D. I was wondering how gravity becomes included in this?

B. She doesn't say here. Anyway, in everything that is created exists this center point, which is similar to like a star and a sun—the light source—which is the foundation of life in general. The galaxy is also a living entity and is considered as such. So, that is what I am saying. I was wondering because it is made by several solar systems that all carry its own stabilizer. BUT does the big one have its own stabilizer?

D. Which one?

B. The galaxy. It has a center point, at least.

D. The scientists think it is a black hole, where all matter is sucked in and vanishes.

B. I wouldn't think so. Because the center point is not a black hole. Not all looks like a solar system, don't get confused. Some are actually more of an energetic form and it's not shining as light. That might be why there is a misperception that it is a black hole. Yet, it is not. It is a similar structure like a sun. It is a center point, the stillness of matter, that exists within all living entities and life forms. A galaxy is merely a bigger one than a DNA string within my individual, for example, or in a plant. There is no difference, really, you said. You say that we are both master designers, because it doesn't matter—size doesn't matter! Huhuhuh. You say it's the same thing. You actually said one time that I maybe do more tricky things, because it's smaller and more picky. But I don't know.

D. I'm like a blacksmith, and you're like a watchmaker!

B. Huhuhuh. So, indeed. But I got that book, anyway. One of the sacred keys, when it comes to geometric forms and the mysteries of creation, is actually those two components. And you should know that gravity is the third. But the two components are the sun, considered the center point, and the stabilizer. And they are acting like somewhat of an opposite polarity to each other. That is why certain things function. When one of these components are not operating correctly, the whole entity or creation will somewhat cease to exist. So it has to have those two components. This is what I know, and I want to make sure that in my solar system the core inside is functioning properly, because that is what I feel is something I have somewhat of a control over. The other, outside stabilizer is also in my hands at the moment, in my solar system. BUT what if it gets affected by outside influences? That is what I don't know at this point, because I only have the book on the stabilizer. But it is, in general, the same, regardless of what you are trying to create. We haven't got to Uranus yet. But I feel like you gave me this book on the stabilizers—you're tricky—because you knew I wouldn't be able to solve it! Because there are pictures of different stabilizers that have been used. Some exist, and some are not operating anymore. So when I say, "Which one am I gonna use? Am I gonna use version A, B, or C from in here?" Then you just kind of smile and say, "We haven't got to that yet, because it has to resonate with the central point." So, in order for me to understand how to create the stabilizer, I have to somewhat return to the center point. Similar like when I created the planet. I had created the form, and then I created the core that would resonate TO that form. I can create the stabilizer, but I have to, in rewind, dissect my center point—which is the sun in this specific project.

D. So, like with DNA, is it created with cosmic light and cosmic sound?

B. Indeed, indeed.

D. So those are two of the components, right?

B. Yes, those are two of the components. And then there is one in the middle that is considered like a vacuum. Matter that is of... oh, how can I explain this? This is probably similar to what is considered like gravity, but it is a (*type of*) matter, or element, if you like to call it that, that is somewhat transparent. And it actually shifts depending on the two components on each side. It is dependent on the amount that exists in that light source (*cosmic light*) versus the sound source (*cosmic sound*).

D. Is the vacuum somewhat like a polarity to gravity, or does it work with it?

B. It's actually a part of it. It is actually somewhat the same (*as gravity*). When Isaac (*or the eighth dimension*) comes and puts (*or changes*) gravity in the fish tank, it still appears like that vacuum. And again, when we talk about the organs within the body that is encased in some sort of a vacuum, that comes from the same source. But it changes depending on what it is supposed to function as and with. Mainly with, than as. Because it has to resonate with, ah... (*Long pause.*) Nay. Ophelia says, nay. We do not have to dive our brain in here with that, because that's not going to get solved tonight, she says. She said I somewhat drifted off.

D. Well, I asked the question because I've been curious about that.

B. Well, she says, just know that there are two major components that have to operate as a receiver and a sender (*transmitter*), so to speak. And in the Solar System, that is considered (*to be*) between the stabilizer and center point, which is the Sun. So, you can see how these two are extremely important. And it's the same, she says. It's also the same as how the spiritual dimensions and realities operate. You have the first dimension that resonates with the tenth. So it's the same structure in everything. Oh, she laughs at this. She said, "This should make it easy for you to solve!" Hehehehe! She knows it's not. Hahahaha, hehehehe. She's tricky too!

D. Well, that won't help at all, but it's good to know.

B. She says you're not supposed to figure it out. You're supposed to somewhat leave the floor for future scientists. You're supposed to give ideas and you're supposed to ponder out loud, she says. "Ponder out loud, but you're not supposed to solve it. That's not what you will do here, anyway."

D. I wouldn't be able to solve it. You would have to tell me.

B. Huhuhuh, and she's not gonna! She doesn't look like she's gonna. Hehehe. "There's a filter," she says, "of certain knowledges that are within your own reach, within your own soul energy and capacity. But there is a filter to certain things, because otherwise all sorts of information that is not helpful at this time would simply just slip out."

Bob: Unity in the Councils (Apr 29, 2018)

Bob covered quite a few subjects in the April 29 session, most of which was included in *Notes, Vol 2*. In the following excerpt, he made an interesting assessment of how spiritual councils operate, pointing out that each member must fully evaluate a topic before a decision is made. Bob feels that several in his council on the second dimension are a bit too slow and thorough when compared to him. What we can draw from his many stories is that soul development moves in stages. As sparkles, they remain in groups while learning. As they grow in knowledge, they are gradually moved into solitary activities related to their specialty. Then, when a level of expertise has been reached, the spirit is invited to collaborate in council work within a group that has a related purpose. Those front–line councils are guided by higher councils, and they, in turn, are aided by higher councils. In *Wave 5*, we will follow the progress of spirits further, where it seems that the advanced entities are directed into a more solitary journey before they merge back with the Creator.

B. Sometimes it feels like we (*in his council*) are not getting anywhere, really, like we are repeating stuff over and over, where I feel like there is more need for action and for results. Gergen is present all the time, because he's not going anywhere at this point in my development. And he says, "Again, this is a new way of learning, to take all angles and aspects into account, and THEN make a decision. To reflect before action." That's what he said. And these individuals in the council, they are actually very reflective, so maybe I will be the engine for action. But Gergen said I don't know all their knowledge yet, so I can't make that judgment yet, really, fully. (*Gergen is Bob's mentor on the second dimension.*)

D. What are you learning now?

B. Well I'm learning with the council for everyone to be on board with a suggestion before we sort of (*thumps hand on arm of chair*).

D. Take a vote?

B. Indeed. So, the difference being, is that in the council everyone has to agree. Everyone has to understand the progress of the idea and the intention, and the end result of this idea, before action is taken. That's why things take a little bit longer. With you and me, there was no need for that because I asked and you said yes or no, and then we put that jar aside. (*When he was learning about the cores of planets, as described in 'Notes, Volume 1'.*) And then I took another one, and you said, "This will work," so there was constant movement. There was nothing like I have to wait for someone to verify my result, if it works or if it doesn't. I got constant and instant response. If I said, "I wanna create like vegetation," you said, "You can't use those jars, you can't use those elements, they don't belong." Then I just put them aside, so we made progress with my solar system, quite rapidly, because of that. And I thought, I asked Gergen, if I could introduce that way of movement and progression (*to the council*). But he said, "Now when you are in a council, everyone has to have their say, and everyone has to be on board with the idea."

Bob: Gravity is a Function of Light (May 6, 2018)

In the conventional view of cosmology, stars and planets are accidentally formed, and if there are any life forms, that too is mere happenstance. Bob, in describing his conversation with a gravitational council on the eighth dimension, makes it clear that planets, solar systems, galaxies, and even fish tanks can be rejuvenated and adjusted when needed. There is an intention behind everything that exists or occurs within the Universe. The area where his solar system was placed (see *Notes, Vol. 1 and 2*) had recently been upgraded, so he was reassured that nothing would happen again in the near-term that might disturb his living planet where his Individual lives. The Individual has been described in our earlier books. Bob refers to the species, which he had created and placed on Earth, in the singular, perhaps because it was originally a solitary creature. But the small bear-like mammal is highly intelligent and was removed from Earth by Gergen prior to the introduction of hominins. It had luxurious fur and would have been hunted for its pelt. When Bob was designing his solar system, he included the pattern for his Individual, so it came back into existence on his living planet.

B. (*Bob came in, trying to adjust the energy that Eli left behind. He was puffing and making noises.*) Ohhh, I wish I had a vacuum cleaner! I'm trying to puff out the leftovers here.

D. Welcome. I'm happy to see you again.

B. So there we go! So I've been having, actually, my first class with a new group of quiet ones. And you (*Lasaray, Dave's higher self*) translate a lot.

D. What are you studying?

B. I'm studying matter, materia, and how receptive it is to surrounding conditions of the gravitational fields, and how the conditions of a living planet, for instance—or even a galaxy, one (*of the teachers*) said here—can be completely different if there is a change within the gravitational field. And the gravitational field can be manipulated with different frequencies of light, and it can change the conditions on everything that is within that region. So, I'm concerned about my system. (*His solar system.*) I wanted to know who is in charge of manipulating this gravitational field, and if it's random, or if it is like a scheduled kind of thing.

D. What did you find out?

B. I did not really find out. But I said, "Because I have a (*solar*) system of my own, I'm wondering if my conditions will change?" And it was a positive response to that. And then I wanted to know who was in charge of that—and who set up that schedule—and why is that occurring? And you're present here because sometimes there is a need of translation. So I asked you, and you asked them. They gurgle a little bit, too, in a way—so there is like a sound response. Huhuh.

D. The change in gravity must have something to do with evolution?

B. Indeed. And it has to do with the increase or decrease of (*cosmic*) light. And I said, "My system is in a very light area already. Is it maybe done?" But there is like no confirmation of that, because, I would assume, that this is beyond the council's knowledge. So, they simply get, I guess, their own manual on how to adjust. I would say this is the gravity group. They are like a group of five, but there are three that are communicating, mainly. I would assume they get like manuals on how to adjust gravitational fields within galaxies. That's what they say, through you to me. I am getting better at this language barrier that we encounter here, because there is a lot of visual here, as well. So, they send me images—I'm not getting a book—but they are EXCELLENT at sending like an image into my chimney so I can understand. And then you help, with the way that you and I communicate, to make the picture clearer, if you like. But they communicate with images. They send me images on how they operate, and I'm learning how to translate that into my language and understanding.

D. Is this Isaac and his people?

B. Well, Isaac, he works with the elements. The gravitational groups here, they don't belong in six or seven, so they are up here at eight. Each level has different groups within them, and they belong in the eighth. They communicate in a way that is very fulfilling. I'm happy about this, because they send pictures so I can see. But because I haven't got the answer of the schedule when adjustments take place and why—so I was wondering about that. But I can't send pictures to them, yet. So I tell you, and you send the picture to them, and then a picture comes back to me. So that's how it sort of moves around here. And I asked about that, "What is the conditions that is the foundation of change?"

D. And you have not received a good answer?

B. Nay, nay.

D. I can't imagine we would have put your system somewhere where it was going to be negatively affected.

B. Nay, nay. You said that when I came in with my solar system into that specific galaxy, it had just sort of gone through their renovation! Huhuh! So they are sort of intact and there is nothing new coming in for a very long time. So you said that I don't need to worry about that, because I'm sure you pictured that these questions would come. You said, "It's like upgrading sometimes, like you do remodeling in a house. It's similar like that." And my galaxy has just gone through a complete renovation when it comes to the gravitation field. That's what you said. So I've been doing that. And then I've been in the vault, because I want to also combine my notes now, because they belong in your vault, they don't belong in mine. And I was like, "Where am I gonna put them?" And you said, "We're going to make a box just for you, because this specific knowledge does not belong in the second dimensional vault. This belongs in the sixth." So I'm getting my own box that I have here.

D. And this is related to your solar system?

B. Indeed. My project. But everything that you do, whether you do it in the spirit realm or as an incarnation, is stored somewhere. But it's stored where it belongs.

D. And all this knowledge is stored in the Library on the fifth, and this is the central repository for all knowledge?

B. The vault is there, indeed. BUT within this vault exists little vaults of other realities. So, in this case, with my solar system project, that specific project belongs in the vault of the sixth. That's where it's stored. So, I have my own box.

D. Very nice.

B. And it's on the third level. You said it belongs on the level of completed projects of solar systems. It's not on the bottom somewhere, or in a closet. I've been going through and tagging certain information and going through (*the boxes*), spending a lot of time there (*in the vault*). [...]

B. So, anyway, I'm gonna be short today because we're saving energy here. But I have been working with different locations, I must say. I have not been with the councils for a while, because they are still pondering about a specific topic. There is like three people in that group who (*sighs*), they are pondering about a specific topic within the topic. And I felt there was no need for me to be pondering about a topic within the topic.

D. Have you already decided?

B. I have already decided my standpoint, and I said I might come back. But Gergen, he said, "Bob, you also have to be present when there are discussions, even if you feel like there are topics that don't belong within your realm." SO, I am indeed heading back. But I felt like I could leave them a little bit. I said, "Why don't you give me kind of a call when you have figured that out, and then I come back and we can just wrap this whole case up." But Gergen said, "Bob, you have to be present and listen to this." And I said, "Well, how long is that gonna take, because I have engagements elsewhere." Huhuhuh. And he said, "Well, now when you are an adult, you have to pick and choose your engagements." And I said, "Well, you know."

D. They're trying to make you sit there and listen. But you never know when they might say something useful, then you'll appreciate being there.

B. Ah, ah. But I thought I did them a favor, to not sit there and look impatient.

D. Can they read your mind?

B. OH, INDEED!

D. So, you have to be careful?

B. I have to be EXTREMELY careful.

D. Your thoughts drift out and fill the room.

B. I thought I will do the kind thing to not be present, so that no one feels like I am rushing them or anything. But Gergen says, "There is a lesson in this, Bob. And it's to also master your own thoughts, and to appreciate the process, regardless of what the process is." I thought I did them a favor to say, "Okay, I will come back when this pondering of the topic within the topic has been resolved."

D. Can you monitor what is going on in the council? I guess it meets continuously, then?

B. Yes, they do, indeed.

D. So, in some way, they are always there?

B. Always there, indeed.

D. Do you leave a little part of yourself to listen in?

B. Ah, that's what I tried to do, like leave a little particle, a passive particle. Huh huh. So I was there, but not there. But Gergen, he's no fool. He said, "I see that you just left like a particle that will not engage!" HUH HUH HUH. I said, "I didn't think you wanted me to engage." And he said, "Yes, I do. You did know." So, I'll go back because I don't want to be expelled.

D. They'll say, "He's not ready to sit on a council."

B. And I am. I am... I think I am.

D. Just imagine, poor Ole has to sit there and listen to everybody prattle on.

B. But maybe Ole, he might have one of those tricks where he goes into hibernation, but he still looks like he's present. But I have not learned that yet. I haven't got that practice yet, so I'm very much a what you see is what you get kinda guy. But Gergen said, "I saw what you did, Bob. You just left a particle, a passive one, so that you can continue your education and your travels."

D. What are you going to give up if you sit on the council? Won't your energy have to be cut back somewhere else?

B. I'm not going to be as much in the vault, there is no need. He said my attention doesn't need to be in the vault. He said, "There's nothing going on there at the moment, so you don't have to go there." Then I said, "Well, I might want to check the boxes." And he said, "There is no need to check the boxes, because you've reached the level where you're supposed to be at this point. There is a long cycle until you reach the next level, so there is no need to sit there and look at boxes." Huh huh.

D. (*Laughing.*) So you're going to take some of that soul energy and put it into the council?

B. Ah, something like 25 to 30, that's probably enough. But I also said that I have classes to go to—and I don't want to be like not participating with the gravitational group. But he said, "Everything will happen when it should. Nothing will interfere." So, he oversees. I can't fool him! I can't say, "Oh, I have a class, that's why I didn't come," because he knows there was no class! Huh huh huh.

D. He'll see you hanging out with Ia, having a chat.

B. Sitting, having a chat, looking at the egg. Then he finds me and he says, "Leisure time."

D. You'll be doing the same thing with Tom.

B. I will indeed. I know what to look for indeed, because I know what Gergen sees! He's like Ophelia, he can just show up. He's like, "Hello!" And I'm like, "Oh, hello." And he said, "What are you doing over here?" And I said, "Looking at the egg." And he said, "Nothing more is going to happen here. Isn't that right, Ia?" And she said, "No." And then he said, "Come on, Bob, let's go." So, I follow. But it's not like I don't want to be there (*with the council*). It's just that I thought when this little group within the group was pondering about something, and I wasn't involved—but he said everyone is involved.

Tallocks, Ophelia: Waves of Transformation (Oct 14, 2018)
This is actually the very first time the Tallocks spoke to us, even though several of their talks were included in *Wave 3*. We held it back because they mentioned the Creator Disk, which was not a topic we had material to develop until now. Since Zachariah first mentioned the Wheel of Creation in November 2016, it has been elaborated on

by Ari, Eli, Jeshua, Ophelia, the Elahim Council, the Council of Nine, the Tallocks, Setalay, the Zeonians, and even Willaby. (Willaby begins sharing in 2022, but is introduced as the last entry in this *Wave 4*.) In other words, it is a critical concept when trying to understand the Creator, the spiritual realities, and the universes of form. As I currently understand their teachings, the Wheel of Creation sits above another energetic disk that is referred to as the Creator's Disk. The Creator's Disk rotates slowly in a counter-clockwise motion, meaning the Wheel of Creation is encountering energies in a clockwise direction, relative to the Creator's Disk. The motion of the Creator's Disk is what drives evolution and changes within all realities of form. The spiritual dimensions are engaged to prepare for upcoming influences and maintain balance as conditions change. The natural seasonal cycles on Earth are a tiny reflection of a larger universal pattern, where all realities move from density or darkness into fog or light. The knowledge and experience acquired during the dark phase of separation is reviewed and stored during the phase of lightness.

Ophelia came in after they spoke and gave a wonderful teaching on rebirth. In her description, when you accept all parts of yourself, both the light and the dark, the doorway to transformation is opened. Within the cyclical nature of rebirth that each soul follows, the darkness carries wisdom that the soul must find. To embrace all experiences as being equally important is to understand the lessons learned from the darkness. Physical death is only a marker along the soul's journey, but within life, there are countless opportunities to choose a path of light.

T. Tallock Council. We are representing the civilization of Tallock, from the great north. North galaxy, 75 distance, light waves. Present with friends: Isaac, Jeshua, Ophelia, present for your convenience and familiarity.

D. Welcome.

T. This great north is where your heart lies, where you prefer to travel to gain and store knowledge. Great halls of knowledge stored in stone walls; replicas found in Sumerian buildings. Builders came from the great north, 75 light-waves north. Portal through. Known constellations. Not in them, through them. Man knew how to connect and navigate. Only a few found the portal to go through, to conquer time, to rest within the puddle of knowledge created by the Council of Nine, combined with the great north, the civilization of Tallock.

D. What name do you go by?

T. We are only Tallock. We are one.

D. Are you related to the Elahim in any way?

T. Yes. You study, you store your knowledge here. Always welcome. Yes, we communicate. Yet Tallocks have never set foot as man on Earth, or like the Elahim as Anunnaki. We supervise travels, cosmology. The great cycles of, what you refer to as, the fish tanks. Fish tanks, your Wheel. The circle is not stationary. All fish tanks travel through different experiences. Your fish tank and your current location travels through the teachings of manifestation and choice. Density, time, that is where your fish tank occupies its teaching. The Creator makes all fish tanks rotate in this Wheel. They are not stationary. All experience different levels of learning.

D. As they rotate, do they change form?

T. Yes. This fish tank, prior to its current location, traveled through the mist of hibernation. Just before moving into manifestation, there were upgrades within matter that exists within your fish tank, in order for certain lessons to be in place, as well as individuals, such as yourself, to be presented. You should know that they all travel. But there is no way for me to give you a timeline, as these great shifts go beyond what you consider time to be. It's simply a cycle of awareness, and for the Creator to see how different models and materia adapt within different settings. I am so sorry for the limited choice of words.

D. I appreciate that. I follow what you are saying, sort of.

T. The great cycles are determined by councils that you have no ability to communicate with. Simply know that you travel through different atmospheric surroundings, if you like. To give you a picture, it's similar to what your seasons represent. There is spring, summer, fall, winter. Same way, travels through different atmospheric shifts that affect the fish tank and those within it.

D. So, in some way, would the dense matter gradually change into sound or light, then move back into density again?

T. Yes. To give you a picture, the right side of the Wheel—if your location is at 6 o'clock and you look at the Wheel—matter, density is on the right side. Whereas the fogs, the sound waves, the shifts of awareness within the wind around you, are on the left. (*He is talking about the phases of change on Earth. To the right are the past influences. The Creator's wind of changes to the atmosphere are coming from the left as the Creator Disk rotates.*)

D. Which direction does it rotate? Towards the fog?

T. No. Fog moving anti-clockwise into density. When density moves and changes direction, moving into the fog, it cools down, it absorbs and it stores the knowledge it adapted as it traveled through the density. It stores, it absorbs, it becomes the fog. This is the closer side to the Creator. Everything dissolves, it becomes the knowledge in the wind. Everything IS. There is no polarity. There are no sides in the wind, is there? It simply flows.

D. When you say you are 75 light-years from Earth, does that mean you are within our fish tank?

T. Not in light-years. Light waves. Each wave would represent 993 light-years. These are waves. Light waves not the same. Don't limit your understanding of distance. We navigate in light waves and sound waves, that is not the same as light-years. But we are indeed within your fish tank. We are solid, dense, because we are in that experience of density. (*The stars in the constellations are much closer than 74,500 light-years. The edge of the Milky Way is about that far away.*)

D. Have you traveled to Earth, manifesting, or did the people of Earth travel to you?

T. None traveled. No man traveled here, though navigating through the portals, (*the shamanic travelers were*) being told about the other side of Orion's Belt and Sirius. In-between lies the portal, the gateway to the north.

D. So they traveled with their consciousness?

T. Yes. Only a few, located within your cone (*pyramid*), your storage of energy. You needed to transform your energy to become the cone. That is the trick the ancients strived for—to become the cone.

D. Was that knowledge available during the second great civilization?

T. Yes. We never traveled here like you Elahim did, carrying scrolls, memories from our Hall of Wisdom. A replica of our halls, our stone halls, imitating them here for man to understand the greater existence beyond the wall, and to never cease to seek within your consciousness, within your mind, the greater existence. The walls represent boundaries. All walls do, even your own homes, your buildings. Everything is a metaphor for boundaries, whether you experience boundaries or not. In other fish tanks... how can I make it easy? You have the ability to de-manifest and travel through materia like walls, no biggie. Here (*on Earth*), you bump into it. Everything of solid matter is a trick. It doesn't exist, even though you observe it. Those who were initiated in the understanding of the north tried to exercise to travel through materia, conquer the solid world, conquer materia using sound waves, attracting light. Combined, connecting points created a third element, which was the foundation to conquer gravity and matter. Using disks, attracting sunlight. That is why the destination and location was in that region—more sunlight. (*The region was pre-historic Mesopotamia.*) You were a part of establishing and engineering the disks.

D. What is the principle by which rocks, and other things, lose their density?

T. The principle is the simple understanding that there are no boundaries. A stone, a rock, is also locked within boundaries, isn't it?

D. Yes.

T. It carries an awareness, though. And in other realities, it has more of an awareness to change, like a chameleon, its structure and density. The principle is to understand that there is no linear matter and time, that they carry waves when they are closer together and further apart. At this time, they are connected close together, creating a line. That is why you experience linear time. The waves that existed before are gone. Before, they traveled independently: light, sound, matter. And when they were apart, you had the ability to travel and change the appearance of form. As long as they are connecting together as a line with no movement between, you are locked within that reality, the reality of form, boundary, time, gravity. Limited. It is by design. I hope I'm not confusing you.

D. No, that's a good explanation. Was that available in the recent past? Or this is way in the distant past.

T. Not recent. No, not recent. Recently is only when your timeline began, when you became trapped. Still, there were those who carried the memory of being outside the experience. There was no big deal to move and mold and transform objects into the way that you wished. You simply observed the shifts within your atmosphere when those waves were available. There were different atmospheric observations. The atmosphere was sometimes less... dense. Still an increase of oxygen, but more spread out.... Dear god, you have limited words!

D. As befitting man's mind.

T. Anyway, this was an introduction to make you aware of the Wheel and how it travels through different experiences. You are, this fish tank, indeed, in the later phase of your journey. Not to say that you are moving, anytime soon, into another experience. But you have already traveled far within this specific teaching, the teaching of matter and how to operate your minds. You should know that the body is also considered a boundary, but your mind is free. Your spirit within travels easier than you know, but you have to conquer the physical, you have to conquer what you experience boundaries to be. Even the brain is physical, you know. Conquer your mind and you travel like the wind.

D. That's a remarkable teaching. When you said, "You became fixed, or when you became trapped," what did you mean by that?

T. Who?

D. I wasn't sure if you were talking about when souls became trapped in bodies, or—

T. Your whole reality became fixed. Animals, plants, cycles of life and death—different. Before, TIME stood still. Individuals could live longer, life span longer due to the movement within your atmosphere. The choice of the Creator, I would assume. Your lifespan, everything, has decreased into a line, which means that you simply experience a little bit of your surroundings. You are limited in this line. If you see a line, at this point, this line is one centimeter. This is where you exist—all animals, man, science, ideas—you are trapped within this one-centimeter line, moving slowly but steady in what appears to be one direction. Before, the line moved and the greater span could be up to twenty centimeters. So you had a different experience, you could travel high and low within this reality. You could absolutely park yourself within this tunnel—that is a way for you to see it—that you are in a tunnel. If you think of when you drive a car and you are in a snowstorm, of how you become tunnel-visioned. That is the same thing. You don't see the sides, you don't see the wing-span of existence. And that is because you are trapped within this line. Before, there were great visitors here, not man. You are not the first. You are not the right, necessarily, heritage to the Earth. You are trapped within the line because your consciousness cannot handle the span. That is why, until you learn how to navigate outside the physical, to conquer the physical, to conquer your own mind, until that is cleared and observed from higher councils and the Creator, you will be trapped in this tunnel, experiencing that you are moving very fast indeed—but fast to what? What are you seeking? What is your destination? If you learn how to stop within this line, within this stream of others, this high traffic that moves in one direction, then you will conquer the physical and your mind.

D. Wow, that is brilliant. How long ago, in Earth years, did that become fixed? Was that before the current hominin?

T. It fully became fixed... there are several cycles here, let's see. One stationary around 500,000 years ago. But then there were tests, if you like. So there were cycles before that when there was a brief lock, a brief fix, but the fix didn't stay. This time it has remained. Before, it was just a pause within the reality of existence and experience. You experience life within this tunnel; one centimeter, that is all you have. Those who try to embark on the ceiling, like you, you embark on something that is greater than you understand. You might fall under the trap of not understanding, even if you pop out your head, so to speak. But you seek, you seek from within the experience of physical matter. That is the wish (*from the councils*), to understand that there are no boundaries, not even in this pipe you are traveling in. You are free, but you have to, in numbers, not only a few, (*be*) feeling sick of being trapped in the pipe, reaching higher, even lower. Lower is sometimes considered as something bad or negative or dark. Indeed, both sides carry different colors, but they coexist, create a wholeness. Man feels like below is a place where you should not involve or head for. It is a fear within your species of falling, not rising. That is why more people tap into the existence of flying, rising. The fear within your consciousness is stored when you fell through layers of understanding your cosmic origin. When you do so, you fall through the layers of understanding all. It is indeed stored within your species and the consciousness here that falling equals dying. Whereas rising, flying, equals life. That is not so. You fall and you rise. You fall and you rise. That is how you travel this big span of existence. Similar like the Wheel, it falls into density, it rises into the fog. Everything falls and rises. Don't be afraid to fall. Understand your protection within.

D. That is really brilliant. Thank you.

T. There, I have occupied your time.

D. I appreciate you occupying my time.

T. We will discuss cosmic matters, distances, understanding how to navigate through the illusion of matter within your pipe, further.

D. I really look forward to that. It's very complicated, but I appreciate you trying to explain it to me.

T. There. Until next time, I bid you farewell.

D. Thank you.

O. (*There was a long pause as Ophelia attempted to bring the energies to her level.*) Hmm. This is Ophelia.
D. Hello, Ophelia.
O. Good Morning. We are trying to adjust the shift that just left, knowing that it is slower within its frequency; more dense for the vehicle here. It creates a sensation of falling asleep, of being taken away into this vast homeland where you belong, where you prefer to travel. Yes, my friend (*she turned and spoke to Bob*), you will have to wait. You would not like this (*energy*).
D. So when he came in, did he come from the spiritual realm, or did he project his consciousness?
O. He projects, Tallocks project. They are visitors from other systems that you will meet on your journey ahead. They will provide more insights about cosmology, astronomical equations, understandings of travels between realities, as well as great journeys of others, as well as understanding the rotation within all life that exists that might experience or be perceived similar as a death. Everything travels through birth, life, death, rebirth. Death, in humanity's consciousness, equals an ending; don't forget rebirth. Rebirth is the greatest joy. When you transform and use the knowledge that you brought—not to be forgotten, simply to be transformed into a higher level of understanding into a higher light—then you increase and you appreciate rebirth. Rebirth is a greater joy than being born. You can only be born once as a soul. However, you have numerous opportunities of cycles of rebirth. Born is only once. Rebirth indicates growth, bringing with you the experience from different realities. You can even have rebirth during a lifetime. Teach that. Teach that you are indeed born once, but you can always be reborn during your journey as man.
D. That has a Christian tone to it.
O. It's a spiritual tone. Don't be confused. Don't put labels. But you are reborn. Being reborn means that you shift your sense of consciousness, you travel without barriers, you understand your equals. You embrace the light, but you also embrace the darkness, understanding that nothing exists without the other. That is being reborn, in one way. Another way is to understand your wrongs and to be willing to do good—to conquer your karmic Coat, if you like. That is also a part of being reborn. So, you see, you have all traveled, being reborn, if you like. If you do not wish to choose that word, chose transformed, since it has a less religious ring to it. There you go.

D. (*Laughing.*) That's wonderful, thank you, Ophelia.

O. Oh, you are much welcome.

Tallocks, Ophelia: Qualities of Fish Tanks (Dec 31, 2018)
The Tallocks are spirits from the sixth dimension who manifest on the planet they call Vlac, somewhere in fish tank eight, bordering to nine. One of the things they mention is that ancient shamans used to bathe or coat their bodies in olive oil to increase their ability to connect with spiritual vibrations. I can only guess at the reason, but it may be that the oil acts to insulate the body from external subtle energies, so the practitioner can focus inwards more easily. There must have been some residual memory of this prehistoric practice, because hieroglyphs made during the Old Kingdom of Egypt depict using sacred oils for healing and preparing the dead for spiritual travels. Many thousands of years later, a contorted version shows up in the theatrics of anointing or baptizing, where a rabbi or priest makes a show of transmitting divine empowerment to a recipient. This is an inversion of the original purpose, where a shaman would use oil as a tool to help connect with their own spiritual power. Religions inserted themselves as middlemen and imperious merchants, selling illusions of sanctity to the naïve.

The Tallock then told how the Little Greys, as they are called by humans, are working with them to help maintain the Earth. Later, Ophelia took over the session and described the characteristics of fish tanks eleven, two, and seven.

T. Hello, friends. Tallock, Elahim, friends from home, introducing knowledge from fish tank eight, where you like to travel. Eight and four, eight and four, creating a mirror, opposite realities. Eight and four.

D. Fish tanks eight and four?

T. Yes. You like to go to the fourth (*fish tank*), the border, visiting your pet (*Siah, on Etena*). The pet misses you. There are scrolls to be found inside temples on the fourth.

D. That's what Ophelia said.

T. You store several scrolls from different realities on the fourth (*fish tank four*), a safe haven within the Wheel. It is known as a friendly companion, the diplomat within the Wheel. The fourth carries the tone that some of your musicians mirrored in the Renaissance time and earlier. They invited the vibrations from the fourth. They didn't know that at that time fish tank four, the border, was actually closer into your reality. That's why it was heard. See it as those jellyfish, going in and out. At that time, when there was a big enlightenment, the fourth drew closer to the fifth fish tank. We observed this, councils, different ones from different fish tanks. There are councils representing all realities observing. The spotlight is on this fish tank for the moment, due to the fact that we do not wish for it to move into hibernation. (*The Creator may send realities into hibernation if there is too much divergence from the intended path of evolution. Bob calls it a reboot.*) We are inviting the light and tones from the fourth. That is what increasing the light means here in your reality. The fourth, where your pet exists and other friends, are making themselves known again. The fourth is a mother energy within the Wheel. This one will understand, as it resonates with the zodiac. She will understand how certain influences affect you. She will assist with certain teachings based on that knowledge. Everything is connected, nothing is separated. Tallock observes. You will visit home shortly. This one knows how, has seen the lightways, how to travel, how to move. Need to not fear the vibration of transition. Need to work with releasing physical energy, transforming to travel on the lightways. Reaching home, meeting friends.

D. So this one will travel?

T. Yes. You can too. You are not afraid of the vibration in the same way. This one easier travels energetically, or in the mind. But in order for the experience to be fully connected, the physical in some way has to be released. It is a science to release the physical and tap into the fourth reality here—your (*the Earth's*) mental realm, (*which is*) the border of transitioning into spirit—without actually dying! Huh. Ophelia would not like that. (*He means if either Christine or I accidentally died while practicing this exercise.*)

D. Too much effort has been put into this project.

T. Yes. This one can do training on how to adapt. We will assist with vibrational impacts.

D. How should that training be done?

T. Your singing bowls are one. It helps. Different tones in the ears helping, assisting. Smells, oils. Use lavender oil, it comforts the soul. Light. All connected. Singing bowls, sounds. Olive or lavender oil. The skin is very suited, if it is not dry. Oil on the skin, olive oil. This is how the ancients traveled. They bathed in olive oil, in big barrels. They were completely soaked. Water or oil has a tendency to react to energetic travels differently. Your skin is key. For you, work with oils on your skin.

D. Is the olive oil best?

T. Yes, something that doesn't dry quickly. No smells on that oil, neutral. Olive oil. Lavender oil simply in a lamp or candle. Smell soothes the soul for travel, assists physical to be released. It's easier to release the physical if it's not dense and dry.

D. When you say Tallock, is that your name, or is this a group?

T. Group. Civilization. Home planet, blue.

D. What fish tank?

T. Eight.

D. Are we on a council together?

T. I join you on the Council of Nine.

D. And what is your name, or what should I call you?

L. We are all Tallock. You can call me Leon, if you like, but we are all Tallock. (*I changed the name abbreviation from T for Tallock, to L for Leon for the rest of his talk. In subsequent sessions, they simply identify themselves as Tallock.*)

D. What dimension are you from, originally?

L. Sixth. Now operating on tenth and nine.

D. Are you related to the Elahim?

L. Friends. Cousin, if you like. Cousin to the Elahim. Tallock never incarnated here. Elahim did. We discussed which group should go (*to Earth*). Elahim took the assignment. We observed. We connect to this reality through certain constellations. We have eyes in the Moon. Huh. Tallock eyes, Little Greys, our friends. Our eyes, when we do not travel.

D. Yes, someone mentioned the Little Greys operate under councils on the ninth.

L. Yes. Great friends of ours. Curious, friendly. Gatherers, that's what we call them. They gather information. They are very eager, thorough, quick. Their communication ability will astound the humans. Quick. You will communicate and meet them and you will see the difference, my son. Different energy, quick. Pay attention, they don't repeat. Huh!

D. I'm glad we have recorders, then.

L. Yes. There. We will meet here soon, again.

D. Do the Tallock have another planet they travel to in fish tank eight?

L. Home in the eighth. This one has seen it, doesn't know what it was. You travel here to connect to the elements. The physical reality that this one has seen is home in the eighth.

D. Is it an Earth-like object, or is it completely different?

L. What do you mean by object?

D. If it is structured differently?

L. Structured differently, less commotion, quiet. That is why you don't like the noise. You can't hear your soul. You can't hear your home calling you because of all the commotion around you. Topography different, no atmosphere (*on Vlac*). The same as here with mountains, big lakes, not all with water, different liquid, resonating with chanting and connections to other fish tanks. Receivers exist within the lakes. Topography is different. Resonates with dark blue. Home, home for you both. This one (*Seth*) visits more frequently than you. You are involved with keeping knowledge in the fourth fish tank with your pet (*on Etena*). You take care of storage within this great library, together with Zachariah and Ophelia. It's similar like the one you find on the fifth dimension, only in a manifested form, if you like. That is why this is a manifested reality where your pet is. It's not a spiritual reality. It is another home. You prefer it. Light, sunlight, different from the eighth. Information stored on all the fish tanks. This is the physical library within the Wheel. There are, of course, libraries and storage in each fish tank. However, this great cathedral stores a little bit of each (*fish tank*). Your pet eagerly awaits you when you travel. You like to return; you like to spend time with the people that exists on this planet or reality. Stronger light, belonging in a solar system of several occupied planets. Grand solar system. This one is small, but your lessons here on Earth are so profound. You will never access more friends in your Solar System that will be occupied, unless you learn the lesson of sharing. You did not know, but a solar system can grow from its intentional structure. Certain events can provide more power to your Solar System, to your Sun, and adding more planets. This system was bigger before. Certain planets out in orbit disappeared. The Sun got dimmed, and the Earth project began. Nothing is constant. But you know that, of course. There.

D. Wow, that's marvelous information. Thank you for that.

L. I'll see you at home! Huh!

D. Alright, my friend. Thank you for coming to join us, Leon. It's wonderful to meet you here.

L. Thank you, my friend. Elahim.

D. Elahim.

O. (*After a long pause, Ophelia came in.*) This is Ophelia.

D. Hello, Ophelia. I assumed you would be doing the clean-up.

O. Hello. Oh, clean-up is absolutely needed.

D. I noticed Christine's hands were shaking, so I knew it was a different energy.

O. Yes, it is. Friends from another fish tank, friends from home. Closer connected to this one than to you, but you both travel and you both visit, and you both connect to the eighth. Simply a preference where you wish to join more frequently.

D. Do you have a fish tank that you prefer?

O. Yes. I do prefer number eleven, and I do like the seventh and the second.

D. What sort of energies are those?

O. Vibrational tones. Energetic realities connected to the mental energetic levels within you, if you like, to give you a picture. No physical manifestation. Realities of non-form and the ability to become one with the tone or the light. Those are experiences, from a human standpoint, like air, resonating with resting in knowledge within your energetic being.

D. It's interesting that you prefer a mental realm, since you come from an emotional, light dimension?

O. Yes. However, the light is highly connected to not only the emotional, but the mental as well. An emotional reality, which is more connected to the second fish tank, is, in many ways, a home base. Whereas there are greater teachings for me in the eleventh and the seventh. Light is not only connected to emotions. On this level, within these fish tanks, they are one. No physical form is detected. You merge with others and simply are emotion. You vibrate as a pulse of knowledge within those realities. It's a foundation for the physical ones to manifest and to become. The pulse, all fish tanks within the Wheel... how can I give you the picture? They balance. If you think of the elements, they are all balanced together. So if you think of the elements provided here—earth, water, fire, air—there need to be a balance to create a physical manifestation that is doable, in order for them to become productive and evolve. No being, at this point, has the ability to simply function with three or two elements. Same within the Wheel. No fish tank has the ability to survive unless it is connected and assisted with all, if you think of the elements. I give you an easy picture here, of course. So let's say that the eleventh and seventh are air, then if those two were shut down in hibernation, the whole Wheel will wobble.

D. That makes sense.

O. The Wheel turns and rotates, so you have to experience, in some way, different elements.

D. So as the Wheel rotates, does the physical matter gradually become something less dense?

O. Not necessarily. Each fish tank is designed to occupy physical matter, or not. So, let's say this one that you have physical manifestation within, eventually the teachings will be moving into the sixth fish tank's position. Meaning it will add simply that element within your reality. At this point, we are increasing the water element that exists within the fourth fish tank, where Siah is. Meaning that water is emotions. Water is fluid, rhythmical, and that is the element that we wish to enhance within the fifth fish tank. I'm giving you an easy way to understand, by giving you earth, water, fire, air. There you go. Let's see. Yes. (*She was looking towards Bob.*)

D. Well, thank you so much for that description, Ophelia. I really appreciate it.

O. You are much welcome.

Tallocks, Ophelia: The Creator Disk (April 28, 2019)
Our friends in spirit have allocated a lot of precious trance time to explaining Creation. The Wheel of Creation was first mentioned by Zachariah in November 2016, and has since been the subject of many talks. To plug the holes in human understanding, our spirit friends regularly return to fill in the details of how the Creator creates. The scientific community only accepts that four fundamental forces exist: gravity, electromagnetism, and the strong and weak nuclear forces. What they fail to recognize is the ability of the spirit realm to manipulate and alter the known fundamental forces, as well as the unknown forces that give rise to matter. The third dimension of Earth, for example, has energy flowing in from several dimensions, creating new conditions and experiences. In this session, the Tallocks and Ophelia describe the Creator Disk that rotates beneath the Wheel of Creation, which itself has several layers. In *Wave 3*, the Council of Nine described the levels within the fish tanks in this way, "In many ways, there are two disks, one lower and one upper. The lower one is the manifested disk. That one is constant. The energy disk slightly above, mirroring the fish tanks, are the ones that move. So, the disk is in two (*parts*), one solid, one stationary, one in motion. It sends the motional, the moving disk, gradually throughout—motion clockwise.

The picture has been sent to this one. You have been given the image of the spiritual realities' center to Pole and fish tanks outward, locating as a clock in this disk. But there are also levels on the disk. One stationary, one travels through experiencing. The stationary disk is where all completion is stored. The ones where you belong to, the second, Etena, and so forth, you belong in the movable disk. You travel throughout." [...] "As the rotation moves in the upper Wheel, the fog Wheel, if you like, that is how it looks, as it has completed its understanding of its position, it simply docks or loses its experiences down to the stationary disk, who is the one that will determine the motion further. At this time, due to incidents in the fourth fish tank versus the fifth, the border is dissolving between them. This indicates that there is a motion where the fourth reality, fourth fish tank, will gradually merge with the fifth."

The combination of their descriptions and the images sent to Christine are a bit perplexing. However, we believe that there are three main disks that work together to make reality. The Fish Tanks in our Wheel are sandwiched between the Creator Disk on the bottom and a fog disk above where the ever-present Master Mind and Master Eye energies are located. This upper layer can be accessed by spirits and is a source of knowledge, as Bob told us during his forays at Etena. The Creator Disk, however, is a mystery, although it transmits intent up into the fish tanks that can be read by the spiritual councils. In the middle are the fish tanks and parallel realities, along with the spiritual dimensions. The upper and lower disks rotate in opposite directions, which has been a point of confusion for me. The Creator Disk goes counter-clockwise and the Fog Disk above rotates clockwise. So there are influences going in both directions that are experienced within the universes of form. We have included an image in the Preface that resembles their description.

T. This is Tallock, here with Ari.

D. Hello, my friend.

T. Let's see who will communicate this teaching. It is the core teaching of the Elahim. Tallocks execute the teachings of the Elahims, in the band between fish tank eight and nine. We are sending images to the receiver in this one of how the Wheel is operating, to provide a new level of understanding of fish tanks versus the grand Wheel. Center core, spiritual. Outside (*are the*) fish tanks (*with*) manifested form. Just because it is a mental reality, it is still considered a manifested reality or manifested form. Physical, mental, emotional all resonate with what we refer to as physical form, as they are non-spiritual. The hub, the Creator, the Pole that penetrates through several disks. See the disks, at this point, horizontal. The disk is a living entity. The fish tanks as well, but the fish tanks are more stationary. The Wheel is not. The Wheel rotates anti-clockwise; fish tanks stationary, appear to rotate clockwise. That means that fish tank five, where you currently are present, the spiritual energy wheel, the disk of spiritual energy flow that radiates from the Creator, the Pole, rotating anti-clockwise, making this level, the Earth plane, feels the energy of the fourth. It's not moving clockwise, in that sense. If you see the fish tank stationary for a while, for me, and then see this mist, the spiritual wheel, slowly rotating anti-clockwise, present in all fish tanks, moving all levels forward anti-clockwise. If you see the image from above, looking down, place yourself on the top of the hub, looking down on this Wheel. The Little One sees it as a clock; we see it from above. When you see this grand spiritual disk, the Creator Disk, like we call it, we don't necessarily call it spiritual, but the Creator's Disk, rotating anti-clockwise through the fish tanks, the fish tanks themselves appear slightly moving clockwise. Do you see the image?

D. I do. That would be bringing the sixth closer to five, the energy of six?

T. Yes. So we reside in the end of ninth, similar as you are in the end of fifth, feeling the presence of the eighth, having the Creator's Disk, slowly and gently, pushing our reality forward; but we're not moving fish tanks, we're not stepping in from one to another. The Creator simply moves our awareness into the upcoming... it is hard to give you a full image, but we're trying to add another level and layer to this Wheel. So if you think of this Creator Disk, each cake, let's say, if there was a piece looking like a cake, brings in a new understanding. So let's say at this point you are pushing into the fourth. But it's not one, two, three, in order all the time. The cake, from the Creator, could be in like trillions of sceons, that is our years, then the cake that we are currently experiencing in the eighth, that piece of the Creator's wheel, will be moving in to the fifth fish tank. Do you see what I am trying to tell you? The image is sent to this one, so even though, at this point, you know this fish tank as number five; it has no number, it simply at this point resonate with the cake, the piece in the big Creator Wheel, resonating with five. In trillions of sceons, this fish tank could be called the eighth. Do you understand what I'm telling you?

D. A little bit.

T. The image is sent to this one; ask after. The Creator's wheel (*Disk*) carries twelve different experiences that slowly move through the fish tanks. You are currently experiencing number five. That is why this fish tank now looks to you (*to be*) at five o'clock. It's not a clock, it's simply in correlation to the piece within the big Creator wheel, at this time, that is lesson number five. We sent you the image as a clock. Now we're adding a new level of understanding to the Wheel, which will indicate that this grand clock that you see will rotate. Meaning that this will appear later on as number six, as the grand Creator wheel brings in the sixth, then this fish tank would be called the sixth. Do you understand?

D. The reality of the fourth and sixth, are they on opposite sides of our fish tank, from the perspective of a clock? Or are these different types of energies?

T. Yes, yes, but it's all designed by the grand Disk. There are two working together on top, overlapping. The engine of them all is the grand disk, the Creator Disk. And if you see that the Creator Disk has, let's say, twelve fish tanks, that's what I refer to as a piece of a cake, a triangle, that's how it looks from above. So the fish tanks look almost square, whereas—let's call it triangles on the Creator's Disk. So we have twelve triangles rotating with different teachings, different components, and events. It's all in combination of light and sound, what sort of manifestation will occur. At this time, you are radiated by the fifth triangle. When the fifth triangle rotates anti-clockwise, it will move into the fourth fish tank.

D. That I understand. And the sixth triangle will move into the fifth fish tank?

T. Will move into the fifth, from the beginning of the fifth, and this grand triangle, wheel, rotates, if you look from above, it appears that your fish tanks rotate clockwise. As they rotate simultaneously, which means that in a trillion of sceons, this fish tank, this universe, this square, could be influenced by the triangle eight.

D. After it has gone through seven?

T. Yes.

D. So they are in order?

T. They are in order, indeed. So everything is in order, but at this time, and you are only going to see this one at five o'clock. But if you see it as a 3–D image, which it is, then the grand Disk rotates anti–clockwise with different teachings. You are now being forced or pushed into the fourth.

D. The fourth triangle?

T. The sixth is moving in, but you are feeling the presence of the fourth, where Siah is. Let's leave it, because I think you have the first understanding of this three-dimensional image. The image is sent to this one. With that, I will leave at this point, to not confuse you. (*As the Creator Disk rotates counter clockwise, the left side of fish tank four is above the fifth "triangle" on the Creator's Disk. Meaning, the energy is similar to the right side of fish tank five. So, there is a blending on the experiencing Wheel.*)

D. That's easy to do.

T. Elahim work with transitions, preparing new teachings to come in; new universes, new fish tanks. You are currently preparing the shift between nine and eight; it's similar there, that you experience here between five and four. There is a band between, an energetic turmoil, that is why this reality experiences turmoil, because on one hand you are still in the fifth cake, triangle, but you are also being pushed closer to the reality of the fish tank of the fourth, meaning the fourth make themselves known. But you're not moving your whole fish tank, it's simply the different triangles that move through you. More will be given, because clearly this is confusing. You did work with this in ancient times before there were historic remains that you now find. (*Prior to all known history.*) Great minds understood the Wheel of Creation and the 3-D activity, and the small contribution that each fish tank provided. You can see this grand Disk as an awareness, moving forward through all fish tanks to get a glimpse, to assist and create new events. You are currently given dual messages from the Creator, in order for the Creator to see how you respond to the light, the light meaning the next level of learning. You are assisted by those present in the band close to the fourth fish tank.

D. Can I ask a question, then?

T. If you wish.

D. If we take our Milky Way as an example, if it is close to the fourth, are all nearby galaxies in the same situation? Or is it based on their own specific frequency, so they might be closer to the sixth fish tank? Do you see what I am saying?

T. Each galaxy has somewhat of an isolated experience. Milky Way is teeny-tiny. It's not even close to the sixth fish tank, it's not going across. It looks from this perspective as a grain of sand. Everything that you experience within your nearest vicinity is moving into this band between fourth and fifth.

D. But other galaxies might be closer to the sixth?

T. Yes, they might still be experiencing the beginning. Let's say—to make it easy so don't get stuck in words or the details of numbers—but let's say that when your Earth was created, it was closer to the sixth, traveling gradually through this reality of the fish tank, being moved gently by the grand Disk forward through its evolution.

D. So the evolution is anti–clockwise?

T. Yes. Physical and emotional and mental evolution, clockwise. Do you understand?

D. I think I do.

T. There we go. Let's leave it before we create confusion. More will come.

D. But within our visible Universe, everything is within the same fish tank?

T. Yes, yes. Your closest neighbors are in that band. Andromeda is a little bit behind. But you experience this duality between light and dark—and again, there is not bad with dark, and good with light. It's simply different experiences. Andromeda is a little bit still behind. They have not entered the turmoil that you experienced yourself in.

D. So, like Siah's world, is it heading towards—

T. Siah's world is just in the beginning of the fourth fish tank, but there are different conditions there. Not the same teachings. They traveled through the awareness and teachings of the fifth where you are currently at, and mastered those turmoils when mental and emotional teaching fly around you like fireflies.

D. So the future of the Earth realm will be much more light–filled and peaceful?

T. Yes. The intention is for you to move into the awareness of where Siah currently is. The fish tanks are simply an experience where the grand disk moves certain objects through, (*like*) your galaxy, you yourself, and so forth. If you can see it as almost like empty boxes where the fish tanks are. These (*empty boxes*) are what the grand disk fills up in order to see different events and experiences taking place. So you do not BELONG in a fish tank, necessarily. Oh, yes, this is tricky. Ophelia says that this is the end of this cosmic class.

D. (*Laughing.*) Is she reading my thought waves?

T. She reads ALL thought waves. But the fish tanks are empty spaces where the grand disk chooses to fill up—in this case (*fish tank five*)—with physical planets and objects and physical beings.

D. So our fish tank will always have physical matter, or will it gradually change to something else?

T. Yes. Siah's world is physical, isn't it? So it's still a physical reality here between six and three. But it's always appearing as a turmoil when the Creator disk moves you through different shifts; and you are in that shift. One (*aspect*) feels more primitive and more connected to solid matter, because you are solid. Whereas another part within you starts to feel spiritual, starts to feel like an energetic being. The duality here is to find balance between a physical and a spiritual experience. Mental and emotional are simply added as an experience in order for you to make decisions. It mirrors the intent the Creator wants to experience in this empty box, where you are currently residing in, as the fifth. All boxes are empty, not just this one. It's just the Creator moving through them. I hope you can see the image; see it as a light going anti-clockwise through all, and the fish tanks are sound responding to that light. This combined creates events that the Creator wishes to investigate. There. Ophelia says that's it. Okay, I'll see you back home. There you go.

D. Alright, my friend. Thank you, that was a wonderful teaching.

O. Good morning to you.

D. Hello, Ophelia. Thank you for that teaching.

O. Oh, you are much welcome. It is simply a reminder to make you aware that the grand design is actually expanding. This is what will linger in your mind until the end of days on this plane. You will try to figure out how this is all connected, with the resources that you have. Don't feel discouraged if you do not fully understand. You are here to set your wheel in motion, similar as the Creator setting the grand Wheel in motion. So see it, if you like, as being that light that radiates, similar like the Creator Disk, through this reality, bringing them forward into what you know now as being (*energetically*) where Siah is.

D. Much more peaceful existence.

O. Yes. But regardless of your actions, the Wheel is still continuing to operate and moving forward. How you meet these turmoils, these challenges that you are facing at this time, is what you know as the power of will. You have your own power. You have the will to do it either in the easy way, or the hard way; but you still have your own will. You are here to simply try to encourage people to surrender to the inner being, to the inner light—who they are. Those who choose another path are feeling locked within the physical reality, the physical events that you see around you. They are staged, many of them, to see how you are responding, what side you take, what trail you follow.

D. Can I ask a question?

O. If you like.

D. It's about karma. Are certain people placed in certain plays as a result of their Coat of Karma or lessons they need to learn?

O. Karma is in the background, if you like. If you see it, your vehicle (*body*), you're steering your experience, your life, in a car and you're sitting by the steering wheel. Karma is placed in your back seat. Karma is the one that creates your roads ahead. So, are you driving on a highway straight ahead, or are you in a car where your lights are dimmed and you cannot see in front of you? Some will experience life as driving in a car in heavy snow. And some will have a clear view of that highway ahead. Karma is simply placed in the back seat, creating all these different experiences for the driver. The driver meaning the soul in a human body.

D. That's a very good analogy. Thank you.

O. There you go.

D. I had another question, before you flee. What does the fifth do? No one has ever said what the souls from the fifth do.

O. The souls from the fifth are closer to this reality. Meaning, if you think of the progress, the evolution of fish tanks, it is similar from the Creator as well. So the fifth dimension, being closer to the fourth and the third, are in their beginning of soul evolution if you like. You transition through levels, but you are born on different realities. The fifth was added later in the evolution of the Grand Disk, the spiritual disk that is, the spiritual realities. It doesn't mean they will not ascend into the light, similar as everyone else. Much of the intention of adding a fifth dimension, for this experience in this fish tank, is unique. It might not be a fifth dimension for souls in, let's say, fish tank eleven. Or they might appear differently, I should say. Here, those who belong in the fifth dimension are normally Earth–bound, meaning that they are familiar with coming to Earth. Some also have gone to planets in Andromeda, but they still feel comfortable with physical matter, physical experiences. Whereas souls which originate from six and seven have in their memory an experience of emotional and mental realities. That is why they struggle more here in this reality than souls from the fifth, as they are more programmed to occupy physical realities and bodies.

D. Okay, that makes a lot of sense.

O. The fifth is known as a great hall of teaching. Souls from six and seven gladly visit the fifth, because they have more knowledge about traveling to physical realties than do you. Great lecture halls, great gardens, things that souls from six and seven might not have experienced in earlier travels. They are your friends, your companions, as you travel to this reality here. Everyone needs a companion within their human family that comes from the fifth. As they are a tour guide for you, they will assist and balance the struggle that you might experience in a physical reality.

D. It suddenly just clicked for me; I totally understand what you are saying.

O. There you go, click–click–click.

D. Wow. Thank you. Wonderful explanation.

O. Oh, you are much welcome. So there.

Ophelia: Linear and Multiple Timelines (Sept 26, 2019)

This particular exchange with Ophelia is uniquely illuminating. Over the years, I have accumulated more than a passing familiarity with the mystical ramblings of the new age philosophers who haphazardly proclaim that time does not exist. The nebulous field of quantum physics has opened a door for scientific theologians to plop a few of their own sophisticated speculations into the hopper, one such being known as the "block universe theory". This hypothesis seems (to me) to be an extension of certain ideas proposed by Seth, as channeled by Jane Roberts. The block universe theory proposes that everything that has ever happened, and everything that will happen, already exists within the universe. And time does not flow, only the observer's perception on the timeline at a particular point in space. However, everything our various spirit friends have said about time, as it relates to the material universe, refutes the notion that the future is predetermined. If your future actions, location, thoughts, physical health, emotions, etc., already exist as a fixed point in the future, then that completely erases free will and karma. My opinion is that the "moving spotlight" and the "block universe" theories are invalid ways of describing time.

I mention Seth (via Jane Roberts) because he was one of the few channeled beings whom I sensed was legitimate (aside from those who speak through Christine). I struggled, and mostly failed, to understand certain of his concepts, especially when it came to probable selves. But looking back, I think his explanations incorporated the fourth dimension (the mental realm around Earth), and even the spiritual dimensions, within the framework of his description of the dream selves and probable selves. After learning about the true structure of reality from our spirit team, I think Seth was examining consciousness, awareness, and perception from the perspective of a soul at home when he said (in *Seth Speaks*), "Progress has nothing to do with time, you see, but with psychic and spiritual focus. Each play (incarnation) is entirely different from any other. It is not correct, therefore, to suppose that your actions in this life are caused by a previous existence, or that you are being punished in this life for crimes in a past one. The lives are simultaneous." Seth talked about lives occurring simultaneously, but he was using a point of reference that is not available to a soul trapped in a human body. I partially agree with his other remarks about the causal relationship of one life to another, but I think it could be misinterpreted as him saying that karma does not exist. Karma is absolutely an active part of the incarnation process, but it operates at a level above the human desires for vengeance or reward. Ophelia gives us a brilliant delineation of how perception determines time.

D. Okay, I have another question about time, as it seems to be something that people struggle with. Does all time occur simultaneously on Earth, or is it indeed somewhat linear?

O. Somewhat linear, indeed. Time is, in many ways, linear like you describe it. Events move through time; matter moves through time, creating occurrences. In many ways, man is not equipped to understand the difference between time and cycles. You have the ability to move beyond the linear time. As you are in body, the normal man will simply experience linear time. As you move into your soul being, expanding your awareness and consciousness, raising your vibration up into the fourth (*dimension*), then you have the ability to experience unlimited time, unlimited time here on Earth. Which means that everything occurs simultaneously in that reality. Once you are—to give you a picture—if you see a man and up to your waist you are in your third reality. The heart and chest will move into the fourth reality. Shoulders, even so, in fourth reality. Head bordering into the fifth and above. Once you are preoccupied from your waist and down, then you will only experience linear time. When you move your awareness up into your higher frequencies, understanding your heart and throat chakras, understanding the different vibrations within your being, then you have the ability to indeed ascend into the fourth reality and experience multiple times at the same time.

D. When I had my near-death experience (*around 12 years old*), I remember what it was like to be outside of time.

O. Yes. From that point, you were hovering above. If you see the linear time, then you see the multiple timelines. Then, if you see above that, you see empty space where you can see and experience nothingness, if you like, as well as tapping into the other two lines. You were in the space of nothingness. You did not experience the multiple time. Once you start, if you had visualized that you had turned around, then you would have been in spiritual time. You would have been in nothingness that will not feel sad. It would have felt empowering, uplifting, because you would have been one with time. When you are here, you are experiencing time—you are not one with time.

D. That's an excellent explanation. Thank you for that. Can souls incarnate backwards in linear time, or is it a forward direction only?

O. Hmm. Forward direction, in some way. However, lessons can be returned to, but not with a full incarnation. From a soul perspective, one can tap into, from the spirit realm, a prior life, but not incarnating in it—simply dressing in the Coat, but remaining in the fourth. So, you experience a past life in the fourth reality, but you cannot incarnate in a past life.

D. I understand. Can you change anything about that life?

O. Yes indeed, if you have risen to that level of understanding on how you can affect your own timeline. You have the regular timeline, but you also have your own. And from the spirit realm you have the ability, after a while, to tap into not only your past Coats, your past lives, and change—which is not something one does without assistance and approval from spirit helpers—but if it's allowed, then indeed, one can go back and do adjustments. However, they cannot go back and delete, from that perspective, delete karma. They can do minor adjustments. But if there is grander issues that took place, you have to be in body in order for that to be resolved.

D. That's a wonderful explanation. Thank you.

O. Oh, you are much welcome. We have someone pacing. I feel pushed. This time he (*Bob*) is the one dragging my arm.

D. (*Laughing*) I can imagine. Separate session. Well, it's good to talk to you again, my friend.

O. See you soon. Bye bye.

Tallocks, Ophelia: Levels of Existence of Elements (Oct 13, 2019)
It would be nice to claim that I understand all of the information in this session, but that would be misleading. In some of the earlier sessions, there have been hints that the energetic atmosphere around Earth was adjusted so that certain elements become locked with the properties we see today. For example, Bob said that Issac told him "So all elements who have the conditions of liquid are stronger. That is why, he (Isaac) said, like before, when gold was used as a liquid form on Earth, that is actually the highest form of a fuel on this plane." (*Notes, Volume 2*). In May 2019, Ophelia commented, "There were eruptions resulting from blending certain elements. Mercury is an element that is used in several different areas; it is the key element for travel and time. They tried in some way to manipulate travel and time. Mercury, in that atmospheric condition that existed, became an eruption (explosion). The blend of mercury and gold are two components of elements that is the foundation for portals and travels. With those, ancient civilizations, even here, knew how to bend time. Bend time means that you can have an access to past and present, because they connect." (See *Wave 3*.) In this session, the Tallocks describe how the elements, at remote times in the past, had more levels of existence. My interpretation is that there were other stable isotopes of gold, silver and mercury once present on Earth, which no longer exist. Or conversely, the visitors (aliens) were able to manufacture stable isotopes through fusion and fission, which were then used for fuel and energy, and also for creating portals and traveling in parallel planes between realities.

Ophelia comes in after the Tallock pulled away from Christine and she gave some very interesting information about undersea power points. She said that oxygen was being generated at various locations on the sea floor to help stabilize the environment and initiate movement of landmass. Although she does not clarify whether the power points are natural or left here by visitors, she acknowledged it is related to undersea volcanoes.

The key from the Tallocks and Ophelia is that free energy is generated by connecting a map on the Earth with a corresponding map in the stars through a link in the fourth dimension.

T. This is the Tallocks. Greetings from the fish tank eight.

D. Hello, my friends.

T. We are here to supply and provide keys for development of understanding physics, to understand the limitations you are placed below at this time. At one point, the veil was not as heavy as it is now. The key is to understand your elements, the minerals and foundations that you are working with. Here, they are simply a dead object, but we see them as spiritual entities such as ourselves. We ask for permission to develop and grow with the elements. Ancients knew how to honor the gateways of what is now known as physics. How to enter the realms where the elements greet you, takes you on a journey to explore them, develop their capacities, how to become new sources of energies, receivers. There are receivers placed here on this plane; a gift from your friends from the eighth. To understand the limits of an element, you have to dissect and understand that it is a spiritual entity as well. To understand a soul, you have to investigate and go through the layers within a soul. The same as with elements. To combine two elements, creating a third, creating a fourth and fifth, was misused by those who did not honor the teachings and the gifts of the elements. You (*current humans*) work differently with physics at this time. That is why you are limited, because you do not ask for permission. You do not seek the treat, the knowledge, within the element. If we take gold, silver, mercury, zinc, creating neutrons, splitting atoms, merging, becoming a different structure, different component within this element. To take gold as an example, gold has ten levels of existence. You know two: solid, or melted. But you don't understand that there are more levels of this element to work with. Seven were available at one point. Ancient Egypt knew how to elaborate and master seven different levels within gold. Taught by those who came from outside, visitors, such as us (*the Tallocks*).

D. Could you explain what the other levels might be?

T. They are different levels within: solid, vaporized, liquid. You only see solid or liquid—two. Solid is not just one form. It was shifting as the ancients knew how to master and agree with the element, agree with minerals. They were given different levels of form, different levels of solid, moving from solid as a teeny, tiny pearl, expanding the solidness, growing into a different form, larger than the original source. Using light, using sound combined, bathing, surrounding the element, the mineral, from two sides, making it rotate; rotate anti–clockwise, moving. The motion was caused by sound. The light provided the conditions of the object, changing the amount of light, increasing, combined with the rotation of sound; two sources operating on each side. Rotation, ascension, motion of object. Sound delivered, similar like drums, tubes—different depending on your mission for the object. The rotation is key. The spinning moves it into, first, the source of what the element is, into what it has the ability to become.

D. So they changed the nature of gold into something else?

T. Yes, yes.

D. And what sort of element did it become?

T. It was still gold, but it had another objective. Possibilities were different, used the power, using, creating the web, energetic web, global web, source for outer influences to read. It was a power plant. Gold used as connecting points. It became the receivers. Silver departed, silver sends off, in its highest form. Gold—receivers. Mercury travels. Three components creating the web; power plants that you once obtained.

D. So these elements were used to generate some power field?

T. Yes, yes.

D. Was the energy used for travel?

T. Yes. Mercury, when the highest form—again, several levels. Mercury has thirteen. Gold ten. Silver has seven. When ancients knew how to master different levels within form, different levels within dissolved liquid, creating form, creating levels of existence, levels of experiencing. It was a vaporized form, silent, that created the web. But the source connecting the strings were solid, but not the solid form that you are aware of at this time. The web is a fog, not liquid. Liquid went below. To give you a picture, let's use a pyramid. Underneath, the liquid that charged the pyramid floated into the pyramid and circled, creating a natural rotation within the solid form of the pyramid. The top was the solid form of either, normally, gold or silver. The connection, the path between pyramids was a fog, vaporized, creating the web, making it possible to either travel or to use, gain, the energy between the power plants. One power plant existed here; you had another power plant above. The remains of the above power plant are now frozen as star constellations, a memory of the same power plant. That is why you see the same pattern here as in the sky; two power plants.

D. That was extremely remote to the Earth then?

T. Huh. Now it is. Also levels, my friend. At one point, it was closer. The replica, the image, was closer. The stars were where they were, but you have several levels in your planet that operates differently. The cosmos, similar. So you have the star map on the ground and you have the star constellations in the sky. Ancients knew how to merge them, raising the Earth map, if you like, the Earth web, meeting the cosmic web. When those two were merged in the fourth dimension, travels were possible. At this time, these two webs, these two connections, are either here on Earth or up in the sky—they don't merge. See it as two levels, (*one*) departing from Earth, (*the other*) departing from the stars, meeting in the middle. The way the ancients knew how to create a replica of the stars was the fact that the star map had descended. It was closer; it gave ancients the information in the fourth. You cannot seek the star map in the fourth at this time. You see it physically where it is. This is the separation of the source to understanding power and the elements. Those who came with the knowledge of the star map allowed it to descend into the fourth, knowing that there were some on the third that will access and understand this map, making a replica. Later, visitors came to refine the plan, helping, creating energetic connection points.

D. You mentioned ancient Egypt as being one of those locations. What time frame did this occur?

T. There was a great effort in understanding these two maps, understanding the star map, making a replica here around 15,000 years ago. But there was a prior civilization much earlier, 50,000 years ago, that initiated the project. Forerunners to those who came later. Same object, same project, used as understanding how to access and gain energy with connecting points. You have the pyramids, but you do it in a smaller way using only a rock. The key is to place them strategically, using gravitationally strong points to place this rock, to place this pyramid. From that point, liquid is added, flowing in underneath, becoming the rock, becoming the pyramid. Rotation, again, is key for any motion, for any extraction of power. Engineering of a higher level, power plants used unlimited resource of energy. Unlimited ways to travel.

D. The light that you mentioned that they added, is that similar to sunlight, or was it something else?

T. Sunlight that was manipulated, increased, using big disks. Solar disks, those were made from copper or gold. Red-yellow copper. Copper—science overlooks the ability that copper has. It's a gift to this planet, a gift to those who engineer power.

D. So the light was added. And the sound that was added to the material, for example, was that done before when it was inside the pyramid or was it done outside? How was the rotation achieved?

T. Inside the pyramid. Rotation inside. Engineering took place inside the pyramid.

D. The light was in some way beamed into the pyramid?

T. Well, beamed... it was given from below, from the liquid. It came with the ability to create light, but the disks were outside, storing light, moving it into vast containers, reservoirs, used later with the liquid. Moving into the pyramid, the beam went OUT, not in. (*The liquid may be the molten copper that is mentioned in a later section about free energy.*)

D. So the light energy and the sound energy was in some way put into—

T. The liquid.

D. And the liquid was then put into the base of the pyramid?

T. Yes. Yes. At this point, we will leave with that, we will continue the topic. But the beam, that you talked about, was when the rotation inside the pyramid had been completed. It zipped through, it opened the pyramid, it radiated and connected with the receiving star in the star constellation. When the connection was complete, that particular travel, that particular access of energy resource was complete and connected. We will continue.

D. Well, thank you for that information.

T. You are much welcome. Okay, thank you.

D. I'll think about that. Goodbye, my friend.

O. This is Ophelia.

D. Ah, hello, Ophelia.

O. Hello to you.

D. Always nice to hear your voice.

O. Just cleaning the energy. We have some friends ready, not just one.

D. We were just talking the other day, this one and I, that we don't get to hear you very much anymore.

O. Oh, you do. You do hear me, not only in your dreams, but you do hear me remotely through the other ones (*who are speaking*). Always present, always popping thought bubbles around, making sure that the general themes remain as planned. But what we do appreciate, and what we wish for you to understand, is that you are taking a step up on the ladder of understanding the higher science and the connection that exists within maps. There are power points around this planet. Some are sleeping. Some begins to activate, begins to come alive from a long slumber, if you like.

The power points that are awakened is to stabilize the motion of your planet. You are both part of motion when it comes to land mass. You are both part of planting different power points, making them evolve, sleep, wake up in a certain time line, in a scheduled development as the object itself, the planet, will tilt, change rotation. It's happened before (*awakening the power points*). It happens over different cycles to create stability in certain regions. We are concerned, as you are aware, of the waters, and there is a need to activate some of the power points, not visible to man, that exist on the seabed. This is to provide more oxygen in the water. The oxygen needed begins on the seabed as it will later rise and fill, gradually, the oceans. This is a long-term project, but the first start is to make sure that these power points, that are located underneath the seabed, will start to awake. There is a power point that has nothing to do with radiating oxygen that is located where the Bermuda Triangle is known. There is another one that is about to wake up, which is hidden in the central part of the Atlantic. Another one, oh, sorry, one, two, three, going horizontally, north to south, in the South Pacific. Those have been awakened longer. Those are operating to provide oxygen to the water in that region. It's between, hmm, the islands of Hawaii and south of there, down to the islands of Fiji, in the middle, south of the Hawaiian Islands, north of the Fiji Islands.

D. Somewhere around the equator?

O. Yes.

D. Are they related to volcanic activity?

O. YES.

D. In what way is the oxygen generated?

O. It's a volcanic eruption radiating oxygen on the seabed. But you don't see, you have no ability. It has not created a tsunami, let's just say that. It's a silent project to not make living beings such as yourself alarmed.

D. That's fascinating. There are so many things the Tallocks are saying about power, which I have a hard time grasping.

O. Just know that there are two maps. We call them maps. One map is placed on a solid object, such as a planet or star. There is another map that it resonates with that is located either in the same galaxy, or in a further galaxy. All maps—and that is what this one works with—is to understand the maps between not only travels, but to replicate a map from the cosmos down to a solid object such as a planet, such as Earth. The intention with the maps are multiple. The Tallocks are engineering power, understanding the resource of how to access and gain unlimited power. This is what you, at one point, incarnated to try to establish once more. To understand that power is free. It's operating, once it is established using the elements, (by) using the maps from below as well as from above. It creates the unlimited resource for all. The stars, if you like, even though they were operated and delivered by visitors, have the key on how to operate, how to gain and access and assist neighbors in their star map. Here the web has fallen asleep. What you see are only remains, such as the pyramids. The connecting maps makes it possible for free energy, for travels, if that is allowed. At this point, the maps are separated. You have your maps that you see, you see the pyramids, but they are not activated. They are only activated once the star map has merged. At one point the star map was descended, merged, available to see, to sense, like a cloud in the fourth reality. At that time, there were also entities, beings, placed here, operating the Earth map, making sure that the pyramids, the receivers, were placed strategically. How could they know where the gravitational points were, unless they were given information from the star map? There. I will leave you at this time.

Teh, Ophelia: The Parallel Realities (Nov 9, 2019)

This new visitor, Teh, gave the most comprehensive description of the parallel realities we have received to date. Teh is a Zeonian, which is a group affiliated with the Elahim. His group travels to Vlac in manifested form. He is a teacher on multiple realities and has, over the millennia, observed the development and subsequent diminishment of human potential to access the parallel bands of awareness. He clarifies, for example, that out-of-body experiences occur within the mental realm (or fourth dimension), but that a parallel reality of a higher level exists. The highest band is outside of both the third and fourth dimension and is the frequency band used by souls when they want to travel and manifest on different locations. The parallel web is synonymous with what other spirits have called 'lightways'. Teh selected the word 'gateway' to distinguish the transition from one parallel frequency to a higher one. It is obviously not a gate, like the gate to heaven in Christian mythology, but rather a change in the state of awareness.

Ophelia came in after Teh left and gave additional information on who Teh was and his roles as a teacher and keeper of knowledge. She follows that with a description of the fish tank boundaries and how they can merge and blend.

Teh. Hmm, let's see. My name is Teh. I'm a friend from fish tank eight.

D. Welcome. What did you say your name was?

Teh. Teh. I travel with this one (*Seth*) between eight and nine. Friends with Tallocks, you. Zeonians. Let's see... the connection is not clear. I wanted to make myself known as a teacher of stellar time; teacher of connection between vibrations; understandings of the whole—merging frequencies, combining elements, travel possible. You lack fundamental vibrations in this fish tank that you are in, fish tank five. Stripped, not making it possible in the same way for travel. It's a lesson in that as well, to grow in your capacity where you're at. Nothing exists or is better than the other, but your lesson at this point is not travel. That is why you are not capable in that little shuttle (*spacecrafts*) to move very far. You will not be able to leave your (*solar*) system in any near future. You do not master stellar time, which is a combination of frequencies, making gateways accessible.

D. I have a question then. Why is there so much emphasis on travel, if we are never going to be able to do so?

Teh. Because you remember within you. Some of you, like the two of you, travel on other places. You remember in your being as you traveled here to be a part of the human project. The human is not able to travel. However, in a distant past, some were allowed to explore the possibility that visitors at that time, here, possessed. Those were humans, but encased in... I can only call it "dust", not a cloud. But they were given a glance on how to travel. Man, however, has never fully occupied that skill set and mindset. But it is a memory within your DNA of the possibility of that, because once you saw it, and a few were allowed to explore and master, conquer vibrational fields—finding gateways. Man has been since then encountering these gateways, but they don't master them. They go through them in one direction, but never return. That was the understanding the visitors, such as myself, taught in different fish tanks—this planet as well. We taught the possibility of mastering stellar time, but only in one direction. Those who are interested in time traveling don't have the key to return in the same way that visitors once did.

D. If someone does an out-of-body projection of their soul consciousness, can they travel through those gateways to other fish tanks?

Teh. Limited, yes, but (*they*) have the ability to return. If you see gateways lined up in front of you, the OBE, out–of–body projection, or remote viewing, take you about two, max three, gateways. You have here more gateways that you can disappear through, but if you leave the third, or even the second, you might not to be able to return. An OBE normally stretches through the first gateway, some to the second. Those who are highly initiated in the art of travel can reach the third gateway and safely return. After the third gateway from this reality, consciousness is lost, dissolved, not being able to return. In that sense, man will be considered deceased, dead. However, they might not be. They are just moved to another frequency—let's say gateway five. But for the rest of you, they appear to be dead.

D. Hmm. Would they then return to their soul home?

Teh. Potentially. But they also have an opportunity to explore the different gateways, which, in some way, are not spiritual. They are in a different frequency band in the fish tanks. They are not spiritual dimensions, but neither are they physical realities, in that sense. For a human, you can accept physical form and spiritual form, not understanding that there are levels between those two, and that's where the gateways exist. You are (*in*) neither physical nor spiritual (*realities*), (*or in your*) soul (*home*). You exist in the frequency occupied by that reality, having the ability to explore. I would compare it to a dream. When you are in physical, awake, you do not dream. But when you are in spiritual, your eyes are more open than when you are in physical. When you reach the parallel universes connected to the reality, the physical one, it is like dreaming—you are a blend between physical and spiritual. It is not captivity. It is a way to step aside from the two realities of spiritual and physical, observing them both through a third eye, if you like. I wish I could explain it.

D. Would the gateway be from our reality into a parallel vibration?

Teh. Yes, yes. So when you leave with an OBE, you can leave and return safely up to gateway three. After that, you are in a parallel reality. It might appear as Earth. You can experience Earth, if you like, but not as physical nor as soul; objectively, like hovering above it.

D. Would it still have the same physical appearance from that perspective?

Teh. No. Visitors knew how to master this. Somewhat visible, but not in the same band of motion as physical beings here. Neither (*is it in the*) soul vibration. It's between the two, but it's not captivity. You have the ability to observe activities on Earth from a perspective of connection to humans, but not fully human. There are those… and where can I place this for you so it makes sense? The first three gateways occupy within the fourth reality. The other ones hover above all. Meaning, you can travel back and forth, hovering above spiritual dimensions, fourth, third, tapping into them all but not being in your soul capacity. You might appear as a human if you were to be seen. But you have the ability to connect to thoughts, feelings on a human level, things that you are not able to (*do*) from your soul level. It is a way to exist between life and death. There are not just two ways to exist, human life, spiritual life—there are levels in–between. And those are the parallel universes, a vibrational band where an entity can occupy and learn and grow, becoming one with the teachings that exists, but being half and half, if you like. Those who fall into those gateways have not the ability to return to physical. However, after objectively experiencing that vibrational reality, they have the ability to return home to the spirit realm.

D. I know a lot of Native American shamans talked about leaving the body and going to different places that are—

Teh. Yes. They went to gateway three.

D. What if they disappeared from Earth life?

Teh. If they did, they left gateway three and continued. But there were a few that mastered to return from beyond gateway three. They were initiated in the art of transforming time and space, conquering vibrational realities, merging them and leaving physical vibration in order to travel. They knew they would not return to the physical. Yet they would appear, once in a while, in a physical–like shape for those left behind who had mastered gateway one and two, let's say. So, your friend, Jesus, he returned, didn't he? He went through the gateways and manifested for those who were taught to travel like him. Manifested and showed himself, but not in a complete physical form. Like a replica, like a dream, like a fog. (*This is further discussed in the next section.*)

D. There are a few Buddhist masters that have done that as well, aren't there?

Teh. Yes. It's a way to bring comfort and to bring knowledge about the portals. To make others understand and eager to learn how to travel. It is a way to exist, co–exist, without existing (*on the physical plane*).

Years 2018 – 2019 49

D. Would the Coat be left behind at that point?

Teh. Those who travel like this don't carry Coats. No Coats. Those who master to manifest in some way for those left behind—no Coats. But those who simply disappear, you have stories about objects disappearing, never to return. Not all come with no Coat, but they are travelers as a soul and signed up for the journey; not consciously aware, of course.

D. Is the only way to access that reality by taking on a physical body and then leaving, or can you access it from the spiritual dimensions?

Teh. Yes. From the soul…if you see two lines, the one below, physical. And the one above, parallel reality. The physical comes to an end, and then it's a jump into the spiritual. Meaning you have to travel through the fourth. The line above has no jumps, it's solid. That train can travel back and forth, transforming existence, tapping into experiences. Visitors who came in a distant past traveled on the upper line, having the ability to fall down on the other line that is fully manifested, and fell down in their physical form. Those who try to travel the other way—and I'm talking here about fish tank five—they disappear. They don't return in physical. The ones who did, such as Jesus and other spiritually developed beings, they manifested in a fog. I know it is confusing.

D. Like when I used to travel as a manifested entity?

Teh. Here?

D. Yes.

Teh. Yes, you traveled on the upper band and you fell down in the particular shape. So, if you see….

D. So, it's the same process, basically?

Teh. Yes, but coming from the upper band you have the ability and freedom to move freely. If you decide to do the journey (*with a*) starting point on the below line, you are limited.

D. Understood. That makes sense to me.

Teh. So, all physical realities belong—if you see a big web—(*that would be*) all the physical realities. And above it you see another web, which is the parallel reality. It's not a spiritual reality, but it's a way for beings to travel. So, you see the below web, meaning the physical one—and let's say we use fish tank five—the below web has not the ability to move freely in the same way. But the above web is where entities can travel, physical travels I'm talking about, not spiritual travels—they do not travel in this web. This web is one physical and the other as well, they just have different options to merge and meet and learn. If you belong and if you have the key to travel in the upper web, you can fall down into the below web, which is Earth and other planets, and you will appear in a physical form for humanity. Aliens—that you call them, we call them visitors, such as myself—travel in the upper web, having the ability to fall down in different objects, such as Earth, and be seen.

D. Is that how you came to visit today?

Teh. Yes.

D. And can you pick specific times that you drop into? Is time also an option?

Teh. Yes. Yes. Stellar time is to understand that the web is both space and time. Cycles, if you like. We will explore this further. The picture is sent to this one, who is a great traveler, traveling easily in the upper levels. Likes to float freely and tap into different realities, exploring different realities. One of his teachings is to be locked and not fully being able to travel. But you can see how the personality shines through. Doesn't like the captivity. Wants to be mobile, free. One of the teachings, indeed. There we go.

D. Thank you so much for that. It was brilliant.

Teh. The picture has been sent. Ask, afterwards, your little brother, and he will tell you and show you. There.

D. I will do that. Thank you for coming today. It was a pleasure to meet you.

Teh. I will be back. Okay, farewell.

D. Farewell, my friend.

O. Hmm. Okay, let's see. This is Ophelia.

D. Hello, Ophelia.

O. Hello to you. It's sort of a struggle to make the bridge and the connection from physical vibration to spiritual vibration, such as myself and also Bob, of course. So at this point, if I can give you a picture, I feel extremely locked in this being because the physical residual energy is still very present. So, here we need to do some adjustments in order for Bob, who has been eagerly waiting. So let's see... hmm... (*She spends a few moments quietly working on raising the energy.*) There. So, you met a new friend.

D. Ah. Do you know him?

O. Yes, I do. Everyone that will come through and talk to you has been carefully selected. Teh is one of the great teachers when it comes to travels, understanding the whole connection of realities and the possibilities that exist or not exist in order for motion to take place.

D. Is he a friend of Seth?

O. Yes. Teacher indeed, one of his teachers. Never been here as a human though, but traveled with Seth to different locations, but not in a human form; tapping in, looking in, but differently, such as yourself.

D. Did he ever interact with beings on Earth?

O. Not humans. But traveled with this one and with others as well, some of them Tallocks.

D. So he's from fish tank eight?

O. Yes. Travels between eight and nine. Prefers to be in the upper part of the eighth.

D. When beings occupy fish tank eight, they are soul beings, but they must spend what we would consider a lot of time in fish tank eight?

O. Yes, they occupy that vibration. Fish tank eight is very much a center for travel—space travel if you like to call it that, with a limited options of words that you have. There are big classrooms or centers where projects and techniques are taught.

D. So when a soul goes to eight, they must take a lot of their soul energy with them?

O. Yes, more. As the two of you travel here, you are only allowed to bring twenty-five percent as a max, normally. But if you travel to fish tank eight, you can bring eighty-five percent. Different. There is no lifespan there. You don't become a child and then an adult. You travel and manifest a full physical experience.

D. Like on Etena?

O. Yes, yes. Like Etena, but different teachings. Teh travels to the libraries and the storage units on Etena, leaving projects, storing projects on Etena.

D. Will Bob ever be able to travel to fish tank eight?

O. He has a wish. He saw at one point how Seth returned, and he could feel that the energy was different than when Seth returned from a human experience; and he was curious about what he could sense. He said, "You are solid, I feel you are solid," because he saw him in your lab as the two of you returned and had discussions. You had not returned. Seth had returned and not fully transformed back into spiritual frequency. Bob, who was present, saw and felt the high intensity of physical vibration and said that he didn't recognize that physical vibration. Seth, at this point, said, "I have not returned from Earth. I have returned from another place." Questions arised.

D. (*Laughing.*) I can imagine.

O. And there was indeed discussions about where Seth had been because Bob is limited in some way, thinking that the two of you travel here and to Etena, but not understanding that you do travel to other places as well. It is, of course, not by chance; it is by design, to bring it in cups. (*To gradually expand the possibilities for Bob to travel elsewhere.*)

D. Just so I'm clear, this fish tank is completely separate from other fish tanks?

O. Which one?

D. Any of them. Like eight, is there some overlap in what we would consider space?

O. There is an overlap to nine. So, both of them are connected, almost becoming one.

D. Eight and nine?

O. Yes, yes. Not separate. There are different—what you would consider space—between fish tanks. At this point, for instance, we (*she laughed gently at her choice of words*), higher engineerings, let's just say, from Source, are trying to make the connection between four and five. Similar like eight and nine, let's just say, to dock them. Meaning they will become more in harmony and symbiosis with each other.

D. Is the fish tank spherical?

O. It's a spherical existence with different understandings and teachings and vibrational experiences, if you like. At this point, we see the need for assistance in fish tank five. How I can give you the picture is that fish tank four has asked to assist fish tank five. Meaning that they would like to dock with fish tank five, similar like eight and nine, bringing more of the understanding from four. Zippering through, which at this point, is a separate barrier. But as they merge into one, they have the ability to be in symbiosis and it is to—you know when someone is about to drown and someone gives them help?

D. Resuscitation? A little bit of air....

O. Indeed. That is what fish tank four is trying to do with fish tank five. Fish tank eight and nine is not the same condition. They are merged into one open, well, I wouldn't say open because it is not freely (*open*) to just move in between, but they are more in symbiosis, operating as one. But it's not like fish tank nine needs to give air to fish tank eight. Yes, Bob, I have taken a lot of your time. So, there we go, energies back to normal.

D. Always a pleasure to hear your voice.

O. Always a pleasure, always a pleasure. So. Thank you so much.

Bob: John 11 and the Bloodline of Yeshua (Nov 17, 2019)

Most of the November 17 session was published in *Wave 3*. This part about John 11 was not, because I wanted time to research some of the details. We are including it in *Wave 4* because it has some historical significance. In October 2023, when Christine was in a light trance, Bob talked about the beginnings of Christianity. He went back to a previous Elahim incarnation known today as Apostle Paul, who was born about 4 BC and died around AD 64. When Bob began describing the lifetime, he first called him Apostle Paulus, which I found odd. However, in Latin, Παῦλος translates as Paulus, so it may be that was how he was known within the Greek communities. Bob only called him that once, and thereafter called him Apostle Paul. For those who are not familiar, there is a story in the Bible of Paul being blinded on the road to Damascus by the bright light of the spirit of Yeshua (Jesus), who had been previously killed by the Romans. A few days later, Yeshua restored Paul's sight through an intermediary. Bob said that the story, like many in the Bible, is a metaphor for a deeper truth. According to Bob, Paul had an encounter with Yeshua's spirit, which triggered an awakening and opened him to extrasensory abilities. He was able to see the auras and life-force around objects, and could read the etheric history of physical locations. Hence the metaphor that he was once blind, but later could see.

Paul himself wrote (per the Bible) that he retreated and studied with Yeshua (or his manifested spirit) for 3 years. He then traveled extensively, converting gentiles and starting churches in several countries. After moving on, he wrote letters back to churches he had established to encourage and give advice to the converts. Some of those letters became an important part of the New Testament, such as Galatians, First Thessalonians, First and Second Corinthians, Romans, Philippians, and Philemon. A few more books are possibly his as well, those being Second Thessalonians, Colossians, and Ephesians. The other books ascribed to Paul, which are the Epistle to the Hebrews, First Timothy, Second Timothy, and Titus were written by other authors with an agenda to corrupt the original teachings of Yeshua. After Yeshua himself, Apostle Paul was the most important person in creating the Christian religion. Paul was raised as a Greek Jew and became a pharisee, a very strict follower of the Mosaic "laws", which emphasize sacrificial rituals as the path to salvation. After his enlightenment, he understood that many religious behaviors are contrary to spiritual impeccability. The destiny of the soul does not depend on engaging in empty rituals, following pointless rules, or killing animals on certain occasions as an offering to their idea of god. Paul established a religion for Gentiles and converted Jews based on the ethical teachings of Yeshua. This introduction is important to the story of John 11 and a more recent Elahim incarnation, Pope Clement III, whom Bob described in a later session.

Bob told us, in an October 2023 talk, that the Catholic Church was created in a treaty between interests to establish a common faith and order, and a pattern of structure and power. The Church does not represent or present the real teachings of Yeshua. Bob said, "All eyes are looking at Jesus in Rome, but secret teachings move around a circle. What you see in Rome is the operation behind the religion and events, meaning social and cultural, wars, etcetera, which are misleading the people. The foundation is in the circle. This has to do with Apostle Paul. He taught there are two ways of existence, living and dead. Meaning, to visit the kingdom of death and come back to life. So, the resurrection of Jesus is an indirect way of talking about reincarnation. Everything in the Bible is surface teaching, but behind the surface is the true meaning, which is hidden. They made the resurrection appear magical, but it is really what everyone does. Jesus showed himself as a spirit after he died. The Romans were afraid of him, and looked up to him in some way. But they understood karma and didn't want the darkness to follow them. So the Romans crucified someone else as a demonstration for the public, for control. They also wanted to control the lineage. Jesus was tortured and died in captivity. When he passed, the apostles knew when he died, but it was 3 years after the fake crucifixion. Jesus showed himself after death."

Bob also said that the true teachings, which Apostle Paul had written on scrolls and parchments, were kept hidden and have remained so to this day. Yeshua had two children, a boy and a girl. The boy was taken west to Spain and Morocco, along with the original teachings. There is a secret group of people who maintain the scrolls and have moved them, along with certain descendants of Yeshua, in a circle around the Mediterranean, from one hiding location (perhaps a monastery or temple) to another. Bob mentioned Tripoli, Cordoba, Zaragoza, a small temple in France, and Damascus as places where the teachings once were stored. They were denoted as the five petals on a rose. So while Rome is the center, the teachings circle Rome in a clockwise direction, being stored in one place for a while and then are moved to another spot, century after century.

With that background, the activities of John 11 can be understood in a larger context. He was part of the hidden group that moved the teachings and descendants of Yeshua to safe locations. He painted flowers on all of his pottery. The ones with hidden messages had a special looking rose, so that others in the association could locate the important vessels. It is interesting that, in the 1600s, the Rosicrucians used a symbol of a cross centered on top of a rose with five leaves and five petals around the perimeter. So it is possible that the symbol of the cross represents the Church in Rome, and the five leaves are the five cities where the hidden teachings of Yeshua and Apostle Paul are periodically kept. Those who are interested in the Bible, as it was originally written, should visit the Marcionite Research Library, currently maintained by Melissa Cutler. As she said, "The original Bible did not contain homophobia, misogyny or the concept of hell: just the beautiful simple message of love."

B. What I would like to mention is John 11.

D. John 11?

B. John 11, he was highly skilled. You were making pottery. This was when you lived in Morocco. You came from the north. You did not like the cold, so you moved to Morocco and you left everything behind. You started to work very much with your hands. From clay you made like things that you drink from. And you were really happy with that and you were actually teaching others to be creative with different material. Your favorite material was that you burned clay and it became a vase, a big plate, cups—

D. That's interesting, because I've always had an interest in pottery but have never done it.

B. Yes, indeed. You had a big shop. You made more than you sold, but you also had it on display. A lot of people came, and you encouraged them to find an interest. After a while there was little ones—well, not children—you had classes in this and you were extremely skilled in creating new models and new ways to work with clay and fire and to mold them into the most fascinating big urns and so forth, and you really enjoyed that.

D. What time frame was this?

B. Oh, this was about 332.

D. AD or BC?

B. AD. You put stuff also—and this is what I wanted to talk about—you put little things in your pottery, in your urns, and you delivered them and there was a secret society that you worked with that delivered messages in these urns. There were teachings that passed between different countries and different regions and they passed through your urns. You were somewhat of a spider in that web, but it was like you were a secret agent in some way. The pottery and everything was a facade. But you were putting, and you delivered, certain messages (*in the pottery*). You were like a post office for different things to be delivered and picked up, when it came to this network of people. It was to protect a bloodline that was in danger.

D. What bloodline was this?

B. It originated from zero. It was a bloodline, and you helped. You were a part of this protection program of a few that belonged in this bloodline. There were messages that went through this pottery-postal–CIA office. Huh huh huh.

D. So you said this started from zero. Did it have anything to do with the Middle East?

B. Indeed, indeed. And you were placed in Morocco and you started this line of occupation when it came to maintaining the bloodline to protect three (*people*) that had to be moved around and separated in order for the bloodline to remain. You came from England somewhere, and you felt like you had to be more central to the activity. You were not a pottery person up there, but you started that as a shield to disguise the real operation behind. And then there were those who came here learning pottery, some were just learning pottery, but there were some in this group—there were like ten young men who came—and two or three of them were actually involved in this undercover operation. So, you taught them the skill set of pottery. You created somewhat of a shield business and you assisted others, and some became pottery people. But others were actually working with protecting the bloodline that originated from around year zero that some were trying to eliminate, to exchange for a higher order (*in the Christian Church, presumably*). These three—one remained in central Europe, one went east and the third one, I don't know if that one made it, but you assisted the undercover operation and for them to be in hiding and to make sure that they were continued. The bloodline is still intact.

D. What was the origin of the bloodline? Where did it come from?

B. It came from that spot, like Jerusalem.

D. Did it have to do with Yeshua?

B. Yes, that was it.

D. What eventually happened to the bloodline?

B. It still exists. It still exists, but it is still in hiding. It's not public.

D. What's the purpose of maintaining the bloodline? You would think after all these centuries it would be contaminated with other mixtures.

B. No, because they are not public. They remain in some way intact, but there are not many. It became, around 1500, it became a drop. There was a peak just around 1100, where there were more, and also more (*who*) protected this bloodline, by those who rode in white suits with the cross. So there was a peak there and then it dropped in the 1500s, and now it is simply a few again. But it still exists, but it is simply like a faded memory in some way. The purpose then when you were assisting this operation, you had a really high position within this, not only within the pottery industry (*he laughed at that*), but in this undercover business. That's why you are a little bit drawn to work undercover and you are more secretive than this one in the way you operate. Because in your soul being, you have not the same desire to share left and right, and this is why, this is the reason. I'm gonna go now, but we might touch on this again. I wanted to make sure that I had my time in the sun, you know.

D. What did the little ones think about your performance last time? (*Bob brought some of his students with him during the previous session, so they could see how he communicated through Christine. Bob later mentions "cherry" life. By that, he means that it is the cherry on top of the cake. It is the pinnacle of how a spirit guide can communicate with his person. The full story is in 'Notes, Volume 2'.*)

B. Oh, they were extremely intrigued. And a lot of them said that if there is a possibility, from this point where they are at, to somewhat put in a request of what the cherry life could be. I said, "I don't know, it's not my position to tell either way. I was not told about that there would be a cherry life." I thought we had several really good lives. And there was also those that were like "Why? What was the purpose here?" Because Jeshua, he had the grander plan at his disposal, but I'm just called in to go and to help. And sometime I wanted to put different things in the pocket. The thing is that when I follow you, I look for potential. I see where you are and sometimes think, "This isn't really going to Lasaray's potential," and then I start to sniff around, like when you were on certain places, I look around and see if there is anyone here who could possibly be a good catch or a good opportunity for some grander shifts or changes or upgrades or footprints. A lot of time I'm looking for what could be a suitable footprint to leave, if I don't see that there is a footprint. But I don't see all the intent behind everything. And you said, "Sometimes I'm not there to leave a footprint, I'm just there to look around. Like Mr. Mustard, he was examining things." But you also left a footprint because you did make people think and laugh. Anyway, they really liked the show, they said. I might do that again. We'll see if it's allowed. Anywho, I'm gonna go now. Ophelia says, "Gonna go, saving energy." So, I'll be back when it's a suitable opening again. (*Charles Mustard is the nickname for Charles Dijon, one of Lasaray's past lives.*)

D. All right, my friend. I don't suppose you want a separate session this week?

B. I do! I'll talk to Ophelia. Keep that in mind, she says. Maybe Thursday. Separate session Thursday.

D. We got way behind when this one went away.

B. Ah. I think Thursday.

D. I'll put that note in the pocket.

B. Put that note in the pocket and send it up, shush, to those who decide, which is Ophelia. I'll just go around the corner and give it to her instead.

D. Alright my friend. Thank you so much for the good information and the stories.

B. Okay, I'll go. Bye bye.

Ari, Ophelia, Bob: Cycles and Polarity (Dec 1, 2019)

As a reminder to the reader, our fish tank is held within an energetic container, whose inside walls are reflective. From the descriptions given in other sessions, it is somewhat roundish when viewed from above, but flatter when viewed from the side. There are twelve fish tanks around the Wheel of Creation, which holds the universes of form and also the spiritual dimensions. The Creator's Disk is positioned below the Wheel and slowly rotates counterclockwise. The Creator's Disk also has twelve boxes, and it transmits intention and scenarios into the corresponding location within the fish tanks above. Councils read and interpret those signals and try to implement them within the universes of form. In this way, cyclical change is always progressing within the manifested realities and parallel planes in accordance with the Creator's intent. Ari and Ophelia both give excellent explanations of how the system operates, even though it is a very murky subject.

Bob came in at the end of the session and outlined some of my past lives, using colored dots to categorize the type of travel. The blue dots represent locations where Lasaray manifested a form. Bob only joins when it is an incarnation, which is denoted as red, yellow, or green dots, so he did not accompany Lasaray during those blue–dot trips. In *Notes, Volume 2*, Bob told how he recreated a female companion for Siah. Bob took the genetic pattern and made an identical animal, whom he named Tess, and raised it to adulthood on the second dimension. When he came in during this session, Tess was still a pup, so Bob was carrying her around in a basket.

One of the corollaries of conversing with our spirit friends is the need to research topics beyond my primary fields of interest. The history of civilizations, for example, held only passing interest to my earlier self. I always felt that spirituality was a reflection of timeless truths, and understanding how a universal principle was interpreted by previous groups seemed like an empty pursuit. However, the spirits are regularly commenting on what our ancestors and various visitors have done, and verifying their statements has led into obscure avenues of inquiry. In this session, Bob talks about a past life in a monastery high in the Himalayan mountains in the first century AD. His description of the monastery and the practices leads me to think it was a very secretive group. The practitioners were generating their own material, finding truths from within and without. Bob outlines some of the knowledge collected by this group. Portions of that information was transmitted to the west, but was probably lost when the Muslims torched the great libraries of antiquity in Alexandria and other cities they invaded. An interesting point he makes is the one about sunrise being an ideal time to access knowledge. When I was younger and exploring the ancestral Native American religions, I spent a bit of time with a traditional healer who lived on a reservation in the western US. He always arose in the pre–dawn hour and would pray as the Sun came up, just as medicine men of the past have always done. The four directions are associated with different aspects of the Creator, which are mirrored within the cycles of nature. The east brings the light of spiritual wisdom and the transformational energy of rebirth, which is seen in the spring of the year. In the hour before sunrise, photons of sunlight begin to interact with the atmosphere and negative ions are generated. The blackness of the night sky gives way to a deep purple color. Light plays a significant role on human circadian rhythms and biologic functions. Blue light inhibits melatonin production and improves cognitive abilities. It may be that the atmospheric changes as daylight approaches assists the practitioner to open the inner doorway to the fourth dimension. Or perhaps our ancient ancestors understood something we do not, and sunrise is when spiritual knowledge is most available to living beings.

D. I had a question. Early on, Ophelia said the Universe is like a jellyfish that moves in and out. One of the main assumptions in astrophysics is that the Universe is expanding, that space itself is expanding. What do you say about that?

A. If you see the disks around the center pole, in each disk you have the fish tanks. What is expanding are the fish tanks here and there. Some fish tanks are bigger than others, so your Universe, fish tank five, is in some way expanding. But on the other hand, it's withdrawing. Meaning it withdraws, in particular, energy from fish tank four. The jellyfish going in and out—if we first talk about the fish tanks—when a fish tank is about to evolve, it normally constricts. If you see like a box or a cylinder, then when it constricts, it looks like a peanut, moving in in the centers. It is like being reborn, it withdraws energy from neighbors. At the same time, this disk is rotating. This disk (*the Creator Disk below the Wheel*) rotates anti–clockwise around the pole. There are other disks rotating other directions, but they are constantly moving. The expansion of your fish tank occurs when... there is no word... just know that before it expands, it constricts. The borders in some way dissolve, but they are still intact. Have you got the picture?

D. I have, yes.

A. The other picture that I would like to send to you, my son, is how it goes in and out, from the pole and outwards. In, out, meaning certain fish tanks merges and becomes closer to the spiritual levels inside. Earlier times, this fish tank was closer. Meaning, the fourth reality barely existed. Fish tank neck to neck with the fifth (*dimension*). In and out. Due to changes within the fish tank, and events, at this point, as you are aware, the fourth dimension is wider than ever. So, like a jellyfish, meaning in and out, closer to Source, back and forth. It is not only to enlighten the species within the fish tank, within the celestial bodies that occupies a fish tank. It is also to bring life, bring new energy that has nothing to do with those inside. It is to change the melody within a fish tank as well. There are several qualities of these motions, and we will discuss them. Just know that at this time, the fourth reality is wider than ever. Way back, hmm, about 1.5 million years ago to 5 million years ago, civilization existed here. The fourth reality barely existent. It was just like going through the surface. (*Souls moved easily from Earth to the spiritual dimensions, like rising up through the surface of water.*) No egos. Civilization blossomed due to the strong presence of spirit, not only in consciousness but in nature, in elements, in the wind, in everything—prosperity. This was a time where climates were different.

D. Souls at that time, though, did not incarnate here, did they?

A. Around 1.55 million (*years ago*), half–and–half's visited and existed in human form. Just know that there is at this time only one way to come here as a soul, if you do not travel differently using grid and points merging for travels. (*Ari implies that aliens can still travel here in physical or manifested forms. It is my understanding that if they do come here, they cannot interfere with the human project.*) Before, there were several ways to occupy a vehicle here. Some—Ophelia will tell you. She traveled inside a body, which will mean incarnation, if you like. Did not come in her regular form; looked like a human. They were here as a group—Shea. Started early. Presence inside vehicles that existed. Humanoid, but looked slightly different. Slimmer, slender, skin white, tall, white long hair. Androgynous in their gender; no male, no female. You might wonder then how they came about. Well, things and conditions were different then; closer to the spiritual levels. Meaning, the realities here mirrored the spirit realm more. It was similar as you travel now to different spiritual realities. You have one side that is where you belong, where you are patterned to travel to; and then you have the other side, where you can visit if you are on that path of knowledge to learn something from another reality. The third reality was simply similar, it was a manifested side.

D. Okay, I follow that.

A. It is easier to see it as an image. I hope my words provides an imprint, where you can create in your mind how this might appear. Use your imagination. Sit in your silence, find the sources and answers within you. You will remember. It might be helpful to draw, for you. There.

D. Thank you so much for that.

A. Okay. There are probably more here.

D. It's always nice to hear you, Ari. I appreciate the wisdom you bring.

A. You are much welcome. Elahim.

D. Elahim, my friend.

O. Just a little bit before Bob has his turn.

D. Hello, Ophelia. Did you have any thoughts to add to what Ari said?

O. As you start to unfold how worlds, spiritual realities, manifested realities, how they sometimes intertwine, how they sometimes merge and become one reality, that is when science will take a step back. They cannot relate to spiritual reality versus manifested reality. It's either way (*one or the other*). And sometimes in the past, as the Wheel rotates, it goes through what would be considered more of a spiritual reality, rather than a manifested one. Those times come and go, and this is hard for those who believe in manifestation only.

D. I remember one time that Ari or Eli said that our fish tank had been parked in this location for trillions of Earth years (*Ophelia gave a surprised "Hmm" sound*). Well, not parked, but had been rotating through this area.

O. The fish tank is locked in the Wheel, and the Wheel itself rotates. At this time, the rotation is not involving this fish tank. It might be other fish tanks that still move. Even though they are on the same Wheel, there are levels IN the Wheel, and they might sometimes overlap. When they overlap, there are times where fish tanks merge. If I give you the picture of, let's say, fish tank four overlapping fish tank five, it doesn't mean that there is motion or development in fish tank five. It simply means that realities are passing this reality to either provide support or just travel over and move into another experience. So even if you are in the same fish tank, in the same Wheel, you still have options to travel in this Wheel. Fish tank five is, as you say, locked, both from the sides as well as in to the pole. Changes will come—time is not important. Is that your question?

D. From a human perspective, I struggle with a lot of the concepts, of course.

O. You have to ignite your inner scientist, your memory, your soul mind, where limitations were different. At this point, you are limited, boundaries are established in many fields, but your fish tank is moving. It's vibrating, even though it is not rotating in the disk. It just needs assistance. You do not need to fully understand, as you, as a human, will never do. But you will bring forward concepts, delivering loose ends, if you like. Toss out a question, "Could this be?" and see how it will be received.

D. You had said at one time that the Creator's energy flows out through the spiritual dimensions into the fish tanks. Would that be considered light energy, and does that fill all space?

O. Light energy, yes. The sound waves simply steer the energies, steer the light, hold the light.

D. And then patterns that are imposed or introduced by different groups that build solar systems and other structures—those patterns interact with those fields?

O. Yes, using different frequencies, different levels of sound and light—neither constant—in order for what manifestation would be available in that specific fish tank (*to be created*), down to what specific existence should exist on a planet. If you see the spiritual realities inside, around the center pole, sometimes the spiritual realities—if you see them as cores, lines—they are closer. Meaning if you see fish tank five, then each level—four, five, six and so forth—let's say that we have them with a decimeter in between, other fish tanks have only a centimeter in between. Do you see?

D. The fish tanks to the spiritual dimensions?

O. To the pole. So here in this cake, in this piece, in this triangle from your fish tank all the way into the center pole, it is wider in between. Other fish tanks, closer in between the spiritual connection and levels, all the way into the core. That is the expansion and constriction, the jellyfish in and out.

D. Okay, I follow that.

O. There. Picture has been given to this one. There we go.

D. Alright, Ophelia. Thank you so much.

O. Oh, you are much welcome. (*Ophelia moved aside as Bob came in.*)

B. Ah. I'm here with a backpack, as there were certain things that you wanted to discuss. So you can have your questions now and I will be happy to oblige.

D. Well, you had gotten through four different locations, and you said there were more places we had visited on our travels?

B. Ah, with you, you do have your atlas book where you put red dots on where you have been. I mean, it becomes a great traveler's book—but it also connects different times and different teachings. There are actually not just red dots. It's like you put different colors based on the level of assignment, the level of consciousness available, and different keys on how that travel went. When I see the red dots, they normally indicate high mission, great prosperity, progress, changes and development, in different ways. Then there are green dots where there were lives where you came down for others, where your assignment might not have been important, or where you came down to learn a human activity. So, there are green dots. And there are yellow dots, which seem to be short lives. And then there are blue dots. And the blue dots, I did not go.

D. No? What were those representing?

B. You went by yourself, without me—the blue dots.

D. Those aren't an incarnation?

B. The blue dot doesn't seem to be. I can't see that you are, because I'm not there, and it's not a human activity. There's several blue dots I can see here around the area of Persia, Mesopotamia, Egypt, southern border of Russia, some around the area which is now Pakistan, a couple over there in the Tibet mountains—the blue dots. In the Tibet mountains there is also a couple of red dots, but there's a lot of blue. There's like a line from here, which would be like Israel, and then it goes like this (*he motions left to right, in a line*), so it's a blue line there, several dots. You, step-by-step, it seems, covered a line here with blue dots. I was not there. There's no me in the blue dots, you say.

D. Is there any way to tell what sort of time frame they occurred?

B. Blue dots were when, you say, very little human activity existed. When you were over there, the furthest away in the Tibet mountains, no human activity at all. When you were over there (*west towards the eastern Mediterranean*), there's a lot of congestion, a lot of blue dots here. There's also some red, but predominantly there's a lot of blue dots around Persia, Mesopotamia, some down in Egypt.

D. This must have been when I was coming in manifested form?

B. Ah. And I was not there, but there was a lot of blue dots there. Like John 11, for instance, that was sort of a reddish-greenish dot.

D. What about John 32?

B. That was a yellow dot. It was barely qualifying to become a dot, you say. It wasn't a human experience at all. It was simply to come in and allowing the Master Mind to look into activities that occurred in the Catholic Army because there were some from the Cell that were operating inside. You really despise that Cell. You have a nose for them and you find them everywhere, it seems like, here. You pointed them out on several occasions—not in the blue dots, they were not here in the blue dot lives—but in some of the red dot lives, you say that they were present, like an infiltrator, in communities, consciousness, science, or spiritual beliefs. There was a huge influence developing (*in the Catholic organization*). So, with John 32, you said, "I'm not going down, but I can be there for the councils." There were councils looking into activity, because there was a Cell developing in the Catholic beliefs. It started to grow from there and it expanded. This was around 1300 and it was NOT good. The Cell traveled, and at that time it had a wish to travel into religious groups, and you wanted to put a stop to it—and you did, in some way, when you were John 11. It started to somewhat ignite before zero (*AD 0*), but then it became calm. Then it went up and down and you monitored this. Then there was a huge explosion of this activity in the Catholic region and you wanted the council to see it firsthand. So, it's a short life. It's a yellow dot, but it barely qualifies as a dot, you say. But you say, "Some of my yellow dots, some of those are actually when I allow councils to monitor activity, and I don't have to be around that long." And some of the green dots, you come down and you just practice to be a human.

D. Was that predominantly before my Coat was folded?

B. Oh, yes. The green ones is before. The green ones are to master human behavior. You can still come down and leave a green dot, but it has nothing to do with you practicing human behavior. It's helping someone else practice their human behavior.

D. I think you said at one time there were twenty–five different levels that souls go through?

B. Ah. They go through different understandings. It's like here you go through the polarity of several different— (*He began clearing his throat.*) I probably need to sing. It seems like something is stuck in this one.

D. Sing away!

B. Na nah na na NA na la la— (*He loudly sang a rousing melody for about 30 seconds, which I did not recognize. We later played the National Anthem of the USSR and compared it to Bob's boisterous melody. It was an exact match. Lasaray had a life as a scientist in south–central USSR, and Bob clearly remembered the tune.*)

D. What's that song? Where is that from?

B. Oh, it's an activity song, a purpose song.

D. Where did you hear that?

B. It was in that big country.

D. Russia?

B. Ah. There is several red dots there. You like, actually, to go there. Especially if you wanted to work in secret. The thing is that you have had several lives as a scientist, but the difference being is that you actually PREFER to work incognito. And you could do that there, because everything is closed a little bit. But THIS time around, you signed up to be more public, which is something you don't really enjoy. You prefer to release things incognito to the consciousness and work undisturbed from the human race, since you did not, necessarily, want to come. I mean, you feel sorry for them, so you come and try to help. But you're also eager to leave. This one sees it more like a play, like dressing up. Huh huh. More like dressing in ignorance. It can actually be kinda fun, this one said. "It's kind of fun to play the fool," he said. Okay, so there we go.

D. I can see that.

B. SO, yes, the green dots represent human behaviors and human activities that you have to master, once you enter the karma program. And each aspect comes with a polarity, even love—giving love, receiving love. You cannot give love freely unless you fully embrace love and feel love. Each has a counterpart that you have to investigate as well.

D. So what would be some of the lower lessons?

B. Oh, the first one is, you know, like coexisting. To not take more than you need. So if we have the concept of taking, on the polarity side of that is giving. So, taking and giving, taking and giving. So, you look into that and that is one of the first things. Taking can become grabbing, and those are the things that you see around you at this point. We see a lot of those green dots that are on that level of understanding taking and giving.

D. That would mean that societies themselves are at a very basic level of development.

B. At this point, yes, indeed. And it's not like it just started now. It started a little bit after zero. (*AD 0*). Because with every upgrade in your consciousness, you somewhat start new in this ladder and different ways of expressing and experiencing certain things. So, if you are given more of a consciousness in your being, how will that reflect in the way you take and give? How will that reflect how you love and receive love? How will that reflect the way you judge or not judge? So, you somewhat start new. As we bump up (*consciousness*) in the future—a new vehicle coming in—that has also, in order to see whether it functions, it also has to go through these different human levels of gaining an awareness or not. So with every cycle that comes, you go through the conditions that are placed here as an experience. It's like placing this in your atmosphere, if you like, and every new species that comes in with a new soul has to go through the levels. So, let's say, here we see grabbing, grabbing, grabbing, and not very much giving. And also, you go through the little things, like how do you coexist with nature? There are little things that you go through here, and as the new humanoid will come in, the Master Mind wants to see, "Okay, we did all these changes. How will this individual now, with a larger soul percentage inside, how will they master the pickle of giving and taking?"

D. They will probably think the lessons are easier, wouldn't they?

B. It should be like that, yes indeed. But we see that there are events that humanity somewhat gets stuck in, like giving and taking is one of those. It doesn't come naturally to the current race to give equally as you want to take. They say, "If I give you an apple, you give me a pear." Before (*among earlier humans*), it was different. They understood that as you give, you also receive. So, if I give you an apple, I gain something that I do not know (*about*). I am not aware of what I am going to get. And it might not come right away—it won't come in a second, like that. But you have to give freely, understanding that as you do, you *will* also receive something at some point that will duplicate what you gave.

D. So the spirits are working behind the scenes?

B. Indeed. But now people are like, "I give you an apple. Give me your pear." So it has to be an instant exchange—and that's not how it works. If I give you something, and it might be way later that I'll get something back.

D. I've often thought that the spirits set up tests for people, put them in situations to see how they respond.

B. That is somewhat of a test. There's a lot of green dots going on at the moment.

D. I know you had brought our book back so you could talk about different things....

B. So I would like us to go here because there are things, since I was present when we were in Tibet, when you were in a monastery in Tibet. Even though there are several blue dots, there's also a red dot. And I was with you then and that's what I can talk about.

D. I'm interested in that because I've always felt like I lived in Tibet at one point.

B. There was a monastery high up in the mountains. If you think of a cave, that's how it was built, inside the mountain. And this was around—the red dot when we were there—that was after zero, but it was not when the Catholic army... it was kinda early. Let's see, was it before John 11? (*Christine later said he was scanning my timeline as he looked for dates or reference points.*) Yes, it was before John 11; we were there before. So around 55 to 75 AD.

D. That was before the Buddhism was introduced.

B. There I was—with you, of course—but I was there. There was a small group, all male, that were operating in this remote monastery that existed inside the mountains, high up. It was facing east, and you have a fondness of east. You actually prefer east more than west. So, in order for you to fully get connected—both of you—you're actually supposed to face east. East resonates with the sixth dimension, in many ways, and you have the ability to absorb information. So, you were up very early and you greeted the wisdom that came from the east.

D. Some Native Americans still do that. They have a sunrise ceremony where they give thanks to the rising Sun.

B. Umm. You like east. You know that there is more awareness that comes from the east. And in general, that's what it is. There's more development in the wind that comes from the east. So, you were there, and you were in this group. There were scrolls, thirteen scrolls, each represented a level of access to the spiritual dimensions. This group, you wrote it down, and the information came from the wind.

D. Are any of those teachings still available?

B. Over there, some, not all. Some disappeared, but they traveled later to the west. But they belong in this monastery. You were a group of thirteen, each in charge of one scroll. But you all had the ability to connect with the wisdom that came from the east. So you sat in the morning when the Sun rose, and you accessed information and you wrote it down. It was all in silence. You didn't speak much, and you actually prefer that. Zachariah was present in that life. You had done this before in ancient times, which would be somewhere in the Greek islands, but it was before known history, and you and Zachariah were there as well in the number of thirteen. Each holding the knowledge of one scroll and guarding it, as a group. I was there, because you were in human form in that time. Did the same thing. You have in your memory a fear of losing what you write down, and it comes from these events. You are very reluctant to leave it out of sight, so to speak.

D. Is there any information in the scrolls that you can pass on or that you remember?

B. It had to do with, first of all, the magnetic field on Earth. How it has changed and how there are rips in the magnetic field that create openings. (*He suddenly looked very nervous and pulled his hands up to his chest. He was quiet for a moment as he listened to Ophelia, then began to rapidly tap his fingertips together.*) In the magnetic field, there becomes like rips. It almost looks like lava coming up. And one of the scrolls is about how to maintain, when there becomes a rip, how to maintain and patch up the magnetic field that exists on the Earth base. That is the first scroll. It had to do with that. It was not your scroll, but it had to do with patching up the magnetic field, so it is intact. Another one had to do with—it gradually goes up to different things—but another scroll had to do with how to use resources, like plants and so forth, and trees and green, in order for you to heal physical and especially also MENTAL diseases. So it's sort of like a medical scroll. It was not your scroll either. You had number seven, that's yours.

D. I like the number seven.

B. You like seven. You were born on the seventh. It's not a big mystery with you—takes the same name, born the same day, it's very easy. But number three, it had something to do with the Sun. It had to do with light and the movement using light. You worked with sound. That was your scroll, that was number seven. But number three here is very bright. It had to do, in some way, with how you use the sunlight and how to calculate solar storms to your benefit; and how that will operate with scroll number one, the magnetic field. Those two (*scrolls one and three*) also determine how scroll number two was accessed or not, as these elements on each side, the magnetic field and the solar storms there, it also made the possibility of growth and accessing in nature the different properties. So depending on these two, it determines the growth or lack of growth in order for certain medical herbs and so forth to be more active. And then there were others here, and then your scroll had to do with sounds. That's why you like the bowls (*Tibetan*). You bonk the bowls and you understand how the waves that travels have an impact on the other ones. The vibration of the sound—if you think of like the biggest bowl, that's what you had. They were HUGE, and you had several inside the cave here. Oh, so you can imagine the sound! If you think of the bowls that existed inside, it was a big space where you had six of these big ones. And each of them were like three or four meters tall, and then in diameter would be also three or four meters. So, there were people, someone like you, that stood on each side and bonked them. And sometimes you bonked one and sometimes you bonked two. All these big bowls looked similar, all of them. They looked like they were made out of copper, very reddish copper. This was in this grand gallery behind the entrance where the chapel and everything was. Way inside you had different chambers. And this was a huge chamber where you operated and understood the sound. You worked on understanding that you can direct frequencies in different ways in order for the magnetic field to be balanced.

D. That must have been mesmerizing.

B. There was a lot of sounds in there, a lot of bonking, and you can imagine these big ones. Sometimes they were all bonking, every one of them were active, and you were moving around and tried to find and mirror the way they moved, the waves, and how that would affect things. So, all these scrolls are uniformly connected. If you take away one, then the mystery is somewhat not complete. It's like taking away a piece of a puzzle, and then it's like, "Uh–oh." It's the same thing here. We will talk more about that because it's time to leave. But it was an interesting experience. One of the scrolls had to do with the different elements and how you combine them. The last scrolls were about opening awareness. And when you say opening awareness, that also meant opening portals for awareness to come in (*to the third dimension*) in a physical form, you say.

D. That's truly fascinating. That was a good story today.

B. So I'm gonna go now. But there are several dot lives where I did not go, and maybe you would like to tell ME about them? The blue dots, for instance. Since I did not come, we might do a reverse discussion where you tell ME about the blue dots, and I take notes for you to deliver in my book. Anyway, I'm gonna go now.

D. (*Laughing.*) Alright, my friend. Thank you so much for coming and sharing today.

B. Always sharing. Sharing is caring. I'm gonna go now. Bye bye.

The Sessions from 2020

Bob: Native Shamans (Jan 1, 2020)
The first part of this session was included in *Wave 3*, when Ophelia talked about native lives and healing the Earth. Bob's talk, in part, was a continuation of her messages. He tells about two of Lasaray's past lives. Chief Eagle in the Dakotas around 1100, and an earlier life in the American Southwest. What is fascinating, to me, is the detailed recounting of how the natives lived and practiced their spirituality before any known contact with outsiders. It is a glimpse into the way those who lived close to the Earth interacted with nature. In an earlier life in the New Mexico desert, there was an old seer who could access memories stored in the fourth dimension during his nighttime vision quests. In that region, between 3000 and 5000 B.C., the tribes were visited by a large alien and his translator. At one point, they instructed the natives to strategically place rocks or structures to mirror celestial patterns and stars. Those patterns activated the local Earth grid to positively influence plants and crops. In a later session, it was explained that shamans were taught how to make an energetic link in the fourth dimension that connected patterns on the ground with the distant stars. One can only imagine the types of knowledge given by the ancient travelers, and how much has been forgotten.

B. And now it is my turn!

D. Welcome, my friend.

B. No one is gonna put me aside this time! If there's gonna be singing, I'm gonna sing myself! (*He was laughing, because Ia came in the previous week to sing and talk, which imposed on his allotted time.*) I have with me your backpack again. In this backpack there is a map of the places that you have been. You said we were gonna roll out this map and we're gonna look at certain points. So, ya' know, I'm all in favor of going places and I have asked if we could potentially start to talk about the blue dots, where you traveled here without me. You laughed and said, "All in due time, all in due time." And I kinda know what that means. It means, not just yet, but it will come. But what we could do is that we could talk about the yellow dots and the red dots. So, we can do that. We're gonna talk about a red dot that you had in this country here (*US*). There are two dots that you wanted me to talk about. One dot is sort of central, where you were a native, sort of a chief, with feathers. I also had feathers, because I like to dress similar like you. I'm thinking like, if there are higher councils observing this play, they will see, "Oh, there is Lasaray, and there is his little spirit helper." So it's not going to be confusing who I belong to. That's what I think. You had like a chief position in a huge tribe and this was about... ah, we were there more times, but you said the later times are not what we're talking about now. So we're looking at an earlier dot. This was around 1050 AD to 1132 AD.

D. Chief John.

B. Oh, Chief John! Huh huh. Your name was actually something with eagle. You had an eagle name and everyone in your family got eagle names. It was like a last name, one can say. But you were like Chief Eagle. You had a wife, and she was highly spiritual. I should tell you that the one incarnating as that wife with you was ACTUALLY Josephine. That's why you like her. She's like an extension of Ophelia, in some way. And Ophelia has been your mother in many lives, but Josephine took the part here, and she was your wife. And what you did—and we were somewhere around North Dakota, a little bit higher, Dakota, you say, is where it was. And you said you actually had several good lives up there, because the further south you came, it became more crowded, you said, even if it was early on. So, this was up in that region.

D. That must have been within the Lakota or Dakota tribes? (*Oceti Sakowin is the proper native name for the Lakota, Dakota and Nakota indigenous people who were part of the historical Seven Council Fires confederacy. Based on Bob's description, he places Chief Eagle in the land of the upper Yanktonai, or Iháŋktȟuŋwaŋna, which means "Little End Village". The Yanktonai spoke in the Nakota dialects. They occupied the area in the 1800s, so I am only assuming the Nakota tribes were living in the same area in the 1100s.*)

B. It was a big tribe. And you had a great responsibility of the development of (*healing the land*). You worked in the corner of this spot—you said it was a big region that was in need of healing—and you were in a corner of that big spot. And you were sending prayers in different ways. You used fires, and it went well this time, with fires. (*He was referring to an early life where it didn't go well and I burnt up.*) In general, that is where this fondness with smoke and smudge and fire, this is where that fondness comes from. Because that is the best way to actually heal. Because you send the wound, let's say, the occurrences—it goes up in smoke simply, basically, like that. But you do prefer to work with heat, and that's why you don't prefer to be in a cooler climate. So, you were working there. And Josephine—who was Mrs. Eagle—she was very spiritual and she was more connected, actually, than you were. You were tall. You were taller than you are in the current body, you were really big. The other ones, they were not that big at all. You felt a big responsibility for your tribe. But you also, due to the connection that you and Mrs. Eagle felt from this specific spot that you tried to heal, there was a huge sadness that you could not fully relay to your tribe, because you knew that it was not gonna be fulfilled within that lifetime. (*The healing of the land.*) And that is a memory in your soul, I would say. It is that sensation of not being able to complete a mission or a work, an assignment, in your lifetime. And it's the same thing now, you said. You have to, in some way, be fine with or settled in the understanding that you are not fully seeing the results of everything that you put the efforts in now—doing your writing—all the efforts are not gonna be shown during your lifetime. And if you feel a sadness about that, that you're not seeing the result, not only of how your work is received, but in the general change around you, then that is a memory from this life as the Eagle Chief.

D. Can you describe the ritual that he would do with the fire?
B. What we did, or you did—
D. You helped!
B. I made sure you didn't burn! That's what I did. Huhuh. So, there was a huge, huge bonfire in the middle. And you were sitting in a circle, but there were several circles going outwards where people were sitting and chanting. And then on the outside there were guards standing with torches as well. They didn't participate, because normally those who were fire-watchers, or guards, surrounding this great circle of humanoids, or the natives, they were younger boys not fully initiated to participate in the ceremony. They were normally doing that at the age of twelve to thirteen. You could actually start to be a fire guard from the age of nine. Your son, for instance, was one of those. But normally, at the age of fifteen to sixteen, you were considered an adult and then you were allowed to join. They went through different initiations to

become an adult. But this was a group, a joined project, so the young ones were participating because it was still a big task. And it was a huge assignment, because everyone sitting in those circles around the big fire, they had their eyes shut. So, it wasn't a little thing to ask of the youngsters standing, observing this and holding torches, because they were actually monitoring the big fire in the middle. They were monitoring that everything went fine. So it was a HUGE undertaking that the youngsters took with great responsibility. So, they were sitting there, and you were walking around inside the inner circle around the fire. You were—I wouldn't say chanting because you were talking—you put things in the fire that made it go poof, a powder that made it go more poof, and it shot off flames, higher flames, upwards. It was a way to call the gods. Maybe you called Jeshua! Who knows? But it was a way to call the gods, and the fire was the way to do so. The chanting was just to create a huge vibrational spot for the gods to enter this (ceremony). And they came into the fire and they showed their faces in the fire. This was a ritual, and after a while... Oh, it was exciting, I must say! Everyone was sitting there, and I stood a little bit of a distance away, but I was there. And the chanting—you should hear it—it was a big wave of humming. Everyone had the same rhythm. It was like uuhhhhhmmmmm uuhhhhh mmmmm and it went on like that and it just increased in sound. And everyone was, in some way, entranced by themselves in this experience, but it was a joined humming. And you were working the fire by sending in this powder, creating something that went up. And it kept on increasing; the fire increased, the chanting, the humming increased, and eventually, you could see the gods, so to speak, in the fire. There were like three faces shown in the fire, and they were the fire gods. So, you honored the fire gods. And from that point, they communicated through you. So you were entranced, in some way. And as you started to talk, the other ones could open their eyes. They could see faces in the big fire; they were still sitting down and they could hear the voices through you.

D. Wow. That sounds magical.

B. It kinda was. But it wasn't Jeshua or Ari in the fire. There was other entities, you said, that came through the fire and showed themselves, like big faces. After the ritual, you never said goodbye to the entities in the fire. They said goodbye to you. And as they did, you sat quietly and observed the fire until it was gone. That took a while because it was a big fire, but everyone sat still in honor of their presence and how they had visited you, until the fire was burned out. Then the remains of that fire was dug down into the soil, you put it down there.

D. How long did it last? Was it a full day or longer?

B. It was nighttime. It started at like 7 or 8 in the evening and it went on until sunrise.

D. And that helped heal the Earth?

B. The intention was that you invited the higher intelligence, fire gods, that would not only communicate to the people, but they also knew what to bring, so that the remains of the fire would be fruitful for the ceremony as you dug it down.

D. So the prayers would go into the soil?

B. Indeed, indeed. So this whole experience—the chanting, the communication, the presence of the fire gods... who knows who they were. We never talked about that. But I did see them and you said that they are like Earth spirits. So it's not someone that I will stumble upon in the hallway on the sixth. Because I did ask! I did ask, "Are these (*entities*) someone that we will later meet in your lab, for instance?" And you said, "No, they are Earth gods." You call on Earth gods, because they are an extension from the planet and it shows in different elements. In this particular tribe, you worked a lot with fire. So you called the element fire. I mean, it's not really gods, it's the extension of the element. So you called them fire gods, because they were the highest level of understanding in that element.

D. That's really impressive. Thank you for that description.

B. Ah. So, that's what you did there.

D. You said there were other dots you wanted to talk about?

B. There was another dot that was further south, like in New Mexico. And climate-wise, you preferred to be there. It was a smaller settlement, and you were there around—well, you've been there also several times—but this particular time you were there very early, around 200 AD. The wound wasn't as exposed, but you did rituals there as well. You showed me this life because that was a time when you felt really connected to the individuals that you traveled with, the humans that you were with. It was because everyone was very intuitive with each other. It was a great community. You still had feathers, but you weren't as big. There was one that was considered (*to be*) a medicine man, that would be like a chief person. But in this specific community, there was no chief position. Everyone operated as equals. But there was an elderly one that had more wisdom and would be considered the leader, because he was a medicine man. But also, he was the one that was connected to the location, you said, that had a memory of several visits. So, this elderly one, he was a great story-teller, I'll tell you that! Because he could hear and sense things that a normal humanoid could not. You could not either. But he sat all by himself on a little hill—it was kinda sandy, it was kinda dry—but he sat in the evening-time, in the night, and he sat there all by himself. And everyone knew he was gathering information, and he was communicating with the star gods. He told stories later, the day after, about what he had heard and what he had seen.

D. Do you remember any of the stories?

B. Indeed. So he could connect to—he flew over the timeline, so to speak—so he could say what had happened before. So, for instance, there were several tribes before you that had put down in the soil different treats. Not food treats, but like maps on skin—they made little drawings and so forth—but there were things buried and he could go instantly to those locations. The whole group was captivated by these stories because they were always true and you found things—it was like a treasure hunt. At one point, he talked about a civilization that had been there 5000 to 3000 years earlier than you. And they had a settlement that he told you all about. They had help from outsiders, he said, and they could build grand cave works in certain red rocks. (*Bob may be referring to cliff dwellings, which are common in New Mexico.*) They didn't live in tents. They lived in sort of a city, so he told about that. He had seen it because he had moved up into the fourth reality and he had flown over the timeline and he had accessed this memory. So he came down and he drew it in the sand for everyone to hear this story. It was a highly developed civilization and region. It was almost like a fort, but they (*the humans*) had help building, moving the blocks, these big stone blocks. He talked about different ceremonies that took place, and how they built all these different circles with stone—similar like Stonehenge—in order for them to invite the gods.

D. Who did they have help from? Travelers?

B. Ah! They did not look like you do! Some were small with strange ears, but they came with taller ones. The taller ones were silent. The little ones talked on their behalf—it was like a translator.

D. Did they communicate with thought, or did they actually talk?

B. The big ones didn't communicate at all to the humanoids that lived there. The big ones were silent, from the humanoids point of view.

They communicated to the little ones with the big ears, strange ears, and the little one—not human either, of course—told them what to do. So the little one was the middleman, so to speak. Much smaller than me! Kinda round, roundish. Strange feet, and talked. It stood next to the big one. So they (*the natives*) could see the big ones, but they couldn't hear it. So the little ones told what the big ones said. They gave information on how to monitor the sky and how to be able to create settlements that would be, location-wise, mirroring certain constellations. So that's why they told them which corner should be east, and so forth—it was to mirror some of the upper constellations and correlate to certain stars. So that's what I was gonna talk about today, and I'm gonna be back.

D. I hope so. This one said she saw you looking sort of despondent that everyone was crowding you up on stage.

B. Well, there's no need to be on MY stage. Maybe they can talk to someone else? I said, "I don't see why this hussle suddenly had to be over here. Maybe they can do it in another way—they can talk to you in your dreams or something." Ophelia said that it is a joint project, and I don't argue that. I know that Ophelia has the upper hand in everything, and she knows best. BUT it felt like just suddenly everyone found this special microphone (*Christine*) and everyone wanted to talk. Then I felt like—because I was on my way up to the stage and then these small individuals ran by me. I don't know who they are. And they were kind of many and they just (*makes blowing sound*) by me, up on my stage. I did not know who they were.

D. You're the one who's been following me all these lifetimes, so you should have priority.

B. Ah, one would think so. But it's a privilege and I don't want anyone else to not be able to talk, of course, because I don't want to sound greedy. But it is my human (*David*). I don't see why they can't talk to their human.

D. I have a feeling there aren't too many people that can do this.

B. Ah. You say that you're sort of a secretary for all of them, you say. Because I was a little bit despondent about this, so we did have a talk about that. And you said, "We are so short of time, because we follow human time." You said that you were sort of a secretary for several councils, several realities, and it's important that we get like a big smorgasbord, bits from everyone. But you said, "We will always make time for you, Bob." You did promise. You did say, "We will have separate sessions if it would ever be too crowded on the stage." And I said, "Who will determine that—if it is too crowded—would that be me or would that be you?" Huh huh ah. And you laughed and you say, "We will always make time." Because there are certain things that only I—due to the archives and being your spirit guide—can reveal. So in this case, today you put the backpack on me, and you said, "Show me and talk about the native lives I have had in Dakota and New Mexico." The one in New Mexico was a very prosperous experience.

D. Back then, it wasn't as dry as it is now, was it?

B. It was dry, but there were spots or regions where you could grow a lot. So it was a mixture, one can say. But it was a big city. And, you should know, that one of these teachings of this individual, who came down with his spokesperson, was actually to teach you agriculture in dry land.

D. Did he bring some seeds with him?

B. He taught on how to manage and maintain soil, to make dry soil into a moist soil, even if it lacked rain. So, he taught about agriculture. And that is also why the tribe that you were in at 200 AD, you had a lot of food and a lot of growth, even though it was kinda dry, because of the fact that your elder accessed this information that your ancestors had put in the grand vault above in the fourth reality. And they—this society that existed 3000 to 5000 years earlier—they had the privilege to be taught directly by a sky god, who came in with a little spokesperson with ears, who communicated and taught you (*humans*) how to grow (*crops*). A lot of it was actually not just to sit around and wait for rain—do rituals and hope rain comes—because what if rain doesn't come? And that is what the little one said, from the big one, "You have to learn how to maintain the high level of produce, even if it comes to a phase where it doesn't rain. And what do you do then?" And he was giving different crystals that you put into the soil STRATIGICALLY, in a pattern in the soil. It was not just one crystal, it was several, that was communicating and creating a map. He said, "We're creating a web in the soil that will increase the flow, and you have to put down the crystals and the stones." And some were just like granite stones and some were more shiny things. So he taught this group how to dig down this pattern based on ley lines; based on the grid; and they put it in a map almost, a grid in the soil and they (*the stones*) were communicating. And then you did like a chanting or a ritual over the soil, and it was, in some way, to activate this map that was put down in the soil.

D. And then what happened?

B. It—not just instantly, it's not that magic! Huh huh huh huh. But you activated this map, this web underneath that you had put down, by using chanting, in some way. You had your hands like this (*held hands outwards with palms down towards the Earth*) over the specific location, and you also used rituals. That is why the stone circles came about, because that was to channel different—not only like winter solstice, and so forth—but it was actually to channel energy from different stars above. So, it was to activate this map in the soil so that the soil itself came alive.

D. How big was the map?

B. It could be any size. The biggest one that you did was not fully a football field, a little bit smaller. Sometimes you did a miniature design. But he, this big one, taught them (*the 3000 to 5000 BC tribe*) how to connect with ley lines and so forth—the energetic grid in the Earth—and to assist that grid by mirroring the flow by creating this map with stones and crystals. Some were dug down inside the soil, and some were put on top. Everything had to do, even the big stone circle, it had to do with activating the region or the spot, in some way. So everything you see, when it comes to like Stonehenge and other circles that you see, everything had to do with using the upper grid, using the upper powers, in order to activate the powers and the location where you were at.

D. Wow, that's really incredible information.

B. Ah. Just the way it is. So, I'm gonna go now.

D. Thank you so much for coming and sharing. It's always a pleasure.

Bob: The Sleeping Oracle of Egypt (Jan 16, 2020)

This is an amazing revelation about life in pre-historic Egypt. The Old Kingdom and later cultures have been exhaustively scrutinized, but archaeologists and Egyptologists admit to knowing very little about the earlier inhabitants. Bob reveals that, around 3400 BC, there was a half-human, half-alien corpse that was kept in one of the temples. It was stored in oil and was known at the time as the Sleeping Oracle. It had been around for at least 20,000 years. The entity had volunteered to stay behind and reveal the secrets of the pyramids and free energy to subsequent groups who came to this planet. Unfortunately, when the Creator and councils changed the atmosphere around 7000 BC, most visitors and manifested entities could not travel here in the same way. Neither were humans able to access the fourth dimension as they once could. Therefore, the knowledge encased and held by the Sleeping Oracle became inaccessible to most people. However, the legends surrounding the ability of the Oracle to communicate were passed along, generation to generation. As Bob points out, the assumption that humans could have their knowledge magically encapsulated in their preserved body was the reason that mummification became a fad among the pre-dynastic and dynastic Egyptians. Bob revealed this information during a July 7, 2019 session, which was published in *Notes, Volume 2*. We are repeating it here because it relates to the Sleeping Oracle, who was the source of that belief. In the July session, I asked Bob, "What was the purpose of the mummification?" And he replied:

B. "It was similar to remain them (*keep them*) in that cone (*his word for a pyramid*), it was like recreating or holding that energy within. In some way, it was said to make them go to the other side, but they were creating a capsule of knowledge that the specific high priest or someone claimed to possess. It was similar to make it not known for someone else to understand the knowledge of what that person knew.

D. So they were trying to lock it away?

B. Lock it away. And some did not have magic powers at all—but they thought they did—so they demanded to be mummified. They said, "I don't want anyone to come in contact with the knowledge that I have, so I want to be mummified when I die." And they say, "Okay, okay." It's like having a portrait—so their followers thought they had special knowledge. Some of them knew things and had that connection (*to the fourth dimension*), but not all.

D. When they mummified them, were they trying to release the knowledge the priest had accumulated over his life?

B. Well, it was to encase it.

D. Within that body?

B. Yes, indeed.

D. And then hide the body away?

B. Well, they felt like the soul divided, but the knowledge that the person had was somewhat locked and remained within the physical. So even if the soul left with a vast majority of that knowledge, some was still available and connected to the person who possessed it; and that is what they tried to encase, like a mummy. And it was also to create different keys—and all this was staged before dying—so the one dying later on could say, "I want it to only be released if someone come across my mummy who has the ability to read this and this and this." So, in some way they believed that certain teachings and wisdoms still belonged with the human, even if the majority left into the spirit realm. But in order for it to not be gone, they wanted to mummify it and connect it to the person.

D. So they would leave the mummies out and accessible, and if someone came along that wanted the knowledge that priest had, they could somehow tap into it?

B. The mummy itself was also placed, normally with guards—it was not like a museum where anyone could come and look at the mummy—it was guarded. Many things was to just make a show out of it. And then people thought, "Oh, it must be something completely fascinating and something that I am not able to reach." So, it was like creating a portrait. [...] The person that was gonna die and leave prayed for some of its knowledge and wisdom and understanding of higher levels to still be locked and remain, connected to the physical. It was also believed that the soul would be able to reenter that life, in some way, into the mummy if it left a particle—let's say it like that—of its consciousness. So it would be able to reincarnate directly into that and just be the same person again."

The Egyptians, as Bob said, believed the soul would split at death. A part of the soul, the *ba*, went to the higher realms, while the *ka* would loiter around Earth and reenter the body when summoned by a priest. By mummifying a human, the priest thought they could encase the secret wisdom of the deceased and make it accessible to future students. One of the most important rituals depicted in the hieroglyphs is called the 'opening of the mouth' ritual. The intent behind this ceremony was to unlock the hidden secrets the dead person had sealed up inside the coffin. My guess is that the high priest would put on a big spectacle to convince people they were giving the mummy the ability to communicate with him or the other listeners. It doesn't work like that, of course, since the Egyptians were human. The Sleeping Oracle was a manifested being who elected to linger in the body and communicate with other advanced or manifested beings, or even aliens. Egyptian kings and priests may have thought they were god–like, but whatever knowledge they possessed went to the grave with them. That does not mean the shamans could not connect with the spirit of the departed, but the mummified body would have no bearing on that process.

Now we will return to the session from January 16, 2020.

B. Ah! And I'm waiting and I'm dressed in my finest!

D. Hello, my friend. What kind of finest are we talking about?

B. I am not dressed in that bib suit! Nay! I showed this one the bib suit (*he showed himself wearing bib overalls, like a farmer*) because of the fact that I wanted to show that I was a handy person, that I'm capable. That was what I was trying to do. I might dress in the bib pants again, but the intention of me showing why I was dressed like that was to show that I was capable.

D. Capable of what?

B. Uh, capable! That I have earned my position as not only a spirit guide and a communicator, but also as a translator for other realities. (*A few hours later, he popped a thought bubble into Christine, saying that it also meant he wasn't afraid to get his hands dirty.*)

D. So, whenever she sees that, she will know that's the message?

B. That is the message, to show that I am very capable in my position! If I had dressed like Henry VIII, he was grand, but he wasn't very capable.

D. He could eat a lot!

B. He could eat a lot, but that made him heavy, and that made his brain and his whole being to not be capable. And you should know that, that what you put into your vehicle will determine how capable, as a human, you can be or become. (*Suddenly the phone rang, and I jumped up to turn it off.*) Hmm.

D. Sorry about that.

B. Well. There is no one else coming up on my stage. I'm not taking that call! Even if someone tries to skootch me over, I'm not going. This is my time. (*Then he began to sing.*) 'This is my time, this is my time to shine, hmm hmm hmm hmmm.' So, I am indeed dressed here in my finest. I'm dressed here similar as Henry VIII. BUT I do not belong in the same era. I belong in pre–history.

D. When you say pre–history, how far back?

B Well, we are gonna talk about the blue dots. But this is when there were three kings in the region of Egypt. And you were there as an adviser. This is not a blue dot life. But you say that what I'm looking at here was the end result of a blue dot life, leading up to this one. There were three kings, three brothers, and you were an advisor to the eldest one, who was in charge. They were dividing the kingdom, in some way, and you were giving advice on where the main minerals were to be found. So, you were the advisor of the eldest one. It was a time around 3400 BC, and it was extremely wealthy, in general. (*This was pre–dynastic Egypt. Egyptian scholars call this time frame the Gerzeh culture, or the Naqada II stage*.) There was no need to be greedy, because the soil was fertile and the river brought growth, livelihood—like animal life and grains, and so forth. It was a prosperous time. What you were trying to tell this individual that you were the advisor to—and in some way, you also mediated between these three brothers. So, you came in like a neutral person, like Switzerland, among them. You said that there is no need to be greedy about the physical matter, because there was enough for everyone. However, there were teachings in temples that were of interest to not fall into the wrong hands, to the wrong brother, to the wrong king. You represented the oldest one, but you were not sure that he was the right one to carry on this teaching, that you placed in this region, when you were there in a blue dot (*life*). There were high negotiations. It was high diplomacy. It was acting on your part, due to the fact that you knew that you had to represent him publicly, but you actually thought the middle brother would be the best to carry on the order of the knowledge that was stored in the temple. This knowledge was not written in a language that was understood by the current humanoids. There was someone like you present, but that one was—he was not in a coma—but he was somewhat still. And the only one who could communicate with him was you. He was somewhat of an oracle, and he appeared like he was in a coma. He was the gateway or the portal to translate these scriptures. And you knew how to communicate with this being, who was half-human, half-not. He was there in physical but he appeared to be asleep. He was known as the Sleeping Oracle. And there was high drama and conflict to be the one, such as yourself—which you hid a little bit—on how to communicate with this oracle. Because you knew that if they understood that you had the ability to move into somewhat of a symbiosis with this being, moving into a similar level—which appeared as a coma—then you could extract information from the being. So it was simply that the shell, the surface, was appearing to be asleep. The inside was fully alert and awake. But those who were as humanoids at the time, and these three kings were, only saw the physical and they understood, in some way, that information was pouring out, but in a way that they could not understand. And you said that this one was a remain, a leftover, from an earlier time when you were there in a blue dot life. So you knew how to communicate with someone that appeared to be in a cocoon. And this is somewhat of the understanding, the leftover, that when you mummified someone, it's the same thing. They believed the physical was mummified but the inside was similar as this being, fully alert and awake, and those who were initiated in that art could still communicate with the one deceased, the one who was mummified. (*The oldest known Egyptian mummy is from around 4500 BC, but the technique is much older.*)

D. If it was half–human, what was the other half?

B. It's a visitor. The body was different. The body was not human. The face looked human, the body did not.

D. What did the body look like?

B. More full, more roundish, full. Not proportionately, as a human. The face looked human, not the body. It was known as it had died, but the inside had not passed. So the inside was still the same as the one who was there when you were here in a blue dot. That's what you said.

D. How long did it exist like that?

B. It was left there. When you were there in a blue dot life, this one was there. It was left as a keeper and a gateway to the knowledge in the pyramid. But it appeared to be frozen—like it was asleep. Didn't breathe or anything at all, so it looked like it died, but it had not rotted or anything. It wasn't mummified, but it was in oil so it was perceived as a relic or an oracle. It, or "it" was a he, so he was in a special pyramid that was guarded. But he was there when you were there in your manifested form as a blue dot. He took the part to remain, to be left there, guarding the scriptures, which could be accessed by only those who were initiated—which none were anymore, because all the blue dot people, including you, had left. So he was there for a long period of time before humans came and incarnated. And then you came in and you incarnated. So you were an incarnation, like a humanoid, but your understanding—it's like we talked about before. If there are a thousand dots in a humanoid, then you were connected very much as a human, but the inside was almost 50/50, like half–and–half. You were a fully physical human, but you maneuvered the body and surroundings as Lasaray. And you were fully aware that you were not a human, but you had the shape of one. Your main agenda was to re–open the knowledge of this being that was like a mummy.

D. What sort of knowledge did he carry?

B. We have to go back to the blue dots to find that, and that's what we're gonna do. But this life here—as I'm here dressed in my finest, similar like you—I have a lot of gold and red, and I do like that. I like when we can go to places, like the Moroccan life, where I am allowed to dress up like you. With John 11, I was also allowed to be dressed in my finest. You humor me, you said, "I know how you like to be part of the play and the game." So, whatever you dressed as, you gave me the option to somewhat mirror that. Sometimes I did not want to, and sometimes I go all in, into character of the surroundings. It's kinda fun. I don't want to engage in the karma program and I don't want to be a human, because I would have to start from scratch, and that seems like a big bother. There's no need. But if I dress up like you do, I can be sort of human like. Huhuh. But the problem is—because I wanted to be known, I've been asking to become known for a LONG time—and you said, "If you want to be known, you have to become a human." And I'm not sure about that. Ophelia or Gergen never suggested that was on the agenda. And Gergen said, "I'm not sure you would want to be a human."

D. This is the ideal solution, then.

B. Ah. But I said, "I want to be known to humans. I've been wanting that for a long time."

D. This is the best way to get your thoughts out, because you can say whatever you like and I'll write it down.

B. Ah, ah. I can say whatever I like, and no one can catch me if they feel offended or something. Hehehe! If I were a human, I might be chased.

D. They'll blame me.

B. So this is much better, but it's been a long time waiting for me to become known. BUT, when we went back and we looked at the blue dot lives, you said, "We're going to go back and look when I was there in a manifested form as myself as Anunnaki, as Lasaray in manifested form." I was not around. And there has actually been—and this just came to my knowledge, so I'm not sure how I'm feeling about this—BUT you showed me the timeline here of where we have been and so forth, and there's a lot of colors and dots. BUT it's not like there is blue dots and there is a stop, and then comes green and red and so forth, like that. What I can SEE, and this just came to my knowledge, among these dots where I was present and involved, you actually came down a couple of times in blue dots.

D. (*Laughing.*) That wasn't very nice to leave you behind.

B. No. This was not recently, but it was around 25,000 years ago. But I was with, I was present. You could see me in the life review films. So, I was known—not for humans—but for councils and so forth. BUT then I saw that you came down in blue dots around the same time. And you said that you did that sometimes to observe either the cycles that were ending, or to kick-start new cycles. And you were perceived, when you came down in blue dot suits, those sort of lives, they thought you were a god! Huh huh huh. And I said, "I would have been a really good god guide!" And you said, "Yes, you would. But the agenda to come down was not a human agenda, it was to kick-start or to plant a seed of new awareness." So you came in—several of you (*Elahim*) were here in blue dots—over several periods of time. So, what I'm looking at here—you said this is what we will begin with—is when you came down in a blue dot appearance around 25,000 BC, and you were in this region. And here we see the strange being that is asleep here, 3400 BC. That one was still there, looking like an egg, almost. Still laying down, not walking around at all. The knowledge… you built pyramids and you stored—there is a gadget in there with pipes and electric, like phuussttt. (*He made a sound like the crackling of electricity.*)

D. And what was it used for?

B. It's a battery. The whole pyramid was a battery. The knowledge, one of the knowledge (*teachings*) that was available, that you left behind, was how to create free energy.

D. That would be nice to know.

B. And the pyramid was a giant battery. And on the top it was like—it's not iron at all, it's reddish. It's like copper and it's a transmitter and it connects to—I can see here what you're doing. You're establishing the foundation for upcoming civilizations on how to be able to use these batteries that were located on power spots. The top is copper, and I can see there is another pyramid further away that communicates similar. There is a connection between them in the top, copper to copper—and it's a wave thing that goes between them. You established like a power plant and you understood the mechanics behind it, and that each battery had to be directed. The sunlight was part of this. You used the disks and you channeled rays, Sun rays, and it charged the pyramid and it vibrated. What I can see is that the whole thing vibrated and it went upwards into the top that had copper and it directly sent out a line to the neighboring battery. They were positioned in a way so they would be at max capacity.

D. Huh. What was the energy used for?

B. It had to do with allowing entrance (*portals to parallel planes*). But it had nothing to do with, "Oh, let's create a lightbulb so people can see in their homes," it was not like that. Maybe someone else created lightbulbs. But you were directing—the pyramid itself was stationary, but the top was flexible, it moved—and you could rotate it, and had somewhat of a receiver. The disks were located in the middle of all these different batteries. It was a grand undertaking, what I can see here, what you're doing. But the main agenda from this, it was not to stabilize the Earth grid, it was to close the portals. You say, "At that point we closed entrances."

D. Are any of those pyramids still standing?

B. Some are still standing, indeed.

D. When was the one that everyone talks about, the Great Pyramid in Egypt, when was that one built?

B. It came a little bit later, around 7000 BC, that's what you say. It's not a battery, but it's a replica. It had the potential to become a battery, but because of the fact that this being was asleep and no one was there to be able to decipher and understand the whole power plant and the whole maintenance and the grid, it came to a sleeping knowledge.

D. Even when I was there and was able to get the knowledge, we didn't use it for anything?

B. You closed it. So from what I'm seeing here, I asked you, "When did you open it?" and you said, 'That's a completely different blue dot." And I said, "Maybe we can go and look at that blue dot when it was open?" And you said, "We closed it, it was an end of a cycle, where we determined that there was not to be entrances anymore."

D. So like visitors couldn't come?

B. No. Not in that region. When visitors come, they navigate by these signals. And when the signals were not compatible to their vehicle, to their craft, they could not merge with the Earth plane, and that was the intention.

D. It would be nice if I understood that whole traveling business a little better.

B. Ah. You came here through this. We're gonna talk more about that, but Ophelia says that was a great window we opened for you. And I'm grateful to be participating, even though I'm seeing here that a blue dot life indeed occurred, in the middle of our joint–life journey, that I was not aware of. And you said there will be certain times I see that there were blue dots.

D. Did I give you thought bubbles that contained images of what happened then? Did I show you?

B. No! No, no, no! That's why I am a little bit hesitant about this information that just came forward, because I was completely left out.

D. I'm showing you now, aren't I?

B. You're showing me now, and we're looking at these blue dots. We're gonna decipher more, you say, and we're gonna look into the blue dots through my eyes. You're gonna tell me, and then I'm gonna tell you, because the human you is a little bit slow—and that works really good for me. So you can't really question me, because you're questioning yourself! Well, I'm gonna go now. But I wanted to tell you that, little by little, we're gonna expose hidden messages and hidden information of visits, of knowledge, of prior beings that have visited before. You say we will look at them and we will see what they left behind on Earth, similar like this being that appears to be asleep.

D. Those three brothers, are they known to modern historians?

B. Ah. They were greedy. They were equally powerful. There was just a shift in their personality, slightly.

D. Were they located in what is currently Egypt or North Africa?

B. North Africa, in that region. They had the whole region, that was the thing they were gonna divide, so it went from like Morocco and down and all the way around to Egypt. They had no interest in the southern part of Africa at that point, but they were interested in accessing the canal. There was a struggle about who was gonna possess the canal, instead of sharing the canal. There's no need to be greedy. There was a lot of—this was a time of heightened prosperity. No one starved, and it was a blossoming society. There was no need to be greedy. As they started to divide it, this is when the region started to have a downfall and it became conflicts between regions, and that canal was crucial.

D. Was it the Nile River? Or was it something else that they dug?

B. Ah, that's the one (*the Nile*). Someone wanted to possess the trade in the canal and put up tolls, which was a completely brand-new thing. So it was a conflict.

D. That's the way humans are.

B. Well, they were humans, so they acted like those. Anyway, I'm gonna go now.

D. Alright, my friend. Thank you so much for coming. I really enjoy our separate sessions.

B. Thank you for showing up. If someone calls you can answer them now, but they cannot come up on my stage—just tell them that.

D. I never get calls, so I'm sorry I didn't turn the phone off.

B. They're not gonna get on my stage, you can just tell them that, because it's mine.

D. Indeed it is. Ask Ophelia if this is the kind of information that is supposed to go in the books.

B. Indeed. It's gonna come in books. There's more of an interest in the Earth's past and how certain things have resulted in the outcome of now and how those are actually reappearing occurrences.

D. I look forward to hearing more, so thank you.

B. Okay, I go now. Bye bye.

Bob: The Zooming Device (Feb 13, 2020)

Bob has an incredible enthusiasm for travel and learning, and one of his favorite places to study on the sixth dimension is the zooming device room. He calls it the zooming device because it is a combination of both travel and learning. The room is like a great planetarium, where objects and structure within the fish tanks can be zoomed in on and examined. Based on his descriptions, it is actually akin to remote viewing. The zooming device facilitates the ability to send part of the viewers' awareness out into the fish tanks, instead of the image being brought into the spiritual dimension. As Ophelia has said in prior sessions, not everything we see in the sky is what it appears to be, as Bob explains here. We published most of this session in *Wave 3*.

B. Ah. So I like to take these classes, because they're better at home. You have like this auditorium, planetarium thing that we can go and see things, and I can see everything. It's a HUGE vaulted ceiling, and we shut the light so it becomes dark and then everything is on display. You just change the screen and I can see everything—it's much easier. You just send me information in my mind about what I'm seeing. And there are like empty zones, which are like portals. They are empty. It looks like a sun or a star, but if you were to come close, you would see it's just a hole.

D. So where does it lead?

B. Next door.

D. To another fish tank?

B. If it's on the border, it might. Otherwise, it leads to another universe or another frequency band in the fish tank, you say. But

I see here, you zoom in on a star and I say, "Oh, look, a star." And you say, "Look closely. It's not a star." And then you zoom in and I can see that what I thought was a star is just empty space with a hole, and it's white. When we peek in, I see something new, I see next door.
- D. Hmm. Next door to some other spot—
- B. Another frequency band, you say.
- D. Oh, like a parallel reality?
- B. Ah. A dot that looks like a star. But when you come close, you'll see, "Oh, it was not a star. It's just a hole."
- D. I imagine there are a lot of things we look at that aren't what they appear.
- B. That's not what you think it is. But you don't have the equipment to investigate fully, like I have. I have a much better auditorium here. And I have a much better tutor, and someone who can zoom in. If I can't see, if I can't go, then I like it to be zoomed in for me—and that's what you do. You said, "There's no need to go to all these places." And I said, "There's a lot of these that are just peek-holes into somewhere else?" And you smiled and said, "Yes. That is true." And I said, "Do I have a peek-hole next to my system?" And you say, "It's not like it's everywhere. If two frequencies are kinda close and in symbiosis with each other, then we create—" And I said, "Who are 'we' because I don't remember being part of this, making holes." It's like making holes in a big sheet.
- D. The last time we talked, you said when they get close to one another, that's when they have the potential to form a portal.
- B. A portal, indeed. But here I can see, when you zoomed in, I can see there is an opening to next door. It's not a tunnel, it's just a hole. Like a window. Someone made just a window, like a hole in space.
- D. Some of the ancients used to think that all the lights up in the sky were just holes in a black canopy.
- B. Ah. Some of them are, like I see here. This one that you showed me is.
- D. Like a big light back behind the hole.
- B. It's a light on the other side. It's another frequency band. And you zoomed in for me so I could see. I like that. It's much better. And you said, "This is like having a documentary." And I said, "How much can you zoom in? Can you zoom in on everything? Can we zoom in on all the fish tanks? Can we zoom in inside the Pole?" And you said, "Easy there, Little Friend." But clearly, you have this

zooming device, and it just depends on what we wanna zoom in on. So, what I see here, now that we have this zooming device using for the Wheel and the fish tanks, I extend that thought and I said, "You could possibility zoom inside the spiritual realities or the Creator. Maybe there's a peek-hole somewhere?"

D. Maybe you could see all the individuals who have made their final ascension floating around.

B. Ah. I would like to see how they look, you know—how they are, how they look. And what do they do? Are they happy? If not happy, then I'm fine being outside. But I don't want to be outside by myself though!

D. It sounds like we have a long way to go before that happens.

B. Ah. But this zooming device, in this auditorium where I can see things, this is great! This is grand! And then this one (*Seth*) comes in and he says that we can zoom in on the project next door, fish tank six. So we're gonna do that, he says.

D. That's one way to go there without actually traveling.

B. Without putting a rocket on me or going into the dryer. I've always been fine with having a documentary, UNTIL I'm not fine anymore and I wanna do! Okay, okay, I'm gonna go now.

D. It was a real pleasure to talk to you. I've been looking forward to it all week.

B. Always a pleasure. I'm here, always here. Okay, see you.

D. Okay. Thank you.

B. You can think of what you want to show me next time about the zooming. We might put up a separate post-it wall about what we should zoom in on, because we only zoomed in here within the fish tank. But now when I know we have a zooming device, which would indicate a documentary, then the world is my oyster, and the world is wide open for me. Okay, okay, I'll go. Bye bye.

Bob: The AD 2178 Life Project (June 21, 2020)
Lasaray's mentor, Jeshua, is the one who planned most of Lasaray's past incarnations. Planning a life is a complex mixture of mission, karma, Coat, timing, astrology, and evolution. It also has to be coordinated with the life plans of other souls who will be participating as family or friends. Bob is a highly skilled spirit guide, so the next step on his ladder of learning was to study that process. To that end, Jeshua gave him an assignment to do all the planning for a future life, which Bob embraced with his normal exuberance. Those steps were detailed in *Notes, Volume 2*. Once Bob was satisfied with his AD

2178 life plan, Jeshua called a meeting to assess the work. Lasaray escorted Bob to the Council of Nine where his plan was evaluated.

In *Notes, Volume 2,* Bob outlined how the Astrological Council uses a combination of the intended personality traits and life purpose to pinpoint when the outer celestial patterns are best aligned to the inner life map. The unfolding of life events is also synchronized to the energy from the stars and planets at various times during the incarnation. The Astrological Council gave Bob the exact time and location for the birth of the 2178 life, so it would be nice if this information is still available for my future self to find.

Bob mentioned Nealon, who is a friend of Lasaray's on the sixth dimension. Bob is quite fond of him, and originally asked him to come down as the father in Lasaray's 2178 life. Nealon agreed, but during the review process, it was recommended that Bob find someone who would benefit from having Josephine as a partner. So Bob exchanged Nealon with a soul from the fifth who has yet to fold his Coat. Josephine is in Ophelia's group of Shea on the seventh dimension. She shared several lives with Lasaray in Europe and North America, and has also folded her Coat. She agreed to come as the mother because she wants to promote community-based organic farming groups.

Bob then reveals how spirits are given access to higher levels of knowledge, which he compares to having foam removed from their ears, little by little. I asked Bob if he could tell anything about the conditions on Earth in the 2178 life. He said there will be changes in the air circulation, causing droughts in Africa. He also assures us that Jeshua and the Council of Nine are monitoring the Cell. The Cell sits atop a pyramid of corruption enabled by their private control of the fiat (fake) currency system, as described in our previous books. Bob suggests that oil production is going to be sharply reduced by the Council, which will cause a financial draught that cripples the Cell. He ended by talking about his friendship with Sniffer.

B. So, you know. I have been promoted from the Council of Nine, my work assignment (*planning the 2178 life*) has been approved with honors.

D. Did you get your diploma?

B. Ah, ah, ah. We went there together because you said I was called, or that I was summoned. And when you said I was summoned, I thought, "Oh, that's scary. What did I do wrong?" And you said, "It's nothing bad. You're just going to get the results of your assignment." So we went together, and I was dressed in my finest, to sort of honor the level of gratitude and the level of the sincerity of this meeting. And Ari was there, and I did like that. Even Jeshua was there, and Zachariah came also. And then you and me. And then, what did happen was that when we got there—you normally are always on my side here (*as he looks to the right*)—but when we got there you took the position of the other ones. So you were over there with the other ones and I was standing all by myself. And I was like, "Ohh, this is different." First, you were all quiet, and I just stood there. Then you and Ari went like, "Okay, we're going to reveal the result of your assignment, and it's going to be here behind us." It was like a big curtain. And there I stood, and I waited, and then it was like drum roooooooll and then the curtains went down. And it was like a picture of me having a star, like there (*as he looks down towards his chest*) and it indicated that I was now like maybe one of you, like I belonged and that I had got my star.

D. Ah, wonderful! You deserved it.

B. And then you say, "Come over here, Bob. Now you can step forward." And I came forward and everyone circled around me and it was a cheerful merging with all of us. And then I said, "Oh, what did you like the most?" And you said, "I liked the part where you said that I was going to go and get the flower, and it was actually that it was not just a flower that I was finding, I was also finding a mate of mine. So, it was a treat. And I liked how you made me go look for a flower when it was actually two treats." And I said, "I did that by myself. I thought, 'You think you're going to chase one treat, and there's actually something else behind that treat.'" So you said that you liked that, and you also were grateful that I had taken into consideration, that you preferred certain places. You said that I avoided London and that I put you outside of London. And also that, "You had taken into consideration that the other ones also should shine."

D. Very nice. Does that mean I have accepted it?

B. It seems so. Yes, indeed. 2178, it's departure time. March. You're gonna be born March 21st or 17th. It's gonna be March 21st, that's what we're aiming for, 2178. You can look at the chart. You're gonna be born in Newcastle and you're gonna be there for a while, before we move you down to the southern part of England, the Southwest part of England. And that's where I'm putting you. But you're gonna be born March 21st. I first thought, you know, let's give him a little bit of a wiggle room. But then those who come in who design the touchdown, they said that it was more optimal, the general flow, if you were born a couple days later. They said, "We don't give wiggle room here. He's going to come in on the 21st."

D. What time?

B. You're gonna be born March 21st, 2178 at 5:38 am, in Newcastle.

D. Alright. Wonderful

B. So this one can put it in to her computer and just look at the chart and see what sort of personality you will be. I must say that I am REALLY fascinated with this group, the ones who decide touchdown. And this is how it goes: A spirt guide comes and has a whole outline for a person, their person, and then they go to this Astrological Council to just say, "Okay, my person has this background, he's been down several times. This is the general intent of earlier travels. This is the intent of his future travel. He's gonna come down, and this is the mission. We also want him to have this and this personality and he's gonna meet a person who has this personality, and the parents are gonna be like this and this, and so forth. They're gonna be in this area of the Earth, and this is the general outline of this life." And then, "Hmm," says the Astrological Council. Then they look at, "Okay, we need to mix and match. Clearly, parents need to come first." Normally when someone like me—when I came, I had created your life—but we also needed to make sure that Josephine was down before. So someone took care of Josephine and the other one from the fifth that's gonna be your father, that I had to change (*from Nealon*). So they were—the parents part in this specific case, because they're not gonna necessarily do that much of a mission themselves. Except for the community that they're gonna be changing, how one works with solar energy and how to learn how to agriculture in a more environmental and earth-friendly way. So it's gonna be this community that they're gonna reboot again. That's the only thing they need to do, in general. I didn't go to the Astrological Council by myself, unfortunately. Jeshua took care of that. BUT I was still participating a little bit with the Astrological Council, since I had an idea of the 17th. But I did not know that the planets were gonna be better suited on the 21st. BUT in this specific case, where the parents are merely there to give birth to you and to create an environmental community. The one (*guide*) who went to the Astrological Council with their lives, their maps, put them together as a unit.

D. So you didn't actually go to the Council?

B. I went to the Council of Nine, and I did follow a little bit on the Astrological Council, but I did not speak, fully. Jeshua took care of that.

D. But you participated?

B. Indeed. I went with Jeshua—and that was a treat. So, I did see the procedure on how to calculate when you're gonna pop down. It's similar like your big auditorium and you can put in different data in somewhat of a box, and then the box starts to rotate. It goes really fast on these slides that I can look at. It spins like a dryer and then it goes slower and suddenly it stops. I can see all the constellations, how the stars are positioned, then I can see Earth and then I can see you as a dot. And then I can see how they somewhat try to zoom in—they're not zooming in geographically because I had already decided that—but they zoom in on the timeline where we're gonna plop you down.

D. That's really high tech.

B. They don't talk that much. I mean, they might to Jeshua, but it appears a little bit like—they're not silent and they don't hum but they kinda (*he then made some random popping sounds*).

D. Apparently Jeshua can understand.

B. Ah. He didn't do the same back, but he seemed to have understood. I did not. So, when we went out, since I was treated with joining, he said, "Mission accomplished. Now we have a date." And I said, "How was that selected? What sort of criteria did they go on?" And he said, "I showed them the general outline and also how certain things—" and it's not just about birth. He told them that, "this and this is the time when he's going to go to school. This is the time when he's going to be by himself. This is the time when his parents leave, when they return home. This is the time when the flower and his treat friend are coming in. Based on that, there was a whole calculation." So, it has not only to do with when we plop you down, when it's touchdown, it's also to make sure that when it's time to find the flower, and you're supposed to be somewhat inquisitive and be a star, we want to make sure that you really ARE a star, that you are under the influence of seeking, of searching, and not being slow and snoozy and sad. So it's a whole system and they can move certain things and, and this was new—they said apparently to Jeshua, and Jeshua told me—that it's not a constant motion, they can manipulate the motion. If they want, let's say, an influence of the energy of constellation Capricorn to last longer, they can do retrograde motion in the system, or make it go slower, slow it down.

D. That would almost have to be on an individual basis, because it would affect everyone on the planet?

B. It affects everyone. He said, "When you're born, you get the astrological map that is implanted inside. But THAT map can be adjusted and go slower than intended from the beginning, whereas the outer constellation, the outer maps, are set in somewhat of a pace."

D. Okay, that makes sense. I follow that.

B. So, you know, I offered to take classes with them. But first I need to learn the language. And then I said, "Maybe you, Jeshua, want to join, and you can translate to me?" And he did this on my back (*patted him*) and said, "You're always trying, you're always ready to go. We will go eventually," he said. I like him. He can make things happen. He made my bubble, and he's quite helpful. He knows my pros and cons, and he knows that I'm interested in going, but I also sometimes don't have clearance everywhere. And he knows that I respond less favorably to blockages, so he always said, "Eventually, Little Friend, we will do that. But first you need to learn the language." And then I say, "I can take classes. I can go to school." And he said, "It has nothing to do with going to school. It's simply that you have to have the clearance to understand it. It's like removing lint in your ears," he said, "That's how clearance is given. You don't have to go and sit and read a book. That's not how it works. When you have clearance, they simply remove like foam in your ears." I wondered who put foam in my ears! Wouldn't it be better if I didn't have foam in my ears, so that I can understand all these different groups? Then maybe I wouldn't have been so shocked about the Moon People. Now I know it's because the foam related to the Moon People was still intact. (*The Moon People are a group on the sixth dimension in charge of designing moons. See 'Notes, Volume 1'. He thought they just stared at him, so he was a little unnerved by their silence.*)

D. (*Laughing.*) I'm pretty sure that everyone has foam in their ears. All spirits are designed like that.

B. And then I wondered, 'Who removes the foam?' And he said, "I remove the foam from Lasaray, when he is granted a new level of access." And then I said, "Oh! Then I know who removes my foam. It's Gergen!" And Gergen never said he did.

D. Have you removed any foam from Tom's ears?

B. No. No. We have not reached that level where foam is removed. But Jeshua said that a part has been removed—because I was a little bit despondent about the fact there was a little bit of foam in me—but Jeshua said that I have actually had foam removed. One part of the foam was removed as I was given my assignment in the Library—I could hear you after a while. He said that was a part where foam disappeared. And then I didn't really fully understand the Council of Nine from the beginning either, and I didn't really hear Jeshua. I thought Jeshua stared, when he was actually just friendly looking. So, he said he had removed foam from your ears.

D. You've made a lot of progress.

B. But Gergen is apparently in charge of when and where. And then I wondered, "Can foam be put in afterwards?"

D. What was the response?

B. It didn't seem like it was like that. Once it is removed, it is removed. And then I wondered, "How much foam is there?" And Jeshua said, "You're all full of questions." And then you came and said, "Oh, what is it that you're wondering about now, Bob?" And I said, "Jeshua said I have foam in my ears, that I can't hear. And I have volunteered to go and learn at the Astrological Council." Because it is highly interesting to know how they work, not just to know when to pop you down, because, okay, we have a date for touchdown. BUT I see that's just a teeny–tiny part of what they do. They work really close with the Evolution Group—because the Evolution Group comes in and they have ideas—and the Astrological Council, they sort of look into conditions when certain changes are best introduced. Backwards and forwards and, you know, halt (*at the best time*). They seem to be extremely close. And then I thought that, because I did not only sketch your life, I sketched something that the Evolution Group might be interested in.

D. Involving what? Fixing the Earth?

B. Indeed. Indeed. And then I can see the whole chain here. I can go to the Evolution Group, I have suggestions on how to proceed. Then they go, "Ohh, great idea! Let's go to the Astrological Council and see when and where and how and what result we can expect then and there." So I can see the whole chain. And now I feel like—I did your life and if you're up to it—I might do more lives with you. But you haven't said anything. You said, "Let's do this one and then we can see."

D. That's a great goal. Can you, in any way, see what the future of Earth looks like? Have you been shown?

B. It's gonna be somewhat of a drought, it's gonna be a drought on the southern part where the African region is. And that is a little bit of what the Council on the Second are discussing, because there's gonna be a shift in the general flow of the wind and rain, clouds and so forth. And unfortunately, there will be a drought.

D. That will thin the population out some.

B. Indeed. It will make less people. But it's also gonna be somewhat of a drop around India, it's too crowded there. In general, it is a little bit crowded on certain places, and then there's all sorts of space on other places. But what we actually are seeking is an improvement of the soil and the way to agriculture the soil. We can't have all these footsteps interfering when we try to make changes, so in that sense, in order for changes to take place, some sort of reboot is necessary indeed.

D. Is the Cell going to be overthrown?

B. I cannot see that. I know that Jeshua and the Council of Nine are looking into that, combined with the Evolution Group who is also a part of that. But the Evolution Group is not part of those monitoring the Cell. The Council of Nine are more involved with the understanding of what the Cell is capable of. And there are several meetings about that specific part of human nature. The Evolution Group are aware, in some respect, but they are not as, I mean they are probably interested, but the Evolution Group looks at a bigger scene. But I know that Ari, Jeshua and the Council of Nine, they are looking into this Cell. It's a monetary drought that is needed, and that is what they are looking into. It's gonna be a drought on several places and they're gonna experience a monetary drought because of the fact there is gonna be a change on how to use energy. Solar energy is gonna increase, even wind power is gonna increase. Oil is gonna be on halt for a while. Gas will be, ahh, it's gonna continue, but oil is gonna drop again. Ari and Eli and everyone—Eli is closer to the Evolution Group, he and Isaac are closer to them. I can see them as—I'm pretty excited here—because I can see the Council of Nine, Evolution Group, Astrological Group, me, council where Gergen is and Ole, fish tank over there (*nodding to the right*). Also, there's a council over there, for fish tank eight, that seem to be in some way in communication with the Council of Nine. Evolution Group is more connected—you say you don't talk with them as much.

D. With which ones?

B. Evolution Group. But I can see here the web.

D. There is also a council on the fifth that oversees the humans?

B. Ah. But we never talked about them, and I've never been there.

D. Zachariah must have some involvement with them, since he teaches so many from the fifth?

B. Ah. Zachariah does.

D. It's a pretty complicated setup.

B. Ah. But I'm willing to learn.

D. I know you are. You're a wonderful pupil.

B. Ah, I am indeed because I'm quite inquisitive. And I'm thinking if you are a teacher, you want to have someone who appears to be interested in what you're saying—and I'm that person, indeed, normally. Unless there is too much going back and forth about the same things, you know, move spine, move not spine. Move spine, make it rain. Make it not rain. Then I feel like, "Maybe we should just make a decision. Hands up if we should make it rain, and then we see." BUT the Astrological Council is involved in that too, in some way. Okay, so I'm gonna go now, but happy to communicate a little bit. Did you know that I've been out with the Sniffer? (*See 'Notes, Vol. 2'.*)

D. No.

B. No? I did, indeed. Me and Old Sniffer, we have bonded on all sorts of levels, and there's no end in our friendship. I don't see it ever coming to an end because there are ENDLESS questions we can talk about, ENDLESS topics to elaborate on.

D. Does he question you, or you question him?

B. Well, we have a system. I ask two questions; he asks three. Then I ask three; he asks two. So it's a back and forth, it's a mutual partnership. He is quite curious about the stars. So what we did, me and Old Sniffer, I said, "Okay, I'm gonna teach you a little bit about the stars, because they are not all what it appears to be." I did ask you if we could come to the zooming device, so I can zoom in and show it to Old Sniffer. But you said that Old Sniffer is not capable of merging to and moving to the lab on the sixth. SO, we laid down (*somewhere on Earth*) and were observing the sky, and we talked about the stars. I said, "Not everything is what it seems to be. Not all are stars." And he's like, "What is a star?" And then I said, "The star is a conductor that makes the rotation of all the planets that circulates around it. Earth is a planet that circulates around the Sun, around a star." Then I told him how I made a star, when I was at Ophelia's place, and then I talked about different things. So he wanted to know about that, and he wanted to know, when I said that I made my own solar system, and I said, "We cannot see it, but it's way, way, way out there behind what we can see here." And then I wanted to know about what took place before the rain or the dinosaurs, and he sent me pictures in my mind and I could see crafts.

D. Oh really? What did they look like?

B. The crafts were just like a frisbee.

D. What were they doing?

B. They were monitoring the DNA, he said, in the mammals.

D. Were they modifying it any, did they have a hand in that?

B. Indeed!

D. Was it predominantly the visitors who created life on Earth? Were they the ones who brought it here?

B. The dinosaurs?

D. I think they had a hand in the dinosaurs, but were they involved earlier?

B. Ah, the ones that came in bigger disks, indeed, came down and put down like poles, created somewhat of a community. They were not humans.

D. That's good that you have such a wise friend.

B. Ah. You know we talk about all sorts of things, and we laugh! He's quite humorous, he has a great sense of humor and so have I, it appears to be, because he likes my jokes.

D. When he laughs, what is it like?

B. It's like (*he makes a little snort, like a baby pig*), like that. And I don't judge. I've heard stranger things. I've heard (*he then makes popping and clicking sounds*), like that. So, you know, I have a friend. I'm gonna go now, but I'll be back.

D. Thank you so much for coming and sharing today. It was really pleasurable.

B. Anyway, it's time to go.

D. Alright, my friend, always a pleasure, as you know.

B. Ah. Okay, okay. Bye bye.

D. Bye bye.

Gergen, Ia, Bob: Earthquakes and Evolution (July 26, 2020)

For this *Wave 4*, we have integrated the storylines and teachings that were first presented in the *Notes from the Second Dimension* series. Gergen, as you may remember, is Bob's mentor or father figure on the second dimension, and Ia is his closest companion. Gergen came in first during this session and told about the changes that the second dimension is planning for the entire west coast of North and South America. In previous sessions, they revealed their intention to move the spine, or the Andes mountain range, of South America. The main reasons are to improve the atmospheric conditions on land and the water circulation in the reefal areas of the horse latitudes. Ia followed Gergen, and she gave information on special groups of spirits from the second, who are soon headed to Earth. They will each act as a spirit guide to a soul from the fifth, who is beginning its cycle of incarnation. Those who are incarnating will have a much stronger connection to their soul particle. One of the groups is being sent to understand and help heal the seas and the atmosphere. Another group will develop knowledge of natural plant remedies, since synthetic remedies are viewed unfavorably by the spirit realms.

One of the points Bob makes is that visitors came from Mars and elsewhere and stored information in large coffin-shaped boxes that were buried near Cairo and other places. It is somewhat unlikely, but possible, that some of the gigantic 100-ton boxes found near the acropolis in the 1800's may have been left there by these pumpkin-headed visitors. If, indeed, those are the same coffins, any useful material inside has been hidden from the public or lost to ancient vandals. Bob proceeded from there to describe how stellar time is not linear, but can be bent and folded to bypass parts of it. However, it should be understood that on the Earth itself, and as far as humans are concerned, time will only be linear. The bending of time is more related to the physics of how manifested entities travel in the fish tanks.

G. Th-th-th-th-this is Gergen.

D. Hello, Gergen.

G. Delivering some updates from the Council on the Second. And also giving the hands up to Bob, who has been participating (*in the council meetings*) with great honor, lasting the whole session through, even during the discussion on whether we should or divert and shift the climate in the region near the Amazon, as we can see the need for an increase of oxygen in that region. So there has been several discussions, and the discussion itself has to do with the region in South America, indeed. The ecosystem is suffering, due to the fact that the trees are decreasing in numbers, and the roots are also decreasing. Meaning, the general web is not singing as it should. There are indeed efforts made from the second dimension, combined with the eighth, as we are increasing certain elements in the region, trying to somewhat reboot the ecosystem. We would ask if man could please step aside for a while, if that would be possible, it would help the efforts made from the second dimension. Bob participated in this meeting and lasted the whole session through, even though it's long hours, huh huh, one can say. He tends to forget, once in a while, that he actually is a second dimensional entity and being. He tends to be more eager to transform his knowledge base outside of home. Nothing wrong with it—he is an explorer, and that is what we also detected in this little egg as he arrived, once upon a time. When he came, you might wonder—and I want to give you an answer—if there was a whole egg filled with little Bob's. It was not. He was selected to join a group of twenty (*explorers*). The other ones are exploring in a different way. They are not selected to have visits and classes on the sixth and seventh, and so forth, but they are occupying places where studies are different than Earth. Bob was told, as he grew up, that if he was going to be a great explorer, exploring different dimensions within the reality of spirit, that he would not have the same opportunity to travel and explore other realities aside from Earth. So, in that sense, they are explorers, all of them, it's only that Bob is allowed to go into training to becoming like what he says, an astronaut. He became an astronaut, that's what he called it. He went into the astronaut program. Similar like saying he went into the NASA training, that's sort of how he described his upcoming studies to his friends. Similar like he was accepted into the NASA training program, that's how he pictured the sixth to be. In many ways, it is. And we are happy to listen to his stories, even though sometimes we—and this is a little trick we have as we progress—that we can not only muffle the hearing device in a sparkle or in an entity such as Bob, we can also mute the information coming from that specific entity. So, he can talk all he likes, but we mute the energy in the room, so it doesn't reach ears or beings not equipped.

D. Does he know he's being muted?

G. He has, as of now, an understanding—because he felt a little bit disappointed at some of his friends who did not go into a high celebration of his exploring activities—as we told him that they never heard it. And he said, "Yes, they did. I told them!" And we said, "We muted the energy in the room." And then he thought that was kind of shady. But there are certain things, little tricks, that one can do. So, absolutely, he knows. I just wanted to pop in and give a briefing on the activity and the efforts made in that region as level of light, meaning oxygen, needs to increase in that region. It would be beneficial for it if man could step aside briefly, so the region has the ability to rejuvenate and to increase its own light capsule. As one shuffle trees and roots, their light capsule is damaged and we are putting great effort into healing these capsules. We do not bring in a new light capsule, we simply try to repair and heal the existing ones. There will be certain activities in the ground in that region. In general, you should be aware of ground activities moving in, starting here in the end of September in several locations on Earth. There is going to be an activation from below your feet that will indicate somewhat of a shift. It has the ability to affect the climate as well and motion of streams of clouds and winds, and that is what we are looking for, and that is why the eighth is involved. You might consider the eighth like the weatherman, in this case. So in some ways, Isaac would be considered the weatherman on channel 1 who will give you the update on weather phenomena coming your way. But it is, indeed, a change in the motion and in the general flow of winds and currents, and that will affect the general climate and temperature in certain aspects. It will rise in certain places, but it will equalize in the end. And that is what we need to improve—the level of oxygen—especially in certain regions, such as the Amazon region. If we could, please, maybe have people be removed briefly, th–th–th–th–that would help.

D. When you say things are going to move, do you mean earthquakes?

G. Indeed. Rumble from below. There is going to be certain outbreaks on strategic places. There will be some over in the Japanese area. Some will be a little bit further south, which will be in the ocean bed south of the Japanese region. There will be some smaller along the west coast in the US country. And there will be some along the whole coastline from the border into Canada, from there, the whole west coast down to the South American region. It's a band, it's a vein that is quite sensitive to shifts, because we have opened up this vein. As we open up the vein, the general flow underneath your feet reaches this vein easier, and that is what is going on at this time. In general, we are stabilizing—but man will not feel it as a stabilizing effect. It might, in fact, be considered as something quite the opposite. But in order for a stabilizing effect or a new phenomena to occur, certain aspects has to be moved and rotated, and that is what is going on at this time. Different scenario in Japan, indeed.

D. What about in California? Are they going to get big earthquakes?

G. Indeed. Same band. From the Canadian border, west coast all the way down to Chile, all the way down. It's one vein. We have opened up the vein. It was long discussions. Bob did not participate in this discussion. He's not a geologist, in that sense, even though he did take classes in geology. But he did not find it quite amusing to move rocks around and flip them. He felt like he was designed for other things. When he was notified about the space program that he was selected to participate in, he said that he understood why he did not have an eye or a fondness for flipping stones. I told him Joel does more than that. (*Joel is one of Bob's Earth-based friends from the second. He is older and was here before the dinosaurs. His area of responsibility is in the Himalayan region. See 'Notes Vol 2'.*) Joel said, "I'm a geologist. I'm not just flipping stones. It's not like I'm just rolling them around." And then we had a discussion about it, about the differences. Joel is quite interested in the space program, as Bob has called it, his training of becoming a space cowboy, of sorts. However, he is not allowing students to come at this time, even though there are some, like Tom, who might be a part of this, eventually. He's quite skilled and interested. But you cannot just have an interest, you have to be designed in that way to master certain qualities. So, it's just different.

D. I was curious about Ia. I was thinking that Ia and Bob were born from the same egg. Did they come separately?

Ia. (*Ia suddenly came in to answer the question.*) No, he was right there. He was right next to me. He was quite bouncy, I remember, even from the start. But indeed, we did participate in the same program, in the same egg. However, we were separated at birth, in that sense, and put into different locations, where we were modified in the way that we were going to continue our journey. So there it is, and so it will be. What we have right now is not just one egg that has arrived from the Creator—from the elevator that Bob calls it—but we have actually three different eggs that we are managing at this time. I would say that the egg that you are familiar with, they have progressed into greater learning and they have also been given their first assignment, (*which is*) to go into human bodies, eventually, here (*on Earth*), in order to assist the seas. Some of them will be divers and some of them will have the knowledge of water biology and how the plant life on the seabed is affected by the atmosphere above. So it's not like they are just going to swim around and make a splash, they are actually going to be quite helpful. They will be taught and equipped in water engineering. They will also be understanding of the atmosphere and the connection to the seabed. So, as they progress into a human experience, these specific sparkles have the training to detect certain motions that is outside of the knowledge of the gadgets. They will get understandings and teachings from within that is not coming from readings detected by a gadget or a machine. They will be somewhat of inventors, if you like, in that field.

D. So, you're saying that you have some sparkles from the second that are going to start the karma program?

Ia. No, not the karma program. They're gonna follow souls who go into these specific bodies. Excuse my confusion for you. They are going to participate, in that sense, that they will be—not incarnating—but they will be somewhat of a split. And this is new, this is brand new information for you. Before (*in the past*), there was a blend between soul and Master Mind. What we are looking into now, in these specific souls that are coming down to understand the waters and the atmosphere, is that they will be a mix of a second dimension entity, as well as a soul from the seventh. So, in that sense, yes, they will go into the karma program. But they will be a passive visitor or a passive observer, in that sense. In many ways, they will appear as that gut feeling. They're not accumulating karma and they're not there to get new karma or to create karma. Bob might like this specific way of travel. But they are merging and blending combined with the soul. Instead of merging with a tree, they are joining with a soul in the human. It's not going to be common. It's a specific egg, and it's for a specific assignment in the waters. So, it's not like it's going to be a trend all over. We are just increasing somewhat of a higher connection and a higher learning, as we are in need to clean the waters. In order for that to happen, that gut feeling that one is hearing—the connection to the soul—it has to be stronger. So the gut feeling would be combined with the soul's own particle, of course. But it would be louder, as the second dimension is somewhat maneuvering the center point differently than in a regular incarnation. As a soul normally travels by itself, it has the pickle to try to hear the center point—that is, hearing themselves. This second dimension sparkle—well, it's not a sparkle, it's actually a well-trained youngster—will simply increase that connection to the soul, to the soul particle. But the human will never understand where this extreme hearing is coming from. Normally, you hear yourself; you hear your higher self. In this case, they will hear their higher self louder, because of the fact that the second dimension entity spirit guide will increase that knowledge with its presence.

D. I understand that. That is a wonderful gift.

Ia. So, they are merging in the center point. They're not going to merge somewhere else. They are simply there to increase the connection and to increase the volume with that specific knowledge that a second dimension entity has in its toolbox.

D. There will still be a tiny piece in there from the Master Mind, won't there?

Ia. Yes, indeed. So, in some way, the body will hold three. Quite crowded! And it is by design, it is a test and it is only for a few. It is about twenty-five souls in the beginning that will be spread out. Some in Australia, some in the Japanese area, some will be in Europe. There will be a big group in training in a Spanish university, and there will also be one in an Italian university in Milan. Some will be in Scandinavia. They're all in the same training program and field, they just address it from different schooling. But indeed, instead of having the second dimension spirit friend on the outside, we have actually merged it in the center point, in this case. And it is a brand-new design. It's not like their energy will go up, so they will not appear like they are stressed or anything like that. Rather the opposite. They will be more calm and quiet. They will have a need for quiet, because they will hear a lot from within, or sense a lot from within. All these 25, coming in around the same time, being born here around—some might come down next year, we're starting the program next year—but most will be born around 2023 in different locations. It is a test to simply allow this understanding to come forward more directly, so one doesn't have to sit around and stumble. Bob would probably like this, as he is more inclined to have a direct link.

D. Maybe they can let him blend a little bit in my next lifetime.

Ia. We will see about that. So, I wanted to stop by and say so. But it has been a great privilege to now have three different eggs coming in, and they're going to be working on different things. One of them, you should know, is in speed training to be more helpful when it comes to changing the way mankind excavates and understands herbs and plant life, in order for that to be helpful in the healing capacity. So we are looking into the field of doctors here, next. We are quite disappointed in some aspect of the occupation of hospitals and doctors. And those who want to make a difference, who really see the dilemma in the physical that could originate or have a source from another part that might not be visible in a microscope or in a stethoscope. It's hard for those doctors to be heard in this gigantic machine of noise which is fired up by the pharmaceuticals. So indeed, we see it and we address it.

D. I think everyone is disappointed with the way it is.

Ia. Disappointed, indeed. Not judging, because one doesn't know better. If one knew better, this would never occur. However, as a spiritual council from different levels are engaging in the project of Earth, we meet certain effects that we see. You are here to meet and to address the mind on how to make choices that are aligned with your center point, to be aligned with others who create a web of knowledge, and to not cave or back down under pressure when someone ridicules the connection to your spirit. It is a way to strengthen the spirit, and that is what you, the two of you, are here to do. We are simply here to color certain side effects we have seen along the way, as humanity has stumbled around on this planet. So, that would probably be it. And Bob is standing with his arms crossed, next to me.

D. Patiently waiting, is he?

Ia. He is quiet. So, in that sense, that is probably his way of being patient.

D. Well, thank you so much for coming and sharing that with us, Ia. That was really fascinating.

Ia. You are much welcome.

D. It's always nice to hear your voice.

Ia. Maybe we should continue to talk and just bump him out. (*Ia giggles as she looks towards Bob.*)

D. (*Laughing.*) He might not stay quiet for long.

Ia. Okay. There we go. Bye bye.

D. Thank you, Ia. Bye bye. (*Bob came in with a quizzical look.*)

D. Hello, my friend.

B. Oh, it became somewhat of a line—and I'm always on time! But suddenly there were friends ahead of me. I'm not saying that they should not have time, maybe just not on MY time.

D. In some ways, maybe it feels like it's always your time, doesn't it?

B. Indeed! It actually does, because I don't have the grand schedule because Ophelia never told me about the grand schedule. In many cases, I see a fog starting to ignite and I know it's time for a session. And then I feel like, "Ohh, someone is calling, someone is calling!" And then suddenly it's like a bump—like a wall or a door in front of my face. And I'm a little bit confused, because of the fact that I don't get the whole outline of the program.

D. You're just put in a waiting room, like at a doctor's office.

B. Put on hold. SO, I want to tell you that I have been to the Evolution Group.

D. Oh, you have? That's wonderful!

B. We have.

D. Did your questions get resolved?

B. It was quite different than I imagined the meeting to go. I thought we were just gonna sit and chit-chat a little bit. But they don't seem as—it's very different than the Council on the Second, where we just talk and talk and things go back and forth. It was a little bit more, I wouldn't say stiff, but they almost appeared as statues. They didn't move. They were three, and they had those purple robes, matching my bag. So now I know why my bag was purple.

D. I thought it was to match me?

B. Well, you have the purple as well, so it's somewhat of a group thing you do, must be. I mean, your robe is not the same as theirs. Your robe is not velvet. But my velvet bag has the same fabric, almost, like the Evolution Council. You have the same color, but you're not soft like a teddy-bear, you're not like in velvet.

D. (*Laughing.*) So what happened when you showed up?

B. They were standing there like three big statues in their velvet robes. I came with my velvet bag, and I did like this. (*He bent forward in the chair.*) I bowed, like that, to all three. I had my velvet bag, and I said, "I'm here offering—", I was gonna say "offering gifts", but then I realized it might not be considered a gift. So I said, "I'm here to offer questions."

D. You're looking for gifts.

B. I'm looking for gifts. And you were there on my right side, like you always are. And then Jeshua was over there (*on the left*). Jeshua was the one that communicated to them, but I could not hear communication from them. But I could see eyes and I could see that they were not statues, in that sense. Jeshua said I needed to let go of my purse, and he was gonna give them the questions. And

I said, "Is it gonna stay here in the room, the purse?" He said, "Yes, it will stay here. I'm just going to give it to the Evolution Group." Then I said, "I don't want it to get lost, or that someone who is not equipped is gonna open it and read it." And he said, "We are in the evolution area, so it is not going to be lost." And you said, "It's okay, Bob. It's okay. Just leave the purse with Jeshua." So I did. Then we stood there in silence—but they didn't even open the velvet bag. They must have understood the questions. I mean they were HOLDING the bag, but they didn't OPEN the bag.

D. They must have been able to read you and the bag?

B. They read the whole thing, it seemed. Because my first question about the grid and the openings, and how it rotates and opens and closes activities and awareness and certain understandings on this level of reality, it was answered by a movie. And it was like—you know how you have that foggy table?

D. Yes.

B. They didn't have a table, but they had it in the floor. So, between us, suddenly, it started to show. I could see like a film, and the understanding was—because Jeshua translated—it has to do with certain conditions based on inside and outside activities. Meaning, who are on-site, and who comes in. I saw certain things being placed in the mountains, like the transmitters, and how it was quite wide-open at that time. It had to do with motion, and it was the time where the continents were supposed to move. So, certain receivers—not the ones on the poles, they were reading the Fork, but these were placed around the same time—but it had to do with changes. All these different activities have to do with changes. I thought it was just changes in the consciousness, but it has to do with changes in general. It has to do with motion, moving continents, moving countries, moving even down to even the smallest river. Like, let's say, "Why does the river flow north to south? Why doesn't it flow south to north?" All these little different things have a plan behind it. In order for those things to occur, this grid moves. It's like seeing a net.

D. Like a fish net?

B. Indeed. As the planet was beginning, like a baby, the whole thing was in this net. The planet was somewhat pulsating, like a heart, in this net. After a while this net sort of became the planet, it sank in. So, you couldn't see the net anymore. This is what I see here in the film in the floor, and Jeshua was giving me words. You were giving me comfort and smiles. I can see here that the net was part of the beginning. At this time, when the net was in place, there was no atmosphere. As the net sank in, it became the planet, became the grid. I could see it's not just on land, it's actually the same web in the sea. At this time, when the sea is suffering, there are rips in this net on the seabed. And that is why they want to do certain shifts and changes. As they moved continents, as they changed the flow of atmosphere, they changed the flow of wind and so forth—and this is way back. This is before Old Sniffer came around. He did not know this, because there is no dinosaurs. There is barely any life forms. I'm not even sure that Ole existed at this time—and we have no idea about me, where I am. We don't know and it's not to be given. So, they are showing me this beginning. After a while, certain influences came in to this level, as they were engineering and maintaining this net. When they were maintaining, a different web was activated or put in this reality. So there were several nets, in some way. This is how the parallel realities started to emerge, because the original net wasn't functioning. Meaning, a new net, a new web took place and came in, and they were somewhat overlapping on certain places. That means that there was a higher concentration of these threads—I can see it as dots because it was more congested, more dense in that region. That specific place looks quite still. It doesn't look like there is a lot of activity in those zones. It's merely portals to come in and out, in those knots. The web seems to be folding on certain places, and as they do, it creates openings between these webs. That's how I see it. Jeshua said that these knots are simply to stabilize the web. It's not meant to be there. It's like a hub. (*The location of the knots inadvertently opened portals between the Earth and the parallel planes.*) And then I can see a hub in the region of England. In that region, there was a hub and it was a lot of activity coming in and out of this hub. There was another hub—not on the coast of north Africa but a little bit down—and in the upper part of Africa there is a hub. And that is the hub, when I see this, where the understanding of—it's like a mathematical group that came in with a certain knowledge of physics and formulas.

D. Was this a long time ago?

B. They're not human. They don't show me what happened in the British Isles, but here they show me the hub where entities came in. There were no humans around. And they (*the visitors*) came in and they placed certain boxes—I see boxes again, but bigger boxes, like a coffin—and they placed it where there is later, now, pyramids on top of them.

D. If this was way, way back, the continents were in different locations. Was this more recent?

B. It's not—I just don't see people when they show me these entities. They are tall and they have dark skins and have a head that looks like a pumpkin, like an oval pumpkin. But it's not going up, it's going sideways. The top of the head is not up, it's back, so it's an oval head. Your top is going straight up, their top is going backwards. (*It sounds like he is describing entities with elongated skulls.*) I can see how they came in. At this time, I don't see humans. I see those who look like the ape–shape people, small. But they didn't engage. There was no regular people, but there was the ape–shaped people. And these entities that had really dark skin, like dark grey, they placed coffins in the ground around the region where now the pyramids of Giza and other locations, like Cairo, and that region. They placed them there and they just left.

D. Was it to stabilize the grid?

B. It's knowledge. It has nothing to do with the Earth. It sings inside it. There are maps inside the coffin. Below certain areas in that region there are coffins with maps and calculations, and they were left there. The only so–called humans are like curved, small, ape–shaped, and they almost looked like animals. They saw them but there are no records, because they did not know how to write. They barely knew how to talk. This is the best way, if you want to come in with some sort of hidden agenda, you should come when there is no way to record you. So what they did, they put them there, and it (*the knowledge in the boxes*) came from outside. It is from nearby—some were from Mars. Earth was like a storage unit and they were leaving them here. Inside, I can see—it's like a big coffin—I can see maps. I can see calculations. And as they left, a big sand storm came. Oh, that was not nice. The little ones, the furry curved ones, they sneezed. That was not nice. But a sand storm came and when it settled, you could not see the coffins anymore. And the little curved, furry ones, they could not really communicate on what they saw. So, it was lost in the dust, so to speak. And they show me the dust was when the grid was closed. So now I can see as that happens, the hub that I saw somewhat dissolved and it started to rotate and move.

D. So if that portal was closed, we are still getting visitors to the planet. So, there must still be other portals open to the parallel realities?

B. Ah, indeed. What they say now is that this hub that I saw here in Africa is closed, but there is now a hub on the poles, because there is no one there to record them. I'm not saying it's those with the pumpkin heads that comes, it might be someone else. But it seems like for those who come (*to Earth*), when there is a hub for them to descend, the conditions (*needed*) are that it is quite secluded, or there are entities there (*where they land*) who are not able to document them. So, that's what I see. I'm looking at this and it's quite fascinating for someone like me. It doesn't seem like there is an opening for questions on my behalf here, so I'm just standing still and observing this movie, and getting some explanations of what I'm seeing from Jeshua.

D. So was that the extent of it, or was there a lot more?

B. It became more. We continued to talk about it, and I will explain it later what we talked about. But I'm gonna make it short, Ophelia says. But I have not left the room of the Evolution Group. I'm still there to continue to talk about it.

D. That's really intriguing. I'm interested to hear the rest of the story.

B. In general, it (*what he was shown*) has to do with when they (*the travelers*) want to leave certain things. This has to do with physical things that they wanted to leave, in this case. But I'm wondering if I were to dig there, if I would find the coffin?

D. I remember the last time we talked, you said sometimes if they dig, even with a big bulldozer, they wouldn't find certain things, because they might be in a parallel reality.

B. Ah, indeed. I also can see here that it is guarded from an outside source, outside on another planet. I can see that they are quite interested in the activity in that region, that no one is sniffing around too much. So maybe it is dissolving a little bit, this net. Maybe that is why the entities are a little bit curious and paying attention to their treasure. It has nothing to do with Earth. These coffins are not Earth's secrets. It's about the location where they came from. Some of them were from Mars.

D. I remember that Ari or Eli said that the Anunnaki were on Mars, and there were other entities there as well.

B. Might be what I'm seeing here. It has to do with crossing the laws of physics. It has to do with bending time, Jeshua says. Oh, bending time. He said that even if Earth has time, once these webs are in motion, it creates a bend or a rip in time. And if you can calculate and decipher when that occurs, then you can conquer physics and you can, in some way, ascend and leave the physical. This is how certain shamans did in order for them to access the fourth reality. They understood how to bend time, and when the conditions were optimal for certain cracks in time. Because first, there is a crack or a rip in time, where you can bend and you can mold and you can manipulate time. And as you do, you can move timelessly, crossing the laws of physics. This is what happened with time travelers. They knew how to dissolve after understanding the bend of time and when the rip was—the rip means that the conditions of time was different. It became first like a stillness, and then it felt like time was speeding up. This occurred at certain times, and that was an indication that there was movement in the web. That is why some people now feel like time is flying. It is because the web is moving. And if you had the same intelligence as you have not only at home, but as you had way back, then you would understand that the conditions at this time, when time feels like it is speeding up, is that you have the ability to bend time and cross the laws of physics. Certain sounds combined with the—it's like a rotation, but the rotation is inside the human. It's a way to leave the physical, to dematerialize. This is what they did when something dissolved and something later manifested somewhere else.

D. So the earlier forms of humans could do that?

B. Not everyone. But what they show here is that once you understand that time is not stationary—it's not going like 1, 2, 3, 4, 5, it can go like 1, 2, 6, 7, 8, 9, 10,11, 3. When one understands that it can jump and it can change, meaning, it can bend—and one doesn't understand this in the head—it is a sensation where time seems to be non–existent. And that is when you have the ability to cross and bend time, in order for a physical manifestation to dissolve and manifest somewhere else. This is how, you know, if you can bend time, then you can have Thursday over there, and if you bend it back to Monday, then you can just go back to Monday. You physically go back and you change Monday, if there was something on Monday that you did not like. Because you bend it, the sheet of time. And that is what is in this coffin, what I can see here and what Jeshua says.

D. That will never be something that humans can do? Wouldn't that undermine the whole karmic program?

B. Indeed, in some way. And that is why that specific web is closed.

D. That is truly amazing, although it is still hard to picture, how time operates independently of the spiritual realities. We humans are fairly stupid, of course, so it is difficult to imagine non-linear time.

B. It's more like a wave or a sheet that folds and opens and folds—that's what it is. And that is why Thursday can meet Monday. And then it is like, "Ohh, what happened to Tuesday and Wednesday?" Well, they are not part of this equation, so they are non–important. So, when you understand how you can make meeting points of occasions that you would like to merge—in this case Thursday and Monday—but you don't have to involve Tuesday and Wednesday. So, they are not part of this sheet that you are folding. That is how spiritual time and stellar time is operating. On Earth, it is linear time—and that is because that specific sheet (*spiritual time*) is closed.

D. So, when travelers come to Earth, do they manipulate time?

B. Indeed. They mainly manipulate the laws of physics, rather than time, in this case, because time is somewhat stationary in that sense, here. What I'm saying here is that before (*in the remote past*), it was a different way to experience time for certain individuals that had the understanding. And this is how time travels took place, because they used the understanding of stellar time—or spiritual time, if you like.

D. But that just occurred in the fourth dimension?

B. Once you were a human, you did not go further—that I can see—than the fourth. So, no. But if you were to practice this outside of the Earth's reality, then you are not just floating around in the fourth. You can, and what I'm seeing here now with the Evolution Group, what I'm saying here is that you can bend realities and cross the laws of physics—what I'm seeing here now, quickly, before Jeshua says it's time for me to go—is that nearby realities could merge. I'm just saying there are connecting points where experiences merge.

D. That is truly mind–bending. I just wish I could understand it.

B. Jeshua said (*he sent a message to Bob while we are talking*), that it is more likely that nearby realities merge. Like what we have with fish tank eight and nine, they have somewhat become one. So, they are sharing time—if time existed there. They are sharing space, and they are sharing the sheet OF that experience.

D. Okay. Those are complicated ideas you are sharing.

B. I'm just looking here at the movie, and then I'm getting information from Jeshua. And then I'm hoping that you will understand, since you are somewhat of a space engineer as well. So, he tells me and I'm telling you, and then you solve it. Then we don't have to talk about it anymore and we can just talk about it at home, instead.

Because then I don't have to be a middleman, since I'm not qualified to be a middleman, in this equation.

D. Neither am I, I'm afraid.

B. But I wanted to know about the grid and how it folds and how it changes conditions and how it opens up connecting points to different realities. A lot of times, when those connecting points, that I called a hub, when that occurs it is to enter, normally, this reality. But you have to pay attention that it's not closing so you cannot leave. I'm gonna go now, so you ponder about that.

Bob: The Astrology of Incarnation (Sept 2, 2020)

Bob describes one of the missing links in understanding the keys to astrology, which is the influence that a soul has on the physical vehicle. As we discussed in *Wave 3*, each incoming soul will make adjustments to the fetus. Personality, future health, mental and emotional acuity, spiritual sensitivity, and other attributes of the body will be coded into the genome, within certain hereditary limitations. Therefore, the soul itself is an unknown variable that astrology cannot forecast. Here, Bob gives a magnificent lecture on the relationships between the soul's journey and astrology.

B. So, finally, we have me, and here I am. And I have had an interesting, uhh—I say week, huh huh, but it's not a week—but I have had an interesting development of my upcoming work as a designer of lives. I have actually been visiting with the Astrological Council. I have been observing their maps, and I have been observing the way they operate and the way they decide, and how one can tap into a body. And here we talk about the little Solar System here (*with Earth*), the little baby one. BUT there is also those who work on the BIGGER ones. If you think of that as a little astrological cycle, the little baby one, but then there is a bigger one that is uniquely designed for the whole fish tank. And, I should tell you, that there's also an even BIGGER one that is holding the whole Wheel.

D. That's intriguing. So, you were meeting with the Astrological Council?

B. Jeshua took me, and you also came, of course, because you know that I'm more comfortable like that. And also, you know that eventually there will be questions. And the questions come to you, because I'm more together with you. So, it's better that you hear what I hear, so that you know how you can answer. It's like playing ping-pong, you know. I say something and then you shoot it back.

You say that it's better that you join—and I think that is why—so you will know how to shoot the ball back over the table, because you know what I've heard. So I did look into, a little bit, how they operate before a soul is popped down in a certain time. You look into the personality, the human personality. But then you also look into the soul personality, because they merge into a common experience that manifests and channels on a physical reality, in this case. So they have to take that into consideration. If we take the 2178 life, and if I were to take another soul and exactly (*having the same mission and personality*) spit it down there in that body, and that soul did not come from the sixth—let's say that soul was from the fifth—it would not be the same. Then they have to modify the human personality a little bit. The planetary positions are where they are, BUT in order for certain lessons and certain missions to fully take form and become, it is not just to have a soul popping in and just, "Okay, there you go. Off you go. Make good." It has to be adapted, soul versus body, and it might need (*to be*) modified a little bit. The modifications are actually based on time. Because the planets are where they are, but due to, or based on, what soul is tapping into that body determines when the person is actually born. So, let's say, normally, the Elahims like to come when it's nighttime. Those from the sixth like to be born in the nighttime. But when you in this case (*the 2178 life*) are gonna be born 5:38 in the morning, they're doing some modifications so it's adapted to your soul energy. And it's also based on... it's like, those from the sixth likes to be born around noon or midnight, 10:30 to 1:30-ish, either in the night or in the day. But also, they have to take into consideration, they say, how much of the soul energy is being brought with. So, in your case, you're bringing more energy in, so that is why you are not born in that time frame. You are gonna be born in the morning time, and it's because you are bringing more soul energy with you.

D. Well, in this life I was born at 12:40, just after midnight.

B. There you go. That's when you like to come. But you only brought 7 percent. You're not gonna just bring 7 percent (*in the next life*), because I said, "I'm not having him bringing 7 percent." I had a claim on like 40 to 45, huhuh huh—and you laughed. And Jeshua said, "45 (*percent*), to Earth?" But you're actually gonna bring about 27. So, you're gonna bring a little bit more. The absolute max, Jeshua said, that you could travel with—normally it is 25—but the absolute max would be 30. That's what he said. You don't go with more. But you do like to be born around those times, when it's high noon or high midnight.

D. The 2178 life will come in like a boom, with all that soul energy.

B. Come in like a boom. But because you're coming in like a boom if you also were born at midnight, it might have been just a boom—and then who knows if any of my ideas would have manifested. When I said what I wanted you to do, and my plan for you, then they took that into consideration, and they modified when during the day you are gonna be born. SO, when you were that big scientist in Italy, you were born just in the peak of the day and you also were very dynamic and you actually had, in that life, you were touching up on thirty in that one, and you could see how well that one went.

D. That was a good one.

B. It was a good one. I was with, of course, and I took credit. I can't take credit for designing it. Jeshua did, but he's been doing this for a while, so he has more skills.

D. That kind of makes me wonder if there is a soul pattern that influences all the lives? Astrology, the way humans look at it now, is pretty lopsided, isn't it?

B. Well, the humans look at when the human body is born, and that's when they determine and calculate based on the astrological signs and so forth. But a good astrological council in engineering also takes into consideration the soul energy, looking into certain keys in the chart indicating what sort of individual this is. In your case, the Elahims, there is a lot of the energy from Pluto and also the energy from Saturn. So those two are the energies that you operate quite well with. For someone to read your chart, they should really look into and focus on those two planets and how they are affecting the other ones in the group around. But it's hard to know exactly, you have to see beyond the physical chart. A great astrologer will understand that once they understand the soul pattern and the soul energy, then they know that there might be another planet that they need to look a little bit more closer to, and then the whole chart could be colored differently. So, in your case, from the sixth, there is a lot of focus to understand the complete, true chart, to understand the soul versus the human. To see the soul purpose versus the human purpose perhaps, and to see that there is a different entity inside versus the outside. In your case, they should look more into the position of Pluto and the position of Saturn, because those two energies are very much linked to the sixth. It's very logical and I would say—this is what they told me—that Saturn is considered to be connected to the sixth dimensions, but Pluto is connected to the Elahims. And that is why we are looking into the both of those. But for another one, if we just want to understand and look into a soul coming from the sixth, then you should probably just focus on reading more closely the effects from Saturn. And from the seventh, there is a lot to look into Neptune. So, a soul coming from the seventh dimension is highly, on a soul level, connected to Neptune. They (*human astrologers*) talk about ruling planets, you know, like the Sun rules Leo, and so forth. But no one talks about who rules the soul. On a soul level, the sixth dimension are ruled by Saturn. Elahims are tapping into the Pluto energy, but you are more closely connected to Saturn. However, when you come into a human body, you tend to channel the Pluto energy. So that is the difference. Those from the seventh, their ruling planet is Neptune. But on a higher level, like if Ophelia were to come in, she would probably also add a little from the energy of some of the moons. That is also connected to the seventh dimension. Similar like you channel the Pluto energy in a physical incarnation, when you reach that level, as you have. Those who reach a higher level from the seventh, tend to channel and connect the different energies from several moons, not just one moon. But they are highly influenced and affected by the cycles of the moon. There are those from the eighth, for instance, those who don't necessarily always come (*they seldom incarnate on Earth*), but their ruling planet is Uranus, because they are very inventive. And those who come from the fifth are actually more connected to all the personal planets—that's what they are called—Venus, Mars and so forth. They are more connected to that group of the closer planets. So the soul is ruled by one planet and the physical can be ruled by something else. And how can one know who is my soul ruling planet? Well, that becomes a little bit when you do soul search, and you can do it through meditation, you can do regression work, and so forth. Regardless of the way you seek information about who you are, you might just find the answers when you, let's say, read the books, like *Wave 1*, for instance. And it might be like a ling–ling–ling, when you read about the fifth dimension, for instance. And then you think, "Ohh, I'm one of those." So then you are more connected to the inner ones. In many ways, I say that they are connected to all personal planets, but they are mostly connected to Mercury and Venus. So, mind, heart. Mind, heart.

D. In that order?

B. First, Venus—heart, and then Mercury—mind. So heart and mind, heart and mind.

D. You see, I don't know anything about astrology.

B. Well, you do back home. You pointed that out and you showed yourself, like, "I was born here and you can see my very charming self here in Italy, being very pompous." I said, "You were kind of pompous," and you said, "Well, what do you expect with 29 percent?" HUH HUH HUH HUH. And then Jeshua agreed and like high-fived me, a little bit like that. Then you said, "Look into how the planets were." And then I can see down in a table (*the fog-table*) how the planets were, because they just rotate and show me (*the planetary positions during that lifetime*). Then I can see the energetic layers, and I can see all the planets. And then I can see you popping down in the Italy life and how that became and how it changed. But then I also see the general—and that is not just based on the little wheel—that's actually also influenced by the big Wheel in the fish tank. Not the big, big, big Wheel, but there is also this astrological wheel in operation, that is in each fish tank. So when I look into, down here at the table, you and Jeshua explain to me. The other ones (*the Astrological Council*) talk, but I don't really understand. So, they mostly point—but they're friendly—and I don't judge. Some (*entities*) are not as verbal as me, but I don't judge. So I look down and I see things. Then one of them pointed to look outside (*the table or floor where our Solar System was being displayed*) and then I looked up and then I saw a different wheel in motion. And that was connecting the nearby galaxies and how that, down to the very little part in our system, how it also affected the general evolution. So I could see that. And that is what is going on at this time. There is a change in the bigger astrological wheel. But man is just seeing the little thing, the little wheel, which is affecting the human personality and experiences. But the big wheel is just circulating, regardless if you're happy or not, it's still gonna affect and do its thing. Because who are you, as a little human, to think that you can affect this big wheel? You can barely go to the moon! Barely! And the moons are mysterious—that's a whole chapter by itself. And that is why it's in some way connecting to those from the seventh. They know more about the moons. You're not so fond about the moons, and maybe that's why you didn't give me a moon! Maybe you didn't think I needed one. But Ari gave me one. (*His solar system, as described in the 'Notes' series.*)

D. You have one now, don't you?

B. I have one now, I have one now, circling around my living planet. And the individual is starting to behave much better. They are a flock and I must say that this flock has expanded. They are (*as he looks in different directions*) flock, flock, flock, flock, flock, like all over, these little family units.

D. That's wonderful! So, I had another question about a soul being born and the position of the planets. Is it when the baby finally comes out that it locks the patterns into its energetic being?

B. They merge. Because the soul comes with an astrological blueprint, if you like, based on the intention. And then when it's born, it merges with the physical map, a physical energetic map, and then those two collide and then they merge and become one.

D. And that happens at the instant the baby is born?

B. Ahh, umm. It's not before, it's not inside the belly. You can see it like connecting wires, and that is sort of an instant action that takes place. And it's not like the soul is doing it, normally, even though you did some of the connecting—you know, the wiring—yourself. But normally it's just like an instant occurrence when you are born. And it's the same thing when you die, when you release your human map, your physical. That's when people say they see a light, and they go to the light. When they start to see a light, that's normally when they let go of the human experience—and the human experience is also related to the human map, the human astrological connection. In that field of the fourth reality, the soul is still colored by the intention it had to become a human. Once it returns home, the soul is just going back, in your case, to become a Saturn energy. But when you die and leave the physical behind, and you unwire and unplug everything, not just the physical, but you unplug the memory, you unplug the data—there is a lot going on when it's time to go home. And as you transition through the fourth, your soul is still colored, and you have the soul map activated. So that is why you feel human a lot of times when you have an out-of-body experience. It is because you have the human map activated still. Once you have left the fourth reality and you move home, then you become the soul energy that you really are. And that is when you are activated again as your color, your tone, and also the true energy, which will be mirrored by the Saturn energy for those who live on the sixth.

D. That's a remarkably good explanation.

B. Ah. So I'm learning stuff here when I go to my astrology school. I'm gonna go more, because I like them, but I do need to have translators. But I'm seeing things on a human, personal level. We look at you, we have you as examples, and we go back and then we can see, "Okay, when you went down into that life of the fire, you had like 3 percent." So, we couldn't really blame me. Well, maybe we could blame me, because if you only had 3 percent you probably needed me to be 97 percent present, and I was not.

D. Live and learn.

B. Based on the percentage that you bring from your soul energy, that's how your spirit guides adapt, so the collective experience becomes 100 (*percent*). So, in your case, when you have 7 percent (*in this lifetime*), then me, Jeshua, Ophelia, and everyone else, we sort of, you know, went back and forth and changed, depending on what was needed. Zachariah, of course, joined when there was schooling. So, we were the other 93 percent, so that the whole experience was 100. And then we sort of talked among ourselves, like when it was time for you to go to school—and no one listens to me about my plans for your schooling—so Zachariah took over. So out of our 93 percent, he was present for about 50 and then the other ones of us, we had to crowd together in the other 43. That's how it works. And when you dimmed yourself, you left and were here for about 3 percent, which is not very common. That is when the other ones of us, we sort of blew ourselves up like a frog and became more so that we filled up the whole experience to 100 again.

D. I've never heard that explanation before. Most people probably don't have multiple guides, do they?

B. No. But if you have one guide, it doesn't matter. Let's say you bring 58 percent, which is sort of a common number, apparently. That's what the Astrological Council said, like anywhere from like 48 to 65, where 58 is the most common number, for some reason. So, even if you only have one spirit guide, that spirit guide will fill up the other 42. But that guide could take a step back and maybe one or two come in and share that 42. That's what they do. So, the whole experience is always 100. That is why a lot people say, and have a sense, that they (*other spirits*) are here—and that is what the Christians say. They say the soul completely leaves. Well, it leaves with its entourage. So, yes, indeed, but it's not just you. But the whole experience OF you is 100 percent.

D. When you say it like that, does it mean the spirit guide feeds information into the brain, or collects information so the human experience is still receiving data?

B. Yes, indeed. Normally during dream state. But the important thing is to know that the soul traveling, being the incarnation, depending on what percentage from the soul bank is brought for that specific purpose and mission, the spirit guides fill up the glass so it is full to 100—and they can shift and change, depending on what sort of cycle their person is on. So, like I said, when you went into school—and no one listens to me about me being more present—that's when Zachariah took precedence. And then I was sitting a little bit, calculating in the back. I do tend to your physical. Zachariah did not do that, so I still had things to do. And Ophelia, she warmed your heart, because she wanted you to feel loved. She was working remotely with activating and sending very strong motherly, loving feelings to your inner being. But Zachariah was the one drilling you to your schooling, and I was tending to your physical. Jeshua, he was also probably somewhere nearby, but we were more present.

D. That's a lot of work you have to put into every lifetime. What do you get out of it? Do you learn anything?

B. But it's a group effort, and that is why I can take credit. I do learn. Because we go way back, I want to make sure that you are protected and know that you have a friend with you, because you tend to pick lives where you are in solitude with no friends. It's a human thing to say, "What do you get out of it?" We don't talk like that. It's like helping a friend. And then you help me with creating my solar system. It's not like, "Okay, I do that for you, and then you do that for me." It's just a give and take, and that is a natural way of being when you think from a soul level.

D. That put me in my place. So, thank you for that.

B. Well, I put Dave in his place, because he sometimes forgets. But what can you expect with 7 percent? BUT the interesting part is that you are gonna increase a little bit from your inner being, similar like you can take it away. And this is gonna be my final thought of the day. But similar as you dimmed your soul when you were in your 20s to around 35—you dimmed there for a while—you also have the ability to bump up the lightbulb. And that is what is gonna happen now. So the second phase here is gonna be that you are bumping up the volume a little bit in the lightbulb.

D. That's good.

B. Jeshua said we're bumping it up to like 11 percent. That's gonna start next year.

D. Maybe I'll be able to hear you better.

B. Hahaha. You're gonna be able to see me. Okay, I'm gonna go now. But you ponder about that and solve things. With 11 percent, we have much more to our disposal, so we can squeeze in more things before the end.

Bob: The Physics of Parallel Realities (Nov 1, 2020)

Bob covers two main topics in this session. The first part is a story about how he and Joel (his geologist friend) joined a group of souls who are planning on incarnating in the Indonesian area. Bob indirectly tells about significant earthquake activity that is going to occur along a line stretching from the south of Japan to Taiwan, then down through the Philippines to Bali. The northern locations exactly define the western edge of the Philippine tectonic plate. Zachariah actually mentioned this location back in June 2016, the very first time he came through. He gave an overview of changes that are coming to Earth, but we chose not to publish the session because it was a bit gloomy, from a human perspective. One of his statements was, "In the not too far future, there will be another earthquake underneath the ocean. The area is north of Australia. There will be a wave going in two directions, mainly. Obviously, it will create a crater on the sea bottom. There is a wave that will move north, as well as south. Smaller civilizations will disappear. Islands will cease to exist." I asked him when it would happen and he said, "Within 10 years. Not in a too far distance." Combined with what Bob says, if such an event occurs, I am guessing the epicenter will be just south of the Philippine plate. The area is a convergence point where the Eurasian, Australian, Pacific and Philippine plates meet.

Bob later gives a very compelling description of the location and characteristics of the parallel realities, and how those realities are used by visitors to conceal themselves. As a final note, Charles Mustard was one of Lasaray's previous incarnations. He was a traveling musician, and Bob's story about him is in *Wave 2*.

I recognized when Bob came in, but he didn't say anything right away. So, I took the opportunity to tease him a little.

D. Who could it be?

B. Huhuhuh. Found me! Ohh, huh huh. I have to sing a little bit because the energies are a bit low in this one. This one has not been following the recipes that we have been giving, so it's a bit clumsy and heavy in the energetic field inside. I poked this one, and he heard, but I'm not sure if he kind of ignored it. SO! (*He began holding random notes for a long time.*) Nay, that did not work. Have to be more boisterous. (*He then started singing the Charles*

Mustard melody, quite loudly.) So, ya know, wakey, wakey. So, I've been on expeditions again.

D. Oh? Where did you go?

B. I have gone into Indonesia. Who would have thought?

D. What were you doing over there?

B. Uhh, well, I was asked because there is a group from the fifth going. I was asked to join as an expert, even though I don't really work with that. So me and Joel went to Indonesia. Joel wanted to teach them about geology and the curves and the activities in the ground. And I wanted to navigate them through jungle areas. It's not my forte, necessarily, since I'm more of a star guy now. But I'm born as a jungle one, but I developed myself. So, I was asked, as a guest, not as a tutor, to join this expedition. It's been quite fun!

D. Who was on the expedition?

B. Souls from the fifth. They're gonna be geologists and they're gonna go into the jungle. So, we went to Indonesia. They wanted to look around (*to decide*) if they wanted to go there and what to do there. There are certain activities in that region that spreads. There are veins everywhere, and at the moment, there is some sort of a disturbance in the veins over in Indonesia. It affects the whole area all the way up to the Japanese island, the water below the Japanese sea, the Philippines, Taiwan, Bali—it's a big region, a big hub where the veins are not fully operating as they should. I mean, who knows if it should, I'm not the Creator. Maybe it's exactly how it should be. However, there is more activity underneath the seabed, and it creates phenomena on land and air. And we (*he and the students*) are here to look into how to maintain (*the veins*). In some way, it is a disturbance. It creates phenomena; it creates tornadoes; it creates disasters—tsunamis, and so forth. But it's also high in the fluid. Meaning, in the fluid in the veins. Meaning, it has a great potential to host these new environmental experiences that are upcoming. So, it is more rich in its capacity to host certain flowers and trees and vegetation, and so forth. And also because a lot of it occurs on the seabed, there is also an opening going on where there are changes in the seabed. For the most part, it's really good, because it will create the continental disks to somewhat rotate. Well, not rotate—they're not flipping—but they're in motion. So, on the surface it will be like, "Ohh, scary!" But underneath, it's a very progressive spot for upcoming changes that are important for the whole planet, when it comes to the environment. So, you know, it's a little bit like sadness on the top, scary on top, but it's actually to make room for this new phase when it comes to the environment and the seabed. I wanted to join them because some of them will come in, as there are gonna be certain disturbances. So, we are looking into the end result and the reason why this is occurring.

D. So, the disks or plates will move around a little bit then?

B. Move around, indeed. Now we're moving it around because we want evolution to take place over in the Indonesian area because it has a great potential to become a very lush environment, both for seabed and upper. That is one thing why we are in motion. The other ones (*reasons*) are, like your hidey-hole up there (*near the North Pole*), where you put boxes that look like those car batteries.

D. I remember talking about that. Those are occasionally moved as the land mass moves, aren't they?

B. The boxes seem to move. They're repositioned—I see here that when boxes are moved, they're not moved that far. And some are just flipped, so they are just like going from that, to that. (*He gestured a 90-degree rotation.*) Like playing with Legos.

D. Does it change the way the energy flows?

B. It changes the Fork, changes the Fork. It communicates with the Fork. So based on what the Fork needs, someone is moving the boxes, the batteries. When I see this, this looks different. You said to not be confused, but I am. And when I get confused, I tend to have questions, because no one likes to be confused. You said, "Eventually, you might not be confused," and I said, "When will that be?" And then you say, "Let's go and have a look–see." And I indicated that maybe we could have a remote zooming device and zoom in on the North Pole and look at a documentary about it. But you said, "It's still confusing, even if we zoom in on it." And then I said, "Would you prefer us to go?" And you laughed and said, "You're tricky!" Huhuhuh. But you know, I do think that the little Elahims might come here, in body—and we've been doing great progress. So over there (*in Indonesia*), I help with trying to locate the veins and helping Joel with the curves in the ground. BUT my heart is still with the ones from the sixth, because they're gonna come down and they're gonna be scientists.

D. You're a scientist.

B. I am a little scientist. And I made a request. I put in a note that maybe if someone should incarnate as an expedition person up north, I'd help! The batteries, the boxes, they read the Fork and they stabilize it. And man thinks, "Oh, stabilizing. Whew, good!"

But it's actually, sometimes, that stabilizing indicates turbulence. It can be physical turbulence, but it can also be experienced as an emotional or mental turbulence. So what is going on at this time is a bit of maintenance in the Fork and the batteries.

D. So there will be some rumbling under our feet?

B. Yes, rumbling. And it's just because the Fork needs to be maintained and upgraded in some way. So it's a shift. This is high engineering, I must say. This requires like a Ph.D–D–D–D–D–D to understand how to read the Fork.

D. That excludes humans, obviously.

B. Ah. But, I wanted to know if we maybe could go to the North Pole and look at what's up there. You said, "You might not understand." And I said, "Try me!" Then you said, "I know you can come, but then there will be all sorts of questions." There are some boxes in the receiving end, in the south. The ones (*boxes*) that are in high operation, that organizes the whole mission, they are placed in the north. There are some, however, in the south also, receivers, so the whole balance through the Fork operates correctly, you say. The ones from the south are monitored by certain entities that comes from a nearby galaxy system, you say.

D. When entities travel from one galaxy to another—

B. Did you know that there is a parallel universe down there?

D. Down where?

B. South Pole. You don't have to have that on the North Pole, because no one understands to go there. But if they did, you might put that there too. There is a parallel reality. Meaning, that man goes and they see something and they try to sniff around, but then the visitors just take like a step to the side. Visitors see both realities. Man only sees one—and this is because your eyes are not equipped. There are certain gadgets that man has tried to develop that, in some way, can read the nearby frequency band, but they don't understand what it is they are reading, because there is no visual.

D. Parallel realities are something that I am really curious about, even though it is hard to envision.

B. It's placed where there is a need for action. A parallel reality is not like encasing the whole planet. It can be scattered. Like I said, I see that there is a parallel reality (*at the South Pole*), a sheet, that's what it looks like, a sheet, like a big napkin. And I see the visitors going across, and they do things in the physical reality. And then when they are spied, they can just take a step to the side and merge with the sheet.

D. Is the sheet physically located in the same space?

B. Ah. But it can be removed, it can move. The physical is where it is, but the sheet is mobile.

D. So when they travel from another galaxy to here, how is that accomplished?

B. They can choose to either travel to the sheet, or to the physical. If they travel to the physical, that's when, you know, space people (*humans*) go like, "Look! An alien!" Then the alien has decided to travel to the physical reality. But then suddenly they are just gone. It's because it went into the sheet. And they can also choose to travel from wherever home base they have, to the sheet. Meaning that they will not be visible at all. This is when certain devices, that man has developed over time, can read that there is an activity, but there is not a visual evidence of the activity. It's just something that appears like an anomaly, and that's what they see. Sometimes they (*humans*) can feel and read that there is a parallel reality, but there is no evidence.

D. Within that parallel reality, are there objects that are similar to physical objects?

B. Indeed, it's a physical. But if I see here, the way you show me in the South Pole, the sheet looks just like a sheet, a napkin, a white napkin. It's thin, it's really thin, but it's quite dense in its materia. So everything exists in the same way as the physical reality, but just more concentrated. So the parallel reality looks like a sheet, really thin, so you might think, "Oh, who's gonna fit in there?" But if I look into it, you say, "It's just an illusion. It has the same volume, the same ability and capacity as a physical reality, it's just concentrated." So, it's like a lemonade, you know. In order for your physical objects to be as is, your lemonade has been filled with water. So you have just filled it up (*he makes the sound of pouring water*) plugh, plugh, plugh, and that's how you look. But it's the same molecules, it's the same DNA structure, organisms in the sheet. They are just—I see what I see here, and you tell me to tell you—but this is also how they moved big blocks and how they did big movements and changes. Man goes, "Oh, megaliths were made using chicken bones," but it's because the parallel reality condenses or it minimizes the object in a way that, in the third reality, there is no way to do so. Nay. I will send this one a picture and you figure it out.

D. A lack of words and concepts. Well, when they move from their home galaxy to here, how do they move themselves?

B. They can move in crafts, if they want to go to your reality. If they go to the parallel reality, that craft, let's say it's big like an airplane, if that airplane chooses to go to the sheet, that same airplane transforms so it fits. Same airplane.

D. So it becomes more like an energetic field?

B. Well, there are objects in there. It's just that the object—if something is this big in the third reality (*holds his hands apart*), it transforms the same object, the same plane, like this (*holds his fingers so there is a tiny little gap*). And then, if that thing wants to move somewhere else, then it expands, it changes based on the conditions. But it is still physical. The parallel reality is a sheet, but it has the ability to manifest and demanifest in a way that, on the third reality, is not possible. So if they want to just observe, there is a sheet as well at certain locations, like over in China, looking into certain excavation areas where they have facilities working with energy. There is a sheet there, but that sheet doesn't engage. It's a sheet like this (*he held his hand out flat, palm down, to show the thinness.*)

D. I know that people say that sometimes when an alien craft comes and goes, it turns into what appears to be light.

B. Indeed. And that is when they move over the barrier between the sheet and the physical.

D. Is there more than one layer or sheet?

B. I only see one sheet here on the South Pole. But I see a sheet there, and I see a sheet there in China, and I also see there is a teeny-tiny napkin over the White House. There's nothing down there (*Africa and South America*). But I can see different sheets, napkins, and that's where they want to have a look-see.

D. Do they interact at all with the humans?

B. Down here on the South Pole, they do. That's why some don't want others to come, because they have spied them. But then they disappear, but the humans don't know there is a sheet, a blanket, there. They see the manifested version of them—I mean, they are still manifested, it's just that they—if you were to put the Earth, the globe, and just shrink it, it's still the same. The human being, two meters like you are, it's just gonna be like a centimeter instead. But it's still the same. You see what I'm saying?

D. I guess it's all a matter of perspective?

B. But in the sheet, it's the same. It fills the same capacity as the outside, but it's just concentrated.

D. There is not as much space between the molecules, maybe?

B. Nay. It's like it shrinks. And this is just in the sheet. I'm not saying there are little people everywhere. I'm just saying that when they merge into a parallel reality, such as I see here, I see that the same individual that is this big outside, doing activities in the South Pole, when they go into hiding, they just shrink and fit the sheet. So they manipulate physics, they manipulate the borders between object manifestation. You say it's not that tricky, so I don't know why it appears to be (*difficult to understand*).

D. Does the density increase?

B. If we were to make you, the same you, and put you into becoming one centimeter, it's still you. You still have the same structure, same design, it's just that we make you smaller. This is how objects were moved, you say, down in Egypt. You took a big block and just made it smaller. I don't know if you put it into the sheet—yes, you did, you say—you took an object and made it smaller and put into the sheet. And then the sheet spit it out somewhere, and it enlarged back to its original size. You said, "This is just a matter of understanding physics. You just take an object and do whatever you like. You can even make it bigger, if you want to." But you didn't do that here, you say. You take a big block and you put it into this parallel reality. You make it the same block and move it into there, and from there, in some way, it was placed, and then back to its original size. Not so tricky, you say. I did not take this class, but you are a great physicist, like a Ph.D–D–D–D–D–D, D–D–D–D–D–D, probably. So you said that it's a possibility, once you understand the laws of physics and how to go beyond the mind. You have to conquer your mind. You have to think of what opens up as a possibility, you say, once you go beyond the limits of your mind. In many ways, magic, you say, is a gateway. Because man doesn't believe in magic anymore—and scientists do not—then they are limited to what they can develop and evolve into, and what they can understand. So you say, "A great scientist is also a magician, because a magician has no limits in the mind, and then it will travel indefinitely and find solutions on how to operate." And you say, "Scientists on Earth are not magicians. They don't believe in endless seeking in the mind. They are limited. And, in some way, that is good, because otherwise they might go sniffing around the North Pole. But a great scientist is also a magician." You are a magician. Jeshua is a magician.

D. He's a good one.

B. He's a good one. "But you have to travel in your mind," you say. "If there were no boundaries, what could I potentially do, or what can I imagine?"

D. The accepted laws of physics limit people's ability to conceive of something else.

B. Indeed, indeed. One of the veils here is that the laws of physics are placed upon you, so that you don't have endless or limitless options in your mind, and not even at hand, on how to solve things. Conditions were different, you say, before.

Ophelia, Bob: The Cave of Dinosaur Eggs (Nov 20, 2020)
Ophelia begins this session talking about the ways that people were manipulated during the 2020-21 flu–fear campaign. The goals were obvious, and it is unnecessary for us to elaborate on the nostrum that the public was cajoled into accepting as salvation from the flu. Our spirit friends have given multiple warnings about pharmaceuticals that impair the functioning of the human mind. The latest injectable nanoparticle concoction can be added to that list, and several other flagitious lists. Ophelia said it is important to have faith in your own soul capacity and not fall victim to prevarications and wild exaggerations conjured up by the media conglomerates and their handlers. People can choose to turn off the mind–control systems and reclaim their peace of mind. I didn't own a TV for many years, preferring to read spiritual books, exercise, or build furniture in my spare time. The yellow journalism of mainstream media should be avoided with the same caution as any other poison.

Bob took over after Ophelia was done with her messages. He began by talking about fish tank six and drifted into an analysis of the Master Mind and the Master Eye. He then explained the difference between a physical body and a spirit body that is only partially manifested on the third dimension. He also gave an amazing perspective on the fourth dimension. His narratives are essential to understanding the difference between the visible and invisible on the third dimension. Finally, he relayed to us something that his friend, Sniffer (see *Notes, Vol. 2*), had seen about 200 million years ago. Sniffer took Bob into the area around where Yellowstone Park in northwestern Wyoming is currently located. Sniffer showed him an energetic memory of a cave that was full of eggs which had been deposited there by visitors. The eggs were different types of large birds and dinosaurs. They left one strange–looking entity behind to guard and tend to the eggs. That area of North America has not been submerged under the sea in the last 250 million years, so it may be that that some artifacts from the cave still remains, but are inaccessible. The message shared by Sniffer and Bob is that evolution is not what we think it is. The spiritual councils and geneticists on the second are the ones who control evolution. However, in the past, certain visitors have meddled with the lifeforms because they mastered the ability to manipulate the genome. Humans, who have only a crude understanding of DNA, are playing god with plant and animal genomes, much like the visitors who filled the cave with foreign creatures.

Scientists have been genetically modifying plants for several decades through a slow process using RNA interference and transgenics. The processes required the mutated organisms to be labeled as GMOs. In the last few years, a new process called CRISPER gene editing was developed. Because it directly modifies the genes without introducing foreign material, the CRISPER defilements evade the language in the regulations. Even though the end result is exactly the same, the CRISPER GMOs are not required to be labeled as such in the US and many other counties. Since these technicians do not really understand the interconnected function of the genes, their bungling mutations could be extremely damaging to various lifeforms on Earth. There have been several studies that show significant increases in unexpected abnormalities in the offspring of the genetically mutated plants and animals. Perhaps more alarming is that the CRISPER process causes many accidental and random structural variations in the modified genomes. One relevant study was published in *Nature Communication* in 2023 (*Tsai et al., s41467-023-40901*) that highlights the dangers inherent to the process. It is important to understand that human derived GMOs are a violation of spiritual principles, and humanity will suffer the results of the aberrations and transgressions.

O. This is Ophelia.

D. Hello, Ophelia.

O. I want to address the human consciousness at this time. The general public, the general individual in the race, is focusing on fear, focusing on the physical fear. This is a rebirth. The turmoil that man experience is similar like a child being born. It is that phase just before someone is born. The turmoil and the changes is actually to awaken the mental and emotional self. The emotional is, unfortunately, in some way hijacked at this time. So the mental has been weaker before, but what we see is that the emotional is following the downfall of being an easy target for influences. As the emotional run wild, the mental is ill equipped to calm, as it's not very functional, as is. So what we see is that the physical reacts to two different centers within your being that have been hijacked and manipulated at this time. It is not a physical fear. The fear, which is not a fear, it is a change, it is a shift, it is a rebirth. You are, as a race, on that threshold of being born. Similar as a child being ready for the world, you are on that step for the new world. But the mental and the emotional are not—how can one say—ready for the next step. It is dimmed. A lot of it has to do, unfortunately, with the pills. (*Many pharmaceutical drugs deaden the mind.*) It muffles the true signals. It hijacks your identity. It opens up for influences not of your own. There are those who seek a need to survive in a world that, in many ways, are becoming more free. You are more aware, you connect. Internet, in some way, is a good tool so that minds can connect. But if someone tries to manipulate the web, they do it in order for that connection to be broken. So, what started out as a good communication central, has also been influenced by those in power—human power, that is. Know that they are few in numbers. But the general experience at this time is to understand (*that*) your physical journey is not depending on your emotional and mental experiences. They can coexist. At this time, they act like three separate units. Those who act in rage, in fear, they are afraid of their physical death. But what is death? They don't understand their soul. They don't understand their potential inside the number as you progress in groups. There are several young souls acting in rage, and it's mainly because they are afraid of dying. They don't understand that dying is simply a transition to being reborn again. If you are in the mindset that death, rebirth, the cycles would not exist, you would have a different opinion about your existence. That is why those of you who have been here for a while need to calm. There is no need to act rage upon rage, wave meeting wave. Be calm. Be still. Lead with confidence, lead with compassion, but don't be emotional. The emotional leads to fear, at this time. Be compassionate, but be confident and strong. Listen. Don't preach—communicate. Few words. If you see those who are just acting out and bombarding others with words, that is a sign that they are afraid. Less words is needed. Simply be the awareness of the soul. Assist others with confidence and compassion, but don't lead and encourage the traps, the emotional traps. The physical is paralyzed, doesn't know where to go.

D. It does seem rather confusing these days to know what to do.

O. Just be yourself. Be strong in your conviction. Just wait, everything will play out as it should. More and more are becoming aware.

D. Will I be able to travel to the US and return to Sweden, without being forced to take their magical elixir?

O. Yes. It will be a discussion, in general, about how to handle this fear. And this is when those who lack the understanding of who they truly are inside will simply cave into submission, cave into authorities. This is the time when authorities should fall. This is the time when you gather as souls, souls encased in a new reality, the earthly reality. But you are still souls. You are NOT humans. You are, first of all, souls. You are here to learn how to cope in a container that is highly affected by influences. There are changes coming, but turmoil first comes. Think of it as a delivery, a child being born. That is similar to what you can see at this time. And this is what I can give you as an image of the current event. We are in labor, one can say.

D. Okay. Thank you for that.

O. You are much welcome. Just don't try to figure everything out. Everything is ready to unfold. We are just staging the next step at this time. Don't interfere, simply be. Don't act out to those who lack conviction on what's going on. But try to deliver the image of the delivery of a baby. The world is in labor. What child you want to be, what child the world wants to become, is not fully in your hands. But we are doing changes in your consciousness. The emotional, however, has been a little bit hijacked, and the (*use of*) pills doesn't help. It numbs, it separates. It makes people passive, not cohering to their truth; acting out because someone tells you that you will die, the physical will die. That is true for some, but also know it is the path that they chose. For those who do not believe in the afterlife, for those who do not believe in a soul, that is terrifying. You will not be able to convince all of them. And that is not your job.

D. Understood.

O. There. So. Bye bye.

D. Alright. Goodbye, Ophelia.

B. Huh! La–la–la–la–la–la–la–la–la–la–la–la. (*He was singing a joyful melody.*)

D. (*Laughing.*) Hello, my friend.

B. Ah, I'm here, of course. I've been here all along. But no one wants to listen to me every day, it appears, even though I'm fully ready to communicate EVERY day.

D. Yes, this one put you off.

B. But this one hears me all the time, gets information anyways. That's what this one says, "I hear you and I know what you're saying. We don't have to sit like this and communicate. I know what you're saying. You can just talk to me directly and I remember." But it's different with you. So I said—I told this one when this one was sleeping—I paid a visit and I said, "Lasaray doesn't hear me as well." And this one said, "Well, as long as one of us has heard it." But I said, "Lasaray might be sad in the head, he might feel lost. He tends to feel a bit lost sometimes, and it's comforting to him if he hears me." And this one was like, "You're just tricky, you just want to talk. Tell me, I'll tell him." That's what this one said! This one and I have been, actually, up in the classroom on the sixth, because you've been busy in haste and I had somewhat of a gap in my schedule. You know, sometimes having a gap in your schedule can be confusing. It's like, "Am I punished? Am I waiting? What is it that I am supposed to do?" So, similar like a human, I felt like that. I had a vacuum in my schedule. The six from the sixth and the spirit guides, they were with their peers having different classes that I was not invited to. My individual is doing well over there. I'm kinda finished with your (*2178*) life, so there wasn't much left to color there. I can't go to the Astrological Council by myself, and everyone seemed to be in their own haste. So this one came and said, "Let's go! I'll show you around a little bit in fish tank six." And then I said, "You know, Seth, I have been sending in my application and showing my interest in becoming a Wheel star." And he was like, "Huh. You want to be a Wheel star? Do you know about them?" Then I said, "Do you?" And he said, "I'm not telling. If there is a group that is considered the Wheel stars, then maybe we will wait to talk about that." And I said, "Have you seen them? What do they do? Where do they go? Have you gone?" And he smiled, and he said, "No, I have not gone. But I can take you to fish tank six, if you like." And I said, "We can begin there." So, you were off in haste because there is something going on.

D. Oh? Where is that?

B. One of the big hastes are up in fish tank three, the one that is asleep.

D. And?

B. Exactly—and? You said, "In due time, Bob, I will tell you. But for now, why don't you go and explore fish tank six. There is an emergency in the dream." (*Fish tank three is in the dream state, prior to manifesting another round of form*). And I said, "Oh? Emergency in the dream?" And you said, "I'll tell you next time." It's hard to understand 'next time'. Does that mean next time we meet? Next time we talk like this? Probably not. But you offered to fill me in, so I'm pretty confident you will. I remember, of course, and remind you.

D. At least you get to go traveling.

B. I'm traveling, because I have a gap and I have a window in my schedule where there is not much going on. I do need to talk about Old Sniffer a little bit. But first I want to talk about when me and Seth went to fish tank six. That one is extremely bright. It doesn't sleep. He said that it is in labor and it's about to become. It has a huge center, almost filled, looking like one big galaxy. Like here, I can see galaxies all over the place. When I see fish tank five, it is like when you fly at night over the US. You see, "Oh, there is a city, there is a city, there is a city," so you see all these little lights. That's how fish tank five looks. Fish tank six is just like one big rotation, one big galaxy. I can see the center here, and Seth said that is where the intention is placed, it's a core. So he works with the core, like you do.

D. So, is it like there is a core and then dots of potential galaxies circling? Or is it just like a fog?

B. One big fog, I would say. But it's very bright, so it's not a dark fog. It's bright. My visual here is just on the center, because it looks like one big galaxy. You can't see individual galaxies or planets, it's like one big one. And he said that it is yours; he said, "Fish tank six is ours." And I said, "Who is 'ours'? Can you really claim one?" And he said, "You claimed your solar system, didn't you, where your individual is?" And I said, "Well, that was much smaller. Have you claimed this whole box?" (*By box, he means the entire universe in fish tank six.*) He said, "Not just me, it's a project from the sixth dimension." And he laughed about that. He likes to sometimes play god. Once, when I was curious about the Creator, he said, "Have a look." And then smiled, like that. So, ya know, he's playful. But then again, I'm a baby Creator as well, and so are you, and so are every soul. Every soul is a baby Creator, so he just sort of played with me. Afterwards he said, "Just stand in front of a mirror and that is the Center Pole. It is just manifested in an individual entity, such as yourself." So, I felt complimented. I felt like I was the Center Pole, just smaller, and with ears. I don't know if the Center Pole has ears… probably has eyes because I have seen the Big Eye. And I want to tell you that the Eye is actually present here in fish tank six.

D. In what way?

B. It's hovering over the center. I can see a disk hovering over the center. And you said that there is also one in your project over in fish tank three. The Eye is an extension of the Creator, you say, but it's a Mother Eye. I said, "Is it like a mother ship?" Huh huh huh. "No," you say, "it's a direct link to the manifestation. So the Eye is like the Master Mind, but it's a mother energy." The Creator is not a father energy, it's a dual energy, but I would say the Master Mind can shift, depending on where the Eye is going. But in general, the Master Mind can transform, being a mental, male observer, or an emotional, female observer. And what I see at the moment, in fish tank six, is that it doesn't seem to make up its mind yet. I see the Eye, but maybe I'm not equipped to determine that.

D. I was curious—when you see the fish tank like that, is it encased in some kind of energetic field?

B. Ah. Like a gel. It's like a bubble, but it's not round. If you were to poke it, like that (*as he poked the air with a single finger*), it would be like gel, soft. I don't know. My next question was, "Is it like a balloon? Can it pop?" And you said, "No, it doesn't pop, unless the intention is to pop." It's not solid, like a concrete wall. It's bending and mobile. It's like a thin layer, see-through, that you can poke.

D. Inside that bubble—

B. There's me, and there is Earth. When I looked into fish tank six, that bubble, I needed him to help me to get there to see this. I didn't go into a washer, so we are kinda watching it from a room on the sixth. It's like the sphere room, but the walls disappeared and it was like I was there. And I like that. Then I can bypass the turbulence program and the washer, I think. And he said, "You are just limited by what you can do in this room." The walls dissolve and then it's like I am hovering around here, like a satellite. But I'm not there, really.

D. To move from the spirit realm to a fish tank, there must be some change in vibration or space? When you say, for example, that you are always with me, is it in some way a physical presence?

B. Here I manifest a part of myself, because a spirit guide, when they go to Earth, they take the conditions that exist, and here it is physical matter. So a part of me manifests myself in a physical vibration. That means that sometimes people can see their spirit guides. That's not such a big mystery, because they have moved into the manifestation form of matter that is physical here. But it's not like I can take the full form, such as yourself, because I'm not incarnated. But I use the materia that is available here. So, that's what I do.

D. From your perspective in the spirit realm, is there a great distance between the part that is left behind in the spirit world, and the part of you manifesting here?

B. If your question is if there is a big distance between the second dimension, my home, and when I travel here—in some way, yes. BUT I can return in a flash. So, in that sense, it is not a distance. But if I don't return into that energetic part of my being, then it would be considered a gap. It's similar like the Tiddles—they are manifested up there in fish tank two—that would be considered a huge, long gap to home. But it's because they have taken so much of their energy. When I go with you, I can manifest my energy for the Earth's experience about 12 percent–ish. And you are manifested like a human around 98 percent. You're still 2 percent that is the unknown. But if someone says, "What do you mean I'm not manifested 100 percent? I don't have toes?" Huh, that's not what it means. That is why this world is so dense, because when you come into an incarnation, you merge with a ready form that occupies 98 percent, or so, of the matter that exists, the conditions that exist here. But a spirit guide, not incarnating, still uses the same blueprint and DNA available, merging the spiritual blueprint with the available blueprint, meaning the physical one here on Earth. So I use like 12 percent, that's why sometimes this one could see me. Because at that time, he was not fully 98 percent. So he had dropped and become more soul, and the soul can see the 12 percent easier. I know this is confusing for you. But the Tiddles, up there (*in fish tank two*), they have taken like an incarnation. They have taken that much up to Tiddle. So, in that way, they feel much further away from home than I do. Because I only use my traveling energy to manifest like 12 percent (*into the material blueprint*). And that's what I do all the time. I never leave you. You CAN see me, and that's also how I can play tricks, that's how I can make a bottle fall and stuff like that. (*Bob pushed a large bottle off the top of a cabinet one time, to prove he was there.*)

D. When you move to the Earth from your home, does it feel like you are moving through space? Do you have the sensation you are traveling to Earth, or is it a shift in vibration?

B. Yes, indeed. I travel, it's a journey. If you see it, it's not just stepping through a door. It's like putting myself in a car and going somewhere.

D. So when someone dies or has an NDE and they report flying through the Universe towards some destination, they are traveling through space, but at some point, they shift into a different vibrational field and leave the bubble of the fish tank?

B. When I say the bubble, the bubble is the whole fish tank.

D. Yes, that's what I mean. So, the soul does leave the fish tank on the way home?

B. And return home, yes, indeed. We are way out here on the border, far out, and we need to go back in. But that can be done quite quickly, depending on how you, as a soul, merge with the physical reality. But it is always a journey, it's always a travel. And it's because this is a physical reality. It's the same with Tiddle, they also have to travel. If you are more used to and trained in physical manifestation and demanifestation, then it takes more of a travel from your spiritual home than, let's say, if I were to go to a mental fish tank. Then it's just a shift. I'm assigned to go here when you go here. But I haven't followed you if you have had other journeys to other fish tanks. I have notes about that, because as soon as we started to talk about the blue-dot lives, I was like, "There might be lives outside that might be considered lives. Just because you don't take a form, it's still a life." But you say, "It's not an incarnation, it's simply a shift. I just travel remotely and investigate and explore and gather facts." And then I said, "We don't have that here on the wall about those journeys, if you would like to share."

D. Well, when you and Seth are standing in the room, observing fish tank six, would that be similar?

B. It's similar like the sphere room, but the walls dissolved and it was like we were just there. He just beamed us in some way, mentally, to explore. I didn't go physically; I didn't take a form there. He showed me like a documentary, I assume.

D. When I die and return home—and I'm sorry to go back to this again—but does the soul move through the Universe to a certain place, like the center point, and then change its frequency back to the home dimension?

B. You don't go into the pole and out. You go through the realities. You have the physical layer, the physical experience in your fish tank. But then, when you're not there anymore, indicating you died, you don't go through all those to return back. You just bump up a level to the fourth reality, and when you reach the fourth reality, you kinda have to be there normally, if you've not been here that long, to explore the Earth's fourth reality. But when that is done, then it's more of an instant motion back to your home base.

D. The fourth reality is just around the Earth—

B. Well, there's one around the Earth, but there is a fourth reality barrier before you leave the fish tank. What I see—the bubble going around—that is like a border, which is similar like the fourth reality before you exit and enter into the pure spiritual vibration, if I talk about fish tank five.

D. That's the one we are stuck in.

B. That's where we are. Here I am, in that one. You are captured by your 98 percent experience in a container, but I'm not. So, I travel much easier back and forth, because I don't have to go through all the junk and experience things. I don't have a fourth reality going, "Oh, Bob, what did you do over here?" I go instantly when you go, I go back and I do all the reflection, if that is needed, directly from home. So, you have a little bit more of a transition phase than I do.

D. To go back to your 98 percent, I remember you said that when souls connect to the body, they attach all these different points.

B. They have to unplug whatever they plugged into the container.

D. Is that the 98 percent you are talking about?

B. Ah. Because you have chosen a physical incarnation, a container, and you have tapped into it. I'm not tapped into (*a container*), I just transform the matter that is available on that travel. And that is why some can see their spirit guides, because they (*the guides*) are in some way also co–experiencing the physical matter. It's just that we don't take 98 percent because we don't incarnate. That's why certain people can see a loved one (*who comes back to deliver a message*)—they normally have higher percent, though. It's easier to see a loved one. When they have passed, they can still return and remanifest that memory of that physical experience that they have (*of their previous life*). And they can, in some way, kickstart that memory by merging their awareness into that energetic memory. When, let's say, a medium connects with that loved one and sees the loved one quite clearly, normally they have bumped up to 20 to 25 percent (*the loved one manifests a form that is 25 percent materialized on the third dimension*). And those who are ghosts and do rumbles in houses and so forth—that's not what you are supposed to do—it is because some souls have a fondness of the physical. And when they die, they might have certain things that they might have wanted to achieve that was not done, or they might have an attachment to a house, or an area, or a belief. Then they get stuck and don't really leave the bubble (*our fish tank*). A soul that comes back to visit a loved one has probably left the bubble, back to the spiritual reality. But those who act like ghosts, who knock on doors and so forth, they are still in the fish tank reality, but they are in the fourth reality within fish tank five.

D. Really close to the vibration of the Earth?

B. Indeed. So they are not in the transition, fully.

D. I think I follow all that, but I have one more clarifying question. The 98 percent, if I bring 7 percent—

B. That's a soul.

D. Okay, then the 7 percent attaches to a form that is 98 percent manifested in the physical?

B. Ah. The soul brings whatever portion—like you brought 7 percent, but we're gonna bump it up a little bit. But the container, the reality, exists of 98 percent, or so, physical bottles.

D. I have said in the past that the soul never becomes the third dimension vibration, that it stays in the fourth. Is that correct?

B. Well, the soul merges with the physical. That's how you try to maneuver the brain, for instance. So you merge, but your soul awareness, your soul mind, is still locked in the fourth reality, observing. But the soul can split again—it's like this: You left your home base and come down to the fourth reality. So, you leave your soul mind by traveling with your soul awareness, the traveling soul energy, into the 98 percent incarnation. The soul awareness is still here, docking off, 7 percent in your case, into the 98 percent bottle. But this is similar like having the Big Eye. So every soul has an eye, and that is left in the fourth reality, observing. But it's not like a younger soul understands this, so they cannot connect TO the eye. Once you have been here for a while, you are encouraged to connect with your soul mind, to your soul eye, to see yourself from above.

D. That's a wonderful explanation.

B. If more were to connect with their soul mind, their soul eye, left in the fourth reality, they would not be as trapped in the 98 percent experience. The new souls, they don't know. They just plop down—

there they go—and then they go not (*the body dies*). Then they come back. But if you have been here for a while, you are encouraged to look at life, to look at you, to look at the people around you, to look at the world around you, from your soul eye. And that is located in the fourth reality. Very close to the third, but it's still an eye, a soul awareness. And that is what is going on right now, is that people do not connect. Even those people who are, let's say, aware of their spiritual nature, they don't want to look from their spiritual eyes. They just want to use human eyes, because somewhere down the line here, the connection has been influenced and it is becoming more of a gap. It's not broken, but there is more of a gap. So even those people who know about this and they know about their connection to their home, they feel a separation at this time. And what I can say then is that you should shut off mainstream information that is just leading you astray, leading you away from your soul mind, from your eye, observing. And this eye is where the Master Mind can also tap in and have a look–see. Let's say that your spiritual guides, normally Jeshua (*Lasaray's mentor*), if Jeshua wants to have a real close look at you, he doesn't have to go hand–in–hand like I do down here with my 12 percent, he just looks into the eye. He can just go like this (*as he leaned forward and cupped his hands like he was looking through a hollow tube towards the floor*), and then he sees everything about you. People might think, "Oh, I'm supervised. Someone is just observing me like that." But it's a friend! It's a friend who has your best interest. And in that tunnel, someone can give information. And then we have me—I don't look in your soul life, that's not my job—I'm supposed to guide you through rocks and hurdles so you don't hurt yourself that much. I'm supposed to be a friend to make sure that the physical 98 percent is maintained. It's a pickle. It's hard, especially since you don't travel with that much soul energy. In many ways, I was concerned about this life being a little bit like the one with the fire, because you said you were going to go down and investigate the mind inside. And I have a quite strong memory about that experience way back in the past. So I was like, "I'm making sure he's not gonna be near fire." So, when you went into those sweat things (*Native American sweat lodges*) and there were fires, I was like, "Ohhhh!" So I bumped up my 12 percent to 15. I paid great attention to that, so you don't fall asleep or sit too close (*to the hot stones*). So, you know, that's what I wanted to talk about, but I also want to talk about my travels with Old Sniffer.

D. Yes, you mentioned him earlier.

B. Old Sniffer and I, we have also been on adventures, and he's fun! He has all sorts of stories. He talks about the big mammals, the dinosaurs—and I can see big footprints. There are, actually, in certain places, where there is now a lot of jungle, excellent remains of these giants. And he followed and he looked, so he talked about that.

D. This was on Earth? You traveled to an Earth location?

B. Indeed. We traveled back in the energetic memory to tap into—he showed me the way that he traveled and what he did. And there were all sorts of things going on at that time.

D. Can you describe any of them?

B. There is a scene here where there is a place just filled with eggs. Big eggs, almost as big as him. Kinda the same form, huhuhuh, but he has legs. But there are eggs here, he said, in a cave, and someone is tending to the eggs.

D. Someone like him, from the second?

B. No, not someone like him. He showed me they (*the aliens*) are not the same as (*what is*) in the eggs. It's in a big cave. This cave is in the North American region. There were those who introduced species and tended to the eggs.

D. So these eggs were types of creatures that were brought here?

B. It's full of eggs. And I can see someone tending to them, and that one looks quite thin, like extremely thin. Dark skin. About two and a half or three meters tall—with a big head.

D. Was it physical, or partially physical?

B. Looks physical. This is somewhere in the US. I see we are not in the middle; we are more to the west, up. There is a crater, up. Oh, this is where the national park....

D. Yellowstone?

B. That's where it is. There are caves. This is an interesting place. And Old Sniffer, he knows about this. You should know... ohh, they don't want you to. That's why they have that bubble bath up there (*the boiling mud and hot springs*). They don't want you to investigate. That's why they put the bubble baths there, so you can't. Oh, that's tricky. Man doesn't have any submarines to go down there! Huh. But this is an interesting place. Here are prehistoric remains. This is like dinosaur eggs, of sorts. You should investigate this, though. There are, up in that region, caves. There are sites, but it's hard to investigate if you can't go into the bubble pool here. It's like a big jacuzzi and if you touch it, you burn. And you burn easily, so this is not for you. So, we don't want to put you there. But Old Sniffer, he showed that what we consider to be evolution is not necessarily fully that. He said, "These eggs were placed here by this gentleman here in grey." He doesn't have clothes, he's just thin and grey. He doesn't communicate, but I'm not saying I feel a fondness to talk to him. I asked Old Sniffer if he knew about him and he said, "No, I only saw him. They don't talk, they just stare." But in some way, he seems to be quite caring about the eggs, and he watches over them in the cave. But those (*in the eggs*) are different mammals. Some of them are birds, like dinosaur birds, and some of them are little lizards that are gonna kick-start the whole project, Old Sniffer said, to become big dinosaurs. So this is like in the cradle of the project dinosaurs, it seems.

D. So this tall, thin fellow must have come from a spacecraft from some other place?

B. I would assume so, because he is by himself there. But he is tending to them. I kind of want him to be like, "Hey, welcome!" when I see him here, but he doesn't. He's quite unemotional. He's very stiff, like those wandering sticks, that's how he looks. (*Bob is referring to insects of the order Phasmatodea, commonly called walkingsticks.*) He's not a bug, but he's monitoring these eggs. And when I say eggs, I can see at least 100 to 200 in this cave. (*In a follow-up conversation, he said he saw many more eggs.*)

D. And there are different species?

B. There are different types of species that are gonna become. Some are gonna be birds and they are more ready. Some are little lizards. I see a little one that looks like a dinosaur, but small, and that one is gonna become. This is in the cradle. So, what man thinks about evolution, you know, huh—here in the cave, someone decided evolution. I'm not saying that this gentleman here brought the eggs by himself. Old Sniffer didn't show me how the eggs got there. But he said that what man thinks about evolution is not fully right, because evolution was introduced.

D. That probably goes for trees and everything else, doesn't it?

B. Probably indeed. I did not take that class, maybe I should have. I was so intrigued about the 4-H farm.

D. But on the second dimension, you are involved in the modification of plants and animals?

B. I am indeed.

D. So you have a hand in evolution.

B. I do. But we never had a gentleman like this. We are a different kind of evolution, where we just follow the clouds and the manuals. This one is just introduced by a higher intelligence.

D. That may or may not be working for the—

B. Spiritual councils, no. Might not be the spiritual councils at all.

D. Is that why you wanted your solar system in a safe place?

B. Ah, because I don't know if someone comes in and puts eggs like this. I'm fully aware about the general evolution and how that follows. And I also have friends now in the Evolution Council group, and Ari might also step in if someone comes. But here I can see, and this is what I knew, I've seen things on my travels, even though I wasn't up and running at this particular time. But Old Sniffer was, and he showed me that sometimes certain events, and in this case, entity species, are just introduced. This is WAY back though.

D. The continents were much more together back then?

B. Ah, it's more connected up there in Canada. And the climate was different too. When this took place, I would consider this to be not spring. It's not snow, it doesn't rain, but it's not super hot. Maybe it's like October.

D. So what else did Old Sniffer show you?

B. Well, he just wanted to show me that evolution is sometimes not what it appears to be. And he observed this with his friends. There were councils on the second and he observed this. So, that's what I wanted to say about that. Ophelia says we're running out of time now, but I'm not on a timeline, so, huh huh huh. But I'll be back.

D. Excellent topics today. And, as always, very informative. So, thank you.

B. Oh, you're welcome, of course. I'm right here next to you. So, when you open your eyes, just the first thing that you do, your physical eyes, try to see with your inner eyes. You can see me.

D. If you bump up my percentage a little bit, like you said, then maybe I'll see you.

B. Ah, ah. Okay, I'm gonna go now. Bye bye bye bye bye.

Visitors from the Past (Mar 22, 2021)

Our general intent is to present the sessions in chronological order. However, we also wanted to introduce a group of aliens who have been intimately involved with the Earth project since life first formed. They will feature more prominently in *Wave 5*. The Visitors from the Past first merged with Christine in March 2021 but they struggled to hold the energy. Since they are manifested entities within fish tank eight, they can only join us by projecting their consciousness into our gathering. When they returned in January 2022, they were able to communicate very clearly. That session will follow this brief one. Their initial talk, below, is a high-level evaluation of the changes that have occurred within our galaxy and Solar System, which they have been monitoring for hundreds of millions of years. They chose to be called the Visitors from the Past to remind us of their important role in the evolution of life on Earth. When they mention that man is repeating the mistakes that led to a downfall on Mars, it means that elements were manipulated and combined to form radioactive isotopes for fuel and creating portals into parallel planes for travel. As many ufologists are aware, there is a great concern among the alien visitors that humans, in their reckless blundering, will unleash radioactive disasters on this unique greenhouse planet.

VP. This is friends from home.

D. Hello.

VP. Friends from the sixth. We are intrigued by the human race. We see potential. Certain aspects within the design is in need of upgrade and to remove certain memories within the brain not functioning optimally. The intention is to drive the species forward in an evolution suitable for the intent of the planet. The intent is not, as of yet, established. Only know that there are adjustments within your design, the human design, in need of replacement. We are friends from the sixth, but we occupy form in fish tank eight. Interesting word for universes—fish tanks. The intent is to move the race into a more suitable form of communication. It occurred and existed at one point, even on this plane. The calling has been sent out to several councils operating and understanding life forms. That is the main assignment we have on the sixth. Form in regard of race (*on different planets*), living life forms, as well as solar systems, planets and so forth. We have never set foot, as you have, in that (*human*) form. We find it odd. We find it slow, and so do you, when you incarnate. That program was established around 25,000 B.C., when there was an upgrade and change within the way entities travel though this layer, the fog surrounding your galaxy and everything within it. Everything inside your galaxy, Milky Way, travel the same. You are secluded, like a bubble, in fish tank five. Andromeda galaxy different; longer lifespans, different agenda for those who wish to travel to that location. The Milky Way galaxy has karma aligned to actions, not only on Earth, but Mars correlates to Earth, in that sense. In the intent of upgrade, we need to make sure that everyone in the system, Milky Way being one, is operating at its highest potential. At this time, we do not see progress within life forms such as humans. We do see the repeat of certain things that became the downfall on Mars. And we see the same events, same actions, on this planet. It carries the same— (*They were interrupted by the Council of Nine, as they were struggling to blend with Christine.*)

C9. This is the Council of Nine, trying to create a bridge. We are introducing to you friends from home, located elsewhere. What we see is a disruption or breakups in the communication line. We will try to establish it. (*Another pause and the new visitors continued.*)

VP. Building bridges between galaxies is not as tricky as one might think. We need to clean the Milky Way galaxy from events and debris caused by outbreaks within your atmosphere. Predominately, the misuse of elements, the misuse of energies, have collapsed your atmosphere and the potential it once carried. We do see the program, the cleaning program, and here we have friends from the second dimension. We have a communication central established within your inner atmosphere, which is the second dimension. The seas and landmasses correlate to a healthy atmosphere. The first way to— (*They suddenly broke off again, and Gergen stepped in and gave a brief talk. He was followed by Ophelia whose beautiful talk was included in Wave 3. When she was done, Bob came in with his story, which is in the proper location later in this book.*)

VP, Ophelia, Bob: Mars and other Calamities (Jan 15, 2022)

While it is never pleasant to think of upcoming calamities, they are a recurring reality of life on Earth. While some percentage can be attributed to natural events, the majority is caused by humans. In the near future, it will be a combination of the two. The Visitors from the Past advise that the spirit realm will cut–off the amount of hydrocarbons in several oil producing regions of the world. The sudden drop in production will cause oil shortages and a rapid escalation of energy prices, which will be followed by a subsequent financial collapse of the fiat banking cartel. When Ophelia came in, she said the turmoil is very near.

The Visitors also mention that they installed "boxes" in the mountains. As explained in *Wave 3*, the crust of the Earth moves in response to changes in the energy flow in the Fork. Visitors used crystal lasers to drill down about 25 kilometers in mountain ranges and install receivers, which are technological devices that can change the direction and current in the Fork. In addition, much larger space-based lasers were used to cut continents apart, which were then moved around using the energy flow in the Fork. Bob was shown how North and South America were separated from Europe and Africa using crystal lasers powered by energy beamed down from a spacecraft above Earth. (See Dec 15, 2019 session in *Wave 3*.) What is now the mid-Atlantic Ridge began as a giant cut in the earlier supercontinent. I asked Evan, a Tallock, about the location and movement of the continents. His answer was, "Yes, more congested. But as the Fork changed tune, the planet tilted, motion took place, creating… oh, what word, what word? What you are aware of, (*human ideas about how*) the continents shift, are somewhat false. They have moved rapidly and slowly due to these receivers. Hmm, you would call it, probably, a magnetic gadget. But it is to redirect motion, redirect the song in the Fork. Planet tilted, waters moved, continents sunk. Those (*continents*) you see and those you are aware of in motion and movement are the latest. The other ones sunk. So there were shifts not only on the surface, but from up and down as well. So what you are aware of as motion in landmass and continents are only the latest. The other ones before, some sunk. No civilization, just shifts to maintain an optimal environment for lifeforms to emerge." The boxes also concentrated mountain energy, which then was beamed to boxes in other mountain ranges. The aliens who were here at the time used those pathways for traveling.

Another topic they touched upon was their past visits to Mars. Aliens and manifested entities, such as Anunnaki, the Tallock, and the Visitors from the Past, colonized Mars while they were preparing the Earth project. Some of the technologies that were used on Earth were first experimented with on Mars. Uranium, for example, was first studied on Mars, but an explosion occurred that forced everyone to leave. The Elahim and the Visitors from the Past came to Earth at that time, but other entities were not permitted entry. This topic has been addressed in our earlier books, especially with regard to the explosion of uranium. The Visitors from the Past said the explosion on Mars was caused by a denser variant of uranium. By denser, I am assuming he means more neutrons. On Earth, the heaviest stable isotope of uranium is 238, which has 92 protons and 146 neutrons. Theoretical physicists predict that stable isotopes may exist between 146 and 260 neutrons, so it remains to be seen if future Mars explorations detect heavier isotopes of that element. The evidence of a nuclear explosion on the surface is verifiable, however. The abundance of the fission products xenon–129 and krypton–80 in the atmosphere, along with concentrations of uranium and thorium in certain areas where there is also surface glass, are reliable indicators of a thermonuclear explosion. (Brandenburg, January 2023 International Journal of Astronomy and Astrophysics.) In a May 11, 2019 session, I asked Ophelia, "Were there disasters that occurred on Mars as a result?" She replied, "There were eruptions resulting from blending certain elements. Mercury is an element that is used in several different areas; it is the key element for travel and time. They tried in some way to manipulate travel and time. Mercury, in that atmospheric condition that existed, became an eruption (*explosion*). The blend of mercury and gold are two components of elements that is the foundation for portals and travels. With those, ancient civilizations, even here, knew how to bend time. Bend time means that you can have an access to past and present, because they connect." And later, "In the Earth timeline, this occurred one hundred and fifty million years ago, the first experiment." That corresponds nicely with the date calculated by Brandenburg.

VP. We are the Visitors from the Past. Visitors is the label, name, community, you can call us. Remember the occasions we gathered for exploring this plane. Let's see, let's see. Isaac, Jeshua, Ophelia, tell this one that they are here. Make the transition comfortable for your baby brother. We are here as a unit. Visitors from the time of change. The upgrade in the magnetic field took a turn in order for changes to occur in the animal life, meaning humans as well. Humans did not occupy the same amount of consciousness. Brain did not connect in all outlets as intended. The change in the magnetic field also sends ripples and changes into the brain. That is why when adjustments from the race, as go on at this time, influences the magnetic field and gravitational network, the channels, the flow between. DA–DA–DA–DA–DA DAH! (*makes a frustrated sound*). Words. Tell your baby brother it's safe. There is a little bit of a resistance. Just know that when modifications occur in the grid—I'm talking about the Earth grid—it reflects on your brain. See it as outlets, disconnect, moving.

D. When were you here originally?

VP Several cycles, several. One time when this one was also here. That is why we gradually introduce ourselves in dreams. This one struggles with dreams. We are sorry. We meet and gradually introduce ourselves.

D. What dimension are you from?

VP. Six, nine.

D. We know each other, I guess?

VP. Yes, yes. But there is still somewhat of a resistance to our presence. Tell (*Christine*) that Isaac, Ophelia, Jeshua, are on standby.

D. (*Speaking to Christine, who was in trance.*) Isaac, Ophelia, Jeshua are all nearby, watching over, protecting you.

VP. We want to tell you about the changes that is upcoming. Sometimes looking in rewind does not necessarily help you to evolve forward. However, it is important to understand where you are coming from. The sixth, the presence of us, tend to generate technological and scientific upgrades. We are here to let you know that there will be, I'm sorry, a blackout. Meaning somewhat of a collapse in your power outlet. This means, not a complete shutdown, necessarily, but we are rearranging the grid. The councils on the ninth are operating the cosmic grid. We are meeting the demand of (*an*) upgrade in the Earth grid. There will be changes in how resources and power will be excavated and used in the future.

D. How soon will this occur?

VP. There will be financial collapse when it comes to power use, shortly. Within the time frame of three to five years. This is not the blackout, but it will be a financial blackout, where interests will falter and greed rise to the surface. The one holding power, meaning energy, will need a re–route.

D. Is there anything that we should do to prepare? Will we be protected from this?

VP. Yes, but there will be a darkness, a financial darkness. See it as it unplugs the amount of power. We are sorry, but the intention is to educate new ways on how to work hand–in–hand with—oh, dear god, what is this? It's completely useless using words. (*He got very frustrated by the use of language to convey his thought–bubble.*)

D. It is very difficult.

VP. (*A long sigh.*) We are the Visitors from the Past. Quite present, observing energetic plants, nuclear powers, solar powers. We are observing the evolution when it comes to energy.

D. Will humans eventually find another source of electricity?

VP. That is the need that has to arise within you. You have to understand that there is not an unlimited supply for you all. Some take more, leaving little to others. There is a need for your planet, your host, to redirect. We are moving around certain outlets that have been known for excavating oil, gas, and so forth. They will dim, shut down, empty. Putting a (*makes clicking sound, which I interpreted as 'stop'.*) And that will create aggression and confusion in the industry. Collapse financial. You have to learn different ways before you can be given the next key. At this time, if we were to bring in free energy and how that can be launched, created, built, it will go lost in the hands of greed. We are waiting for incoming friends from the sixth to take on human form in places in the industry. New ways—similar as when suddenly apps were launched, it became a big success for those who understood how to create and make apps function and successful. This is the same thing, we're creating and launching a new app, but it's not ready for the current human.

D. This will be after our lifetime?

VP. It will begin when you, my friend, are in your late seventies. You will see it. You will recognize—you will not meet them physically—but you will recognize your friends. You will recognize the way they operate. You will recognize the methods they are using. You will understand that friends have come to take your place. We are simply here to let you know—a preview, if you like—that you need to modify the way you use energy. First, it might be simply a financial adjustment, a collapse that will create a ripple of anxiety. It's not (*for*) sure that a blackout, that it will go dark physically, so to speak, is necessary. (*A complete blackout may not happen.*)

D. It seems like those in control can only be taken out of power through revolution.

VP. Exactly. Taken out of power. (*He makes a popping sound.*) Plug out, unplug. And how do you unplug someone who is in charge of power? You unplug the connection they have to that power source.

D. Which is money?

VP. Money, as well as the source, the generator of power. Meaning, some known areas where oil, gas have been rich, will not be so. We also want there to be protection of the area around Alaska. There are others from the second dimension that are in operation. We want them to be supported. Meaning, if man does not find oil, if they don't find the resources they are looking for, they are more likely to remove themselves. Similar as what we see now when man are not easily movable. Meaning, if you do not fly around, the atmosphere has the opportunity, the grid above, has the opportunity to generate, to be healed (*in the*) connecting points.

Overall, the current work from spiritual sources has to do with maintenance in grids. Above, so below. We work with the below. Isaac and others are maintaining the cosmic grid, making sure atmospheric conditions are correct for adjustments. Unfortunately, the human race is squeezed, like a hot dog, in the middle. We are sorry. But then again, you are only here a short sneeze, and then you're gone. We are here to look at the overall sneezes coming in. That's how we see it. Never walked as humans, of course. They are more like insects.

D. The insect population is going to be decreased, isn't it?

VP. Yes. Change. Need to be relocated. There are too many on certain places and less on others. We are happy to see that you are in a country with a lot of space around each insect. I'm sorry to call you, my friend, an insect. You are not. But you are taking the form of the insects in order for the rotation (*to be understood*). In this case, the rotation has to do with the understanding of one's place in this big play. Others are assisting the rotation and movement physically. There will always be conflicting sides when it comes to evolution and understanding and education. Some are afraid of education. Meaning they are not (*he paused*)—it's like their harbor is not open for ships. The ships cannot enter the harbor. It doesn't matter how grand the ship, the boat, looks, they still are not capable of anchoring. It's not your mission to create harbors. You are here to create ships, ships of information, education, understanding. Understand that some boats will never reach the harbor, (*and will*) go somewhere else. It's a rotation in landmass. There are adjustments in all grids. Ophelia and her friends adjust the filter within (*humans*). We work on ground control (*Earth grids*). Isaac, cosmic grid, with friends.

D. Were you in any way involved in putting the boxes in the mountains?

VP. HUH! Who told you?

D. Joel. (*Bob's geologist friend from the second.*)

VP. Joel?

D. Someone from the second dimension who was observing.

VP Oh, yes. That's true. Yes, yes. (*He was getting information from Gergen and others.*) I remember Joel. He saw us coming in a craft, dropping, drilling, leaving the boxes. He tried to wave us off. He was not welcoming.

D. The boxes generated some field that affected the natural grid?

VP. Yes. And he was not part of that project. He had a different mission. He was very proud of his mountains, and the conditions that he, probably with friends, established. Unfortunately, Joel does not—and neither do we—see the big picture. We simply execute on demand. The demand was to put in sensors, receivers, in the mountains to read the currents below, and to also work as batteries, connecting points between mountains. It was a way to create (*connections*) between mountain ranges across the globe for crafts to move. Mountains carry the energy needed—mountain energy. And we placed sensors, receivers, geographically on different locations, (*such as*) the Himalaya. Also—but Joel is not seeing this—also placed in underwater mountains. There was a whole grid that came about.

D. Was the purpose to monitor the Earth, or was it to power your crafts?

VP. It was to create power also between (*the mountains*) for transportation, for travels. Mountain to mountain. Mountain energy. Receivers between (*the mountains*) created the opportunity to transfer between (*different locations*) rapidly. The receivers registered the life form in each mountain. Transformed the life form in the mountain to an energy form. Quartz, in particular, created the highest way, and the fastest way, to travel. The receivers simply collected data, transformed the potential in the mountains (*using*) the minerals that were high in those areas. That's why they were strategically placed on certain locations. Those in the water, seabed, those mountains simply held the line. This was a time when we created grids. We do it now as well, simply more in disguise. And some, like you, through the insects (*humans*). We will return at a later point. Simply refer to us—and tell this one to welcome us—as we are the Visitors from the Past.

D. Is that how we should refer to you?

VP. Visitors from the Past. We are not in spirit form when we were here. We were solid, as were you. We did not incarnate. We came in craft.

D. Were you within this fish tank, this universe?

VP. We are operating in several at the moment. Mainly here.

D. I had a question about how you travel between fish tanks. Can you go in crafts? Or do you in some way travel energetically?

VP. It depends on the border between realities. It's the same within fish tanks, as well as between them. If the borders are allowing physical manifestation, physical entrances, then craft is used. If the next reality is not complimentary to where you are coming from, an adjustment and transformation takes place. Sometimes we need to return to the spiritual (*dimensions*) inside—to give you the picture—in order for us to transform to a new reality.

D. That I understand.

VP. Otherwise, we can travel directly between. Some are visible, some not. We can travel to Andromeda in craft. We can travel between Andromeda and Milky Way in craft. We do not need the pickle to go home and change suit.

D. Do you have a planet somewhere in these galaxies that you occupy?

VP. Yes, yes. Several.

D. And you've been involved with Earth for a long time?

VP. Yes, yes. We were friends on Mars as well. We did similar upgrades. There was just an explosion due to uranium, due to the particles in the sand. Ignited.

D. This was on Mars?

VP. Yes.

D. Was it an accident?

VP. Yes. Accident.

D. Is it the same form of uranium that we use in our bombs on earth?

VP. Yes, but not as strong (*on Earth*). Stronger on Mars. Higher in its structure, higher density. The amount ignited in the combination of the atmosphere. That is why the atmosphere is important. You cannot upgrade and change minerals, resources, or chemicals, if the atmosphere is not complimentary to that upgrade. We do not want a repeat, like Mars.

D. Are you involved, in any way, with the pyramids on Earth?

VP. Not built. We didn't build. It was a similar model, like we did earlier with the mountains. Similar, just the same. Just using little cones, instead of a whole mountain range. They were easier, we did not have Joel protecting. Huh huh. He shushed us away. Ran around, shushed. He waved with a flag, almost. Like a red flag.

D. When the boxes were first installed in that part of the world, the Himalayas weren't in existence, were they?

VP. There were existing mountains, yes. (*That is a true statement. The geology of how the Himalayan mountain range formed after the boxes were placed was detailed in the Oct 6, 2019 session in 'Notes, Volume 2'. Prior to their creation, there was an older mountain range in the same location on the continent.*)

D. It must have been in the last hundred million years or so?

VP. Earlier. There was no human life form. It was animal life, but not in the extent that it created problems. And that is why there is a need to decrease the amount of bugs, insects (*humans*), because you cannot do too many upgrades if there is motion. At that time, before the mountains, were way before. We have been back with similar, like you mentioned, pyramids. But that was like yesterday, from our way of seeing it. It's almost like this morning, for you. With Joel in the mountains, it would be considered, in human ways of thinking, millions, millions, millions, and millions of years. Way, way, way back. Mountains existed; they were formed earlier than you know. Joel was formed earlier than you know. There were no animal life to take into account—some, of course. There were some small, furry creatures, bear-like. And some great (*numbers*) in the ocean. But they were not affected by our establishing the network.

D. That network helped to create the current mountain range, didn't it?

VP. It created and changed the receiving, the hearing, of several entities, such as mountains. When I say entity, I mean mountains; I mean seas; I mean landmass. I don't mean the bug. The Fork was in change. And so we adjusted and used the outlet (*energy source*) from within, the Fork. The mountains rose and land masses broke off, started to move. (*He is describing the breakup of the Larasia and Gondwana landmasses into the smaller tectonic plates.*) It was a grand design. We wanted to do something similar, but it's not possible with all the animal life, insects, and so forth. It's a smoother transition than it was then. At one point, it was quite rapid. We modified and created the motion of landmass. The uplift of continents, as well as mountain ranges that rose.

D. Was that to assist with the atmosphere and lifeforms?

VP. Lifeforms to come. Atmosphere were working independently before us. Atmosphere came first and was in place. We used the power of the atmosphere in order for us to connect the Fork and different focal points, in order for the grid to be established.

D. I have a question. How was oxygen first introduced to the Earth?

VP. From the eighth. It came in like a star fall, like a capsule. It landed like a meteor. It landed on several places. It was established from this—it almost looked like a diamond. Six-point diamond. Beautiful. It dropped into the ocean. It dropped on land. Several places. It emerged, the ability to breathe. At the same time, winds, climate. It came—the way I can show it to you would be to show a star fall. You have seen remains, some found in caves. It's like crystals. It was introduced. The spiritual source behind it, eighth.

D. That's fascinating. Thank you for that.

VP. I will give you more information about it, if possible. There are several phenomena, not just life forms. But as you mentioned, oxygen is also a lifeform. Water is a lifeform. It wasn't just big rain, even though it increased, of course. We will talk further.

D. Those are fascinating subjects. I appreciate the information.

VP. You are welcome. I've seen your friend.

D. My Little Friend?

VP. Yes, yes. When you walk around, we see him. He looks like Joel. Joel is a little bit older.

D. They're friends too, my friend and Joel.

VP. There you go. We will be back.

D. All right. Thank you so much. I really appreciate the visit.

VP. You are much welcome.

O. This is Ophelia.

D. Hello, Ophelia. I kind of assumed you would step in.

O. I needed to step in and somewhat create a passage. The energy from visitors are more materialized. They are more solid, which will also take more energy (*for Christine*). We have mentioned before that you can alternate between the way you access information. Sometimes, this one can lay down and you can lead through experience. It will be easier, in that sense, and you will be able to have more frequent release of information.

D. Without her doing the heavy trance?

O. Yes, laying down, more relaxed. Guide her through. Seth will tell you. Seth will meet. They will talk, but in an easier way than this. It's more complimentary to the physical. It will not bring too much intensity to the experience.

D. How frequently should we do that?

O. If you use the other form, you can do it more frequent. You can do it more than once a week, if you like. You should alter. Bob, of course, will not come in the same way. He needs his own time. But you can alter. This one will know which one. We will tell this one. So, there we go.

D. They (*the VPs*) were talking about a time of darkness, a financial collapse, stuff like that.

O. Yes.

D. Obviously, from a personal perspective, we would like to prepare for that.

O. There is no need to fear. There will be changes in the financial structures. There will be a halt in imports and exports, due to aggressive feelings between countries. There is no need to fear, but to be mindful. Simply go within and don't fear. Be calm. Find your breathing. Find your breathing means the focal point of who you are. Returning to your breathing exercises will give you the calm and clarity of the human mind, when the human spins. (*It is notable that this session was about 5 weeks before the NATO sponsored Ukrainian conflict started. Since that time, there have been many sanctions and financial seizures that caused massive inflation in the West. The dollar is rapidly losing its reserve status as a result of these actions.*)

D. Okay. Well, thank you so much for the advice.

O. There. We will briefly allow Bob to come in. But it might be a separate session for him, as he's been waiting. And the energy needs to be addressed.

D. Thank you, Ophelia.

O. You are much welcome. (*She moved out and Bob instantly came in.*)

B. Mmm.

D. They finally opened the door for you?

B. Well, there is still some sort of cough, you know, bad air that's lingering around here. Maybe this one smoked. It's still a little bit of that left over.

O. Ophelia said it came in somewhat materialized.

B. Ah. I did see. And I'm grateful for that, because otherwise I would be a little bit disappointed if it would just be like a door again. But I did see them, and they're quite grand. They are wearing like dark capes with crystals that are all sort of colors. Mainly dark purple, blue, white.

D. Did they look like physical beings, or did they look like spiritual beings?

B. Oh, if I were to go there, I could probably poke them in the belly. But I'm not sure I'm supposed to. You know, that's not really what we do, just go poke. But if I did, I'm pretty sure it would be resistance. I'm quite fascinated, because I wonder where they came from. And I don't remember seeing them that much. But they look similar like you. Their cape is dark purple, and the thing that goes around like this (*draped around the shoulders into a V-shape in front*) was in crystals. And one had like a belt with a big crystal that's red, like a ruben.

D. (*Laughing.*) Ruby?

B. Ruby.

D. So they had crystals around their chest and shoulders?

B. They showed off. You know, I also want to have now a belt with like a big crystal!

D. You know who would recognize them?

B. Huh?

D. Joel.

B. Joel is friends with them?

D. He's seen them.

B. Oh, I'm gonna go talk with Joel. He's a bit grumpy when it comes to like visitors and those he's not familiar with. He's not like the most social guy you can find. He's not as curious. I'm curious, you know, like, "Who are you? Where are you from? What is your purpose? Where are you going?" You know, like that. But he's not. He is more like eyeballing. Similar like the Moon People, he just stares. And I said to Joel, "Maybe you need to polish your social skills a little bit, because you don't know. These might be quite fascinating friends." But he doesn't have that in his make-up. He's quite content to work solo, which is a little bit unique from the second dimension. But his capsule, his being, sort of detached from the group quite early. And he doesn't like to be disturbed, necessarily. He doesn't even really reach out to me all the time. It's mainly like when there's a question. And then there's like no end (*to the questions*). But otherwise, you barely see him.

D. He's very mission focused.

B. Well, indeed. And he likes to work solo. He doesn't like commotion. He doesn't necessarily always come to our, you know, like our festivities (*on the second*). I invited him and I said, "It would be good for you to have social interactions. Look at the little ones." I said, "You don't have to engage." But I have invited him. And last time when we had a ceremony, he did come. And I said, "Just sit here in the back. You don't have to do anything." He's a little bit like you when you are in a human form, and I have to somewhat help along.

D. Give a little push.

B. Give a little push. Very much like that. He's same generation like Gergen, in some way. So he's a little bit set in his ways. And so are you. When you come into human form you are more set in your ways than you are when Lasaray and I talk. You go with the wind a little bit more. Even though you kind of know the schedule, you are more accommodating and you are more flexible. So, okay, I'm gonna go now. I'm going to have my own discussions because there have been changes. But I wanted to tell you that I invited Joel, because I feel like we need to polish his social skills a little bit. It's helpful, you know. I said, "Maybe you wouldn't have seen these visitors as intruders." And he said, "Yes, but they were, because they came to my mountain."

D. They said that he came and was kind of waving a red flag at them.

B. He told me. He said that he ran and he didn't leave. You know how they do, like those to demonstrate, when they lay down on the ground, so that no one can come in and tear down something, for instance?

D. Yes.

B. Similar like that. He planted himself there with his flag. He didn't move. He's quite particular. He's a really good friend. He's quite intelligent. He knows a lot, probably more than all of us combined, when it comes to mountains being a living life form. And that's what we're gonna talk about. But you have to set off a lot of time when it comes to Joel, because he can get quite excited to talk about his topic, individually, one on one. But this whole social scene is not his forte. It's mine, though!

D. I know, you're very social.

B. I'm quite social.

D. You're quite popular, too. I have to say that a lot of people who are joining our group tomorrow are hoping that you will talk.

B. Well, maybe I will sometime, if it's allowed. We'll see.

D. You're admired by the people who have heard you speak.

B. Well, you know, I want them to be excited. I want them to know that they have maybe someone like me that sort of tags along. And I want them to pay attention in nature. They might see someone like Joel.

D. Waving them off.

B. Waving them off. Nay, he's not allowed to wave humans off. We all have a manual, we have a guidebook on how to interact with humans. But he said that they were not humans, those who came, because humans were not around when this happened. Okay, so I'm gonna go now, but I'll be back.

D. Okay, Bob. Thank you so much for coming.

B. Okay. See you. Bye bye.

Bob: The Highway of Life (Dec 31, 2020)

This session ended with Bob giving a very nice way for us to visualize how spirit guides are able to anticipate when an incarnated soul may need help during its life. He said it is like seeing a highway from above, where detours, roadblocks and clouds are visible to the guide. The highway represents the life plan and the movement of the vehicle shows how it is progressing. The clouds and offramps depict where lessons are scheduled. The incarnation can sometimes pull over and stop, or perhaps take an unscheduled side trip, and that is when the spirit guide needs to assist the most.

D. I was curious—when you see this future life, I guess you get glimpses of how it is going to proceed that is out of the linear timeframe?

B. Ah. I see the linear experience, and then I see it sort of hovering on the side. Sometimes it's merged with the timeline and sometimes just sort of tagging along on the side. When I see that it tags along on the side, that means that the life is open for changes and evaluations and modifications. But when the life trots off, I see it like a little fog, a little cloud, and when the cloud moves back into the timeline, that means the predestined activity that are sort of cut in stone, they will occur regardless if I try to modify. So a life looks like that. Sometimes you are on that timeline and then you are directly on track with whatever purpose or activity that you designed, or someone designed for you. BUT when the life on certain times moves to the side a little bit, that is when modifications and choices can be made. In this life, for the both of you, you do not have that many times when your cloud, your life, is next to the predestined timeline. Everything is sort of in there, so I can't put in notes in your pocket as easily that I thought I would. But I will monitor—and this is what Jeshua always does—and now it's my turn because I'm part of the 2178 excursion. So now I'm here (*reviewing the life*) and I'm looking with the Astrological Council and I see the timeline and I see the different impacts, depending on energetic flow from the planets and stars and so forth, which I thought was the only thing. But then I was taught here (*that there are more influences*), and Jeshua is trying to translate, which I'm pretty happy for. In many ways, I'm like the

Old Sniffer there, I need someone who translates—so I can see here the timeline. And he said, "Here everything goes according to what we have designed. But when the little fog, the little cloud moves to the right, modifications can be made. This is how I see Lasaray when he's out and about. I can see if there is a need for me to engage. If he is on that timeline, moving along according (*to plan*), I don't need necessarily to engage that much. I simply supervise and look into certain activities. But when the little cloud moves to the right, from my visual perspective here, modifications and downloads and exchange of data can be made. However, occasionally, unfortunately, the cloud can move to the left of this timeline that one can see. And that's when," Jeshua said, "that the soul doesn't hear. It moves into depression, it moves off–route. As long as the cloud is on the right of this visual highway that I can see, the soul is open for modification, for choices, and so forth. Once one is on the left side, one is not open for modification and choices and will not hear the spirit guide's efforts."

D. What if it is directly on the line? Is it doing what it is supposed to?

B. If it is on the line, then a spirit guide sort of relaxes a little bit. It's like, if I give you a visual, if you are on the line, I would have this position (*as he relaxed back into the chair*), "Okay, moving along beautifully. Driving the car, everything is fine, following the speed limits, everything is fine. There we go, good." And then, "Okay, going to the right side," so I put myself like this. (*He leaned forward, looking down attentively.*) "Okay, what's happening? What should I do? What modifications are needed?" Because I have the objective view here—I'm like a helicopter—I can see like over there, there is a new entrance ramp to the highway. If so, "What do I need to prepare him for, as the journey continues?" And sometimes the cloud stops. So, this is how we (*the main spirit guides*) see it. I never did this with you, since I was always inside the line and inside the cloud. (*Bob is beside me during the incarnation, not observing from above.*) Jeshua said, "This is how I see and can monitor and assist Lasaray." So I asked, "If I want to have a two percent life, how will this cloud act if I am in control?" Huhuhuh, and Jeshua laughed. He said, "It's not a two percent life that is coming up in 2178." But I said, "But what if it comes up in 2278? How would it look?" He said, "If you have like a mole, or a two percent life, it could be on the line, because it sniffs and investigates. But it moves slower. If you compare it, in a regular life on the highway, you should drive around 90 kilometers per hour. But if it's a mole life, they normally go much slower, like 50. So, from a spirit perspective, it's easy to see if there is a mole. Sometimes a mole will just sort of move to the left and just park while spirit guides or higher councils investigate the highway. Then THEY put it back in." But in a normal human life, don't expect, if you go off route—if you don't engage in life and you find your life on the left side—don't expect someone like Jeshua or me to come and just move you back in. You have to move yourself back in. So, if you are not a mole—if you are not a two percent person—or if you HAVE a Coat, then you cannot have someone move you. You are supposed to move yourself back on track. You are supposed to move aside, take a listen, take a pause, reconsider options, and then move yourself back again.

D. So how would someone pull themselves back on their track?

B. Well, what we see here is that when someone is paralyzed out of fear, for instance—like we see now (*during the 2020 flu lockdowns*)—there is a lot of those who are on the left side, who are just waiting for someone, and to be saved back to the highway. You know, like, "My car broke down." "Yes, your car broke down. But you have the manual in the car on how to kickstart the battery again," just to give you a visual of what's going on. But if you are a two percent or a mole, then spirit helpers will do that for you because you are remotely steered, in some way. If someone is—Jeshua wants to make this clear, because no one wants to be like a car broken down—but you are supposed to find the manual in the car, to plug in the battery and jumpstart the car again. However, if the spirit guide sees great effort in trying to jumpstart the car, and if it doesn't really do so, a little help can come in. It's like a flash.

D. What if you have no Coat and drift off to the left?

B. If you have no Coat and you drift off to the left, then you're probably a mole or a two percent. Those with no Coats rarely are on the left, unless they are a two percent or a mole.

D. The Council of Nine, the last time they talked, described the ones who are off to the left as sitting still in a rowboat out on the ocean, not realizing they have oars. Just waiting for someone to lead them somewhere, to save them.

B. Sometime one of these little boats sitting there, looking exactly the same, paralyzed, can actually be a mole investigating this paralyzed flotilla around them. And that is what we see, a flotilla of nothingness. So this is what Jeshua said. Since I'm gonna be put in the seat where I have a visual of you—I've never been in this seat! I've always been inside the line or inside the cloud. I've never felt like, "Oh, now we are on the right." Or, "Now we are on track." I mean, I could see if we were not on track, and I could help you, steer you. It's all about training! It's all about growing and understanding. And now I can see how Jeshua sees you, or how Isaac sees this one's life. Ophelia probably sees as well.

D. What about a life that has already occurred? Is the pattern there?

B. The pattern is there. You can see, you know, drifting in, drifting there, and so forth. And sometimes, let's say someone had sort of a tricky life and one is just down to help others or just have a few little experiences, then they normally are just on the highway with their car.

D. So, in this future life, when you look at it, is the whole cloud off to the side of a line, as a probability?

B. Which life?

D. The 2178.

B. 2178. I'm looking here on the intent. I see the line, the intention that we have. And I see there is a little exit, where the cloud could possibly make a pause. It's not a U-turn. I'm not allowing U-turns. I said, "We're not going back. I want progress moving forward." And I said, "I don't want to have circulations (*roundabouts*) because what if he just circles there for a long time?" Ha ha ha ha ha. So, I said he can have those little, you know, like you see up in Colorado where trucks can stay. (*Rest stops.*)

D. So, every soul would have its own path of intention that it follows when it comes to Earth?

B. Indeed. And sometimes a spirit guide can create the path, and that's what I'm doing here. And the Astrological Council is helping me with WHEN to put in those little side tracks, if you like. And it doesn't mean that you will take them. It just means that it's there if you need a ponder. That's when you normally, as a human, feel like you are standing with two choices. When you are like that, then your car has turned off the highway and you are in a side cloud. But what I see here (*in the 2178 life*), I see this line. I see the whole life and I see half-way, or a little bit less than half-way, there is a shift. And that's where the spiritual enlightenment is coming in. And after that, there is not that many side roads.

D. That's really interesting.

B. Okay, I'm gonna go now, so hoodily-hoo. I'm continuing to prepare and it's quite exciting, now that I'm sitting in the observatory and

I can see the life. I've never been having this view of your life. I've just been right in there with you.

D. You'll be like the Big Eye in the sky.

B. I'm like the Big Eye! Huhuh. Okay, so I'm gonna go now.

D. Alright, my friend. Thank you for all the information, and it's always a pleasure to hear your voice.

B. Okay, I go now. See you soon.

The Sessions from 2021

Tallocks: The Changing Ecosystem (Jan 7, 2021)
When the Tallock began speaking during this session, it was a bit choppy. But as their energy adjusted to Christine, the sentences became more complete. When they describe changing the rotation of the circular veins, it has a more complex meaning. As the veins are altered, it is a precursor to landmass movement or atmospheric changes. When that happens, earthquakes or tsunamis are to be expected. So a simple statement about changes to the rotation of the veins is an indirect warning of destructive change. The Tallock have participated in the Earth project for hundreds of millions of years, along with the Elahim, executing the will of the councils and the Creator. In this session, the Tallocks describe how the human is periodically adjusted, and they seem to play a direct part in some of those activities.

Even though their talk was brief, it is packed full of thought-provoking ideas. For example, they say, "Landmass is a living entity, as well as the seas. The sea is a living entity that you are not, as humans, aware of." If that is a statement of fact, then it is imperative that we re–evaluate how we interact with the Earth. Native cultures, who understood that truth, have been supplanted by societies that only see lifeless dirt, rocks, water and air. The enlightened may concede that some of the flora and fauna have some spark of awareness, but it is rare to encounter a person who feels compassion for a rock or the elements and minerals that support those lifeforms.

T. This is the Tallock. Greetings from Vlac. Greetings, greetings. Earth not feeling well, not feeling well at all. Tending to your host is necessary. The minerals are out of balance, out of place. Rotation underneath your feet, establishment within the core necessary for progress. This is the turmoil that manifests as chaos in your species at this time. It's the rotation within your host, needed for progress and evolution of new species. There are new species incoming to your planet. Ecosystem failure needs to be repaired. Ecosystem not operating properly. The changes made from within, core, minerals, implant, rotation of the circular veins within your host needs to be attended to—the operation is ongoing. The result is what you see in your species as fear. You sense the ground shaking underneath you, in some way. The work is ongoing. We are sorry for the experience. We are aware of the effect it has on mankind and other mammals. Ecosystem, however, is in greater need than your wellbeing at this time. You have to excuse the language. You have to see the bigger picture. The intent is to repair the ecosystem, plant new insects, new minerals incoming. Vlac, on expedition. You are friends of ours. We know you do a different job than your nature normally requires of you. You are engineers in creation, when it comes to manifested worlds and forms. You have a preference, though, to enlight the mind, where mind is existing. Here, it is existing, but the level is questionable. We are here to assist the race of consciousness. But hand-in-hand with that operation is the operation that goes on within, where we kickstart certain species, kickstart events. Your Little Friend saw, in the store—he called it a store—when friends of ours bought something that he saw. (*Once, when Bob was in the store on Etena, he saw three entities picking up some star-shaped objects. The stars are programmed to alter evolution on planets bearing lifeforms. Based on the description, alien visitors can place these objects on a planet and new lifeforms will suddenly appear, perhaps by altering the DNA of an existing creature. It can also be programmed to put certain species into hibernation, if that is desired.*) Your friend, why don't you bring him? He seems different.

D. To Vlac?

T. I'm not sure if he would like it. It's not the same surrounding as Etena. It's a center of research, a center of engineering, science. I'm not sure if he is interested in that, but we see him following closely to you.

D. I'm pretty sure he'd be interested.

T. When he is ready, invite him. He saw the star, I know, because I saw that he asked about it. He asked you. He follows you at home, in the hallway. I see him talking, asking questions.

D. He has a very good mind.

T. We could need someone like that in research. What is his expertise?

D. Plant and animal life on Earth, but he's been working on learning the solar systems.

T. Well, we are operating in close connection to the council on the fifth and on the second for this project. They are the ones in charge of what area needs to be rebooted, kickstarted. Some will go into hibernation. Within the area around Australia, there is a concern. The ecosystem needs to be rejuvenating differently. Needs to sleep—hibernation. As we rotate, as we fix and patch up certain holes within your host, Earth, then certain places are enlighted. Others fall asleep. You can see it in the consciousness within your species. Don't judge, just know that there are differences within both events, mammals, landmass. Landmass is a living entity, as well as the seas. The sea is a living entity that you are not, as humans, aware of. But the sea is not a cohering intelligence, necessarily. It's different. Certain lakes have more consciousness than others. Certain streams are considered babies, or veins. Certain oceans are actually in need of sleep. So it's not a collective consciousness in your waters here. Normally, an element carries a similarity in its potential and consciousness. When it is in a manifested reality, such as here, we want to see the different scenarios that can happen within an element or a species. That is why you see different behaviors, not only within your species, but other mammals as well. And also, how certain waters and forests, even rocks, appear differently. It is because the elements have a different evolution and progress here, (*that are*) not always available on other places. So, you are not the only mammal or species going through a cycle of evolution. The whole entity, the whole body—meaning the world itself—is an ongoing project. We see how elements evolve or dissolve, such as a mammal, or waters, or forests and trees, and we try to balance outcomes. The little star—tell your friend, since he thought it was a magical creation, and it is—it is a tool used to plant events, new scenarios, new outcomes. But also, if you rotate it anticlockwise, it pauses the evolution; it pauses your consciousness. So, this little gadget is used on several areas, in several expertise. When we dimmed the consciousness in the mind, a little smaller version was placed within the body, the human container. So the mind was rotated backwards (*regressed*) a little bit. It's not as tricky as it sounds. And some might think it's an implant. And yes, it is. Your current species has this implant within you. It is a chip within the physical. That is why a soul cannot channel its full potential. It cannot access the soul mind as easily as it did before, because the chip is implanted in the brain of the vehicle. This is by design, and it is decided by higher councils on the tenth, and even eleventh. They execute where these modifications should apply. There.

D. I'm sure Earth is only one of many places, is it not?

T. In this area, no. It's not the same in your little corner over here. It's a fond project. We see Earth as a greenhouse, similar to how man plant and pot and tends to things in the greenhouse in their backyard. We see it as a project, where modifications and the result of certain impacts—not only in the flora and fauna ecosystem, and especially the atmosphere—there is an interest in how a physical, manifested form responds to these adjustments. And that is what we see right now, for instance, because of the ecosystem and the temperature being too high, in general, in your atmosphere. We are adjusting from within. The result, unfortunately, is the collapse of the mental. It is not just this year. It is a progression that's been going on since the 50s. This is when it started to really come to term, that putting in a pill (*psychotropic drugs*) would help the consciousness or the mental balance within the being, instead of understanding the surrounding environment and the impact it has on a species. Certain animals react and respond better. You can see it similar as why most animals understand when there is an earthquake or tsunami, how they flee. But man stands still on the beach, watching the disaster come to shore. Similar. The animals don't have this chip in their mind. They are more equipped to follow the frequencies and vibrations they sense through either their feet or other senses. Man's senses have been stripped. We are trying to see the impact of a higher consciousness, a higher brain capacity—when outer influences increase—how this mammal, such as human in this case, how they respond. Do you understand the project as a whole and the importance of calming the mind? To sense the energies, to sense the events, with a different approach. The chip is by design in your vehicles that exist at this time. If it is rotated again, which it is designed to do, your experiences of these disasters to shore will be perceived differently. You might even react as an animal and find shelter, instead of standing and watching it overwhelm you.

D. When was this chip installed, roughly?

T. The other mental capacity of the chip has been in (*since*) 3300 BC. That's when we started to dim a little bit, but not the entire population. What I mentioned in the 50s was that the humans tried to meet or control the mind more. It became a business of high interests to work with medical treatments, but it wasn't new.

It operated before, just in a different manner. But the chip, it was placed in some regions around 3000 BC. But not everywhere. Not Egypt, for instance. But that's why you can see little progress, like tribes and no monuments at all in certain places, whereas other civilizations rose to greatness. So little-by-little, that's when it was started.

D. Remind me, what dimension are you from? Are you from the sixth?

T. Yes. Six is home. Just a different location of six. We are connected directly with fish tank eight. So, there. Wanted to come by and tell you of our presence and what we do.

D. Thank you. It's been a while since we've talked, so I appreciate you coming and sharing with us today.

T. You are welcome. See you on Vlac.

D. Very good. Thank you, my friends.

Bob: Sniffer and the Dinosaurs (Jan 7, 2021)

Bob revisits and elaborates on the November 20, 2020 session where Sniffer saw an alien creature guarding thousands of eggs in a cave in an area around Yellowstone Park in the northwest of Wyoming. Sniffer sends thought bubbles to Bob that are like holographic movies. Bob then narrates from Sniffer's perspective, as if he is there. Aliens brought several new species to Earth, which they wanted to occupy or control. When these eggs hatched, Sniffer could detect the difference between the normal reptiles and mammals, and the ones brought in by visitors. He said they were occupied by a different energy, meaning they were not animated by the Master Mind. And now, all these millions of years later, Sniffer said that some humans display the same characteristics of the aliens who once occupied the foreign dinosaurs. Other spirits have implied some humans are inhabited by alien life forms, not all of whom are benevolent. The Cell is one such group, which may explain their attitude towards humans.

B. Ah! Ah! Mah mah mah mah mah. (*He was tuning Christine's vocal cords.*) I'm in full operation, of course. I've been with Old Sniffer. I did not expect or foresee that it will take such a jumpstart of interests and questions. He's extremely enthusiastic. Sniffers do see the world as a grid, like a puzzle. So they can move and rotate puzzle pieces to find certain things and to optimize the general grid itself. They're not just, like someone said, they're not just there to find things. It's not just like a search dog. I mean, he's highly equipped in understanding how to rotate and fix puzzle pieces. So he's an extension of the second dimension when it comes to the lower grid, meaning the foundation of life forms, and so forth.

D. You're probably glad that you got Old Sniffer as a companion, aren't you?

B. Ah. Because, you know, like we have been talking a little bit about the dinosaurs. I want him to tell me about his life, you know, where has he been and what did he see? And then he said, "What did you see, when you went to that place where the big, furry animal is? (*Sniffer was asking about Etena, where Siah is.*) What did you see?" I said, "You're tricky!" Then he said, "Let's share." So, we do share. And he did say, about dinosaurs, that some came gradually. But some actually came from one day to the next. It was because the general grid kinda changed direction, and he said it seemed like it was overnight. And certain dinosaurs came in, and it appears that it was not just the Master Mind in those. It was actually like parts were incarnating in the dinosaur. And that came quickly, he said. He said, "You can see the difference in the eyes. You can see the difference in the way they operate, whether they are just Master Mind experience, or if they operate as an intelligence, a different intelligence." And when he saw that, he got baffled. I'm pretty sure those who were around—like Ole probably saw this. But Ole doesn't say. Because I went to Ole and I said, "did you see this? Did you see like incarnations in dinosaurs?" And he hummed. And I know all about what humming means. It means 'not now.' But Old Sniffer, he saw firsthand a difference between the different entities that occupied a dinosaur body. He said some was an intelligence inside, and they could lure on other prey differently than those that was general Master Mind. He said there was a difference in the way they walked, there was a difference in the way they communicated, and he said that he observed this. So now when he sees humans, he said, "It's similar how I can see certain humans. They are operating a little bit like that dropped (*by visitors*) dinosaur. They are operating from a different brain, a different mind," he said. So, from his perspective, it was overnight that there was a shift that came. And he wanted me to ask you what really took place, what happened, because he didn't see the back story about it. So, I'm here, of course, on both the behalf of me and Old Sniffer to ask. And maybe we go to the Evolution Group and see what this was about. I don't see, because this was pre-me. But I'm highly interested in seeing this, because I know you talked about coming like in a manifested form. BUT here we also have someone who came in somewhat of an incarnation.

D. You remember the dinosaur eggs you saw in the cave? Do you think the aliens hatched bodies, which then they occupied? Maybe those eggs are related to what some people call the reptilians, who are still here on Earth.

B. I'm wondering who we can ask, though.

D. Ask Ophelia. Maybe she can give us a hint?

B. She said that I see things so that I can report to you. But the one in the cave with the eggs, that was part of something here. If it's the same as Old Sniffer was talking about, we don't know. But like I said, it was different when I saw that cave with the eggs and the one guarding them—that one was odd. He guarded the eggs, big eggs. Not as big as me, of course.

D. If visitors came and made their own forms by modifying DNA, then maybe they occupied them as well, blended with the body.

B. Ah. This is gonna be explored more. But Old Sniffer told me this, and I'm highly interested, of course, in knowing anything about pre-me. But yes, again, that cave with the eggs, that was different because it was a colony of eggs. I mean, it was not a million, but thousands. There were a lot of eggs in that cave, all looking the same. White, uuhhmm, maybe the size of one foot, or one and a half feet.

D. Half a meter?

B. Ah.

D. Those are pretty big eggs.

B. Big eggs, but the being was much bigger. But it didn't seem like it was his babies, his eggs. He seemed like he was like a keeper of them. So it didn't seem like a mother. You kind of think of a mother looking a little bit different, like Ophelia, like white and shiny and tender.

D. It was just a job for him?

B. It didn't radiate that maternal vibe, really. I'm not sure, but I don't think it was a parent. So, I did ask about the zooming device that we have, if it's possible to zoom not just around the fish tank and the Wheel, you know, and inside the Pole, huhuh, which you were not in favor of. But I said, "If we rotate the lens, can we zoom back in time?" And you said, "Yeah, we can. We can zoom in, but it's a different lens. We just adjust. But yes, we can zoom back and forth, if you like." And I said, "I like!" Then I wanted to know about certain things pre-me. And that's when you said, "Well, we have to have clearance from Ole or Gergen to watch anything pre-ourselves. If I want to look something pre-me, I have to ask Jeshua for sort of the code and the lens." But you said we can ask Ole and Gergen. And then you asked if I had asked. And I don't lie, so I said, "Huhhuh, I haven't asked." And then Jeshua came, and Isaac came. Then I asked, "Can my bubble go also back in time?" And Jeshua laughed, and he said, "Yes. It's a different bubble, but yes, you can go back in time." And that's what's gonna come, he said. He said we're gonna go back in time and we're gonna explore prehistorical experiences. I hope I'm not excluded, just because we're going back pre-me. That would be disappointing. Old Sniffer, he might tell. But Jeshua said what we're gonna do now, moving forward, is that we're gonna go and find hidden keys in the past. So we're gonna travel on the timeline. We're gonna adjust the lens, you say and zoom in on certain events and we're gonna detect shifts of consciousness. And we're gonna detect where things were on a peak and a high, and where things went wrong—and what did go wrong. I'm signing up for this class, to zoom back. I'm more interested in zooming back, actually. One might think it would be more moving forward. But I'm limited to moving forward, I'm fully aware. So there's no need to ask about that too much.

D. Yeah, I'm interested in learning about the past, too.

B. Well, Jeshua said that's what we're gonna do, we're gonna travel back. And that's why also we have Old Sniffer, so that maybe Old Sniffer will guide us to the right location, the right coordinates on the map, so to speak, on the Earth, so we know what to do. We're gonna talk about a lot of the blue-dot lives and we're gonna see more of the events that took place in manifested form. BUT what Old Sniffer said here about the dinosaurs coming in, they were NOT just Master Mind. It was a blend within the species. He said you can see these different changes within a group of mammals, whether there is a presence of the Master Mind in that race, or if it's another higher intelligence. But he didn't know where and how that came to term, because he wasn't told. Then I said, "Maybe we can go ask someone."

D. Were the newer versions that came from elsewhere, were they bigger and more aggressive?

B. They were darker in their skin and they were standing more upright. The other ones walked more on four, whereas the other ones, physically, were more upright on back. More like the Rex.

D. More like a carnivore?

B. Indeed. They had a different brain. We probably need to ask Ophelia about this, or someone who is willing to talk, because Old

Sniffer was there, and he now tells me. But at the moment, the only thing that Jeshua said, when I was with you, was that we're gonna go back in time and we're gonna discover certain anomalies and how modifications within the mammals were made. Something about putting like chips in them. Jeshua said implants, he was talking about implants. So there are several things we're gonna go back and look at.

D. That's great to hear.

B. So, I wanted to come in quickly and just say hoodaly-do, and so forth. You know, like I still have certain things on my own, even though it takes a lot of time to be with Old Sniffer. He has so many interesting stories, and I'm in that phase where I want to sit and listen to his stories. And now I know that there was not just Master Mind moving around, there was another intelligence. And he said that they came overnight, it appeared. Maybe they hatched in the cave overnight, because yes, indeed, those eggs, they were different.

D. They must have been, at one point, eliminated? Or are they still here, do you think?

B. Not the physical. The physical is not here. But the mind, he said that he can see certain behaviors that remind him of those.

D. In humans?

B. Ah, in humans. So he said that, in some way, the mind or the behavior is similar. There are certain activities going on that remind him of those beings.

D. Well, they probably just changed forms

B. Ah. Changed forms. So, you know, like I'm going to go now. But wanted to stop in and say whodaly-hoo, and happy birthday to you, to Dave you. (*The session was on my birthday.*)

D. Thank you! And thank you for being by my side all these years.

B. Ah, you are much welcome, because where you go, I go.

Bob: The Creation of the Fish Tanks (Jan 9, 2021)
This was one of the few times the origin of the fish tanks was brought up. At one time they did not exist, but grew as extensions out of the spiritual dimensions. The fifth dimension came later, after form and destinations had been established in fish tank five. Even though the fish tanks are structurally made from the first through forth dimensions, the higher dimensions also have a vibrational presence throughout the universes of form. Evolutionary cycles exist in everything made by the Creator. Within a fish tank, there are stages

that we can related to as seasons of the year. Hibernation is the depth of winter, and is a time where no matter or form exists. Bob describes that as a dream state prior to the emergence of new structures and manifested realities. He learned this when he met his Helmet Friend and takes a brief visit into fish tank three, where he experiences the dream of creation and intent. He points out that specialists enter the dream state of the fish tank to read and understand what the Creator intends. They then create scenarios based on the Creator's intent, which are planted like seeds. Those seeds will later manifest as a part of the realities of the fish tank when it wakes up from hibernation. For example, the sixth dimension would read the Creator's intent for a galaxy, and then prepare the pattern in a lab on the sixth. At the appropriate time and location, the pattern would be "planted" within the energetic soup of the third dimension, where it will grow into the desired material and form. Other dimensions participate in creating suns, atmospheres, gravity and life forms, all in accordance with the general intent of the Creator and guiding councils.

On a small scale, spirit guides do the same thing when humans dream. For example, when I fall asleep, Bob will follow my soul into the fourth dimension to protect my soul energy. Because of the population on Earth, the fourth is full of people dreaming at the same time. So he will flute away any energies that I should not encounter. Occasionally, he will watch a dream unfolding and plant ideas or images within the dream. All spirit guides try to communicate with their person in this way. At a certain level, people often understand the meaning of significant dreams. The majority of dreams are not divinely inspired. As Charles Dickens wrote in *The Christmas Carol*, they could be the result of "an undigested bit of beef, a blot of mustard, a crumb of cheese, a fragment of underdone potato." However, dreams that feel more compelling or thought-provoking should be given a bit more consideration in the morning.

B. You do seem to be working on something big with your friends. I haven't been invited to that gathering, but I know that when you come back and we meet, you're sort of very focused and concentrated. Sometimes even a little bit tired. It doesn't have to do with the Earth. Oh, you say you're about to wake up the fish tank three. That's what you say. (*Lasaray, who is always present at the sessions, sent him a thought-bubble.*)

D. Have you seen the dream?

B. You said that you ARE the dream when you work on it and that's why you're tired, because you become the dream. So you enter the dream, you say, in order for it to become. It's not like you look from above and just say, "There it dreams." You engage in the dream. It's like a play. It's almost like when you see the play on the Earth, but you move into the dream and you create scenarios, and you participate directly in the course of action of the dream. That's what you do. You merge. I can see you in there in the end of fish tank three. I don't see the beginning of fish tank three. I see the one closer to four.

D. I guess the universes, the fish tanks, have been around for a long, long time?

B. Ah. I asked. I wanted to know, "When did the fish tanks become? Who organized them? Why are they organized in this fashion—and why do they rotate?" I said, "If we go back, pre–me, pre–, pre–, pre–pre–, pre–, pre–me, was it the same? Was it always twelve boxes, twelve fish tanks? Did it change over time? Did one start, like, 'Oh, let's see with one'?" And you said it was not like that. You said that this disk had twelve, it's just that they expanded. They were small from the beginning, but in the course of time, you say, they expanded. So they gradually, one–by–one, little–by–little, they started to connect. And what I see now is that some are like (*he makes a sucking sound*) glued together, and some has a little bit of a gap between. You said, "In the beginning, there was vast space between. So when the disk was created, this disk, the fish tanks were there, but they were like seeds to become. And then gradually they expanded as events and occurrences took place. That's how they become. Everything is like that," you say. "It begins from small and it expands. Just think of a human," you say. "Mind being small, it expands, it grows in potential."

D. Okay. That's a good description.

B. It expands from the intent. So we have boxes, and it would be indicating like twelve different intents. But in the beginning, they were probably like intent seeds. Maybe I'm an intent seed? Everything is an intent seed, you say. So then I thought, you know, I'm like a fish tank. I'm expanding in my awareness. But fish tank number three is about to become and it's about to expand.

D. I guess the spiritual dimensions also would have expanded?

B. They come closer to the fish tanks, meaning the spiritual realities versus form. When I say form, it doesn't mean that it's a solid rock. Like a mental reality is also form, because a thought is the same as a rock. It's like it goes in and out, like, from the Pole, in and out gradually, like that. (*Bob made motions like he was playing an accordion, in and out.*) So it started like very close with the seeds, and the seeds were almost in the spiritual center. And then it expanded like that. Everything grew from the core outwards. (*He made a gesture like a balloon expanding.*) Then the fish tanks become like that, like constant expansion. But in the beginning, it's going like this, like a jellyfish.

D. I remember that Ophelia said that it was still kind of like a jellyfish.

B. Ah. Certain fish tanks are more like a jellyfish than others. And they feel good about that, because they're moving more into the spiritual reality. Fish tank five is more static. It doesn't move back and forth in the same way, it seems. But fish tank two, they move more inwards. Okay, I'm going to go.

D. Alright. Well, thank you so much. That was a really good talk today.

B. Okay. See you at home. Bye bye.

Ophelia, Bob: Celestial Astrology (Jan 27, 2021)

This is a perfect example of how the title does not capture all the topics in the section. Bob begins by telling us about a new class he is attending on the sixth dimension with three other students. They are studying how the changing alignment of celestial bodies affects the perception of humans. As different energies flow into Earth, it influences the way people interpret their surroundings. Because everyone has an inner map, it does not affect everyone in the same way. He then makes an important observation that miscarriages are often a result of the time of birth not being optimal for the incoming soul. The soul and its guides can make the choice to leave before birth, but once born, souls do not have the right to terminate their union with the body. Near the end of his talk, Bob outlined the relationship of solar systems to the grid within the galaxies.

Ophelia came in first with some guidance about the path ahead for our work. We are publishing some of her advisements because she said we should expect a group of aliens to communicate with us. It was a full year before the Visitors from the Past finally got a chance to speak. We presented their January 15, 2022 earlier in this *Wave 4*, so they have already been introduced. However, Ophelia's foreshadowing reveals how much planning is behind each session. From the perspective of the councils and Ophelia, every topic is a nontrivial piece in the unabridged story of creation, which they want us to know.

O. [...] There are new entities—perhaps fifty-fifty spiritual, fifty-fifty physical, some relates more to the mental capacity—and they are ready to move in. The information, the supply radiating from these zones, will be less warm than you are used to. It will be more choppy and you will have to connect information, puzzle pieces. We will always be present, as well as the Little Friend, of course, to warm up the topic a little bit for you. But those who come in, welcome them, even though they might feel odd and they might feel, from a human standpoint, out of place. They are not. They were here before and around the time of the dinosaurs, and are interested in telling about the project of these big mammals and prehistoric times when there were different events taking place. Some highly evolved, some less. Technology will be something that will be conveyed in this information, but it might appear choppy. Meaning, you will not be given the big picture. You will have to create the picture. [...] Just know that there is a different zone, different entity, a fifty-fifty spiritual versus mental realm, physical reality that is ready for entrance. (*Ophelia was talking about the Visitors from the Past.*)

D. Are they from this fish tank?

O. No. (*She laughed a little.*) No, they belong in the ninth fish tank. Eighth and ninth, travel between. Friends to the Tallocks, so you have, in some way, made a connection. But the other ones are, from a human standpoint, robotic, choppy in the way they communicate. Listen to them. They are your friends.

D. Is this the next stage of what we are going to be taught?

O. Yes. You're moving a little bit away from the human—the human would like to just reside in the comfort of an angelic reality. However, the two of you are more comfortable with more structure, more logic, less warmth, higher intelligence. From a human standpoint, it is experienced as less warm. From your soul self, it is not. Try to see these friends from your inner self. Know that you are similar, you are just dressed up in a human form among others.

D. I understand, from what you have said over the years, there are different entities here, who are not from the fifth, that are occupying human bodies—such as the Elahim?

O. Yes, but you (*Elahims*) are not great in numbers. You are spread out. And normally, that is how it is organized. It is not common for the two of you to join. Sometimes you help each other, being parents. A parent isn't there, necessarily, for the whole lifetime.

But it raises and provides comfort for the journey. What I would like to say is to simply be in the mindset that you are welcoming, always, new friends. And even though they might appear different, everything is set beforehand, before coming here. The two of you are the receivers to establish this information. Similar as creating a satellite, this is how the two of you operate. You are a satellite for us to navigate and transmit our message. One through the word, one in writing. The two of you together will need more solitude, as you are embarking on new territory which is less common, even for a spiritual community. They might not fully understand the connection that the two of you have. Meaning sometimes it will be a conflict for the human mind to embrace these energies that are perceived as less warm. A higher intelligence is creating a cell memory within the human consciousness that creates fear. Unfortunately, there is a history where entities coming into this plane did not embrace the earthly laws, the cosmic agenda radiating and surrounding this plane. This has created somewhat of a fear within the human consciousness. So, when a soul travels in, there is still this memory connected to fear of what is a foreigner. You can see it similar as a foreigner from another country, it is the same thing. You have somewhat of a leftover (*memory*) of what is not familiar to you, to be at a distance. Just know that there are friends coming in, and this one will start to feel their presence. She did so in 2010 and 2011, did not fully understand. Isaac is moving in more, presently, to this one's vicinity, making sure that she doesn't reject these newcomers. They are friends. They just appear, from the human standpoint, somewhat odd. I wish we could have put wings on them. It might have been more angelic. Hmmhmm.

D. Are they from Vlac, or somewhere else?

O. They operate sometimes on Vlac, but they don't have Vlac as their home. But they operate in the same family as the Tallocks.

D. Very good. I look forward to their arrival. Did you have any specific advice to share with either one of us?

O. Just be happy to allow this journey to unfold, to rest assured that you are taken care of. [...]

D. Well, Ophelia, it's always a pleasure to hear you.

O. Someone is dragging my arm. I could have continued.

D. I always feel so comforted by your presence and your words.

O. We are here to assist you. We are here to bring you the comfort that you, as a human, tend to need. You, as a soul, simply need to reside within, and the voice to your home, to us, is there. But sometimes, in the midst of everything going on in human energetic realities, that creates a disconnect to that voice. That is why we seek (*instruct*) man to find peace in nature. Nature doesn't rumble in that sense, making man deaf. As you move further into your soul—yes, Bob, you could have said this. I'm moving into someone's territory. Anyway, I wanted to say that you are guided moving forward, and there are gifts along the way.

D. Thank you, Ophelia. (*Bob immediately took over.*)

B. Ahh. Oh, Ophelia came today.

D. Hello, Bob. I guess she always comes.

B. Well, she's always present, of course. Always present. And I'm happy about that, because when she talks, I get to listen because she doesn't muffle my ears anymore. SO! I have been taking classes up on the sixth. I have been given new mentors. One is actually Nealon, who, lo and behold, actually had knowledge from the Astrological Council. I did not know that, but he's actually a great astronomer and also astrologer, connected to Earth. He had great knowledge in what a human would consider astrology.

D. You have a new friend!

B. I got new friends. First, I was extremely excited. I thought it was gonna become like a partnership, like you and I, but it did not turn out like that. I was placed in a group of three. It's been a while since I was in a classroom with others. They were from the sixth, and I was placed in this little group. I was treated as an equal, which was kinda nice, but it's been a while since I was not the sole student, like I am with you. So I had to adapt. There's been a lot of homework in my study, and it's also been a while since I was given homework, in that sense.

D. What sort of homework?

B. It's astronomy. It's more to understand the connecting work between galaxies and why they are where they are. I'm getting a little bit of a preview of how someone, or Jeshua, was pondering when he created my solar system environment. Like, it has to be a match. And I'm given a little bit of a teaching here on how solar systems coexist within a galaxy and also how the galaxies are interconnecting within. It's like, you have a solar system and the solar system is in a galaxy with several other solar systems that somewhat resonate similarly, having the same melody. But then the galaxies, they also dock and they merge. And this was part of my homework. I'm supposed to come up with ideas on how to, at best, create a galaxy reality. It's like, within each fish tank there are galaxy families. Your Milky Way belongs in a galaxy family, and they resonate similar. All the way from the big one all the way down to the Solar System, creating for humans the conditions on when to be born, and so forth. It's a great science and I'm in that science class.

D. I would think that is extremely complicated.

B. It is complicated, indeed.

D. Maybe you can share some of your learning, at some point?

B. At some point, when I'm more in-phase with my training and my understanding. When I understand, then I can tell you, so you understand.

D. That sounds fair.

B. Anyway, when we are talking about the Astrological Council and when the soul is being born (*in a human*), it's quite interesting to see the amount of effort that this council takes into consideration when each soul is born. It's not like you just drop them down. And sometimes, one should know, that when there is a miscarriage going on somewhere, it can actually be that the conditions were not ultimate and it wouldn't have worked out from the intent that soul had. So, a soul, normally combined with a spirit helper, can make that decision. Sometimes when there is a miscarriage, that can indicate that the dropdown wasn't following the intended plan.

D. Huh. I know there must be a huge amount of coordination involved in putting souls into bodies.

B. Ah. It's a big coordination, not only to make sure that the parents are suitable, but that they are connected to their astrological cycle as well. So there are, in this case—normally with the mother and the soul coming in—there is this merging point that needs to be exact. And when they sometimes don't interact accordingly, there can be a miscarriage. Then the soul tries again and comes down again. And sometimes, a soul might try to come down with the same mother again, but the mother might have been traumatized, so then the soul will have to come down in a different body, maybe that the mother will meet it as a friend later on in life, and the soul will impact the mission through a non-family unit or bond, but still the mission can take place, just in a different way. So there are all these strings that are connected between souls. But sometimes, they say, especially when there has been a miscarriage, the soul in the mother can sometimes become paralyzed with grief and not be suitable for that soul to merge into that place again. And then the soul comes down, let's say, in the sister to the mother, so it will still have an impact and the lesson will still take place, just differently.

D. And the objective of all this is to help people unfold their Coat of Karma?

B. Indeed. But sometimes a human experience can create like a fog, like a numbness, over the Coat and the intent. So, let's say that the soul came down and it didn't work accordingly for that touchdown, so the soul decides to step back. Meaning, it becomes a miscarriage. The soul in the mother might be traumatized and clouded from the experience. And when that happens, the soul will try to intervene and help the mother soul by just coming in, in a different configuration. And if it doesn't work at all, then they might do it next time around.

D. I guess part of the lesson would be about dealing with grief and seeing it from a more spiritual perspective?

B. Ah. Ah, dealing with grief. A big part of the Coat of Karma is how you deal with grief. And here, I'm learning about the first kind of grief, which would indicate miscarriage, for instance. There are different kinds of grief when someone leaves for the spirit realm early. And here we talk about grief when it comes to departure, but there is also the kind of grief when one feels misplaced. There are a lot of people feeling misplaced, and maybe they would hope they could be like a miscarriage and go home. But you wouldn't want to say that, necessarily. But a lot of souls at this time are calling the spirit realm to go home. And these are the younger souls, because they don't want to address numbness and grief. So they are calling from within to be called home early, knowing that is an option if something is wrong. Like in the scenario of a miscarriage. But once you are born, you can't claim that anymore. You can't claim that you want to come home and be a miscarriage anymore. Now you have to deal with it. And this is what they say. But a lot of new souls are asking, because they do know that they can be called home early if the conditions are not as suitable. But the soul doesn't understand what is suitable, it is the councils who do. So I'm looking into that a little bit, on how to navigate among the perception of that everything is wrong, like, "Ohh, ohh. I'm misplaced!" And we say, "No, you're not misplaced. You can't play that card any more. Now you have to deal with it, you have to create your place." A lot of people don't know how to create their place, they just sort of shout from within, "I'm misplaced! I'm misplaced!", like you're drowning, like you don't know how to swim. "Oh, I'm drowning! I'm drowning!" "No, you can swim. You just have to use your arms, you don't just use your feet. You have to use your arms as well." So there are a lot of those, at this time, who wants to be called home and come down at a later time. BUT what the Astrological Council is saying here is that the energy at this time is speeding up certain life lessons. Especially last year and, moving forward, there are contradicting energies. And this is provided by Jupiter and Saturn—very different energies. A lot of souls, especially those from the fifth, they just want to be in the Jupiter energy. They don't really want to be addressing the Saturn lessons. So, at this time, because the Saturn lessons are very strong on man—meaning authorities and a little bit of responsibilities and restrictions. Restrictions meaning that you cannot move that far. So the souls are calling out, "Ohh, I can't swim! I can't breathe!" And then the spirit realm, they don't just call people home, like, "Okay, you don't feel like you belong, I'll just take you home." Spirit guides are kinda pushing them back. And there are those—and this is tricky to talk about for a human—but those who try to make suicide, there is a great effort right now, where spirit guides are putting in a great effort for people to not end lives, just because they think they can't swim!

D. I know there are a lot of suicides now, especially among young people.

B. And that's not how you're supposed to solve, because you just postpone life lessons. So there are certain things that sometimes people forget.

D. So the effect on humans, astrologically, is something you are studying with Nealon?

B. Ah. I have my little model here, and he said, "Put Lasaray in the middle." And I put Lasaray in the middle. And then he said, "Now start motion in the Solar System." (*Bob had a model of our Solar System that he could set to any desired time, in order to see the energetic influences on my past lives.*) And I can see how the planets start to move. I have you here in the center of this little model, so I can see like, "Oh, here is happy," like spring. There is sunshine, there are flowers—and when I say springtime, I'm not talking just about the seasons, I'm talking about your perception of life. I can see that. Then I can see where clouds come in, so I know, "Okay, here comes something that is gonna be somewhat of a lesson." Then I can see how these planets interact, with you in the middle.

D. I'm not still being subjected to lessons, am I?

B. No, but this is like an experiment. So you should be fine with whatever forecast I'll put on you.

D. (*Laughing.*) Are the primary influences coming from within the Solar System, or does it reach beyond that?

B. If you have a Coat, then it's mainly from the Solar System. Those who do not have a Coat—and this is something we need to take into consideration, since you don't have a Coat—you are actually influenced by the galaxy that you reside in. So I'm looking into the influences from outside the Solar System. It sounds like a merry-go-round, like la-la-lala-lala-la. And then I see that a lot of people are affected by what's going on in this little merry-go-round thing. Those who do not have a Coat, they are affected by what's going on outside (*the Solar System*) because you sense and you hear the music in the web and the web of the galaxy.

D. That's fascinating.

B. Ah. So, I've been in training. I was given a pile of books, so I'm having homework.

D. Where do you study when you're doing your homework?

B. I'm just down the hall from your office.

D. Do you study in a group or by yourself?

B. Nay, I'm in this little group. We are three, and they are from the sixth. But they've been here for a while, so I'm new into this little unit group. They have proceeded a little bit longer, so they have already been given each a galaxy. I'm learning about the Solar System at the moment, just making sure that you are born when you're supposed to, and to see what the general intent is. And then I wanted to know, "Who decides the speed and everything going on with the planets? Who decides the general intent and rotation? And why do they go retrograde? What's that all about, and who decides that?" Because there are clearly effects going on. So there is someone sitting and deciding this. It's not the Astrological Council. It goes higher up, because there is an energy behind them that I could sense, but I could not see them. And there is someone, like a higher mind, if you like, behind the whole intent of the rotation. I don't feel like it's a council, it feels like one big—you know how I saw that one Big Eye?

D. Yes. Maybe it's like the Creator itself looking through.

B. It's similar. Both you and Jeshua said that there is like an extension—like the Master Mind actually manifests in several different ways. The Big Eye is actually the Master Mind, in one manifested form. The Master Mind is like a chameleon, depending on what it is investigating. It's like the Creator transforms into whatever entity it wants to be, in what way it is suitable. So when I saw the Big Eye, that was the Master Mind. I mean, I saw it as a Master Eye, but it was an extension of the Creator. It clearly wanted to look at something.

D. Huh. Another twist of complexity for me.

B. Anyway, I wanted you to come, but you said that you had engagements elsewhere. So that's why I'm here now. I'm gonna be here for a while, you say. So I was like, "Where are you gonna be?" And you said there is a galaxy suffering trauma, you say. I don't think I'm gonna get that galaxy (*to study*), I don't want to have someone who is traumatized. I want a happy galaxy.

D. When you see the galaxies, do you read them energetically? Can you tell, just by gazing at them, what kind of condition they are in, and what level of vibration?

B. Ah. Ah. Andromeda, it seems like they've been doing work on that one, because it looks more radiating. It's more glowing, it's more solid, it's more dense. Whereas the Milky Way is tilting. The other one is horizontal, whereas the Milky Way looks like it's tilting, like a ski slope. So someone needs to lift it up a little bit. That's how I see it; I don't know what it means. It seems like the Andromeda project is further along.

D. That's what the others have said, that it's in a more advanced state.

B. The borders around Andromeda, the galaxy, is also more established. The other one is more in motion and doesn't seem to be holding on together fully. And he said, my friend here on the right who has that galaxy, "It's not a problem. We just need to rewire it." Huhuh! And I said, "Rewire?", and he said, "We just need to rewire certain things, and then it will be lifted up and the borders will be more solid. Then it will look exactly like Andromeda." Huh. And I said, "What are you rewiring?" And he said, "Mostly we look into the suns, all the suns, because they are the stabilizers for the whole experience to be in balance." And I said, "I know also something about stabilizers. I know about Uranus." And he said, "Oh, okay. You're on that level. Uranus, yes, I remember. It's the same, but then they get bigger." And I said, "I have a stabilizer in my system. I created a system, you know. I also have a system."

D. You do have experience.

B. (*Looking pleased.*) I do have experience. So I said, "So, when you rewire—" And he (*Bob's classmate*) said, "Yes. We connect and we recharge by connecting stars and stabilizers. Because the star in each system is also a stabilizer. It's the one that makes the whole thing rotate and go into motion. So it doesn't wobble," he said, "you use a planet like Uranus. First, you make sure the suns are connected correctly, so the rotation is going correctly. And then when all the systems within the galaxy are within a suitable motion, we activate the stabilizers, meaning all the different Uranus's. And that's how the system lifts up and becomes like a less wobbling ocean."

D. That's really complicated.

B. Ah. So he's rewiring the Milky Way at the moment because, he said, that there is not functioning rotations among the interior designs, meaning the interior solar systems, like the Solar System here where humans are. He said, "It's like having a bug in the computer, like a virus in the computer." That's what he said. So when we reconnect the galaxy it is about—he made it so I can understand—he said, "We're sort of maintaining the firewall in the general computer. But," he said, "the Solar System where Earth is, is considered at the moment as a virus in the general system." There are others who are tending to that, while he is doing the general maintenance with rewiring, at the moment," he says. He said that you will understand this. So I'm just repeating, really.

D. I do follow that logic, but that is all. I am curious, are most of the suns electrical in nature, or what we would perceive as electrical?

B. They're static. You mean electricity, in some way, like you will get a shock if you touch it?

D. I sometimes think that people have a misunderstanding of the nature of suns and the energy that feeds the suns.

B. Well, the energy that feeds the Sun is a little teeny, tiny intention spark in the middle that comes from the great design. So when they try to establish this virus that they want to isolate, meaning the Solar System where Earth is, they look into the Sun and the core of the Sun and try to modify the general core. I see what they do. And they also replace certain suns with something else. He says sometimes they're non-functional. So I said, "Who decides that?" And he said, "The one behind the door!" Huh huh huh! He knew that I had been down the hall! He said, "We all watched you go. It's the ones behind the door!" (*When Bob comes to lab on the sixth, he is not able to go to certain areas. He left class to look for*

Nealon, their instructor, and encountered the 'fog door,' which he is very curious about.)

D. I guess they didn't go in either?

B. Nay! He said, "We saw where you were heading." So anyway, I'm gonna continue my class. Nealon is back and I'm gonna listen to what he has to share; he has summoned the class. I'm gonna be given my assignment. Of these two, the one with the Milky Way, he's a little bit friendlier. He's a little bit more sharing. The other one is more silent. He seems proud of his project.

D. I hope you get a good one. It's going to be interesting to hear what Nealon says.

B. Ah. Apparently, I'm going to learn about how to isolate the virus. Meaning, when you find something that is affecting the whole unit, meaning the galaxy, how you isolate it and how you work on it in order for the rewiring to take place properly. He said that I'm going to be working with that first, before I take on a galaxy. Makes sense.

D. It does. I have a question though. Since the Solar System is considered to have a virus, is that caused by humans or soul activity on Earth? Or is it from something else?

B. Nay. It's not so much human activity, it seems. Well, the human activity, when it comes to excavating certain fossil fuel and so forth and not being mindful of your environment, that has an effect. But it has nothing to do with if you're not friends with your neighbor or anything like that. But what you do with factories and the environment, that has a huge effect. I'm supposed to be more listening to the Fork, because the Fork tells the story. Everything is programmed within the Fork, so you learn how to tap into that. Once you tap into the Fork, you can start to maintain. And each planet has a Fork, so that is how you know what to do, you say. I'm feeling like I'm gonna look into those boxes on the poles because they have programmed and stored and registered all activity *(from the Fork)*. So I'm probably gonna be in that sort of excavation group to go pick up boxes, I'm thinking. I'm really excited to be helpful here, and to make somewhat of a mark.

D. They showed you the boxes a long time ago, so there must have been a reason for it.

B. I'm mostly intrigued about the North Pole. The South Pole is more like a decoy, like, "Oh, look over here! Here I am!" That's to make sure that no one looks over there. But I see! I know what's up there. And Ari has shown no interest in the South Pole, only in the North

Pole. Then I'm thinking, if Ari is interested and you're interested in the North Pole, that's where, clearly, I'm gonna go.

D. I'm sure you'll share when you know a little bit more.

B. Until then, you can share when you know!

D. If I ever come back from where I went.

B. Ah. You went somewhere with a trauma, you say. I don't know who has suffered trauma, but it didn't seem to be here. Somewhat of a collision, you say.

D. A collision between galaxies?

B. A collision. And when there is a collision, there is somewhat of a cosmic trauma. And then I got concerned, you know, collision, I heard that word. And then I was like, "What about MY solar system?" You and Nealon said that the borders around my solar system area is like a big bumper. So there's not gonna be a problem. You know those cars in a tivoli (*amusement park*) that just bump into each other? If someone were to come close to my solar system, you say, it's similar to those bumper cars that bump and go out.

D. (*Laughing.*) Yes, bumper cars.

B. Ah. Okay. I'm gonna go now. I just wanted to stop and just tell you where I am. If you ever wonder where I am, I'm just down the hall.

Setalay: Finding Joy (Mar 7, 2021)
Setalay is a seventh dimension entity who lives on Etena, after completing her incarnation program on Earth. She and Ophelia are both Shea, as we have described in most of our previous books. They have similar energy, which is calming and compassionate, yet quite powerful. Setalay is the one who takes care of Lasaray's pet, Siah, and his companion, Tess. Tess was recreated by Bob as a gift to Siah. (See *Notes, Volume 2*.) Setalay came in first during this session and gave some lovely advice about finding joy in your life as a key to finding your light.

S. This is Setalay.

D. Hello, Setalay.

S. I'm here to tell you that your friend Siah is doing alright. He is playful again as he has his companion (*Tess*) once more and he is connecting and docking. And we are delighted to say that there are probably little ones on the way. We have observed the activity in Tess, and the amount of solitude the two of them have been engaging in. I also want to tell you about the storage, where we have the infinite capacity of storing information from other celestial bodies. Your Little Friend came and visited once and did not get that far. However, the intent of the storage is to be of help when there are celestial bodies in need or in distress, such as your planet at this time. The planet itself is feeling fine. It is getting its strength back. The species, however, is feeling the same sadness, entrapment, that your planet did before you. So, we are simply engaging and increasing the aid for your planet. We are grateful for the decrease of travel, as we see the pollution is starting to become less of a bother for people. What we are concerned about, however, is the lack of connection within your race, as you are again dividing yourself. We see the cause, of course. Because of being trapped within government rules—and that is nothing we support. We encourage you, as a race, to find the light that connects you. And to see beyond the veil of a few, to not be discouraged by information that is flying around you (*which is*) not necessarily true. When you are in that vicinity of disorder and illusions not benefiting your being, it is wise to take a step back and find your own solitude. (*She paused and looked to the left, towards Bob.*) I see you. I saw you before, as well. (*She turned back.*) My friend Ophelia is here with the Little One. The message, however, from Etena, is to find the common joy within your life; to gather around that sense of happiness. Whether it is a hobby, whether a task, a person or an animal, just find something to gather your mind around, because that is light. Once you find that cause of happiness, you just, in your mind, embrace that happiness, embrace that animal, hobby, or whatever makes your heart sing, and that will increase your light. It is hard for some to be in the mindset of finding their soul or finding a light. They, in some way, equate it to a lamp or a candle, but it is simply to find your happiness—that is light. And once you find it, imagine that you embrace it, and it will become you. You will become the happiness; you will become the light. That is the first step of disconnecting from what is going on. Find your source of joy. That is YOUR light. Each light is different. When you say "find your light", people become disoriented by that sentence alone. But when you say, "Find whatever makes you happy." Perhaps it is singing. Perhaps it is doing puzzles. It does not matter, it is the joy, it is the light, it is the love for something that you love that will give you the love in return. That is how you find your light and disconnect from disorder. So, just wanted to pop by and give you the advice from Etena.

D. Wow. Beautiful. Thank you for that.

Bob: Helmet Friend at the Store (Mar 7, 2021)

In this story, Bob talks about a trip to the store on Etena. When Bob travels to Etena, he is in a manifested form, as is everyone else he encounters. Lasaray and Bob met another entity from the sixth dimension, and he is with a younger peer who is wearing a helmet. In the case of his new friend, the helmet seems to be a physical device that enhances his senses so he can read the dream in fish tank three. Bob extrapolates the concept of the helmet to energetic changes that either improve or suppress perception. In his example, the filters that were placed between the incarnating soul and the human physical mind before 3000 BC are like a helmet that acts to muffle signals sent by the soul, which is the opposite of how it worked on his Helmet Friend.

Later in his talk, he mentions the pyramid on Etena where all memories and patterns from all creation in all the fish tanks are stored. As Setalay revealed, it has infinite storage capacity. Bob described it as a museum. If someone sees a lifeform they like in the museum, they can go to the 'store' and get the energetic pattern that matches the destination where it is intended to go. The pattern is then submitted to the various working councils on the fifth, sixth, seventh or eighth, who evaluate it and, if approved, load the manual into the cloud. Bob said the manuals from the cloud were used by those on the second dimension to create or modify DNA and make a new lifeform (See *Wave 1*). Obviously, this is a simplistic way of explaining creation, but the beauty is that we understand it very well, which is their goal.

B. I want to tell you that I have been, once more, to the store. We are collecting seeds.

D. Seeds?

B. Seeds. I already have, of course, the intent of my plant. It's in my manual already. But I'm wanting to create somewhat of a surrounding around my plant, so I'm looking into vegetation. Some will be for disguise, to hide my plant. And I also had a little bit of an agenda to go to the store. The public agenda was to find seeds. The hidden agenda was to go and look at the individuals in the store, and to also go down the different aisles, because I could see that there were some interesting developments going on down one aisle.

D. So you were curious about looking at the other shoppers?

B. I'm curious about the shoppers, because NONE looks like me. There are some that looks like you, but they also go with someone, like their person, a friend. (*Bob means they are in pairs, a mentor with an apprentice.*) I'm looking and I see someone looking like you and I'm wondering, "Should we go over there and just make new friends?" And you said, "That's not really what you do at the store. People are here to go shopping." I said, "Well, it's sort of a good opportunity, I feel, to make new friends and just pass information back and forth. Maybe someone is interested in ME?"

D. So did you encounter anyone?

B. We did meet another of your companions that you knew, that was there with his friend.

D. What did his friend look like? Was he also from the sixth, or somewhere else?

B. Noo! No, not from the sixth. Outside, he was a little bit round. Inside, he was like a little computer. It was like it remembered everything—but he talked oddly. So you talked with your friend and I tried to talk to his friend. But it felt like he was reading me. I could feel, when he looked into my eyes—I say he, I'm not sure, but it felt like he—and he downloaded ALL my travels! Everything that I have gathered over my travels, he just looked at me and instantly (*Bob made a slurping sound*) sucked it all out!

D. That's sort of invasive, isn't it?

B. Well, it wasn't mean. But he just looked at me and could read my whole experience. I don't know where he belongs. But he was a little bit more manifested. It felt more like a visitor, like he came from one of the fish tanks. But he instantly knew everything about me. I did not know anything about him. I had to ask, "Where are you from, little spirit?" Ohh! (*Bob was given the information.*) That's why he had that skill set! He is working on fish tank three! He's working with the sleep. He said—well, he did not say to me. He said to his person—to you—to me, apparently, that he had added somewhat of a layer in his brain, like a helmet, that made it possible for him to read my mind. Because that's what he does in fish tank three. He reads the dream! You said, "He is on a special assignment. You can see that he is a little bit different. He just came to shop, but he belongs now in a manifest form in fish tank three. He has that on—like a little helmet." It's not a helmet that you can see. It's an energetic addition to the brain. It is an energetic helmet added to his brain that connects his original soul mind to the fish tank three mind." Depending on where you travel, that helmet brain is what you get. So when you go to fish tank five, or to Earth, there is a specific energetic helmet that you get. In this case (*as a human*), it numbs. So you don't have the opportunity like before when the helmet was different. Meaning the species on Earth before could communicate telepathically. Now there is a different energetic helmet when you get here, so you cannot. But his helmet is to read the whole fish tank, to read fish tank three. So his helmet merges with his soul mind. He said that, "When I go there, I transform my energy. But it's not like it is transforming my soul being. It's mainly my soul mind. So I numb my mind a little bit, I make it passive, and I absorb the fish tank three mind (*that is*) available." He just hadn't taken off the helmet when he came to the store! When he saw me, he had the opportunity to read me, because everyone who is in fish tank three has the opportunity to read everything that is going on. They are creating something new and they have to be able to read the dream. So his helmet is different. But when a soul comes to Earth, it doesn't get that sort of helmet. I said, "Has this helmet EVER been on Earth or in fish tank five?" Then he said, "Fish tank five was also in hibernation at one time and also slept. So those who came there to kick–start fish tank five also had this sort of helmet—if they are engineers." What is his profession? (*Bob is pondering out loud what his Helmet Friend did.*) Creative Engineer of Evolution.

D. That's a nice title.

B. He asked for my title!

D. You're a Great Traveler! Which he knew when he read you.

B. Ah. We are in aisle 5. But he's heading to aisle 3, and you know why?

D. No.

B. Aisle 3, fish tank three. We met here in aisle 5. Fish tank five related. This is where I've been going back and forth—I shouldn't say back and forth, because I only took a few steps in. The aisle goes on for a long time, but it's not like I have full access and have fully explored aisle 5. So he was heading to aisle 3. And I said, "Why don't we all join? It seems like we're having a very good communication going on." But you said, "We're going to shop here in aisle 5."

D. Remember the seeds?

B. The seeds! I had already forgot about the seeds. I was just so excited about this new friend and the information that wherever you go, the soul mind is colored by the fish tank and you are added (*given*) an energetic helmet that mirrors the mind. When they had a lid on the consciousness on Earth, they changed that helmet, the energetic connection to the soul mind, so that it went down a little bit. It has nothing to do with the soul coming in and out. It's in the design of the manifested form that exists on Earth.

D. You read my mind! I was going to ask you that question. Is it part of the Coat, or is it part of the design of the human form?

B. The design. The Coat is more connected to prior visits and what you do, but the general mind and the general helmet is very different. His helmet, when he merged into that manifested form—which is kinda round! He said, "I'm not round, normally. I just came from fish tank three. We're just popping into the store and I'm gonna go right back. There was no need to dis–form." And I said, "I'm like this, but sometimes I have a peanut suit!" So I told about that. His peer, your friend, he smiles! I like him. He's taller than you.

D. Is he an Elahim, or someone from the sixth?

B. From the sixth. I said, "We're gonna make a flower soon. I'm creating a life for him (*Lasaray*), that's what I'm doing." Now I understand why Ophelia said I could not bump up the light in the brain, because the helmet would not allow it! Even if I had been pufft, pufft, pufft, trying to pump up and blow you up like a balloon, it would not have worked. There are limits. Ah, if I had done that about 30,000 years ago, it might have worked. This is what it is; the helmet is glued to the human mind. Before, it was more rhythmical, so you had the opportunity, with some exercise and some practice, to make it detached.

D. So you would be more able to communicate?

B. That's why some could merge to the fourth and get information. And some could communicate telepathically. And then some were like, "Huh? Fire?" So, that's why. So, now the energetic helmet—meaning the ability—it has to do with the communication. And when I say communication, it's not just about talking, it's about the information that you receive and send off. What I now see, what you show me, is that the energetic helmet on the current human, it's almost like a napkin attached, glued onto the brain. The soul mind hasn't the same ability (*as it once did*). That's why it's really hard for you to communicate telepathically. Some have little windows, like a déjà vu, when you kinda feel like, "Oh, something happened here." Or you communicate, "Oh, I think of you," and someone starts to have a hiccup over there and it's like, "Oh, you thought of me!" So there are a few little windows where man goes,

"Ohhh!" It's a memory. But in general, you say, the design at the moment is that it's not as flexible as before.

D. Is that what allows or limits the ability to communicate with the fourth dimension?

B. From fish tank five and Earth, yes.

D. So when you're on Earth, if the helmet were more flexible and opened up, that person could be communicating with the fourth?

B. Easier. And now it is a gap because the helmet has merged, it has sort of sunk in. The soul mind and the human become almost like one, because of this lid. (*The soul mind cannot communicate as easily with the physical mind, due to the filter.*)

D. That makes sense.

B. Ah. Makes sense. This is what I said—when you say there is no need to go to the store—clearly there is. And then they're off, and we're not. And now you said, "We're not going to talk with more people. Now we're just going to find our seed and then we're going to leave."

D. (*Laughing.*) So, when you travel back and forth to Etena now, can you just move there instantly?

B. Ah, instantly. But not by myself, though. I'll go with you, together. I think it's also because of the fact that you want to make sure that I come back, because I might set tent. There are so many interesting things to see—it's almost like Disneyland for someone like me.

D. Yes. All those pyramids you can go and investigate.

B. There are pyramids with storage. There are pyramids like with the museum where the gift store was. You don't go shop there, but you can go and have a look–see. That's why I said, "How would I know what to buy in the store, if I don't know what has existed or what is possible to exist? Or what is not suitable to exist?" It's like a storage of history. They have also fish tank three in there before fish tank three started to dream. That is now stored in there somewhere.

D. That would be amazing to go through the museum and see all the different realties that have existed.

B. Ah. So, ya' know, I got my seeds, or the pattern of the seeds. And now they didn't stare as much at the cashier. I just went right through. I could probably go shop for myself next time and you don't have to come. I said, "I probably can do this all by myself." And you said, "You would like that, wouldn't you?" Huh huh huh.

D. I had a question. The pyramid with the historical remains, can entities go in there to get patterns?

B. Oh, they get more insights. They don't take it from the pyramid. They study it, and then they go shop in the store.

D. And there are probably little modifications you have to do to get it to match the destination?

B. Ah, to get it to work. If someone were to come in here and just go shopping, undetectable, it might not work. Because you have to get the manual to make it cope and to make it work together and to connect. And if you don't have all the different aspects of the (*DNA*) map, then it's not gonna be a flower.

D. So when you get the actual pattern, who does the matching with the destination?

B. I do it by myself! If I was younger, I might not. But now I'm perfectly skilled to create a flower by myself. Sometimes I get help from Ia because Ia has more patience. And sometimes I get frustrated with details. It's actually a lot of detail work, so sometimes I ask Ia to come.

D. Well, she likes the DNA modification work.

B. Ah. When it comes to connecting DNA—I did take the class. It's not like I missed it or skipped it, it's just that I get impatient because they all look the same. But Ia says, "No it doesn't. It has a different ring to it, it has a different melody. If you listen to the little dots that you're connecting, the DNA dots and the strings, you will find that when you start to meddle and to connect, suddenly it's like, "Augh! Wrong melody!" And then, "Ah! Here we have a tune!" But that's the thing that takes time, or cycles. So sometimes I get Ia to do this. So, that's where we've been.

D. That was an interesting trip.

B. I'm pretty excited about this store, and I don't know why we didn't go earlier.

D. I'm sure there was a reason.

B. Not a reason that I understand. But this is where you went to get all the stuff for my solar system and my individual and my planet, and so forth. This is where you went to create the jars.

D. Oh, I remember. You said I had jars of material waiting for you when you came to the lab, and you didn't know where I got it.

B. You went to the store, but you didn't bring me. This is what you do when you're gonna go and patch up solar systems. You say, "We all shop here." It's like never ending. You should know that there are hundreds of meters in the aisles, and I only went in five or six steps—in aisle 5, I should add. I never even went to aisle 2, for the second dimension, I never even went there. Ole went. This is where they get stuff into the clouds, into the manuals.

D. Huh. Is that where the manuals are located?

B. The manuals are located in the pyramids, but how to make a manual and what to put in a manual in the cloud, exists in aisle 2.

D. That makes sense and it all ties together.

B. You would think so, wouldn't you? I am in, but I'm not so far in. If I stand here in my aisle 5, if I turn, I see the cashiers. (*He had twisted to the right and seemed to be peering in that direction.*) Right there. They're tall (*the shelves*), like 20 meters up. (*He leaned backwards and looked upwards through his closed eyelids while he studied his inner vision.*) I can't reach.

D. I guess you can't walk out with something undetected?

B. Oh, no one steals.

D. Or lies.

B. Or lies. You're not supposed to. It doesn't get you anywhere if you lie or steal. Even if no one catches you, YOU know. Anyway, I'm gonna go now. We're gonna leave the store, you say.

D. Alright. Thank you for describing all that. And, as always, it's a pleasure to hear your voice and learn what's going on.

B. Well, I've been around, of course. Things to see and learn. Okay, I'll go, but I'll be back. Okay, bye bye.

Bob: The Creator's Hand (Mar 22, 2021)

Parts of this session were the last entry in *Wave 3*. Bob's portion of the talk was saved for this *Wave 4*, because he gives some additional information about the cycles that begin and end with hibernation. In describing the Creator Disk, he also calls it a fog disk or the intention disk. The experiencing disk is what we have identified as the Wheel of Creation. The intention disk seems to be a mystery to all the spirits that we communicate with, since we are all part of the experiencing disk. Based on certain statements made in other sessions, it seems that the Creator Disk sends intentions up into the experiencing disk, where the spiritual dimensions can then read and interpret what the Creator's plan is at that location and "time". I readily admit that there is a grandeur and complexity that is hard to grasp, but this is a core element of the spiritual design. In the Preface, we included a simple drawing of how we interpret these layers. Later in this session, Bob's

Helmet Friend gives a very good summary of the process. On this grand scale, entire universes go through cycles where all matter is dissolved back into energy. The memories recorded since the previous hibernation are transmitted down to the Creator Disk. Then a new dream of intention is sent up into the experiencing disk. The spiritual councils read the dream and make scenarios and patterns that will manifest new structures within the formless state of hibernation. And thus begins a new cycle of creation.

After the session, Bob sent a thought bubble to Christine that the even numbered fish tanks are more aligned with emotional or female energy, while the odd numbers are more mental or structural.

B. Huh huh. Ah!

D. Hello, Bob.

B. So, I did have a travel card here. I was looking into certain things, and checking off the boxes where I've been. I do get intrigued about traveling to new places, now when I have a new friend, huhuh. So, we did go back to the store because I said that I forgot my basket! Huhuh. And you said, "You did not." I said, "Maybe I wanna go and see my friend again from fish tank three!" So, we did go back. And I stood in the same spot, just to make sure that if they come back that they maybe would see me.

D. Did they?

B. Ah. They came back. And I was like, "Oh! Here we are again!" I'm intrigued about this new friend of mine that I have. It's going better with the communication, even if it's not going great. But we—with your permission, probably—we were allowed to communicate more. And I'm quite fascinated about fish tank three. So we did have a meeting, and that's when I said, "Maybe you can sign off on fish tank three on my travel card?" I have five, four and I'm heading upwards to two with Tiddle, so we have three there in the middle. So I'm trying to begin to complete the circle here.

D. How else are you going to become a Wheel star?

B. How else? And number six, I have only sniffed on. So it doesn't seem like anyone is there. There is something peculiar going on, you should know, on fish tank twelve, three, six, and nine. They are like focal points in this Wheel. Number twelve is a big mystery—we do not talk about it. And when I say WE don't talk about it, that means that you do not give me any information.

D. I might not know.

B. But wouldn't you think that it would be easier for you to just say so then, that you do not know? BUT when you say that you don't know, I do tend to say, "Maybe we should ask Ari, or Jeshua? Someone must know." BUT there is something extremely interesting with the focal points. Meaning, twelve, three, six and nine. Three is asleep. Number six is about to become, so that one has already slept. And Seth did say, about the rotation, that it's not like the fish tanks are MOVING in the Wheel. They rotate over a disk that is established. The fish tanks rotate, so when I saw that, meaning that fish tank six, at one point, were positioned where fish tank three is at this time, sleeping. Meaning that fish tank five was where Tiddle is now. So it's like a solid disk, the Creator disk, that no one goes to. You said, "There's no need to ask about that, because no one goes, not even when you have dissolved!" But I said, "Someone must do maintenance, of some sort? Someone must tend to it?" And you said, "No, it's solid. It's established. It doesn't go anywhere." Oh! Then Ari came, and everyone came (*probably Ophelia, Isaac and Gergen*). I like when everyone sorta chips in when I have a question. You all said, "The established Wheel that is positioned, that is the intent of the whole experience. The rotation, when the fish tank travels over the intent, is that they come in contact with that intent of that position."

D. That makes a lot of sense.

B. AH! Ah–ha, ah–ha! So between all disks, there are intent disks, and then there are experiencing disks. And the spirit realm belongs in the experiencing disk. That didn't seem to go down either, as I see this. (*The spiritual dimensions are part of the Wheel.*) I see the fog disk, which is the intention of the Creator, holding that intention and holding that experience of that specific location. Whereas fish tanks are slowly moving like that, over. (*He held his right hand palm upwards, finger spread, and about 5 cm above, the left hand palm down, which he then slowly turned clockwise.*) And they move, actually what I see is that they seem to move clockwise. So I see this big Wheel, meaning that fish tank six at one point did sleep. I understand that the position on this intention disk at 3 o'clock, that is sleeping. So everyone who comes in contact with that specific location, geographically, sleeps!

D. What about fish tank five then, because that came across three later than six?

B. Ah! We do have four and five, and four is just brand new, popped out from its dream, so it operates perfectly. Whereas fish tank five, this is where it sort of... oh, I don't know. I don't know what happens when it comes to all these focal points, like now at number six. It's much brighter in number six; it's sort of dimmed in five. Oh, no one tells me. But what I can see here is the intention disk, and hovering above it is the experiencing disk. And that's where I am.

D. I guess the patterns in the intention disk don't change much, but it expresses differently as the fish tanks move above it?

B. No one knows about the intention disk. I asked Ophelia; I asked you; I asked Ari; I asked Gergen; and I tried to ask Ole—everyone knows it exists, but how it came there and what the purpose is, no one knows. I mean, the purpose is to experience. I find it interesting to know that the experiencing disk is rotating and that there are crucial focal points—twelve, three, six and nine.

D. And then the spiritual dimensions are also connected to the experiencing disk?

B. Indeed, indeed. But I can't see that the spirit realm merges down to the Intention Disk. So, everything that is experienced and where there is activity, whether it's in a spirit realm or whether it's in a fish tank, it all exists in that disk. The other one, it's just a fog.

D. Can you flash an image into this one's mind, so she can describe it?

B. Ah. This one sees. He said, "We know all about it." And I said, "Why didn't we talk about this?" He said, "Well, we are doing it now." But I have my travel card. And I said, "I have seen glimpses in fish tank six." But fish tank six is about to—it's almost like an explosion in there. It seems for some reason it's going clockwise. What I see is that it rotates. So once fish tank five is positioned over the position of 6 o'clock, there's gonna be much more light, like being reborn. Whereas, coming out from fish tank three to four, there's a huge gap from three to where I see Etena. Etena is extremely close to number five. But number five carries its own experiences. So just because number four will be positioned where five is currently, it doesn't mean that it will take on, exactly, the pattern and behavior of fish tank five. It just indicates that they are moving into a different level of experiences.

D. I know it's hard for humans to think in terms other than physical terms, but are the planets and the density of matter in fish tank four similar to fish tank five?

B. I can only see the border. If you see all the fish tanks being, let's say, 10 cm wide. If they are 10 cm wide, then they would be, let's say, about 15 to 20 cm long, from the edge into where the spirit realm begins. So they're more like a piece of cake. And fish tank four, I can only see 2 cm in from fish tank five. The other 8 cm of fish tank four is sort of hollow. I don't know what's there closer to number three, where the dream is. It doesn't seem to be much activity there.

D. So the fish tank doesn't all start experiencing the same thing at the same time? As a part moves across the Creator intent, different parts of the fish tank are activated separately?

B. It doesn't seem so. It depends on the geographic point on the below disk what it is there to experience. The below disk determines the experiences. And Ari said that it influences and it causes events that might be to teach that fish tank something. So that could indicate there are a lot of things going on. The below disk, that is the Creator. The pole simply holds the whole matrix, the whole design together. The fog disk is like the hand of the Creator, sending up its intention. The intention is, in some way, stationary, but also depends on behaviors that occur in that specific fish tank—even down to the smallest galaxy—is looked upon. It's almost like a hand holding it. This is how I see it now when I look at the fog. It's like a hand with twelve fingers, and in the palm is the pole; and above each fingertip is a fish tank. I can see like this (*extends his right hand out as if he is holding a large ball in his palm*). It's doing something, and I'm curious about this. And I'm quite fascinated about this hand, holding each disk.

D. I guess the Creator Disk gets feedback from the Master Mind on what the response is within the different universes in the experience disk?

B. Ah. So each fingertip on the hand, connected to a location, carries a certain experience. And when the fish tank comes in direct contact, certain things happen. But based on free will and choice and what goes on—it doesn't steer it, everything that goes on—it leaves the experience to BE an experience. But the finger reads. I can see it almost like this. (*He wiggles his fingers up and down to show the connection to the experience disk.*) It reads. Huhuh. It's big. I'm not sure I wanna go. I have revoked my interest to go to the hand. I'm not sure. But I can see the Big Eye. I'm not sure. What if I fall down here? I'm concerned. I remember also that you said you patched up holes. And then I wondered about those holes. If that is not patched up correctly, do I fall down in the hand? And then is it like a trash can? If things don't work, you just pop it into the holes, like a trash chute.

D. Ophelia was talking about sending entities back to the factory for reprogramming, so who knows?

B. I did ask about that. And that's not in the hand. The hand is clean, it's not a recycle station. But I was just concerned when you said that you had to patch up holes, because I do remember that we did see holes (*into parallel planes*) that looked like stars. So I said, "Could we potentially angle a hole, and instead of looking sideways, could we potentially look down and just see (*the Creator disk*)?" Ari said that I might not be ready for that yet. Maybe I should read on TripAdvisor about this place! Huhuh! It's not yet to be given whether I'm putting that in my travel card. I was still focusing, looking into this, but then you came and Ari came—and Zachariah, he talked about the factory. (*In 'Wave 1', Zachariah said that some souls are recalled for repair, like bad toasters.*) And then I wondered, "Is this the factory?" And Zachariah said, "No, it's not. No one goes." But I said, "Why do I see it, if no one goes?" Because, clearly, there will be questions if I see something. So I don't know why I and everyone else can see it.
D. It's good to pass on. Now that you've told me, I'll write it down.
B. Yes, you write it down, and then you solve it. I mean, we cannot expect that the human you will solve this. But when I ask Lasaray, he solves things all the time. I know that you solve things and you've patched up several galaxies. It's not like your first project! In general, it feels like, on so many levels, that it's busy, that there is a lot of things going on. Because I can see that Ole is running around, Gergen is sort of serious and running around, with a lot of tasks on his agenda. I asked Ole if he wanted help with anything. "Later, Bob," he said. And Ia, she's just singing.
D. Is she still taking care of the little ones?
B. Ah, the little ones. She's establishing songs in a new group. So there is a lot of singing going on at the same time. Like I said, it's not a time for rest, it's not a time where the spiritual realities are sleeping. It's high action and there are things going on.
D. So the little Helmet Friend from fish tank three, you said you met him again?
B. We, ah. I did not go by myself, so WE met. He talked about the dream and they are establishing the next phase. So he's deciphering—not by himself. There's a HUGE group of those, similar like him, that are operating this. It's like, first you download (*the accumulated experiences*). "Something has to die," he said. "It's similar to what I heard about humans dying. So, the fish tank and all its living life forms has to, in some way, die. Meaning, they just go blank. And in that blank phase is where data is taken out and

moved into a hibernation phase." He said that in the spiritual realms where he comes from, dying is considered an upgrade. "Here (*on Earth*), dying seems to be," he said, "connected to fear, instead of an upgrade. People think that being born is the peak, and the dying part is connected to an end. But," he said, "the birth part is quite primal, and the dying part is the good one, because that's when you have gathered all your knowledge. And that's when you leave off data and you move into a changed aspect of yourself."

D. So the fish tank is in a dream state, do you think, based on what they have said, that there is any matter there?

B. Energetic. I can see, in fish tank three, I can see all the objects, slowly moving. And it comes to a barrier. And that's when he said, "Here they died. It stopped. And then there is a light. So it's a quick transition. And there is a center in this fish tank three where they extract information. And the end phase of fish tank three is just the dream state."

D. If there are galaxies, what happens to them?

B. He said they are pulverized into the—when they dissect and extract data, it becomes pulverized, and that is later shooshed out in the end phase of fish tank three as a dream. And that is just merging, so all experiences merge. It doesn't become like an individual experience, like, "Okay, Earth did this, Mars did that," it's just gathered as they dissect one–by-one, pulverizing, moving it into the dream. And once in the dream, that's when they really read the intent and how to move forward. And so you have to understand, also, the position it's going TO.

D. So when it starts up again, what happens?

B. Because it is blended—that's why Etena, being close to fish tank five, operates very similar to an Earth reality. Whereas the beginning of fish tank four is very much mirrored by the dream. So the end, the last 30 percent from fish tank three, into about 50 percent into fish tank four are somewhat looking the same.

D. And then form gradually emerges from the dream?

B. From the dream. So similar like it was pulverized over there (*matter reverted back into light*), once it transitions and moves through the dream—with a little bit of help, or deciphering—it later becomes objects and goes. So that is the experience between three and four. It might not be the same experience, he says, when four goes to five in the rotation. I think that he is probably the guy that I should talk to because he seems to know about this rotation. You said that he is a friend from the sixth, he just has a different form.

D. Oh, so he is from the sixth?
B. He's from the sixth because he's an engineer. Every engineer comes from the sixth. Unless you are a different engineer when it comes to...
D. Atmosphere?
B. Ah, that's from the eighth. But he's like a cosmic engineer. Someone has taught him about the rotation (*of the experience Wheel*). And I said, "Who do you go to school with? Who is your teacher?" Anyway, it's quite fascinating, of course, for someone like me. So, I'm gonna go now, but I've been around a little bit, and I'm having my card here and we're looking into certain things.
D. I'm sure we'll go some more. Ophelia didn't seem to mind that you had a travel card you printed up yourself.
B. She said I printed it myself?
D. She said it wasn't originally part of your travel card.
B. Nay, nay. I'm just sort of helping evolution along a little bit. Sometimes I think that my evolution might come to a halt, and then I'm just sort of helping it along. HUHUH! And then you say, "But you don't know where you're heading." And that's when I said, "Well, if no one tells me, then maybe I create my own evolution." Like, I am my own creator. I just don't wanna fall down into the hand. And I don't want to go into the pole yet. I wonder if it's like an elevator—where do you go? We still haven't found anyone to ask and to talk to.
D. Then you would go into the dream.
B. That's a different dream. Who knows if you ever wake up. And if you do, what do wake up as? Are you spit out in a different dimension on a different disk?
D. Probably don't want to find out, at least right away.
B. (*Bob had looked left.*) Ophelia says, "No need to know." Ah. We'll see. I'm gonna go now, but I have indeed modified—well, it hasn't happened yet—but I have put in potential dots in my travel card. I'm saying that I might be interested in becoming like a dream engineer.
D. Right after you become a Wheel star?
B. Maybe first I become a dream engineer, and then I become a Wheel star. I said, "If I can understand the dreams, and I can understand the focal points—like three, six, nine, twelve—maybe that will just speed things along a little bit. You said that I would probably not be comfortable in certain locations.

D. I remember you said that some of the tones—
B. Are not suitable for my being, you say. It might make me feel dizzy, or it might make me feel nauseous. And I don't think that is what I want. Ohhh, okay. I go. See you. Bye bye.
D. Bye bye, my friend.

Ophelia, Bob: The Unwinding and Crystal Energy (May 3, 2021)
Ophelia, when she addresses a topic, gives a magnificent analysis that is both penetrating and gentle. Very early in our work, Ophelia talked about filters being added to the human, which muted the spiritual input. She says there are two paths that the mind and emotions can follow, one from a soul awareness, the other from the human ego, and they are intertwined like two strands of a rope. She foretells of the unwinding of the strands, and those who have followed the human or ego strand will no longer come to Earth.

Bob came in after Ophelia was done and talked about going to Etena, where he was invited to join a group lesson on ancient Earth history. He gives a very interesting description of the activities of visitors who were using light energy to create lasers to separate land masses. Manifested entities did this work under the direction of the councils. He mentions there were several types of crystal energies used by multiple alien and manifested civilizations in the past.

O. Oh, Bob, my sweet, dear friend. So eager to speak. So eager to be of assistance—as we all are. But he, in particular, has a great investment, one might say, in the direct speech that he delivers, and the communication. Yes. He pointed out that it is not just him speaking. It is the communication that he is intrigued by and sees as his greatest accomplishment so far. And indeed, he has been silently observing you for so many lifetimes that we understand his tremendous joy to be noticed and to be of real assistance, as you are now aware of his presence. He will, of course, have his moment in the sun, as always. Yet, I feel it's important for me to step in and simply provide a little knowledge for humanity. We wish this to be publicly announced. There are two paths ahead of humanity at this point. Two strings that have been intertwined, but now separates the race, the race of humans. Those have been connected and intertwined up to this point. See it as a rope that is opening up. The spirit realm has sought this opening for a long time. The intention is to separate the minds and the hearts. So, you will see, first, the mentally inclined trying, struggling a little bit more than the emotional, the empath, like you wish to call them. I would not say that the empaths are necessarily a true empath, always. It is a word that the human, the human ego, wishes to place on oneself. There is a difference between being spiritually intelligent and emotionally intelligent. Those who proclaim to be empaths, normally are human or ego directed. What we see now is a combat within your race, within yourselves on the direction one wishes to take, logic verses emotion. You have to drop the sense of the human intelligence, the human logic, the human emotion, in order for you to understand and direct the soul's intention. This is what we see and what we are asking for you to declare: that there is a human path, and a soul path. Both, in some way, have emotional and logic in its string, they are just driven by either the soul or the ego. At this time, unfortunately, due to the fears that have been placed upon humanity, most are in the human string. Those who are driven by the soul—and they are few in numbers, or less in number—are struggling, due to the fact that they (*feel they*) have a need to help those who are in the human experience. It is important to understand that you are not all here to help. You are here to clear a path for new incarnations. If you feel a need or a drive to assist those who are ego or human aware and are not carrying the soul awareness, please don't put it as your responsibility to assist them all. You are here mainly to create a new path for new souls, new incarnations. Those who are in the human string will not come back for a while. Have that in mind, and observe, simply, your own trail. What would you like your future self or your future children—your soul children, your spiritual children—to come down to? Believe and understand that one string will disappear. It doesn't mean that you will not be humans, but you will be different—warmer on the inside. At this time, there is a division in your race. Allow it to be so. You do not have, as humans, the full outline of the plan, the grand design, this new chapter in your history.

D. Is this something that is going to happen soon, in human time?

O. It's a gradual transition. Think of it as a 50 to 100–year cycle. It's a longer human cycle than you might be aware of. But know that there are, within 20 years, a big amount of those in the human string that will be removed naturally, and not return for a while. Don't feel the need to push your awareness on everyone. It doesn't mean that you should not raise your voice and your opinion. It simply means to hold your energy, to hold your light. You are creating a new path, a new development, if you like, for new incoming souls. That is your primary goal. Just see the other road, that it might be diverted elsewhere. Your intention should be how would you want your future self to be returned as (*or to*).

D. Is the gene therapy vaccine that they are pushing going to speed up the elimination?

O. Yes, yes. Unfortunately, that is the—it is a tool, indeed. Don't judge those who seek a quick entrance to the light, to freedom. They will access light and freedom. Just not here. They are not lost, they will simply access what they seek, elsewhere. There. Bob, don't push. (*She said that very gently towards her left.*) He is bringing a book. Apparently, there are some things that are missing in his notes.

D. When you said that there were two strings that were intertwined, that was the human ego and the spiritual?

O. Human and... simply see that the experiences here were intertwined as one. Now the rope is dissolving, opening up, becoming two strings, two threads from that same rope. Both are logic and emotion. Mental and emotion. Just one is related to the human understanding of that experience, versus the other, which is spiritual intelligence and spiritual emotions. They are just being separated. Before, they were more connected as one experience, and one could access the spiritual level of oneself easier, in some way. But the filter creates a division, making you take a stand, making you see the reality around you and within you in a different light. That is the filter coming in, it is for you to make decisions that might feel uncomfortable from a human standpoint. Those who simply seek—and this is also based on survival—those who feel that there is no continuation, they are locked in that reality, in that string. And it is meant for that string to be separated so the other string can grow in strength and power. It is like cutting off, in some way, a limb on the tree that is not alive anymore. There. I wanted that to be said. And I'm pretty sure that Bob has an opinion that he could have said it himself.

D. Is that something we should release in one of our books? Do you want it put out? Or is this more for us?

O. It is public information. We want this to be shared. Thank you.

D. Thank you, Ophelia.

O. Oh, you are much welcome. And indeed, we will leave the floor for our friend.

D. I did have a quick question. When we first started communicating, was it intended for Bob to become as involved?

O. As a frequent speaker?

D. Yes.

O. Perhaps not to the extent that it became. But he was claiming his space, and we saw the response. So the reaction and the level of joy that he provided increased his stage, built his stage. So it was not perhaps intended to be as frequent. But yet....

D. Have the general teachings changed from what you intended to talk about originally?

O. It follows a plan, a guideline. We simply have paused it a little bit, due to the change of direction in the human consciousness. It is simply going in a slower pace at the moment. The general outline is still the same.

D. And we'll have time to finish?

O. Yes. There is, what you call, time. There you go.

D. Well, thank you, Ophelia.

B. (*Bob came in a gave a long sigh.*) And finally, we have me. And I'm last, even if it doesn't seem to be somewhat of an order. Or the order seems to be that I'm always last. It's never changed.

D. Perhaps it is just holding the best for last.

B. Best for last. The grand finale! Like I said one time that I wanted to have you as my grand finale. And that became a HUGE success. So, if that is connected, like grand finale equals success, then I'm happy to be last. (*Bob is referring to a show–and–tell he did for the little sparkles on the second dimension. See the story in 'Teaching Tom' in Notes, Volume 1.*)

D. Did you hear my question to Ophelia?

B. Nay. I did not.

D. I just asked if it had originally been planned for you to be as involved as you are now.

B. I planned! Ohh, I planned. I made a plan. I made my own agenda.

D. Well, it seems to have been adopted.

B. Ya. I feel that it's important, because I've been with you for so many lifetimes. A lot of times you did not hear me. I mean, you did not HEAR me, but you heard me as you slept and I had night watch. So that's when you heard me. But I also wanted to be acknowledged to the greater community here on Earth.

D. Well, we're happy that you're involved and here with us almost every time we talk.

B. Ah. See, it works good for everyone. You're delighted and I'm happy and content. So it comes together beautifully. I kinda knew it would. I would have been surprised if you did not want to talk to me, since I've been your long–term friend. I wouldn't have been angry or blamed you, of course, if you did not. But there have been lives where you did not believe in me, or in light, and so forth, and you didn't believe in the spiritual realities. I never blamed you, because I knew that the mission was different. BUT I still knew that you heard me on a subconscious level, and I just needed to be more patient with you and see you more as a bucket. You were more like a container, and I can see you differently. Sometimes the container is more like a barrel, you know, the lid is on. And sometimes the barrel is open and I can see the connection is there.

D. I appreciate your persistence.

B. Anyway, I have indeed been in the storage units.

D. Oh? Which one?

B. The one where I thought I might get in with my rhubarb leaf. (*Bob tried to sneak into one of the pyramids on Etena as told in 'Notes, Volume 2', the April 15, 2020 session. This time he was invited on a tour.*)

D. So, they let you in?

B. Kinda. I signed myself up for a tour. Huhuh. You granted that wish, and I went in to explore. So I passed the gift shop. I'm not by myself. You are given like a light and the light—if you think of a candle, but it's not a candle—and the light is activated so you can see where you are allowed to go. If you were to drift off, the light shuts down! And the reason I know this is because as I went in with this group that I was with—it's not a field trip, but it's like a little group of students. They're older than me, they don't look like me at all. No one looks like me. They look like Julia, all of them. (*Julia is a younger soul from the seventh.*) But they are male and female gender, in some way, or they portray that energy. But they're slim and smiling and dressed in white. I'm more small, a little bit round, and dressed in blue.

D. Blue is a good color.

B. Blue is my finest outfit.

D. Are you wearing all your awards and stones?

B. No, I don't want to brag. I have them at home. But I'm dressed in my finest.

D. So how did you find out your light went out?

B. I was walking here in the back of this group. I didn't know whether you were with or not. So the whole group went left and then I saw something extremely mysterious. I wasn't gonna leave the group. I was just briefly gonna have a little look–see. And as I took that extra step away from the group, my light shut. And there I was. The group continued on with their lights on. You can see it as candles, but it's more like a little torch, a little golden light bulb in the top. So there I was and I couldn't go either way, and I didn't know how to ignite my stick. And then Setalay came, and I said, "My stick broke." She smiled, and she said, "I'll give you a new one, but you have to stay with the group." And I said, "Well, it was because of the stick. It broke." It was actually after, when I told you about the experience, it seemed like you already knew. That's when you told me that the stick shuts down, the light bulb in the top of the stick shuts down, if you are off route. I laughed and I said, "Well, I told Setalay that it broke!" Uhh, huhuh. I understand now that she knew that I had taken a step to the side.

D. Did you catch up with the group?

B. I had to catch up. She came quickly and said, "Hurry, so you don't miss your group, because it's not good to walk all by yourself here. You're not going to like that at all." So she just sort of ignited my stick and said, "You run off now. Go together with the group." So I took off and was like, "I probably should not do that again."

D. So what did you see on your tour?

B. We went into like a vault that is part of Earth's history. It's a time when crystal energies were highly in use. It was similar used like now, when you use like cell towers and satellites, you simply just directed and used crystal energy. We came into a room—it almost looked like a cave. And since I was a little bit behind, when I came in everyone had positioned themselves around this hole in the ground. So I took my position quietly in this circle. The cave, you should know, it's quite magical. But it's quite dark, so I'm glad my stick is working again. And when I looked down, I could see Earth, and I could see the activity on Earth with crystal energy.

D. Do you have any idea of the time frame?

B. It's come and gone several times. When I looked here, it was not the latest time. The latest time was around 25,000 human years ago. But I looked back to when Ophelia came, Shea came, and used crystal energy. And you should know that it operates differently, depending on whether the crystal energy is activated in water, or on land, or in air. You can also use crystal energy to its highest potential using the element of fire. As you use crystal energy combined with the element mercury, you travel. I'm pretty sure Joel, geologist Joel, knows about it because this is like rocks. I did not take that full class. I did not take the Ph.D. in geology. So we are standing here and we are observing how crystal energy, combining with other elements, are creating power, energy. But it was also used like a laser. And the laser was to divide land mass. So the crystal energy was directed from within, but there was also something coming from outside. It became a HUGE light—almost like you see the Center Pole—but it was directed from a flashlight in space. Looking closer than the Moon. Looking like the Moon, but closer. Creating like a laser, and it divided continents. There was no human activity.

D. Was it used benevolently, or was it something that was not supposed to happen?

B. Oh, it was intentional. Umhmm. I don't see who does it. I know that Ophelia is with, because the Shea were involved. Their knowledge, in their core being, relates to the understanding of manipulating light. When humans think about manipulation, it is something bad. But this was manipulating the light, working with the light and using crystal energy combined with different earth elements, welcoming in and directing the light from this flashlight ball in the sky that looks like a moon but closer. And it was a laser that divided continents. There were no dinosaurs; there was no me; I'm not sure even you. Ari knew. You said that you were a sparkle when this activity took place. You did not do this. Ari knows, so I might need to ask him. But here we stand, and we look and we see how continents are dividing, using lasers. I don't know why. It's AMAZING for someone like myself.

D. So before they started doing that, was there only one mass of land?

B. This was in the beginning of baby Earth. But what we are looking at was not just one, so this (*dividing*) must have been done before as well. What I'm seeing here, I see at least two or three separate lands, so it's later. But there is no effect to the ocean, there is no bubbling, the ocean is completely still, which was surprising to me. I'm trying to see if it started to bubble. It did not. It did not create disharmony. Here, you should know, everyone is silent, BUT there is information coming into my being, coming from the Eye above. There is an Eye in the ceiling and the Eye is communicating. It's not loud. I hear the information in myself, in my being. And you said, "The only way to hear this is if your stick is lit up." If I had come in here and I hadn't had someone fixing my stick, since it broke, I would not have heard the information inside. It is complete silence. But the information about what we are seeing is heard within, and I see the Eye. This is the part of creation of this baby planet. I can see how it was fixed. And the Eye—what I was gonna say—it must have heard my thought. Apparently, it's a two-way communication, because I was thinking, "Oh, I wonder why it's not bubbling in the ocean when they do all this laser work?" And then I heard the answer in my being. Because it was my question, it's only me hearing the answer. So who knows what the other ones are asking and getting answered. I was thinking that afterwards we might get together and just share.

D. Compare notes?

B. Compare notes of what we asked and what we received. Hehe. Mainly what we received! So I asked in myself, in my thought, "I wonder why it's not bubbling?" And then I heard in myself, from the Big Eye, that because sea life was already ongoing, they didn't want to disturb them.

D. So the laser is not hot, I guess?

B. It is hot, but when I see how they cut and make things move, divide, I was thinking it should start to bubble in the ocean, like a tsunami, of sorts. But it did not. So I was thinking that, and it must have heard me because I got the answer inside my being. There was no wish for disharmony for sea creatures, because the sea creatures were there. But no creatures on top, no land entities. Nothing on land.

D. So this must have been many hundreds of millions of years ago?

B. It was like in the beginning. We're talking billions back. Because I'm not here, I'm not sure even Ole... maybe Ole. But I'm not sure about Gergen. Ari said that he knew about it, but he was young, he said, when this took place. Ophelia says that her mother participated, so she also heard about it. They read about it in school, she said. It's amazing. But I simply stand here and I see baby Earth becoming. Sea creatures already existed and one did not want to disturb the peace in the sea. (*Bob's statement is correct. There have been microfossils and stromatolites found in cherts and shales that were deposited 3.5 billion years ago. Oil and carbon isotopes ratios in some sedimentary rocks in Greenland and Australia point towards even older sea life.*)

D. So once they divided the land, what happened?

B. Moving, slowly moving. It's a cut. Then Canada floated down, and that one went right, from where I'm standing. I don't think that I should walk around too much and try to change position and go around the circle to see if there is a different view of what happened to, let's say, Africa. But I see a continent go down there and then Greenland goes there.

D. The continents have moved around a lot. Land has moved all over the globe.

B. Ah. But the Eye is the lecture conductor. It gives us information on what we see. So there are no living life forms on land, but in water they are there. That's why they had to be careful when they did that division with the laser, making cuts and shifts. Even on the seabed, one was extremely careful not to disturb wildlife on the seabed. Because you think, "Oh, move country there, move Greenland there," but underneath there is also a complete turn and shift in order for everything to be optimal. Created canyons, for instance, on the seabed. And things sunk, certain boxes sunk down.

D. So the crystal energy, is it something humans could use?

B. They did, before they became like greedy professors. Then it became like a mayhem when they overused it.

D. Where does the energy come from?

B. From the Earth. It's an energy source, a power source that comes from the Earth.

D. Is it electromagnetic or some other form of energy?

B. Gravity. It's a combination, but gravity is the predominant source in order for the crystal energy to be... what word can we use? Not directed. To expand... Oh, they took it away, the whole thing was deleted. Ophelia deleted. Someone came in with a sponge and deleted my thoughts.

D. I guess we're not supposed to know.

B. Nay. It just became blank. That happens sometimes. I'm probably not gonna share too much more. Just know that I had an interesting afternoon, huhuh, with new friends here. And everyone is standing here looking at how the creation became.

D. Did they tell you anything else that was surprising?

B. We're gonna continue the class outside, where we're gonna try to use crystal energy and we're gonna modify and learn how to use it to the highest potential of its existence, based on if we use water, air, earth, fire, and last comes to master the crystal energy combined with mercury, because that's how you travel. You also said that even a higher level exists, using crystal energy combined with gold. There's also a biological component that works great. But you said that mercury and gold comes last. First you learn how to use earth and water, in some way. Then comes air and how to extract and use crystal energy as a power point and a power plant, and how to use crystal energy waves in the air in order for it to become a power plant. And then comes using it with fire, which was what they used, in some way, here (*as a laser*). But in order to create that whole laser thing that I saw, they were using all Earth elements, but not, you said, not gold and not mercury. Crystal energy using those two minerals are to travel and to open up, you said. You use the gravity combined with the Earth elements.

D. You'll have to maybe explain how that was done, unless we're not supposed to know.

B. Well, something was erased in my being. But I'm going to class now, so I have to go because we're gonna compare notes. I don't want to be left behind again, so I'm not gonna miss my group again.

D. If you hadn't caught up, you would have missed out.

B. I would have missed the whole thing. And the Eye is shut now, so the show is over. I'm gonna go now with my class and we're gonna see what happens, and maybe I'll be able to share. Ah, okay. I have to go. I have to be a little bit short, but I don't want to miss my group. Okay, okay. Bye bye. (*This was one of his fastest exits from a session. He wanted to catch up with his group.*)

Zachariah, Bob: The Grand Play (May 16, 2021)

It had been nearly a year since Zachariah had blessed us with his presence, so I was happy to hear his voice and wisdom again. Hidden within the casual talk is a somewhat serious message to humanity. He has been busy on the fifth dimension preparing a new wave of souls for their trips to Earth. In his comparison to changing the type of tires on a motorcycle, he is stating that souls who are not aligned with the upcoming program will not be returning to Earth. This observation is identical to what Ophelia said in the previous session about the unwinding. Those who have followed the human mind and emotions will be moved to another learning environment. In addition, many geographic areas will be cleaned of the karmic residue left by those permanently departing souls.

In this story, we learn that Bob had gone to the fifth and was roaming around trying to get information from the young spirits who are headed to Earth, and the conversations between him and Zachariah are quite amusing. Bob then gives a really good explanation of how the traveling part of the soul carries the life plan into the Coat of Karma and then into the physical vehicle.

Z. Huh.

D. It's been a while.

Z. Oh, Bob, Bob. He's so eager to join, to understand the greater shifts and changes. And indeed, there are new levels of soul capacity coming in. There is, however, a need to understand that there is no judgment in the ones who lack the ability to remain in the current cycle. It's like a bicycle—we are just changing the tires. We are upgrading the tires because the roads ahead will have a different foundation. Meaning, the bicycle itself will have to be adapted. It's similar like with your motorcycle, it had different tires depending on if you wanted to go and climb on gravel roads, or if you wanted to go flat—similar here. As we change the general way to travel, commotion and disturbances take place within the flock. Meaning, souls who are currently in body. But believe me when I say that they are aware, inside, that they are leaving earlier, in order for a general change to occur. We are, indeed, training in what Bob called 'life study camp'. And believe me, he has tried to join and simply see. This occurs in libraries and study halls on the fifth—and he is not invited to all of them. I see him, however, and I say, "Bob, this is not a study hall for Lasaray to train for his upcoming journeys. Can I help you with something? Why are you here?" Oh, he's just looking, he says, because of the fact that he, apparently, is part of a calculating program. Meaning he calculates and draws your upcoming life. So he simply wants to see the new souls. (*Zachariah looks to the left and observes Bob for a moment.*) Oh, Bob. He tends to see it as you are the leading actor, and he wants to see about the support staff, what they are looking like and what they intend to do, or "if they are going to be a problem", he says. Huhuh. Oh, god—he cannot come in. I stopped him at the entrance. He was going to be quiet, he said. But when I asked him what his agenda was, then he told me that he is creating this (*2178*) life. Of course, I knew already. Jeshua told me. But he also wanted to see the surrounding souls coming in, if they would be "in the way" of your mission. He said that because you were going to find a plant and that it would be coming into somewhat of a—it had to do with the medical industry. He wanted to see if there was anyone here who was going to work in the medical or pharmaceutical departments, "if he could have a word", he said. He really doesn't seem to be so eager for things to go wrong. Of course, we understand, but there are several at play. (*He turned again to the left, listening to Bob.*) Yes, Bob, I know the intention. I'm aware. I'm aware that it's a big mission, a big project. Not all of them are gonna be in the way for you. So, I wanted to come in briefly and tell you, tell you all, to not fear the unknown. To not trip over your own feet. To remain strong and stable on the feet that you have. Allow your feet to take you without interference of the winds around you. (*Zachariah then gave some personal advice before stepping back and letting Bob join with Christine.*)

B. AH! AH! That was a treat! He's not been around for a while. He's been busy with the study camp going on. I see a group there, there, there. (*He nods in different directions.*) And I'm looking into WHEN are these specific groups going down. Are they gonna be down around 2200? Because around 2200 we are in high action, and I don't want there to be interference.

D. Did you learn anything?

B. Well, I was trying to communicate with some (*of the students*), but it seemed like I was discovered by Zachariah. And he said, "What are you asking?" And I said, "I'm simply asking a question about when and where they are gonna be down, and what they're gonna do." They're quite eager to share, so I don't know why we could not continue the discussion. But I was escorted out. I just want there to not be any interference. I said, "If you don't know, really, what you're gonna do—so that you don't just tumble around—maybe you can just stay away from England and New Zealand, if you can go elsewhere." And they were fine with it.

D. What if they were going to be helpful?

B. And that's also what I wanted to know, "Are you gonna be helpful, or are you gonna be in the way?" Because if someone here is gonna be like that specific doctor guiding you through the maze of regulations—because regulations might still be around—then they are welcome to join.

D. I am curious about something. You develop a life plan as a play, but you have all the other spirits around the area doing the same thing. How does that all get merged and blended together?

B. Into a grand play. First, I make my play, and this is what Jeshua has always been doing with you. So, he creates the play and sometimes you participate in the planning. Sometimes you don't, you just accept a mission and allow someone to draw the general outline of that life. But then you go together and you have all these different councils that work to patch up and match these plays. It's like a puzzle that you have to create, so a grand play takes place. Normally, it has to do with, let's say, a location geographically where we want certain things and shifts to occur. It's also sometimes to release karmic energy that has been stuck. There are certain countries that have more karmic energy stuck—

then you have to flush the toilet so that it cleans out the area. Because geographically, there is also a suit. So you have the soul, the soul comes into the suit, and you have to mix and match. So, soul personality versus human personality either collide or become like one. Depending on what sort of personality your soul is, it is easier or harder to adapt into the suit, into the human experience. If I place you in a country or a geographic zone in need to be flushed, you will act one way. But if I place you in a country where the flushing has already occurred, where it is clean, then it's more likely that your mission will be successful. So that is also why you are placed later on—because we need to flush England.

D. How is that going to transpire?

B. That's beyond my capacity. It's done by the Evolution Group. I had the desire and a wish to place you there, but then, in order for that to happen, we need to also look at the general evolution of that region. And that region needs to be flushed. And when I say flushed, it has nothing to do with souls going down the pooper, it's more that there are karmic residual energies that is clogging up the system. It needs to be cleaned. Actions are certain things that can create problems in the pipes, so to speak.

D. So after 2178, England has been cleaned?

B. The area where I'm placing you will be flushed. And it's also so that Josephine can create the green community. In order for that to be received, it needs to be clean. So you can see we are putting different things in play. But if we were to put that into play NOW, it will simply be lost.

D. So the area will be peaceful by 2178?

B. There's still gonna be a little bit of fires here and there, like bonfires that we need to navigate around. But the general outline of that region is that it needs to be stabilized and flushed. There are other places that need to be flushed as well. [...]

D. How much of my soul energy are you going to have me bring down?

B. I was thinking about 15 percent.

D. Am I going to be a spiritual person?

B. No. That was the thing I had to delete. You will be spiritual, but just not in the way that you think now. You will be a scientific person, but your information will come from within. So you are spiritual, but it's a spiritual intelligence. The information is placed within your center point so that it radiates like a little heater. It's just an instant knowing.

D. Am I going to find and read our books?

B. Ah! You're gonna recognize that.
D. Will I recognize this life as my previous life?
B. Ah.
D. Will I think about you, then?
B. Ah. You understand reincarnation, you're not dumb. It's just that you don't say, "I'm spiritual". You're not religious at all. But you act like a psychic, it's just that you don't see yourself as a psychic. You simply act on intuition, which is much stronger. But it's basically ME bumping up the intuition. It doesn't matter what you call yourself. You don't like to be vague, saying "I believe." You say "I know." And the thing is, that knowledge is correct.
D. When you see this future life, from your perspective, is it like a play that you can visualize?
B. Ah. And I can modify your behavior, because there were certain times where I felt like you were not very social. You've been like that. It's sort of a trademark when you come into a body. So, I'm deleting and I'm polishing and I'm fixing, changing colors in the color map. I was talking with Jeshua and I said, "I want him to be more outgoing. I want him to be more charismatic and talk to people." Different color patterns in the suit are triggering different human personalities. And sometimes they are aligned with the color map that the soul comes in with. You, however, tend to be very much as is. Whereas this one is more like an actor. At home he is similar like you. Oh, this is tricky. I only took one class, as of yet, about the soul pattern. The soul color map indicates a little bit about your soul personality. A lot of those who come from the fifth, they just (*he made a sucking sound*) merge and become and they just go and they start a life. When it comes to you, you struggle, you kinda resist to merge with the suit. The thing is, you wanna come down and do your thing and go.
D. It is fascinating, but such a complicated process.
B. Ah. But you say to simply give you the manuscript when I'm done here with my role plays and everything. So I'm just gonna give you that when it's time, and I know that you can simply look at it and you will instantly know. Here, it takes a little bit for you to comprehend. So I'm not gonna do that, I'm not gonna give too much information. (*Bob next describes the life plan as being similar to a programmed chip.*) It's like an energetic chip that I charge, with help from Jeshua. That's how a life becomes. When the whole role play, the whole outline is established, it becomes like a chip that merges into your soul being, and it becomes part of the traveling

part of the soul. It doesn't merge with the whole 100 percent (*of the soul*), it merges with the percent of the soul capacity that is gonna travel. So it is someway separated from the soul. The soul can observe the traveling self as a separate unit, like an extension of one's self. And then it (*he made a popping sound*) releases and it takes off, and then it goes into the suit. The chip and the suit are more alike. Whereas the soul can observe the suit and the chip. Meaning, the chip is the one that left the motherchip (*the higher self*), so to speak, for travel, as an extension to participate in a play in the distance. [...]

D. That's a good analogy of how the soul travels. (*The motherchip is the part of the soul that remains behind in the spirit realm. The traveling soul is colored by the life plan, but those influences are only temporary. At the end of the incarnation, the traveling soul part returns in pure form to rejoin the motherchip.*)

B. You should also know that the traveling chip, on its way into an incarnation, can get drained and it can be affected so much by the suit and other suits and the environment on Earth, and different things. Similar to what you see right now. At this time, there are a lot of chips that are not functioning in the host, meaning the suit. Like I said, suit and chip should be like one, and they normally are. But when there is turmoil going on, those two are not in contact. And what they (*the spiritual councils*) want, Ophelia says, is that the chip and the suit should be more aligned. At this time, it's just suits, and the chip is trying to activate the suit and trying to send signals back to the motherchip, meaning the soul at home. It's a chain reaction that is not working as well as it should. What Zachariah is doing in his study camps is that the chip will be upgraded, so it doesn't become a separation of suit and chip. The chip is the traveling soul energy, the percentage that left, that docked away, took off from the motherchip to experience something. At the moment, the suits are experiencing, chips are kinda limping behind, and the motherchip has no control.

D. You've talked before about the suit. So, we have the suit in the fourth, and then we have the body. Which piece are you calling the suit?

B. The body. The chip is a traveling percentage of the soul.

D. What about the pattern that exists in the fourth that carries all the soul's intentions?

B. The problem is that there is separation, so the fourth becomes a little bit of a problem. When suit and chip are divided, they are more subject for disinformation that exists in the fourth reality. So the fourth reality somewhat descends and interferes with this entity. Do you see what I'm saying? When suit and chip are aligned, connected, operating together, they are less influenced by disinformation that travels above their head in the fourth reality.

D. I just wanted to clarify, is the chip merged with the Coat in the fourth?

B. The motherchip is the higher self, looking down and seeing what is going on.

D. You remember when you took the students to the tailors?

B. Ah. That's the suit.

D. And then you have the physical body.

B. That is the suit. Body is the suit. The (*pattern of the*) suit transforms into a body. The Coat of Karma is so connected to the physical experience that it dresses the physical—but it's like one. But you want to see them as four, when they are not.

D. I just wonder which part the chip was merged with, the Coat or…?

B. The chip merges in the suit. As the suit becomes born, suit and body are one, maneuvered by chip. At this time, the chip cannot maneuver suit and body. Suit and body are experiencing and making decisions by themselves. Disinformation is easier to travel and to affect a large group of lost suits if they send it off in the fourth reality. A lot of what's going on is that disinformation and fear are placed in the fourth reality by those who are aware that it transmits easier when suits are running around with no drivers. The cars are body and suit, merged. As soon as the body is born, the baby is born, the suit becomes the physical. But the driver is still the chip. The motherchip, and when I say chip, it's not a boat, it's a computer chip where you put in data. A microchip.

D. Oh, you're saying chip, not ship! (*I had mistakenly thought he was saying "ship". He obviously read my mind, which shouldn't surprise me anymore, but it still does.*)

B. Nay. It's a computer, it's a microchip. That is the driver, that is the soul. The micro-CHIP left the mother-CHIP. You're so slow. We did have this discussion at home, because you told me this story. And this is what I said, it's better that I give the manual and the manuscript to Lasaray, because after micro-CHIP left the mother-CHIP, it's less likely to be fully heard. That's when the walkie–talkie is not working that well. The microchip is the driver, that is the departing soul energy. In your case, your 7 percent. It's time to go now, but we're gonna continue this story, because there is a whole chain that needs to be looked into.

D. I really enjoy this type of conversation, because it helps me to picture what is going.

B. Well, so do I, normally. But it helps if you understand. When I have a conversation like with Ari and everyone at home, it's them teaching me. And now, I'm like the spokesperson—but I don't complain, because I did want to be the one telling you. It's just that it takes a little bit more effort. I have to be more clear. Maybe I should have used a different description. Maybe I should have just said the driver, meaning the traveling soul energy, when it docks into the car and takes off, it's the driver's skill that is important. Is it trained well, or does it just know how to drive an automatic car? And here we have a manual with a stick, so how is the driver managing that, and so forth?

D. I was kind of hung up in my mind, trying to figure out where the Coat of Karma fit into the picture.

B. The Coat of Karma is the suit. But the suit, as soon as the body is born, Coat of Karma is activated and becomes (*or merges with*) the body. Suit and Coat become one. Whether the driver is equipped to navigate remains to be seen. It's like, you have a cell phone and you take out the sim card, it doesn't work. In your case, your American phone did not work here (*in Sweden*). It died. It's like saying that there is a disconnect between the microchip, the soul energy, and the experience, which would be the phone.

D. So now all the bodies running around are without—

B. No drivers. No drivers. "It's okay," Ophelia says, "We don't judge. We simply see that there is a time in the human evolution when there are just cars with no drivers."

D. Headless horsemen.

B. Indeed. Like a cell phone with no sim card. Ahh, huh huh huh! Who you gonna call with no sim card! That will make people understand! Just empty phones, like a shell with no sim card.

D. When the Creator calls, no one answers.

B. No one answers. It's a little bit sad. But Ophelia says to not judge. It's happened before. It's no sadness, really. It's just that, when you remove sim cards, when you take drivers and you put them in the Tesla car and then say, "Well, there you go. Off you go." But the car is triggered and follows the influences from the fourth reality, where a lot of disinformation and fears are just hanging over your head, so to speak. And winds are taking this car. It's similar like that. People want to have an easy ride. But they don't want to steer life, they don't want to navigate life. It's like having someone take you to a destination, taking you to a nice job, giving you that good position at work, giving you a great companion—maybe even come in the mail. This whole trend of being passive and lazy is exactly what those who want to influence the cars want. The problem is, with no drivers, or no sim card activated, that everyone thinks that is the best choice, the best option, because they are disconnected.

D. That's a really good explanation.

B. Ah. So I'm gonna go now, before you lose interest and lose understanding in what I've been saying. Huhhuh. Okay, I'm gonna go now.

D. Alright, my friend. Thank you so much. It was a brilliant teaching.

Council of Nine: Interstate Highway of Humanity (June 24, 2021)
The Council of Nine came in to offer comfort about the turn of events in 2021. It is interesting that they focused on NATO, as that organization has planned and executed several wars since they delivered this message. The war in Ukraine officially began in February 2022, but was started by the main NATO players in 2014 when their mercenary groups overthrew the elected government and installed a puppet regime, which then started a civil war. NATO, of course, is an appendage of the Cell, whose goals are always destructive. In 2024, just before this book was published, Sweden also joined NATO, which occurred without a public voting. The Council of Nine discloses that there will be several more years of turmoil, probably peaking around 2025. A financial collapse will trigger societal problems and widespread discontent. People who have suckled on the groupthink disgorged by the media are going to be confused and angry about the many ways the rulers have misled them. Again, they advise people to not follow the crowds, or surrender their own power to others who are ignorant of the soul. The comfort for us is knowing that the spiritual councils and visitors are the ones who will prevail.

CN. This is the Council of Nine. We are here to enlighten the world at this time about the hiccups. The hiccups has to do with the lack of ability to move forward. The human race at this time is paralyzed. They are unable to move forward. When we say move forward, it does not necessarily mean physically. It has to do with finding solutions. That is the biggest trick at this time, whether man sees solutions, or if they are asking for someone to bring one solution. One solution doesn't exist. It is a time for you to find your path, and to allow that path to transform and become you. What we see is that the human race tries to squeeze each other, crowd each other, on one path. That is how we see when a consciousness is going astray. We see the change within your emotional selves. A need to align, a need to hug each other. One of the things that this hiccup the world has experienced the last one and a half years—yes, it started earlier than media wanted you to know—it is to see whether you connect with your kinfolk, or if you are more eager to separate. When you separate from those who are your friends, families, and so forth, you become lost in your mental capacity. When you are lost in your mental self, you are astray and you try to gather as clusters in roads with others. (*People tend to seek solace in the company of others, even when the group may not be spiritually oriented or compatible.*) That is simply physically being with others. But you are disconnected mentally. The emotional within you are screaming for support, screaming for help. Some recognizes this as a human heart, a human emotion. Another will feel a different calling from within, your soul heart, if you like. This is a time to try to separate the human mind, the human thought, versus your soul thought—similar as the emotional state of existing. We see, however, the flock paralyzed in this path, this road. I can compare it to that everyone wants to go on E4 (*an interstate highway in Sweden*), instead of taking the smaller roads to their destinations. E4 is what Google Map told you to go on, and there you sit in bad traffic, not going either backward or forward. But you are content because Google Map told you to go on this E4 road, instead of taking the smaller ones, where perhaps you would be able to see the countryside and where you will be able to navigate by your senses, your eyes, to see the world around you. But there you sit on E4 in bad traffic—to give you a visual. However, what's going on is planned. Nothing is by chance. There are those who want you to believe in evil, that there is an evil hand placed upon you. I wouldn't call it evil. I will call it a human need, a human desire to collect and to be superior over others. There is no evil force set upon you. The force that is set upon you are spiritual realities, but also extraterrestrial intelligence. Those who appear—yes, Bob, you saw them in the store. Yes, in the store. Yes. (*Turns back towards me and continues.*) Just want to let you know that there are higher powers observing your behavior. One spiritual, one extraterrestrial. The extraterrestrial entities are parallel realities. They've been here before. They know the land. They know the human race well. They know the traps that you might fall into. Those who talk about an evil force, I'm sorry to say, are only humans. It is nothing else. Everything will be fine. But you have to, as a group, rise above your fears. You have to open your eyes and try to take different roads. Don't get stuck on E4.

D. Are the extraterrestrials in human form, or are they observing?

CN. Hmm! Yes, some are, some are (*in human form*). Not part of the incarnation program, in that sense. A special request given at this time. Yes, some are. Geographically placed to observe technology, bases, certain industries such as military, government. So yes, some in disguise. Some sitting just nearby. But because of your eyes not being equipped at this time to see parallel realities, you do not see who sits next to you in your UN council. There's an interest in NATO. Concerned about NATO. So, yes, there are extraterrestrial eyes on that organization. (*NATO is being closely monitored by alien observers.*)

D. Are they concerned they might start a war?

CN. Differences between progress. It's not a uniform agenda in that organ. There are differences in how to progress. There are battles unseen, undetected from the regular public. There's an interest in how debates are going in that organ. The spiritual realm doesn't necessarily look upon it. We have hands-on eyes reporting, looking into the activity within that organ.

D. I remember one time you or someone had said aliens were interested in the resources on Earth and wanted to reduce the population. Are those similar to the ones you are talking about?

CN. There are different eyes, different presence. Some look into NATO, as I mentioned. Some look into oil and gas industry; those are your friends, the Tallocks. They look on resources, minerals, how much supply exist for certain changes to occur. When we say changes, it means moving landmass, changing direction of the weather system. For the weather system to be optimal, we have to make sure that it corresponds correctly with the amount of gas and other minerals in that region. There are changes within your weather systems, how the winds are flowing and how the oceans respond to those currents that needs to be adjusted to not have a bad impact on seabed and so forth and animal life, specifically, in the sea. There are certain interests, Tallocks being one, looking into how man is behaving when it comes to resources and energy supply. We do wish travels to be reduced. So, that is a good effect of what has occurred (*lockdowns*). That is a spiritual response to the hiccup of man being too mobile. There is no need to be that mobile all the time. Try to sit and listen. Otherwise, you are just following the current, like a wind, back and forth, like a powerless leaf. There we go. Do you have any more questions?

D. Yes. I am curious about the aliens you mentioned at first. Are they working with the councils, working with you?

CN. Yes, yes, of course. They simply are the spy, the eye, the report organ, the level of interacting with Earth, animal life, humans and so forth. But they report, similar as you do, to spiritual councils. Not necessary our council, all of them, but different organs within our system. To be able to collect data is something that we have both humans incarnated, souls such as yourself, as well as, in some cases, transformed extraterrestrials. You will see it, or you could see it, in their eyes. They are not many, so don't try to find them in a crowd—you will not.

D. Is there a longer game plan with this hiccup that is going on?

CN. The hiccup is a 10-year phase. The big hiccup will be about 5. There's going to be a change around 2025. Until then, the world will be in the hiccup.

D. What type of change will it be? Like natural, political or financial?

CN. After 2025, man will have had enough. Humans will understand what it means to have enough of superior impact. But they have to separate themselves from the E4 first. They have to understand how to navigate on smaller roads, to listen to the silence. At this moment they are stuck on a highway, a highway making loud noises, where you cannot see where you are going. There will be a change. However, certain things need to crack.

D. What type of things need to crack?

CN. Financial systems being one.

D. Alright. Very good. Thank you.

CN. There we go. Until next time, I bid you farewell. Elahim.

D. Elahim.

Koh, Bob: Filling the V-Shape (July 7, 2021)

This was the first time that Koh came in to converse with us. He is a member on the Council of Six and closely follows the activities of the Elahim when they incarnate. He describes an esoteric method used by ancient mystics to acquire knowledge in the fourth and higher realities. It should be noted that the practice requires the body and mind to be adequately purified of earthly contaminants. The mind, for example, must be freed from any attachments to the human drama in the grand play. Likewise, the body should be cleared of alcohol, sugar, meat, wheat, pesticides, and other chemicals. Then, the seeker must be in stillness; mentally, emotionally, and environmentally. Meaning, no cellular radiation, noise or other disturbances, and preferably surrounded by nature. We have been told in other sessions that the language of the spiritual realm is symbolic, and Koh is instructing us on how to access that knowledge. The key to admission, it seems, is living like an ascetic. Done properly, the visualization using the V-shape will lead to igniting the inner Merkaba. As Koh says, "This is the way the ancients saw and understood the cone. As you add more cones, more V's, they will start to rotate and you will be able to embrace and invite more realities into your cone. This is when the Merkaba is established. The Great Merkaba will rotate in your center, the six-pointed star. Understand that the beginning starts with a V." Humans often are misdirected to believe that spiritual knowledge is something that can be found in a book or passed on by others. But ultimately, the attainment of an activated Merkaba comes when perception is no longer clouded by the transient nature of the human emotions or mind. And that is always an inner journey. Although he does not say, my feeling is that the different Vs in the Merkaba represent types of knowledge and experiences available within the human form. The V symbolizes the openness and ability to receive input from your soul and guides. The inverted V symbolized the body and its ability to hold and transmit pure spiritual compassion in thoughts and actions. There are levels of advancement in each area, and a personal Merkaba is complete when all aspects of being a soul in human form have been mastered. At that point, the body is like a pyramid that holds the soul's awareness without the emotional or mental centers being colored with human desires or impulses.

After Koh pulled away, Bob came in and, since he heard the Council of Six talking about the V symbol, he began to describe the V-shaped vestment that he wears sometimes when traveling. It has symbols and awards that represent where he is from, his level of knowledge, where he has traveled, and what he does. Later, he tells how to fill the V-shape during life by being joyful, which will fill the cone with more colors.

K. Greetings. We are here representing the Council of Six. Meaning, we follow the progress from the sixth, looking into shifts on Earth. We have never walked as man. However, we have great knowledge about the behavior of man. You, in many ways, the two of you, are our eyes and ears. We follow you closely as you travel into body. You can call me Koh. I follow your progress closely. You report, both of you, when you dream. It is important to make sure that your dreams are clean. That is why you need the solitude as man. When you are colored by activities on Earth, your dreams are hard for us to interpret. We need to be precise in the information you transmit. It's like a fog from the human self, where the soul blends in passing. The passage meaning the fourth. We descend into the fourth and try to interpret what it is you are revealing. When your soul is colored by activities around you—that is the importance of solitude—your dreams are colored as well. It takes great training in order for us to decipher a clear dream, and most are simply a fog. You have been on Earth when we revealed codes. These codes, we will again bring to your knowledge. Codes that, when interpreted correctly as man, open doors to higher realms. Don't simply focus on the fourth. Those who could navigate in the fourth reality as humans used different ways. We are here to assist you to navigate to higher, close by, realities. Not necessarily spiritual realities. Codes that will decipher and open portals to nearby realities, (*which*) means parallel worlds. The spiritual reality is an umbrella hovering, encasing, warming all realities below. At this time, we invite friends from parallel realities. (*There are*) open windows, so to speak. In order for that to occur, you have to cleanse yourself. You have to drop ideas on what to expect. Believe me, it is nothing of the sort. (*Meaning, it is not what you expect.*) Friends are on standby, providing the same knowledge that you once possessed (*during an*) ancient time when you worked with little pots, urns (*as John 11*). You knew the language then. You could decipher the codes. Your channel was clear. Both of you need to let go of earthly information in order for you to receive the codes. These codes will come as symbols. You have to, within you, decipher the meaning. In order for you to do so, you have to be in stillness. We are on that threshold where this work is about to begin. It has not, as of yet. These symbols provide more information than any words can. However, at the moment, you are trapped within the information of words. We will ask of you that you meet us in the middle. Using the words in order for information to be revealed. But interpreting and understanding the meaning of symbols is crucial for you to fully grasp the greater reality around you. As we move forward, we will provide different signs. The first sign I'm bringing to you looks like the letter V. V. (*He holds his hands up chest high with the heels of the hand and thumbs touching. The palms were flat and leaning outward, but facing each other. From my perspective, in front of him, the edge of his hands looked like a V.)* This indicates meeting points between two spheres. Let this image be an imprint in your mind. I ask of you to close your eyes, to see this symbol V. The two points above, place them on each side above your ear. Let those lines draw downwards into your Center Point. Let the V become you. As you sit in stillness, this is the first level of concentration to understand the greater realities. This is how you center yourself. Two dots on each side, above your ears. Lines drawing downwards, one over your heart, stopping at the Center Point. The great, grand V. Allow that V to become you. Drop your physical form and simply be the form of V. This can also look like a cone. Imagine that you fill this cone with the water of knowledge. At this point, you will only have water a little bit in the bottom. The more you learn, the more you progress, the more you use this ancient technique of the symbol V, filling up the knowledge from above, like water, the more you will understand. The ancients knew how to be the V, the cone. In this case, the bottom is up, it's open. Pyramids symbolize the encased knowledge, meaning the cone flipped. It held the water; it held the information within. This is the way the ancients saw and understood the cone. As you add more cones, more V's, they will start to rotate and you will be able to embrace and invite more realities into your cone. This is when the Merkaba is established. The Great Merkaba will rotate in your center, the six–pointed star. Understand that the beginning starts with a V.

D. Does each side represent something?

K. Male and female, in this world.

D. There were a lot of symbols in antiquity with a V and a sphere or circle inside the upright arms.

K. Yes. The circle indicates the Eye, the all–seeing Eye. It is what you will reach when you fill up your cone. But first you are the V. The easiest (*way*) to do, to center yourself and become the V, is to (*mentally*) place two points above each of your ears, on the sides. (*He touched a point not far from the temple on each side.*) We will continue to help you. This is the first symbol we give. Practice it, both of you. Together and separate. You possess joint knowledge, but also different. You need to find your own solitude, even though you work together. We are providing different cones, different information. You are receivers. Become the V, fill up this cone with the water of knowledge. Water also represents feelings in this reality. Embrace the high and low of feelings. That is how you will understand and separate yourself from human feelings. Understand that spiritual feelings are different. It's a compassion to simply be a different kind of existence. You will find that in the circle you talked about. That is to encase any spiritual knowledge, spiritual compassion, in the shape. To be centered in that V shape is to understand.

B. (*Bob suddenly came in, coughing.*) Oh. Excuse me. I thought it was a group activity.

D. He was not done.

B. I didn't think he was done. I thought it was a group activity that I should sit in. But Ophelia says I should wait. But it was not a group activity. It's not a choir, she says. I find this interesting. Earth-based but fascinating. But Earth-based is—oh, I just want to say this—Earth-based is also cosmic, and I'm a cosmic engineer in the making. I kinda already am, of course. But it's how to connect above and below. It's a grand mystery and I'm interested in listening to this individual. Okay, I'll step aside. I didn't want to interfere. I simply thought it was a co-listening experience, but it was not. I was too close, it seems.

D. Alright, we'll talk in a few minutes.

K. (*Koh came back in.*) Well, where was I?

D. Water and the higher and lower emotions.

K. Yes. The V shape will give you the starting point on how to interact with all worlds and also how to separate and understand your place in the world that you are currently in. When you activate the Merkaba, you simply operate from a higher knowledge. It is a rotation of a feeling within, where you transmit that knowledge to others. At one point in the history on Earth, all Merkabas were activated in the race. This was a time millions of years ago, and you were not here as human. They were prototypes, one could say, of a human. Less hair than the later form. It was to understand how to activate the Merkaba within you, that you, as souls, always have activated—but how to do so when you move into a form not suited, potentially, to hold it. We will continue the lecture. Simply be aware that the first step is to understand the shape V. It is a cone. Once you have the cone filled up, you can flip it, and that is the meaning of pyramids. It is to hold the knowledge. When you hold the knowledge, it activates and generates energy. The ancients knew how to use the pyramids, the cone, in a way to transmit energy as well as holding it. It's a storage device in order for free energy to be transmitted. But free energy is also available between humans. You can be a cone without taking the form of a pyramid. But you, in your soul energy, become that form. As ancient man knew how to activate all different devices, all angles, all V shapes, they became a pyramid, a holder of encased knowledge. You can do the same. We will continue to talk. [...]

D. Thank you so much for that.

K. We are part of the Elahim group. We simply operate on a different agenda. We transmit symbols and read and decipher information that moves between realities. At this point, we are interested in the Earth reality. And be aware that there are several parallel worlds surrounding this field at this time. That is why there is a turmoil of information around you. Some decipher the signals correctly. But the majority feel pressured about energies they don't understand. It is because of the high interest and high presence of other realities around you. That makes it hard for a human brain to calm. You feel the energy, even though you don't understand it.

D. Are entities involved with the other energy fields, or is it just an energy itself that is disturbing?

K. Clarify.

D. Are other entities coming to Earth and interfering?

K. Yes, yes. On behalf of other councils, yes. We are also tightly close to councils operating on the fifth—those who hold the Earth, your planet, in their hands; those who look after the environment; those who work with transmitting levels, waves of knowledges. The waves of reading human behaviors is very much occupied by the councils from the fifth reality. Zachariah travels between. Great Ambassador for us all. The libraries are filling up on the fifth. Zachariah assists. We all assist, simply with different expertise and interests.

D. Is there anything I can do, personally, to clean up my dreams?

K. [...] Establish the V–shape, breathe in, fill up the water in your V–cone. Fill the water, draw it down. Breathe. You can breathe through water. The blockage you feel is when you feel that you cannot breathe in water. This is on a subconscious level. The V–cone is already established. The human feels it cannot breathe because the cone is filling up with water. Use all elements. There are no boundaries on how you can activate and work with all. As you understand that there are no boundaries between water and air, breathing and swimming, if you like, in this cone, then you activate the fire element. The fire element are the borders, the lines from your ears down to your core. As you establish that, you can draw that energy though your belly area, activate the earth element. Meaning, activating the third reality. Earth represents the third reality. Fire represents your home base. Knowledge and communication—emotion and compassion—represents water and air. Use them in your cone. Draw them down, holding this experience by fire. Draw it down, let it merge with earth, which is the third reality, and you are whole.

D. That's a wonderful description.

K. There. Your friend, is he always this eager?

D. That's one of his primary qualities, curiosity.

K. He's curious. We see him, of course. I know he has seen us. We will help you. You can call me Koh. I'm here as a representative. More, perhaps, will transmit information, but there is no need for confusion. But yes, we come with these teachings. It is important to understand to be humble with knowledge. Okay. Different energy. (*He sniffed like his nose itched.*) We will return.

D. Thank you so much for the information. I really appreciate the knowledge you gave us.

K. You are welcome. Elahim.

D. Elahim.

B. Now I didn't interfere!

D. Hello, my friend. At least you know what the V is now.

B. Ah. I might be interested in taking more classes of these different signs and symbols. Because you said that "the whole universe, all fish tanks, are resonating with symbols. And it's easy to know then, where someone is coming from. Because they have that mark of different symbols." I don't want to say they are branded like cattle, but in some way, it is! It's similar like you are somewhat branded also where you come from, like me from the second. But in a human mind, it sounds like you are branded like cattle.

D. You probably wear symbols on your robe?

B. I have several symbols on my V–shape, here. (*He looked down at his chest, where there is a V–shaped collar or vestment on his robe.*) That's why you kinda wanted to know why there is a V–shape on all the robes of knowledge that we have here. It is because it represents the cone of knowledge. Inside, we have me here, as you can see. And there is a V–shape going like this here with all different medals and symbols. (*He was looking down at his robe again.*) It represents where I've been. This is my travel robe, so that when we go places, they can see like, "Okay, he's been on Etena on fish tank four." So we have here different things here representing where I've been. This is one here (*as he looks down towards his right shoulder*) that says I am a spirit guide for an Elahim, an Elahim spirit guide. You put it here. And then there is different things to kinda show where I'm at. You might wonder why the necessity to flaunt this greatness, but it's a way to establish a relationship. So you kinda know who you are talking to. That's why I was quite confused when they (*Koh and the Council of Six*) came in those brown robes, looking like peasants. Because, clearly, they should have all sorts of tingle-tangle on them to show their level of knowledge. But he says that you have to be humble, and sometimes it's important to kinda hide where your knowledge level is situated.

D. That's a lesson for Earth, I guess.

B. And for me, apparently, because I do like my travel robe. But maybe this robe is like a keycard when I go through different doors. Like, ding-ding, and then I can come through. I don't know, but I put different things on it, on my V-shape, like that.

D. Did Gergen hang anything on you?

B. Ah. But that's another robe. This is my travel robe. And when I say travel, it also indicates me being a spirit guide traveling to Earth with you. So, all spirit guides have this sort of diploma, because of the fact that they are companions to a soul that is trying to navigate in this fog, in this maze, on Earth.

D. That's probably a pretty difficult task.

B. Ah. And I did not have training. It was merely like, "Oh, okay, Lasaray needs someone. Who can we find... oh, there is one." Maybe that's how it was. Then I was just fetched to start this journey. But Gergen said there was actually more planning behind it than if we just stumbled upon each other, even though I perceived it as such, that you just stumbled upon my path. But there was probably more planning behind it.

D. Well, when I came down for the first incarnation, there wasn't a system of training guides at that time, was there? (*Lasaray was half manifested, half incarnated in a Yeti-like creature, about 450,000 years ago.*)

B. Nay. When you came the first time, it was—I mean, the second time was the fire—but the first time, you were sort of similar looking. We kinda had a little bit of training on what to eat, what to not eat and so forth, because we needed to put that in your memory bank. Like certain mushrooms you should not eat, for instance. I taught you that. It was also to understand the elements and when and how to navigate in order to rest, to eat, to harness your physical energy. You tumbled a little bit with that. You ran a lot and then you became tired. And then I said, "Save your energy." So we had all those different systems. And this first time you were down was over in what is now northern India, bordering into the higher, cooler climate. So you were there. What took place, and I followed you, was that it was quite a long life—you didn't die. So I also had to help you die. I said that it's gonna be sometimes a little bit like, "Ohh, how to exit?" But you just kept on going, so I felt like we also had to talk about dying. And this was the first time (*in a partial incarnation*) and every time I tried to teach you about dying, or maybe assist you a little bit to die, you just kept going. You became older, and older, and older. But I said, "Eventually, it stops. And we have to prepare for that. We have to prepare for what happens when it stops, you know, what do we do? Where do we go?" So I needed to help you with that. But you were quite physically strong and your organs lasted a long time. You were not so clumsy, like you became later. But I think that they kinda adjusted the strings within you. So the first time you were a little bit of a superhuman. You did have a little bit of fur, so you were quite like a yeti. So I had my hands full. When you burned, you were not a yeti, you were more of a little shaman. So we adjusted certain things. BUT one of the big things in becoming a spirit guide is also the pickle to take on the fact that we have to teach you how to die, how to exit and make that transition as comfortable as possible. And also, to understand that when you de–dock, when you release the physical, moving into the fourth reality, there are certain things that you have to navigate through. That's also part of the spirit guides duties, because we don't want you just floating around like dirt in the fourth, not knowing where to go. So there are certain things that we have to, as a spirit guide, take care of. And since you didn't seem that eager to die, I had my hands full. Eventually, I led you to a berry that you were not supposed to eat. And then you fell asleep and then I assisted you.

D. At least you didn't push me over a cliff.

B. I did not push you over a cliff, because I did not want there to be a bad physical imprint of your first travel. So I guided you to a berry, several berries, and then you fell asleep and then I assisted you. Because you didn't really know how (*to die*). It's tricky. You always have assistance, of course. But because the physical was not a regular human, like it is now, where loved ones (*spirits of deceased relatives*) could come and assist. You know, a jolly group that sort of goes like, "Rise!" (*He turned his palms upwards and made a motion like a preacher telling the congregation to stand.*) We did not have that, we did not have loved ones, and you were a yeti, kinda. So we had to improvise. And when I say we, it was mainly me trying to assist you moving forward through the fourth reality. There were hiccups, I must say, during our program. When I say hiccups, it was like when you left the yeti and you had to move through the fourth reality. I was aware of that, because that was the only training they gave me, you know, "Help him through the fourth!" Huhuhuh. I was like, "Okay." But the dying, no one told me I had to assist! I thought that was gonna come automatically. Later on (*in other lives*), it did. And then it was like, "Whoa! I did not give you a berry! Why are you dying?" But in the beginning, since you were different—I think you wanted to have more like an Elahim form, like big. The furry thing was just a human attribute, of course. You're not furry at home. But Gergen did help, and also Ophelia and Jeshua, absolutely. I did have help. It wasn't like I gave you a berry and then let you float around all by yourself in the fourth. So I did have help from Jeshua. He created like a wind underneath your feet. You almost looked like a rocket, a NASA rocket, but it didn't go that fast. It was just like a breeze under your feet as you ascended. And I talked! I said, "Lasaray, here I am! Here I am! Look over here. We're transitioning. How did you feel about it?" Jeshua put in wind underneath your bottom and made you go up so you didn't stop. So, he did that. Ophelia came with somewhat of a blankie. It was a transformational energetic blankie, in some way. And I talked. First of all, I apologized for giving you the berry. I said, "You didn't want to leave, so I did not have any options. In order to come back, you kinda have to leave!" Huh huh huh. I asked Jeshua, "How long is this gonna go on?" Because you didn't have the regular human life expectancy of like up to the age of 80, tops. We were up to 112 when I gave you the berry. I didn't know (*what to do*). And then Jeshua and Ophelia said, "He's not going to have that form. It's just his first time. It's sort of freewheeling. He doesn't have a purpose, in that sense. It's just to come down in a form, and he wanted that form."

D. Like a test run.

B. Like a test run, indeed. After that, you never came in the yeti form again. You came as a shaman, but a smaller version. But as you can see, there are certain things that a spirit guide needs to take care of, and that is one thing. We don't want you to be as debris in the fourth reality and not moving forward.

D. Sometimes spirits do become like debris for a little while, don't they?

B. Debris, indeed. When there is too much debris, there is assistance that comes. Mainly from the councils from the fifth dimension, who are more connected to the Earth reality. And there are cleaners that come.

D. Vacuum up the strays?

B. Vacuum up the debris. And when I say vacuum, it's like a cone that comes in, and there is like a tube. So it is a vacuum, the cleaners.

D. People are always talking about shooting through a tunnel during an NDE, so it seems similar.

B. Ah. And now we have to shoot them forward into their home base. They can't just be stationary in the fourth reality. There are souls coming in, and people dream, so we cannot have too much debris. It cannot be too cluttered. You should know, also, that there are councils who operate in the fourth reality. Did not know that, did you?

D. I did not.

B. Nay. They are somewhat like spies, directly from the Creator, and they report directly into—I'm not saying into the Pole. They don't live there (*in the fourth*). They simply are visiting. Like the Tiddle-Taffles, they belong from the second dimension, but they have currently migrated to Tiddle in fish tank two. So there are councils who have migrated, briefly, into the fourth reality. It cannot be cluttered—and this is what I heard—with more than about 65 percent. When it reaches 85 percent—like during the 1900s where there were souls that left who did not find their way home for various reasons—cleaners came in.

D. There were a lot of people who died all at once during the pointless wars.

B. Indeed, and they did not know where to go. And that was not good because it became too cluttered. And then when people dream, because you should know that when you fall asleep and you dream, all of you, even those who don't believe in the spiritual reality at all, all become psychics. And that is the thing—that is the gift from the spirit realm—that when you dream, you are all intuitive. So those who don't believe in anything at all, at least they believe in their dreams.

D. At least they should.

B. Well, they kinda do. They ponder about the dream.

D. So, when you dream, is it all spirit or is it a mixture of human and soul?

B. It's a mixture. And depending on how often you've been in body, it varies how much it is a human experience that dreams. Those who don't have Coats, they can dream simply by being the soul, because when they detach, they detach completely. There are certain cases, when someone lacking a Coat, take on lives that are traumatic, in order for others to learn about trauma. So there are souls with no Coat who take on traumatic physical experiences in order to teach what trauma does, not just to the physical, but to the mental capacity within you. Those souls who take on that is to teach, in some way, the world around them—the medical establishment, hospitals, and so forth, but also the general consciousness—how you relate to trauma. And those souls who take on that to assist others can be colored by the experience. Because trauma doesn't exist elsewhere. It can exist a little bit in the first layer in the fourth reality. But as you move through the fourth reality, higher up, no trauma. Also, I was gonna say, these Coatless souls who take on those sorts of experiences can sometimes be a little bit affected and colored by the human experience. But when they sleep, they go through and are ascended to merge with healing teams.

D. I know the ones that were just here, they talked about our dreams being cluttered.

B. Ah. And if you engage and encounter all this debris—meaning, those who have not moved on, or dreams that are not clean—it is hard to navigate. And those who still have Coats can sometimes be affected by that dream. Meaning that those who try to read and interpret dreams have to take that into consideration when they tap into a certain soul. So when you (*Lasaray*) dream, for instance, not having a Coat, you are more clear. But you tend to also be drawn to human negativity. And THAT can influence your dreams, but not the soul. So, try to be drawn more to joyful stories than to negativity. Because that has a tendency to disturb your experience when you dream, and the cone. And when I say cone, it's because when you leave the physical reality, you also leave from your center and you exit up, so it looks like a cone. And hopefully, whatever knowledge you have drawn into your life, into your cone, you also take that with you as you ascend. But if you simply de-dock and leave, and not knowing how to harness the experience and the beauty that you found as a human, then you can be lost. So, find the beauty, fill your cone, fill your V-shape within you with beauty, joy, happiness, giggles. I know you, Lasaray, don't necessarily giggle that much. But a giggle fills up the cone with all sorts of colors. And again, nothing bad can travel on colors—so we (*guides*) can see the cone. Meaning, the soul experience and how you connect and combine above and below, the way you fill up your cone, and the colors you fill up the cone. Your cone is currently greenish-blue, which means that there is still a little bit of rest and recovering. I would say that what is needed is to bring in more of the orange. If you breathe in orange-red into your cone, that will help the physical. Don't get just stuck and content with blue and green, even though that's your favorite color. Both of you, that's your favorite color. But you have to embrace human energies, and that represents other colors. Your core color is blue-greenish, both of you. In order for you to feel whole and to also be at your best in your experience, you have to embrace the colors that is on the opposite scale. And in this case, for both of you, it is to breathe in orange, yellow, and red.

D. When you say our core color is blue-green, is that an Elahim, or is that a mixture of human and soul?

B. Nay, it's the Elahim. Dark blue moving almost into dark purple. And the green represents the ability to self-heal. And green tends to be part of several soul colors, in that sense, because green represents the ability to heal. It's a healthy color, it relates to health. And souls, even if you think, "Oh, a soul is always healthy," but souls can also need to rest, save energy.

D. You also have to do that too, sometimes?

B. I do. I have to maintain my light capsule. And when I do, I focus on green and I focus on white. Because the Center Pole is white and gold. Gold and white.

D. You've seen the Center Pole?

B. From afar. I've asked if we can maybe move a little bit closer. Huhuh. I know that I cannot travel there in my peanut suit or in my little sphere, in my bubble, but you have the zooming device. So, I still, now and then, with some sort of distance in between, I bring it up.

D. So would it help to put colors in our cone if we find a quiet place to be?

B. Ah. And exercise. Breathe. Go out and walk, breath, exercise, that's what you need. It does help when you swim in the lakes.

D. Yes, I enjoy that.

B. And it helps. It fills up the reserves. So I wanted to come by, and we're gonna continue to talk.

D. Does Ophelia have any thoughts she would like to pass through before you go?

B. Yes. She says the intake of food, of eating fruit and so on, you will feel like your energy is coming back. She says it's like, here is your skin, your human skin, and when you eat fruit—you remember when I shrink–fitted the bubble?

D. Yes.

B. It's actually working the same way. You feel like you are shrink-fitting your soul.

D. Okay, we'll do that.

B. Okay, I'll go now. That's what Ophelia says, she likes it when you eat fruit because it shrink–fits the soul. So I'll go now, but I'll be back. Maybe there's a separate session coming up, but we'll see.

D. Alright, my friend. Thank you so much, and Ophelia.

B. Ah. Okay, I go. Bye bye.

D. Bye bye.

The Merkaba and the Coat of Karma (Commentary)

Our spirit friends will talk about important concepts from a variety of perspectives, in the hopes that we piece it together. The Merkaba, as it relates to the center point where the soul attaches to the body, is one of those. Mastering the Merkaba is an active process that begins with the first incarnation, and ends when the Coat of Karma is folded. It has only recently occurred to me that Ophelia's description of the inner dimensions, in *Wave 1*, may have been an introduction to the inner Merkaba. The Merkaba is the common name for a star tetrahedron, which are two interlocked pyramids, where one is inverted. Each pyramid has four corners, so the Merkaba has eight areas of knowledge and experiences on Earth. When it spins, it has the appearance of a six–pointed star, which is how some of our alien friends see the center core in a human. In Ophelia's teaching, the bottom point would represent the first dimension, and the very top point would be the illumination of spiritual knowledge. The soul, when immersed in the physical, must seek to find a balance in the physical, the mental, and the emotional aspects of being a human. In *Wave 1*, Ophelia said:

O. [...] "So, if I may, I would like to draw a picture for you.

D. Please do.

O. The physical you, meaning where you put your feet, if you see yourself standing, and you can see a rainbow going through you that represents different layers of your being, the center, meaning the soul, or the spirit that we actually prefer it to be called, goes through all these layers. So you have the possibility to connect to all different dimensions, if you choose to. That is the secret of those who are initiating the higher order, or the higher… how can one say… master all the spiritual realms that are contained within each being." […] "This is what the ancient civilizations knew about, a knowledge that has been lost over centuries. It exists in all individuals, yet most of them are not connected to this wisdom. There are actually seven layers that you are connected to, seven dimensions from this specific reality. One to seven. One to seven, where your spirit connects through them all. The eighth would be considered leaving this specific reality. The eighth layer and above is not accessible for you at this time."

In *Wave 2*, Ari introduced the concept of the Merkaba meditation as a way to access knowledge from the fourth dimension, which he calls the fog above. During the April 15, 2018 session, he was talking about pyramids and how the ancients practiced their skills.

A. […] "It also serves to access the fog as you sit in a cone. This is the meaning of the image of sitting in a Merkaba, like a pyramid or a cone shape. That is how the natives learned how to go out of a physical, parking it, and accessing the fog above.

D. You said a Merkaba, what is that?

A. It is a sacred symbol, geometric form, how you can exit out of the physical. It's similar, like if you see the pyramid and you imagine that you sit in this pyramid, an energetic one, that is, the shape of the pyramid is also sacred. And you imagine that you sit in this pyramid. This is not new. Several individuals use this in meditation, but they don't have the ability to transform the pyramid into a Merkaba. The Merkaba is like the pyramid spinning, becoming several in shape. And that is how the ancients knew how to exit the physical, leaving it parked, and ascending to the collective consciousness, the cloud above, gathering information. This is how you see there are certain similar temples, symbols, in different areas within the world. You can study the Merkaba and you will also get a key on how the Elahims operate."
[…]

A year later, on July 7, 2018, Eli again suggested using the Merkaba visualization as a tool. We are repeating a small portion of his talk here. *Wave 3* contains the original and full version.

E. [...] "Put yourself in a Merkaba, visualize yourself in a Merkaba. Sit in that power. Visualize this pyramid energy rotating around you. This is a way for you to access the memory within, your soul memory. It is a way for you to leave the body as well, if you choose to. But it is easier for you to visualize that you sit in an energetic cone. Use what colors you like. Visualize and ask it to rotate. You will not rotate, you will be centered, but it will open the portal and the gates within. The trick is to be centered and still, as the outside, the atmosphere in this cone, or whatever spiral you wish to use as a tool. If you follow the spiral, you simply leave the body. If you center yourself in the cone or in a spiral, gates open. This is what the ancients knew. They never used the free energy in a way that caused harm, and they knew how to access different states of awareness. If they wished to explore the fourth, then they rotated and circled with this energy flow, the Merkaba or a spiral was also used; in that way, they lifted, they ascended into the fourth and accessed new information. Collective memories, a collective knowledge bank, just above your head. If they wished to open soul memories, portals within, they sat still and centered. Two different ways to use this vessel." [...]

In another session, which will be in *Wave 5*, Seth gave a discourse on the Merkaba that is quite fascinating. Before the Coat is folded, each person has a spinning Merkaba that represents the knowledge needed for completion of the journey. Once all the understandings are reached, the Merkaba stops rotating and forms a pyramid or trinity of knowledge for that soul on this reality of Earth. Seth explains it in this way.

S. [...] "It is acceptance. It is compassion. It is matter. The matter represents where you are at. The Trinity, in this way, means the matter of the human form. But you have to connect acceptance and compassion in order to gain the trinity here, meaning in the human form of matter. If you travel elsewhere, the trinity looks different, matter is different. The Merkaba simply indicates work in progress. Trinity means completion, full acceptance and understanding. You have to love the three parts. You have to love (*have compassion for*) the matter that you are working with, the human form. And that is the trick, that is the hardest part of the Trinity, before it (*the Merkaba*) stops. You have to accept the journey. You have to love (*feel compassion for*) that part of yourself traveling. You have to love (*have compassion for*) the form holding the trinity, in order for it to become a Trinity. As long as you do not love yourself, your form—(*until*) you accept form, you accept the journey, you accept the mission, and you accept differences in that form—then the trinity is not established. It is still Merkaba in rotation. The problem is that not many know about the Merkaba. It is accessed by different practices, such as breathing. During out-of-body experiences, those who travel have the ability to observe the Merkaba. In the beginning of a journey, the Merkaba is where the soul connects. But in the beginning of a journey, when a soul travels, in this case here (*on Earth*), it rotates quite fast. It slows down gradually, based upon progress, until it finally stops and becomes the trinity. There."

When the Merkaba meditation technique is used to recapitulate past lives and previous experiences, the practitioner sees from the soul's perspective and is no longer attached to the mental and emotional responses of the human self. The sadness of childhood, for example, which may have been a haunting specter of the past, becomes less personal. The soul views the scene of its previous self with tender compassion, and within that framework, understanding and acceptance are acquired. As more and more of the human impulses are supplanted with soul awareness in everyday life, the trinity will be complete, and the Coat of Karma will be folded.

Ophelia, Bob: Silence and Door 33 (July 28, 2021)

We do not publish most of the personal instructions and advice that we receive because it wouldn't be that helpful to the reader. Ophelia's part of this session is personal, where she is encouraging us to meditate and cleanse the body. However, it may be interesting to those who are also seeking a connection with their higher self, so we are including it here. When she was finished, Bob came in and gave a very insightful talk about fish tanks three and five. When he was moving into fish tank three through the door in the pyramid on Etena, he became silent and seemed enthralled with what he experienced (or re-experienced). He explains fish tank three was put into hibernation because there were entities who were creating problems with the web. My interpretation of what is meant by hibernation is that the energy maintaining the manifested forms is pulled back to the center points so that the intent can re-emerge in its original pure form. An animal species can be put into hibernation—meaning that it becomes extinct on the physical plane—but the pattern and intent of the species continues to exist both in the memory of the planet and also in the museums of previous life forms. It can be re-created at any time the conditions are right. On the massive scale of the universe, hibernation could have various degrees. The most complete would be a dissolving and merging of all forms back to the center pole of the fish tank. Everything in the fish tank has a center point, from the smallest element, the planets, solar systems, galaxies, families of galaxies, all the way up to the center point of the fish tank. Each part can be put into hibernation and restarted. In many ways, it is like a software program that gets a glitch and needs to be rebooted. The Creator is the master programmer who makes changes to the intent being projected up into the Wheel.

O. Greetings. This is Ophelia.

D. Hello, Ophelia.

O. How are you, my friend?

D. Well. I thought that might be you.

O. Oh, yes indeed. We are several here. We are celebrating the steps that you are taking. The cycle that you are currently on is about to come to a close. You don't necessarily see the beginning and end in your progress and cycles. But we follow it and monitor your development closely. At this time, you are moving into new territory. And with that said, vacation is over. And when I say vacation is over, yes indeed, it also unfortunately entails your intake of food. More liquid in your vehicles are required. You need to become less dense in your energetic systems, especially this one. But you as well, because your role will change. At this time, you both need to be able to move freely within and among frequencies. Frequencies meaning spiritual dimensions as well as manifested visitors. There will be a shift in the information, and this has already been revealed. With this said, it is important that you pay attention to messages that come. Some will feel unfinished. Some will feel lacking the point. The point is for you to try to find within your own system, within your being. Your change, my friend, is upcoming. Your transformation is about to come. Meaning, that you have to open yourself up like a lotus flower. Step–by–step, it is your development that we are now monitoring. You have to want to understand your origin. You have to find your treasure within. You have neglected yourself up till this point, following too much of your human mind. At this time, we ask of you to ignite your spiritual mind. You need the solitude; you need the peace. Both of you thrive better in a cooler climate. And with cooler climate also comes the darkness, and that is beneficial for your growth. Healing will take place within your cells, physical cells, but also highly connected to your spiritual cells. When I say cell, in a human mind that resonates with DNA. The spiritual cells are intact, but can be contaminated if the body is too human. In this case, you have no Coat of Karma, but you have memories, never–the–less. Those memories, in some way, attack your soul DNA, making it hard for you to reject signals that are of human origin. You need to find the solitude, find the peace. Start your breathing exercises once more. Water is good for your physical body. The swimming that we have advised you has ignited the sensation of cleansing. We are not necessarily looking for physical improvement, meaning muscle tone. We ask of you to enhance and increase your spiritual muscle tone. That is done in a different manner. The mind needs to calm. It needs to be released of human influences for a while. Some exercises are individual for you, but mainly it has to do with YOU finding a space to settle your roots, to listen to the silence, to be in each other's company without demands. To simply be is a gift from us to you. Don't rush to find chores. Believe me, they will come.

D. Is there anything I can do specifically that would help the process?

O. Unplug from human influences. Both of you. This has been said, and it is now repeated. We want you to find the peace. The mind is boiling. The human consciousness is boiling. Don't let that lead you astray. This is what we ask of you, to simply sit in each other's company; to not have a fully booked calendar as a human is something that you struggle with. You might not struggle in that sense that you feel like you have chores to do, but your mind is constantly seeking information, seeking something to learn. But it is on a human level. And this is what we ask of you to adjust. To simply sit quietly somewhere in nature. You can sit together, but you can also sit with about 5 meters apart. Sit silently and listen independently to how nature, how silence, resonates with you. This is what we ask of you this fall, is to simply recharge, to release information in your brain, in your human brain, allowing your spiritual brain to awaken. Your cells, your spiritual cells, need to increase in numbers, and this is what your Little Friend, Bob, talked about, with your breathing. To breathe down the energy and fill up the bottle. (*She laughed and looked to the side, so Bob must have said something.*)

D. Well, what about food, since you said we need to clean?

O. Try to eliminate the wheat products as much as possible. Eat vegetables. Dairy is not so bad, but it needs to be in preparation for the digestive system to be able to receive the intake. The main part, next to sugar, is the wheat. So, sandwiches, unfortunately, picnics, are....

D. Not so good? What about meat?

O. Meat, if the meat is prepared correctly, it's not so damaging. But be aware that there are side products in the meat that will increase the human cells. And that is what the industry is seeking. The body becomes heavy. Back to the fact that your energetic self, your inner systems, organs, and spiritual self, need to be slimmed, needs to be trimmed in its nature, in its design. As the human eats too much heavy—sugar is bad, but the heavy energetic food such as wheat and, in some way, meat—it's damaging to the energetic levels. The balance becomes, hmm—it runs too quick. Needs to be cooled down. Soup, mushrooms, tomatoes, we highly recommend. Tomato soup. Garlic, eat a lot of garlic. It cleanses your breathing; it cleanses the veins. Garlic is one of nature's many medicines. Use a lot of garlic. It doesn't matter if you smell, since it's just the two of you—with 5 meters apart.

D. (*Laughing.*) What about potatoes?

O. In moderation. Heavy, but not off the list, just in moderation. Try to eat more steamed vegetables, that is good. Tell this one, kindly. There.

D. Thank you for that advice.

O. You are much welcome. Simply be in the mindset of love. To be, and to know, that you are cared for. To enjoy the present time as humans, but also to enjoy the fact that you are aware that something much bigger is taking place, and you are a part of it. How would you set your footprints? How do you want to be remembered? The important part is to find the answers within. When you know the answers within you, it's easier to ask the right questions. Questions, you have in numbers. But you pop them left and right. And when I say you, I mean humanity as a whole. Try to focus on the answers, and you will find that there are few answers, because of the fact the questions are irrelevant. You find the answers that you need, the few that makes your life important. Try to neglect too many questions, and you will see that there are just a few, a handful, of answers that you need. (*Ophelia turns left to address Bob.*) Okay, Bob. Yes, you are.

D. That's really brilliant. Thank you, Ophelia. I always enjoy hearing your voice.

O. You are much welcome. It is a delight to follow you. Bye bye. (*Bob moved in, seamlessly.*)

B. Ah!

D. Hello, my friend

B. What I have been doing, aside from continuing to scrubble down details about the 2178 life, I have also, actually, been back in the store.

D. What happened now?

B. Well, I don't know. It felt kinda empty on the shelves. And I'm thinking like maybe this is like a Monday, you know, when everything is delivered on Tuesdays—something like that. But then you say that it was similar like my torch. (*When he wandered off course in the pyramid on Etena, his little torch went out.*)

D. Oh, yes, I remember.

B. It disappears, magically disappears. It's not a fog, it just looks empty.

D. The only thing left to see is some electrical tape and a broom.

B. Haha. And some nails in a box. But you actually humored me and said that we are gonna trot down silently along aisle 3. It's where they store things for fish tank three that is in hibernation, that is sleeping. So helmets, I cannot see. But I do see my friend, way down there. Way, way down, and he has the helmet on. But for some reason, he doesn't hear me. When I came in, you said, "We're going to go down aisle 3 because I have a surprise for you." And I'm all in favor of surprises. I think that's fun. You said that I have to be quiet, though, because this is the sleeping aisle. I'm not sure about that really, or if it's just that I should be quiet. I mean, it kinda worked because I was quiet. So we were walking down this aisle, and on the left side is the shelves. There are certain things, but not much, I must say. I don't know if there has been, you know…

D. Like a big run on merchandise?

B. Like a big sale and someone just came in a snatched everything from the shelves.

D. A big Covid sale.

B. Huhuh, like a pandemic. Then everyone is like, "Need to buy those nails and building stuff." But far down, I do see my friend, and this is where we're heading. On the right side of the aisle, though, are, in this case, doors. And we are passing closed doors. And you there on that side, so I don't see fully. I'm on the left side, looking at the empty shelves. But you say we are heading down to door 33, and that's where the surprise is gonna be.

D. That's an interesting number.

B. Ah. 33. You said it's a holy number and it has a significance when it comes to geometry and also gravity, you say. Anything with 3s, in some way, in different combinations, creates—it has to do something with the vacuum field and gravity.

D. I know Tesla was obsessed with 3. He would circle a building 3 times before he went in, things like that. He said that 3 was a magic number, for some reason.

B. 3, 33, and 333. 3s and then you puzzle them differently. It's a magical number. And here we are on our way to door 33. And it has to do with fish tank three, because that's the aisle that we're in. So I'm heading down here and I can see, the closer I come—I see my friend. And he's standing there, and now he waves. But he's not by himself. So he also has somewhat of a mentor. I don't know why you don't just let me be like with him. You don't have to accompany me.

D. Don't you still need a translator, or can you talk with him?

B. Well, if I had a helmet, I don't need one. He didn't need any translation when it came to me. He just looked at me and zoomed in on me and instantly knew. So his helmet is somewhat of a translator.

D. I don't think you have a helmet, do you?

B. Nay. Maybe that is my next gift. Christmas is coming up! Huhuhuh. I do get presents from you and Gergen and so forth. Ophelia tends to give me presents now and then.

D. She gave you the plant.

B. She gave me the plant. It's in a container for now, but it's gonna be launched. But on the way down here, there is like several doors. But we're going to door 33, and here I am. And my friend is standing there, also, smiling. So, he knows, probably, what this is all about. You said, "Once we open the door, you will have a look-see into fish tank three." So for some reason, this aisle is not just a store, it also provides....

D. It's like a zooming device.

B. It's like a zooming device, it's just that I use a door. When I'm standing here, I'm asking like, "Am I supposed to go by myself?" Uhh. And you said, "No, the three of us will go." So the door opened and my little friend, he's just smiling. I think he's really happy to show me around. I don't know why it says 33, but it has something to do with the molecular setting, building blocks, you say. Everything has building blocks with 33. It has also to do with some keys when it comes to understanding the gravitational differences. (*Bob was really struggling to find words to describe what he was experiencing.*) I don't know why you don't share that much, though.

D. That information would be nice to know.

B. But I'm gonna open the door and we're gonna have a sneak–peek here and look inside. So, it's just a threshold. And when I open, ohh, I see! Inside it just goes like this (*he moved his hand up and down, like it was riding a wave*). It's like a big snore, perhaps. It's just wobbling like a big breathing, like that.

D. So what is it that is wobbling?

B. The energy is wobbling. Not like this. (*He held both hands flat with the fingertips pointing toward the other hand, then made waves with both hands.*) It's like one big wave, one big breathing. There are certain tones, very silently. But you said that we're gonna investigate the dream. It has also something to do with the building blocks of 3 that will bypass, you say, gravitational conditions. And you say that man are not aware of the portals of 33 and 3s, and the magical keys that resonate with 3. And 3 is like the trinity to understand the blocks that you can use in order for different… (*He was struggling again to explain.*) I don't know why I'm trying to tell you, since you probably already know this. But the gift is to go into fish tank three. And you said, "Sometimes, you can come directly from the store into a fish tank. There are doors."

D. So when you look, is it like you are inside of the fish tank? Or are you observing it?

B. At the moment, I'm just standing here in the doorway.

D. Does it look like, if you step through, that you will be in the fish tank?

B. I will be in the fish tank. And now we're gonna take a step into the dream. You say, "Once we take a step INTO the dream, we become actors, in some way, in the dream. And we can not only just look, we can also modify and change the course of the dream." But I'm not sure I'm supposed to meddle with that. But I'm gonna observe my friend here with the helmet, the way he works. I did get somewhat of a little lamp on my head. But it's not a helmet, it's mainly, perhaps, to see, because it looks quite foggy to move around there. But we're gonna go and we're gonna investigate the dream, and we become part of the dream. And this is a gift, you say. So here we go, and I'm all excited. I'm in the middle—here is him (*nods to the left*) and here is you (*to the right*), and we're gonna go now. So, ohh, now I go! (*He then became quiet, as he was observing.*) Oh. It's like one of those sounds from those big trumpets that makes a mmwwaaahhhh. (*He made a deep tone, like a foghorn.*)

D. Is it a steady sound, or is it rising and falling?

B. Rising and falling. Fish tank three had somewhat of a turmoil in the beginning of its cycle. Now it's not happening, but this is why they shut it down. There were conflicts between forces, and it had to do with possession of certain minerals. These minerals do not exist on Earth, you say. But there were certain things that were used and harvested as an energy to move around. Huh–huh, you with your little rockets, you have your fires and go like this high (*he held his index and thumb about 1 centimeter apart*) and then, "Oh, need to go back." But this had to do with the ability to use free energy for transportation. And I can see almost a vehicle, of sorts, they put themselves in a lane and it just sucks around. It was an engineering and also a prototype on how to have free movement, huh huh, like the EU. HUH HUH HUH. He says the conflict was not so much about the material. It had mainly to do with the web where those vehicles traveled. Like, "Okay, this is my road," like tolls, almost. And this one (*Seth*) was with, trying to mediate, trying to create this web of connections between realities in fish tank three. This was way pre–me. Oh, my friend says it was not pre–me. I was at the 4–H Farm when this took place, so it was not that long ago. I do remember the 4–H Farm quite fondly. But that's not here. But I did exist, he said, my friend here. But they observe these road systems, if you like.

D. So is this like an interconnecting energy field within the universe of fish tank three?

B. Indeed, indeed. In fish tank three. In quite the early beginning of it, quite close to fish tank two. But there is a real border to fish tank two, it's not like between four and five, where it's sort of dissolving a little bit. It's a real border. But it took place in about the first 10 percent of fish tank three. The purpose of fish tank three is to find prototypes and connections, like interconnections for travels. So it's sort of like a road map. I guess this one (*Seth*) goes here a lot because he likes maps. Because of the fact that it was not optimal to connect all realities, it became a little bit like those mad professors, using energy too intensely. Here they were connecting too many points, and it became a mish–mash of signals. What they are learning about is to, in some way, reduce the amount of travelers.

D. Are those travelers from that fish tank?

B. Manifested. These are fully manifested; they are like solid. If you were to poke them, they would feel that.
D. Do you know which spiritual dimension they came from?
B. Some of them came from six, mainly six.
D. So they had enough influence over the fish tank that they caused it to go into hibernation?
B. Ah. It was too many options of travel. It didn't become free movement; it became tolls. Not payment tolls, but hurdles everywhere. It became like a conflict between engineers, if you like, on how to solve this specific motion between. It was a prototype that had nothing to do with just fish tank three, it was about to be launched. So, each fish tank creates different things, in order for it to be beneficial and adapted into all fish tanks. And fish tank three had to do with motion and the ability to send and receive signals. Signals could be like a dot, like a physical entity, but it can also be an energetic dot, like how you transmit and move energy, and so forth.
D. What contribution does fish tank five make to the Wheel?
B. Fish tank five very much has to do with the contribution of nature, like plant life, and all the elements like water, soil. In fish tank five, you merge and combine all the elements. You have air; you have everything. So, in many ways, fish tank five blossoms, it has the potential because all these different things that others have been doing in other fish tanks are put into high action, into fruition. You can put in stuff into (*a different fish tank*) and hope that it will blossom. But there is also a wave that goes from inside and outward, like this (*he made a rolling wave motion with his right hand, palm down, fingers pointing outward*). So you have this that has to do with—almost like free will. And then you have the intentional plan going like this (*with his left hand he showed a wave going across his body, perpendicular to the free–will wave*). So, at this time, Earth is in the middle of intention and free will. And that is why it looks like this (*he held both hands palm downwards and showed the two waves crossing each other*). So in fish tank three, it had to do with just intention. It had nothing to do with free will because it was mainly like a workshop. In fish tank five, you merge intention and free will. It's almost like time and space merge—free will and intention merge. So it's like one wave going like this, then the other goes like this (*repeats his hand movements*), so the whole thing wobbles. And the sleep is about to,

it has to do with releasing the experience. It's not gonna go anywhere, but it's gonna become. It's still a workshop.

D. So when it goes into hibernation, do all the manifested entities leave?

B. Ah. Back home. No motion anymore, it's completely silent. It's only that mmaaaggghhhh. (*He repeated the foghorn sound.*)

D. They were conflicted with each other?

B. Indeed. And with the plan. When it's conflicting with the plan, someone can come in and say, "Stop."

D. So that's why, when you went in there, you felt like you could impact the dream and the end result?

B. I could impact. I'm not supposed to. I don't think I'm supposed to. You said that I should also be careful about wishing that, because I can BECOME the dream. I can become part of that project. And do I really want to become a dream? Meaning, I would assume, that they put me in hibernation as well. So you said, "Be careful where you poke around." And that's why he has this helmet, because he's not affected. He can sniff around and he can adjust and participate in the dream, and he can change the outcome and the evolution of the dream, because he sees the bigger picture. His helmet is somewhat protecting.

D. He can also sense what the Creator intended?

B. Indeed. "This helmet is like an extension of the Creator," he said. "It's like you have a little bit of a Master Mind. When I have this on, my mind is almost like the Master Mind." That's nice! I said I had a hat with stones sewed into it, but it didn't do much. So then it feels like I'm just dressing up, whereas his outfit actually means something.

D. That's a lot of responsibility.

B. But the gift here is not a helmet. However, what you gave me is a little device on a necklace. It looks like an eye. So you said that I can look through it and I can see, but I cannot touch and interfere. (*He gestured like he was holding a flat object in front of his eyes.*)

D. So you hold it up, and then you can gaze—

B. And I can see what he sees. But as soon as I drop it, I'm free. I like to be free.

D. I suppose a lot of the stories that you hear about fallen angels, in some way, that is like souls coming into a reality, like a fish tank?

B. Yes. And in this case, those who were removed could be considered like fallen angels. It just came in like, "Stop." I can see those like

10 percent, and then everything else is just like a big fog that is breathing.

D. So if fish tank five were to go into hibernation, could they put parts of it into hibernation, like the Milky Way galaxy, and leave the rest of it alone? Or does it all go into hibernation?

B. Well, in fish tank three, they took it all down. But there are more galaxies in fish tank five than in fish tank three. And some of them are, if I look at fish tank five—I have my eye and I can kinda look now a little bit—some of them are about to merge.

D. There are billions of galaxies, or at least it appears like there are.

B. Ah, but they merge, and that's also part of fish tank three. Because when it's closed, they merge, like that. Things can merge like this, then it becomes like the disks, you say.

D. One over top of the other?

B. Overlapping like that. But what they don't want is for them to go like this (*palms down, fingers pointing towards the other hand, and then colliding*). And fish tank three is very much about order, you say. And when some entities became a little bit too forceful with their way of order, it came to a stop. And now we're dreaming about it, to just sort of resolve it. But it's a lot about order and it's very— again, fish tanks three, six, and nine create the holy three. So we have that here. In some way, they resonate as well. There's gonna be more talk about this, you say, but you wanted me to see the dream. And when I see the dream here, I can feel the presence of someone that is like a big hand. It's like a hand is holding fish tank three, almost, and it's like pulsating.

D. Is there light or anything?

B. Mainly foggy.

D. But you sense that it is being supported?

B. It's supported.

D. And the support is like the intention?

B. It holds the dream, it holds the intention and it holds its position. And now we're heading back to the door, you say.

D. I hope we can find it.

B. Huhuh. Well, it's just behind. I didn't go that far. But it's just you and I going back. He's not done.

D. He's off to work?

B. He's off to work.

D. That's pretty handy to be able to go out into a fish tank from the store.

B. So, I'm back now but it was quite interesting to see different things.
D. It's really interesting about how all this works, the grand design.
B. Ah, it's a grand design. And you say all fish tanks have different agendas and they're designed differently. And some are, at the moment, dreaming. It's more of those workshops, like a factory, where certain prototypes are launched, worked on, and adjusted. But it's also part of a dream as it's absorbing.
D. I guess the dream exists in all the fish tanks, doesn't it?
B. Ah. But this one really snores.
D. I mean the dream in some way is the intent, so no matter what stage it is in, it's part of the dream?
B. In a human, the dream is the intent. But waking self is the executive and the free will. To learn that is to master both realities and both levels of existence. So I'm gonna go now, but we're gonna have a separate session here soon.
D. Well, thank you for all that. It was really interesting.

Bob: Sewing the Big Sheet (Aug 15, 2021)
Bob begins the session by talking about vacuums during my incarnations. That usually means silence or a lack of feedback. But in this case, he meant an absence of meaningful activity related to the soul's purpose. He said Jeshua, Lasaray's mentor, sees my lives as a map, where he leads me from one important step to another, always with the eventual goal in mind. In this life, it was to find Christine and fulfill our part of the project, where she and I receive and deliver their teachings to humanity. If we look at Christine's map, the steps to becoming a pure trance channel had to be perfected before the spirits could share their wisdom. Regardless of where she may have been living, Isaac would have guided her to the situations and people vital for that ability to flourish. This is true for all souls, since no life is fully scripted. Bob also explains how the main spirit guide weaves together all the influential moments from each lifetime to create a tapestry. The map on this tapestry should eventually match the Coat of Karma for that soul. The mentor unerringly guides the soul through all the steps needed to fold its Coat.

Later in the session, Bob talks about tumbling. When he was first preparing to travel, he was told that going to some destinations would make him feel like he was tumbling, like being in a washing machine. He has yet to work up the bravery needed for that method of traveling, but he still mentions it from time to time. In *Notes, Volume 1*, Bob talks about traveling to Etena the first time and encountering birds guarding the planet and controlling who was allowed to enter. We have since learned that the manifested entities change their appearance, depending on who is observing them. When Bob approached, they saw that he was from the second, so they chose to present themselves as an animal he was familiar with.

B. Hello to you, there.

D. It's been a while.

B. It's been a while. Well, not a while, because we put you on pause. So it's not really a while. For us it's like a pause. We pause time, like you call it, so there is no gap. I've learned this, because I did complain a bit when I felt like a vacuum. And then Jeshua said, "Well, you know, we don't have to make vacuum, we can just sew two events together, like that. So it's like no vacuum." What I feel, as a spirit guide, is that I'm in a ditch, feeling vacuum, feeling like time is passing. But for Jeshua, he just connects events. So, it's just a pause, and he's sort of like sewing them together. So I'm learning a little bit about certain tricks that I can use moving forward. Then I said, "So, all these journeys, I was in the ditch, and you just sewed and had a continuous experience? Is that correct?" Huhuh. And he said, "Yes." Huhuh. And I was like, "Why didn't we teach me this earlier?" He said, "Even as a spirit guide, we evolve and we learn different things." So, for him, all your lives are sewed into a continuous sheet. Whereas me, taking care of day-to-day life and activity, I'm sort of falling and rising like that ditch—highs and lows in this big sheet of experiencing. But for Jeshua, he doesn't go up and down like a roller coaster. He just steadily moves on and calculates and creates this sheet. So basically, what you do when you come into body is that you create a sheet. As a soul, you are not aware of this sheet that you're creating. But as you pop down, the main spirit guide creates like a map. So, for Jeshua, depending on what happens, he just redirects the map. But he just sews them together. It's like a living map, a living sheet. It would be similar—if you see the map—and you are like, "Oh, place him in the US." But then suddenly, you go to Europe. So it would be similar like we would connect the Europe Continent and the US. He just sews them together so they become like a sheet. Whereas me, I'm going slowly here in the sea, ditching, falling down, not aware of this whole creation of this sheet.

D. I'll have to think about that.

B. But I wanted to tell you that I've been in the Library a lot with Zachariah. There were certain things that I wanted to study up on, like your lives, in order for me to—because Jeshua said that now when I'm creating something for you, then that also has to patch up in this big sheet. So, he was interested in understanding my ideas for you, so that he could sew that experience into the general sheet. All souls have this map that the main spirit guide attends to. And then those sheets overlap with others, creating like a scenario that belongs in the Earth's reality. And, you know, some say, "Okay, is this stored in the fourth reality?" And in some way, they are. But they are also stored in the Library. So you don't have to sort of dip your face down into the fourth reality to access it. You can go to the Library (*on the fifth*), and that is what humans call like a book. It is similar like a book, but it's more like big doors, sheets, that you go through, like that.

D. Are all the lives on one sheet, or is each life like a page?

B. When you are in body, then Jeshua sees like a big map. He can see and he can zoom in, and if you make different decisions, then, like I said, the map also changes. But for him, he doesn't have to sort of go down and up. He just sews the experiences together, so he wanders straight across. It's like he creates bridges, whereas I have to take the boat, swim, fly—I have to do all these different things with you. And that's when I experience the vacuum, because I am in–between experiences. Jeshua is not. So I said, "That would have been helpful if I hadn't been between experiences."

D. Is this similar like a book of life about all your incarnations on Earth?

B. Incarnations, indeed. When you incarnate, it looks like a big sheet, flat, horizontal, and like I said, he just sews the experiences together. But when the sheet is done and you fold it—it's similar like the Coat of Karma, in some way—but it's not a karma sheet. It's basically like events. Some are events that you, yourself, participated in, you know, you took actions and created an event. But it's also sometimes—and Jeshua said, "We can also, if we feel like there is a need to redirect and change the sheet, the map, then I can make him go other places. Then I sew in a new event. I tie two events together, if I feel like there is more progress or assistance or aid in another area." So, it's also like a geographic sheet, if you like. And that is done on an individual level. So when I said that there is a vacuum, he said, "No, there is not. I just tie events together. So for me there is no waiting around." And I felt like we have had lives, several visits, where there has been a lot of waiting around. Especially for me, because you did not hear me all the time. So, I went through and was looking into like when the walkie–talkie is on or off, what I can do to improve the receiver in you. Because you're gonna be different in the 2178 life. You're not gonna hear me like this—which was my first idea, of course. It's not going to be the same. But I'm gonna have like a receiver—so you will not hear me with your ears—it will be like you have ideas. But it's me directly communicating, putting those ideas into your center point.

D. It won't be as nice as this.

B. You're not gonna know the difference because you're in body. You're just gonna feel like you just have a lot of ideas. It doesn't matter. But in some way, it would be nice if you could talk like this, but I couldn't do just everything. So I've been in the Library with Zachariah and we've gone through certain things. I've looked back and studied up on certain things. But not just study up on you, because I have that fresh in my mind, so to speak. It's not like I forget. As a spirit, you don't have like amnesia. Once you know something, it's there. And that's why I felt like maybe if we bumped up the brain a little bit so that you didn't have to relearn everything, it would be more like whatever I put in there, whatever we put in there, just stayed.

D. I could use that help in this lifetime.

B. Well, I have asked, on your behalf—or mainly on my behalf because I feel like I'm repeating myself a lot—I said, "If I could make you not need to be repetitive, if I could adjust, maybe just a little bit. But Ophelia said there is a limit on what one can do with the brain that is currently available. But it's changing! It might not be changing until 2178, but I'm hopeful! So I've been studying up with Zachariah. And Zachariah, he also is helping with my little students, little Elahims and spirit guides, and so forth, because I feel like I have neglected them a little bit. So I've been with Zachariah and they've been training on amnesia, because they don't understand that they will forget their mission. So we have classes on how to handle amnesia. I said, "In the beginning, it will be more of a constant memory loss because the soul has to put all the effort into maneuvering the physical." Like a robot, a little bit. You can see that in certain people. Like they don't really know how to maneuver the physical. Huhuh. Like maybe they don't have the rhythm when they dance, for instance. They stand out, like an odd human. Don't judge. It's just that that soul is trying to figure out how legs work independently from arms, and so forth. We've been there, of course. You don't like to dance, but that's a different thing. It's not like you don't know how to maneuver your legs. But you claim that you don't, but I know you do because you don't have a Coat any more, and I know you can dance. I've seen you dance. You know when you were Charles Mustard? Well, there were other times when it was almost like (*the Irish*) River Dance, you know, sideways. I knew that you liked it. I saw that you liked it—and I know you know how to. But you said that it preoccupies the mind from the real intention. But I said, "You can make someone happy by dancing." Anywho, I've been with Zachariah and we've gone through certain things, and we've also been helping the little ones coming in. I have my hands full.

D. What has Zachariah been doing lately?

B. Zachariah, he has big classes in big auditoriums. There are a lot of souls coming back and reporting on environmental imbalances. So there's a lot of those reporting classes that he also sits in—it's like a boardroom, in some way, that he sits and listens to data. There's a lot of souls coming home at the moment that are reporting certain things, so he sits in like life review councils, but also in study groups. And those are bigger, like big auditoriums where there is a group—so Zachariah is not by himself. There are several (*other teachers*) that are also educating (*students*) because of the fact of changes in the environment, the temperature and so forth changing. We're looking into understanding how to adjust the living quality for the body. So there are a lot of studies, because there are cycles going on. And there is an environmental cycle that he is also teaching, with the group. So he's a lot with the councils on the fifth, at the moment. As a guest lecturer, perhaps. I wasn't invited. But I like to sit and talk with Zachariah. I like to hear stories because he's quite wise. And again, he doesn't forget anything either, so we have quite interesting discussions. However, he's not like a sharing kind-of-guy, always. So you have to ask, he doesn't just tell. It's a good fortune, huhuh, that I'm quite inquisitive! Otherwise, nothing would have been shared, because he doesn't share by himself. But I ask by myself, so that's why our relationship is quite prosperous.

D. He's a wise one.

B. Ah, but he's also a little bit busy. Then I've been creating a lot of events on your life, of course. But it's also to tend to your energetic levels within you at this time, since you've been not been feeling well. So I've tended to those mundane Earth changes as well.

D. Thank you for working on me. I was aware that you did.

B. It's not like you are this spring chicken that I can just fix in a day. Sometimes it takes a little while. It's also a little bit because of the fact that your soul is not fully connected to the physical. I don't have so much to work on sometimes, because of the fact that you don't fill up the whole body.

D. I worry sometimes what's going to happen in the next few years when people start dropping dead from the injections.

B. Well, they go home and they report. It's not like a big uh–oh about that. But it's important that you unplug from the world, now and then. And this is what we have talked about. We told this one, when the two of you met, that it will be that you go out and do something, and then retreat.

D. Are we going to have enough time to continue working on the books?

B. Ah, ah.

D. Like Wave 6, 7, 8…?

B. It's not like you're super busy with other things. And that is a pickle for this one. Not for you. Once you find your silent spot, it will be different, because you cannot run around in the same way.

D. I feel like I've been getting behind on our books.

B. Well, the human you feels like you are behind. But no time has passed, just sewing events together. So this is just you feeling the same way as I do, like a vacuum.

D. Okay. That's good to know.

B. Anyway, Zachariah, he seems to say, "You have to ask the right questions." And I say, "Why don't you just give me the answers? You kinda know what I want to know." And he said, "Ask the right questions." So I made a list of new questions and went back to Zachariah. He said, "You made a list?" And I said, "Ah, ah. I have certain things that I thought we could talk about, topics." He looked at it and he said, "Did Gergen approve?" And they are friends, Huhuh, so I said, "We didn't go through the list because I didn't find Gergen." And he said, "That's not true. Gergen is always around for you, my little friend." So, I have different lists. I have a list for you where I want to zoom in. I have somewhat taken a step back of going everywhere, because it seems that it involves a lot of turbulence. Then I felt like, "Am I ready to tumble?" I was ready to tumble to go to Etena, but you said, "That's not really a tumble, we simply passed through the mist and we were welcomed by the birds. But if you're going to go to other places, it might affect your being." And then I said, "Maybe we don't have to tumble. Maybe we can just zoom in and I can sit safely in the zooming device room. That will make me learn, but not necessarily be in an experience that I might not be ready for."

D. So have we been doing that?

B. A little bit. We're looking at fish tank seven.

D. Hmm. I don't hear much about seven.

B. Oh, seven is fascinating. It's similar like five, in some way. It's divided a little bit, the even numbers and odd. There are more—how can one say? It's more emotional in the even numbers. It's a different color in those. They're more like orange, yellow. Whereas the odd numbers are denser in some way and it's a different kind of experience. In fish tank seven, what we've been looking at are actually engineering of planets. It's like a lab. So I've been in a lab situation.

D. This one said she has seen you in a lab.

B. I've been in several labs. This one (*in seven*) I did not go to because I wasn't sure if I wanted to cross the barriers of tumble. So I said, "Why don't we zoom in and I can have a look–see?" There are places there that have like—the place that I have been looking at—it's like glass pyramids, a location. It doesn't have an atmosphere like here, so it's more of a logical environment. Tallocks live in eight, bordering into nine, but you've been in seven a lot. You say that there is a lot of mental experience.

D. Are there manifested beings there?

B. Ah. And they have vehicles, they have crafts.

D. Can they travel to fish tank five, or do they?

B. There is a link. I don't know how they go, but there is a link between. But fish tank seven is more evolved. It has a different tone. It's not as warm and welcoming as Etena. It looks a little bit robotic, but they are intelligent. What I see in this star system here is that they live in glass pyramids. But you might think, "Oh, glass. You can have a look and see inside." It reflects so I cannot look in. But you zoomed in and you said that it is a lot about energy in fish tank seven—how to store and recycle energy. So there were certain ideas from fish tank seven that were used by Tesla. He took information from here, fish tank seven. We never went. I don't know how I go there, and I said, "It's okay. I don't have to, I'm comfortable here in the couch," kinda. But you wanted to show me where ideas of science (*can be found*). And a lot has to do with energy and how to make crafts fly and (*how to*) ride, you say, "We ride energy, we don't take it. We ride energy waves." So we're looking into that. Fish tank three still sleeps. It actually snores. And you said, "Once it starts snoring, which is a way to detect changes, because there is a different melody." Like a volcano, it starts to rumble and harvest the data, and then it's eventually going to blow up. And once it's blown up, it is ready to become." Like a big sneeze.

D. So then everything will start remanifesting?

B. Indeed, in some way. I'm seeing certain things here in fish tank seven, though, that I am quite interested in. And you said the Tallocks goes there also, even though they seem to belong in eight. We didn't look so much in eight. Anyway, I'm probably gonna look more.

D. That's really interesting.

B. Well, I'm gonna go now. I just wanted to pop by.

Ontorio, Bob: Cosmic Time and Evolution (Aug 29, 2021)
This is a wonderful session, for those who are interested in exotic metaphysics. This was the first time that Ontorio, one of Lasaray's teachers on the sixth dimension, came through and spoke. He delivered a brilliant lecture on space, time, and how the human can master the understanding of both.

When he left, Bob stepped in and talked about his living planet where groups of his Individual live. He gives a very insightful analysis of the relationship between evolution and stress, which he then applied to the modern human. Finally, he told how changes are brought to Earth by travelers from the parallel realities. One of the examples he cited was from *Notes, Volume 2*, when Joel saw visitors putting boxes in his mountains. The boxes were activated to change the energy flow in the Earth and cause the tectonic plates to move in a specific way. The result was that the Indian Plate broke away from Gondwana around 130 million years ago and made a 6500 km journey northward through Tethys Ocean to crash into the Eurasian continent and form the Himalayas. The speed of movement has remained a mystery to modern geophysicists, but the tectonic rearrangement was planned and executed by the spiritual councils and alien visitors.

In this session, we have included Ontorio's advice to Christine and me about fasting on the full moon. He gave no additional information, but I assume it has to do with the flow of energy at that time. Back in 2016, Jeshua said "the cycles of the full moon represent the polarity between the male and female." In a future session, perhaps they will clarify if fasting during a full moon is the optimal time for everyone, and why that is so.

B. Oooooohhhhh! I'm too close! There's someone here. Ooooohhh! Someone grand! You brought him. Oooohhh, he's like bigger than you. Ohh, and I get to tag along! He's an old friend, he says. I'm here, so clearly it wasn't like a door in front of me, but I'm gonna bow away a little bit because he's so shiny and grand. He's dressed in his finest, I would assume. I don't know who dressed him, but he looks grand! I don't know what it means, but there are several symbols on him and like a belt with crystals. I don't have that. I don't know where he shops for his clothes. Maybe it's in the store, like a different department that we have not gone to. But I'm gonna go and sit here. Ophelia just came and put a chair right there, so I guess that indicates me sitting there for a little bit, so we'll see.

D. At least you'll be close.

B. I'll be close and I'm gonna look. Okay, Ophelia now stands by the chair, meaning that I should probably go sit on the little stool here that she brought.

D. Well, good. We'll talk here in a little bit.

B. I'll go sit over here now. Ophelia doesn't seem to leave, so I'm sure she's gonna stand there with me.

D. Alright, my friend. Thank you.

On. (*Ontorio*) Transition from a higher level, we are here to greet you. I am your friend from the sixth, your teacher. I'm here to bring your notes from our joint work back to— (*He didn't finish the sentence.*) You can call me O... oh, what can we use here? Huh huh. Oh, I know this one too. You are both excellent students. You are a pride and joy to observe. I will not take up too much of your time, but I'm here to give you information from home. You can call me On... unfortunately, we work with symbols, and now I have to find a letter that resonates with the symbol. On... On... Ontorio. Great! Huhuhuhuh! Translation, symbol to letter!

D. I'm really interested to hear what information you brought.

On. The classes we work with, with both of you, resonates with gravity and the cosmic time. I'm here to help you to understand the concept of stellar time, and to understand the importance of closing and opening portals. The portals of time create opportunities to expand and grasp space. As we move between levels, fish tanks—as you call them—but also spiritual realities, we have to in some way manipulate or adjust space. When space changes, time is an option. Here, the space is in a certain fashion, creating the illusion of time. The foundation for all experiences comes from space. The time barely rides the different foundation of the space it is connected to. That is why we say that time is an illusion. If you focus on space, you will see beyond the illusion of linear experience. Once you grasp that you simply occupy space—you occupy that bottle, that space, for instance—anywhere and any, huh, "time" you travel, you occupy space. When it is an incarnation here, you shrink your energy at your disposal to the bottle holding that space. When you travel elsewhere, you can merge with the space available. Meaning that you do not have a form. Once you are, similar like in the spirit realm, without form, then you can transcend and become the space. Once you become space, then you are beyond time, you see beyond any illusions. That is the trick. And that is why coming to Earth is more problematic. Because you first come into a container that will lead you THROUGH the experience. And that is the limitation each soul needs to try and navigate around and through. Once you understand and go beyond in your mind, from your solar plexus, once you expand from your physical—and you do not have to have an out–of–body experience, but it will feel as such—as you transcend outwards and try to think of, from your solar plexus, that you expand beyond your limitations, then you will see beyond the illusion of time. Time simply rides the captive space. Once you are beyond the feeling of captivity, such as a body, you will see beyond the illusion of time as well. Time simply rides the experience that exists here. So, stellar time means that you see beyond yourself and you can become the experience. You become your surroundings. The time—that will indicate growth, evolution—once you reach the understanding of (*the reality*) outside your captive form. And even the form of a fish tank is the same as the form of a body—you have to rise above and become the location, if you like. And that is the trick here. We talk about this on the sixth. We teach how to ride time.

D. I've always been really fascinated by time, space, and gravity.

On. Gravity is the measurement, here, that time can use and ride on, because the body is captive by gravity, but the soul is not. As long as you are body, you will experience time. As long as that is your reality, you will be captured in the wheel of time. The body is always going to be captive by that experience here on Earth, but the soul has the ability to expand from that captivity and see from a higher level. You transcend into the fourth reality, and once you are there, you see the play of body, gravity, and time. The shamans from the ancient times easily just took a step out of their physical container. It was easier then. The bottle wasn't as complex as it is now. It was easier to enter and exit. What we see now is the body being too contaminated. Meaning, the soul struggles, even those, such as yourself, who are aware of the opportunity to exit. The bodies that you have available, all of you, are heavier. In order for you to be able to navigate through the bodies available, we are asking you to change your diet. That is the only way for you, unfortunately, since you do not have the prototype bodies anymore. The fast is something that we would like for you to return to in some capacity. It will help you feel lighter in your energetic self. (*Ontorio then gave Christine and me certain exercises to do together, which are omitted here.*)

On. Human emotions are putting like a lid around your soul. They need to be understood, be experienced, for you to not be stuck. It's similar like the physical when you fill it up with sugar, things get stuck. On an emotional level, experiences such as abandonment create the same problem. What we are aiming for is the experience to understand space and time, to rise above the illusion of time. You will experience gravity quite differently once you access the fourth. It's not heavy, it's a friend holding you like a vacuum, not pulling down. Holding you but still offering a variety of experiences and possibilities to move. Here, gravity only allows you to move back and forth, around with your feet. Whatever comes up in a plane needs to come down, eventually. And that is what we want you to rise above in this experience upcoming. There. Your friend is here.

D. Just one more question. Should we do this exercise after I have fasted?

On. You should fast around the full moons. Releasing. One day before and at the full moon. This one can also do a one day fast with juice, but needs more energy. Fruit, vegetables only. Make it a routine.

D. On the full moon day, or the day before?

On. On the day before and on the full moon.

D. For me?

On. For you. For this one, pick a day out of the two. Probably directly on the full moon.

D. Okay. Wonderful. Thank you.

On. There. I will probably return.

D. I hope so. I really appreciate you coming.

On. Interesting how you need to transform symbol language into those little limited letters.

D. Everyone struggles with the human language.

On. My name was like one symbol, one letter, but it didn't translate into the O. Needed to add. Ontorio. O–N–T–O–R–I–O.

D. Thank you for spelling it.

On. Huh. There we go. Elahim.

D. Alright, my friend. Thank you so much. Are you also Elahim?

On. Elahim.

D. Are you friends with Jeshua?

On. Yes, yes. Good friends with Isaac. We're all a group of friends, of course, on the sixth. I do have a lot of discussions with Zachariah as well. But Zachariah is moving around, belonging on the ninth. Okay. I'll go for now.

D. Alright, my friend. Elahim.

On. Elahim.

B. Oh. Hee ho–ho! I got to see your friend. He's a teacher. He's also a friend with Nealon because I've seen them in the area of study, further down the hall. There is like a hallway where we never go. And at one point, when we passed that corridor, I did see Nealon. I know Nealon because of the fact that I did plan on having him in your life (*the 2178 life*) at one point. But he was talking to someone, and now I know that was this friend.

D. Good to know.

B. Ah. So I've been a lot on the sixth, lately. I'm trying to also have a little bit of—I do want to look into my Individual and my solar system. I don't want to just shoot them off and not tend to them anymore. They are in their location and they're doing well, but I also wanted to kinda look into how they're doing. We didn't go again (*in his bubble to visit his solar system*), but I went to the zooming device.

D. What are they doing now?

B. The Individual has become a flock and they are plenty in numbers. But there are no predators, I don't like that. I said, specifically, that my living planet will not have predators. So everyone will just mind their own business. No one eating anyone else. No one trying to take over someone's space. So I'm creating a friendly experience and environment. But you said, "In order for evolution to take place, friction needs to be introduced." And I said, "You mean friction, like a change in diet? Like not eating my red berry, instead having them eating leaves? Just a change of mind?" And you said, "No. That's not friction. Friction means that another way of existing, or something that looks different, or appears different than you, is introduced." And that's what we see here on Earth, of course. But I never went to that planning meeting about that. When I see that, I can understand Earth, because it's just full of friction. Everywhere you go, almost, you are encountering friction. Whether you go on the Metro, you know, it's always like, "I missed the train, or I missed my appointment." There's always these like eeee, eeee (*he made a squeaking sound*) moments. So if you think of like a rail where the train is going, there are those things that make it go suddenly that way, and then it goes that way. (*He gestured first to the right, and then the left, meaning the train switched over to the wrong track.*) And here comes the train, meaning the incarnation, the experience. And then they are all aligned on going to the left, but what happens is that they took the wrong train, So, you know, it's actually like you thought you were gonna go south, but now you're heading west, creating friction because you're lost! So that alone is constant friction here. And then you have everyone having an opinion, which is also friction. So I said, "Maybe I'm not going to introduce opinions." And you said, "Well, that's part of evolving. Don't you want your friend to evolve? Do you just want him to be there and eat?" And I said, "Well, why not?" And then you said, "That would be like me saying you're just gonna sit and be a secretary in the council, and that's where you're going to be." And then I thought about that. Do I want to do that to my Individual? Do I want to tell him to just sit there, like Gergen would say to me, "You just sit on that stool and you are a secretary—for life. Forever." And forever means until you dissolve. And we have still not fully taken on that whole subject (*of dissolving*). I'm kinda hoping here that on the sixth (*dimension*) that it might be resolved. Because it's not gonna be resolved on the second. It's not gonna be resolved, of course, huhuh, on the third! Huh huh. And the fourth is just like all sorts of mayhem at the moment, so there is no need to go and find solutions there. Because I do have, now when I'm more—I mean, I've always traveled with you THROUGH the fourth, so I encounter things. Sometimes when you leave (*Earth*), I help you through the fourth. We go, "All rise!" and everyone goes, including me. Then I say, "Leave that behind, Lasaray. Leave that." Like when a rocket takes off, the NASA thing, they drop the, ah....

D. Boosters?

B. Boosters. And that's what we sorta do when we go through the fourth. But I can also see, "Oh, there goes you with your person. How did that go?" (*He was looking to the side at other spirit guides helping their deceased companions in the fourth.*) I'm not allowed to fully understand someone else, exactly, on details. But I can see colors. I'm not blind, I'm not color blind. So I see and I can read the energy and the speed of someone else transitioning.

D. These are people who are leaving permanently, who have died?

B. Yes. Others leaving sort of the same time as you, when they die. And here we all are in the fourth, and I'm helping you. But you're kind of navigating and steering by yourself, so I'm just helping you to release. You are doing it by yourself, at this point. But in the beginning, you did not. I had to somewhat lure you along. And that's when I created—because I understood that you respond well to that—so I created a song. I have like a flute. (*He whistled and mimicked playing a flute with both hands.*) And you followed that. I've actually done that, so if you hear like a whistle inside your head, that's me. It's me trying to get the attention. (*He then whistled again.*)

D. I actually have heard that before.

B. Ah! Ah! I use my flute for different things. So, don't think that if you hear a flute, you are dying. It's not only like when you transition. So don't be like, "Ohhh!", human scared. And don't tell this one, "I hear a flute. It's time to go home." It's just me trying to direct your attention. Like, "Look over here, Lasaray." (*He whistled again.*) That's what I do. But I can see others. They don't have like a flute, but they might have other tricks. And some are really trying to push their person out of the third, like that (*he holds his hands head high and shoves upwards*), push. Like you're trying to push someone up a ladder. That one has a long way to go before flying by himself. But it's okay. Oh, I went off track here. My Individual, I don't want him to experience friction, but I think it is important that he does. But not by a predator.

D. So, what did you settle on?

B. I settled on the change in climate. And here Isaac came and helped because he's like a weatherman. Huhuh, like a weather god! I never took the weather class. I'm not really sure about how interested I am in the weather class. It's not like I'm not interested, I'm just not REALLY interested. I said, "I can wait. You can just come in and do." It's not like I need to know everything. Sometimes it's nice to be able to delegate.

D. It's nice to have help from an expert.

B. Ah. And I'm happy to delegate. So, Isaac came in and helped me. We're gonna separate a couple of continents, and when that happens, a shift in climate takes place. Meaning, one is sort of continuing in its old fashion, but the new spin-off group will encounter more of a cooler climate, encounter snow. And the first things we're gonna do here is we're gonna monitor the development of someone who does not evolve in that sense, who just sort of eat, sleep, and mate. So that's this group here (*the ones in the same climate*). But to see what happens here when there is friction—meaning, there is not the same abundance of available food—and what that group does with friction. And then you compare the two, that's what you said. And then you look and you can see, "Okay, this group suffered a little bit." What we're seeing is that they decreased in numbers. (*Then he looks towards the first group that has no friction.*) Whereas this one just thrived. However, not a lot of growth took place mentally in this group. Whereas this one became more intelligent, more interested in solutions. So friction gives solutions, whereas the happy group, they just ate and mate. They just existed.

D. Similar to human development on Earth.

B. Indeed. It's similar like if you have shoes or no shoes. So, this would be considered those with shoes. (*The group with no friction.*) Whereas friction indicates barefoot. Meaning, you have to find a smoother path. Or, in this case, food and hidey-holes, like caves. That group evolves mentally. Whereas this (*no friction*) group evolves physically! And that's what you said, "It's similar like Earth. We put in friction and then the attention from the spirit realm," huh huh, meaning, me (*Bob*), "goes to those with friction." So that's when you said, "It's important that you understand that friction provides development and evolution." So that's what I did.

D. That's really wise. I had a couple of questions about your Individual. You call him the Individual because at one time he was a solitary creature, but you changed it and made him....

B. A flock.

D. And obviously, they have a lifespan, so they live and die?

B. Ah. Yes, indeed. So there is a cycle going on. If I were to compare to human years, they live about 25 to 35 years. It's 50 here (*nods towards the group in the cold*). So, I'm introducing all different kinds of experience. But this will be the first, and then we will evaluate.

D. That's really interesting.

B. I said, "Okay, I put in friction." And then I thought, "What sort of frictions have been put into my path? Because a friction is a way to evolve. It's like penetrating certain experiences."

D. There have been a lot of stressful situations along your path.

B. Ah. Like my bubble. That was one that was like a love–hate relationship, if you like. Because I loved the fact to go—I don't use hate, necessarily—but I disliked the unknown. There is like no steering wheel, so who is steering this bubble, for instance? And since you did not go in a bubble, then I felt like, "Who controls the speed? What if my bubble suddenly goes in a different direction?" Because it wasn't like you had hooks on it and dragged me. It was like my own experience. That was friction because I had to overcome my fears. And that is also part of friction. Maybe not with my Individual, but on Earth one of the frictions is to meet fears and to see that there is nothing to be afraid of. Even if it's just that little teeny, tiny thing that your train went to the west, and you planned on going south. Some will experience that quite fearful, not knowing where they are going. Others will be, "Okay, okay." Then they take out their little phone and go, "What buses goes from here to there." They kinda are in the mindset of resolving things, finding solutions. But others become paralyzed if something goes in another way. So that is a HUGE friction that is put on mankind at the moment. How do you solve little frictions? How do you navigate things that you experience as fearful?

D. Fear seems to be a very prominent sensation here.

B. Because what we see here, when someone becomes trapped by fear, they become immobile and they just stop. And what we see is there is a lot of that stiffness. And back to the fact that the soul is not stiff, but fear makes everything stop. It's almost like the human holds their breath. When you hold your breath, you somewhat pause the experience. It's not necessarily like a good pause. It's almost like dying. It's like a pre–dying kind of experience. Unfortunately, a lot of humans are sort of almost dying, even though they are not.

D. Because they are paralyzed?

B. Because they are paralyzed. A soul that is in motion, a physical that is in motion is not paralyzed. And that's why we give you different tricks, like find your inner hobby, find a human hobby, find a soul hobby, you know, activate the inner rhythm so you are not so influenced by others. Because sometimes it's not even your fear! It's like, "That one is scared! Ohh, if that one is scared, then I am too!" And then everyone goes, "Ohh!"

D. Like a flock of sheep.

B. They go (*he makes a deep inhalation*), like that, and hold their breath. And that is sorta like a death. It's not a reboot, which can be quite positive, but this is like a death. And a lot of people are repeating like a dying sensation. And it's unnecessary because it's not even your fear, so why are you dying? Why are you taking on someone else's fear? And then (*makes a sharp inhalation and holds his breath*).

D. They choose not to live.

B. Choose not to live. And it's like the human experience completely takes over the soul. And that's what I mean, that in some way it's a death, because the soul shrinks inside. So normally it should be like this. (*He holds his hands up with the palms facing each other. The left hand is the soul, the right is the physical body.*) Like fifty-fifty, let's say. That's normally how it is experienced in a regular human. You want the soul to kinda warm up the physical. But if the physical takes charge, then it just does this on the soul. (*He wraps the fingers of his right hand over the left hand, which he made into a fist.*) That is when it's like (*makes an inhalation again*) a death. It's a soul death, not a physical death. But the soul kinda dies a little bit.

D. So the human self over-powers the soul.

B. It just pushes it down, and it's like a soul death. That's why I say they kinda die a little bit. One thing to be aware of is if you hold your breath, it's like your soul is checking out briefly. (*He inhaled and held his breath, and then let it go.*) Then we're back on track.

D. That's a good teaching.

B. Okay, now we talked about that. I do want to talk a little bit about my continuous training program.

D. With the students?

B. No. With me.

D. Oh, YOUR training program. Where are we now?

B. Where we are now is that we have been with the zooming device a lot, and we've been looking into gateways between existing realities. We are still in fish tank five. So I'm looking into the parallel realities and to see, first of all, where they are. Even around Earth, the parallel realities are closer on certain places. Like there in the desert in the US, in New Mexico, there it is thin.

D. I remember we talked about that.
B. You can go there and kind of experience—It's not on a daily basis, you have to kind of wait a little bit. It's not even like, "Oh, when the full moon comes, it opens up." There are like calculating programs when they occur. It's like an exchange, you say. It's not just that the third will have a visit from the parallel reality, it's also that something from the third is also ascending, so it's like an exchange going on.
D. So, what is being exchanged? Is it energy and information?
B. Energy, information, and sometimes it's actually like planting a seed—like a new, let's say, flower. Or like putting in new—it's almost like they are rebooting certain things.
D. If a seed gets planted, how is that done?
B. It's the Master Mind that uses the parallel reality to, at certain times—and I must say, when I see this on the zooming device, when this has taken place, there is no one around. So it's like very secretive. Huhuh. A secret operation going on, almost. Because I'm trying to see if there are like little tribes or something observing this, but they're not. It occurs on, huhuh, not a daily basis, but it occurs a lot. But normally when there is no audience.
D. There are always new species being introduced, but I thought the second dimension was involved.
B. Well, the second dimension receives. Something comes down from the parallel reality, which is not a spiritual reality. It opens up an experience that is somewhat in resonance with the third, and something can be dropped through the Master Mind, through a manual. But someone from the second has to kickstart it.
D. So, do you get involved?
B. Well, not me personally. But like Joel, for instance, that's why he was concerned about when someone put stuff in his mountains, because he didn't know what to do with that. And then I said, "Maybe it's not the same thing." But it was from a parallel reality that that information came. So sometimes there are creatures in the parallel realities that are visible. You experience that a lot on both the poles, but also before in the mountains over there. (*There was an older mountain range where the Himalayas are now.*) So the boxes, the receivers, also came from a parallel reality, and that's what Joel saw. But he didn't know what to do with that! Huhuh. So sometimes it's not a plant. With a plant, someone like Joel is eager to take it on. He was working on water channels through the rock, so that's when he saw those (*boxes being*

installed about 120 million years ago). They came in and just landed in (*the area of*) his project. And that's when he asked me if I knew anything about that. It came from a parallel reality. He didn't like that it disturbed his work a bit. So I'm looking into the parallel realities and I can see like sheets. On certain places they are kinda close and interactions take place a lot. And sometime the parallel realities are a little bit—and this is like a physical thing in some way, an energetic physical level, it's not a spiritual level—so there are entities here that I can see. But because of the fact of the human eye, they are not detected. So they stripped a lot in the human eye.

D. I have a question about the parallel realities, to help me understand. Can you see where those entities might have come from? If it is somewhere outside of Earth, did they travel through the parallel reality, like a highway?

B. I see like some sort of craft.

D. So when they move from their planet to Earth, and obviously we don't understand what time and space are, but they have to traverse what we perceive as distance.

B. Well, they ride the parallel barrier and they just use that as a way to move between different galaxies and star systems. It's simply like accessing a highway, if you like. So once you are there, that's when they can travel in like the speed of sound.

D. The speed of sound is not very fast.

B. The speed of sound is moving—well, it's like human sound is like bong—but this is like space sound. Like we talked about before, light is not constant.

D. I thought light was constant and sound varied.

B. Light can also change. The speed of light can change, and the speed of sound can also change. Here, from Earth, the speed of sound is like 'bong', and that's it. You can imagine your craft going at that speed—it would not go anywhere. But you have to expand your perception of motion. Nothing is constant. Much of the parallel realities are lifted because gravity and vacuum follows sound, whereas light is different. It's like two different ways to travel. A spirit (*coming from the spiritual dimensions*), when they merge, they travel on light, if you like. Whereas a physical entity, traveling, uses the heavier, more concentrated form of energy, which is sound.

D. So it is a spiritual sound?

B. It's a cosmic sound, it's not a spiritual sound. Cosmic sound and cosmic light operate in different fashions. From here, light and sound are what they are. But you have to first and foremost start thinking about that certain things behave differently, depending on conditions. So here sound is what it is, like, bonk. And light goes ssshhhttt (*something going by very fast*). But in the parallel reality, it can go faster, or it can even go slower. So, when I look here and I see the parallel reality—and this is just one—moving into the Earth's reality, the way they use to move is sound, gravity. And sound and gravity are linked together.

D. This is truly a fascinating subject for me.

B. Well, you told me this. Like I said, we're having a class here (*on the sixth*). Because nothing is constant. That was the first thing you said to me, "Always know that nothing is constant, Bob." And when you said that, you can imagine how many questions started from that single platform in our program.

D. I also remember you said that in one of the parallel realities, things were much more miniaturized.

B. Like planets?

D. Maybe I misunderstood what you were saying about the parallel reality near the South Pole.

B. It's more obvious on the South Pole, but I'm saying that on the North Pole, that's where you REALLY should look. That's where the sixth have bases. There are Little Greys on both. The ones on the North, they don't want to be detected. So a lot of what is going on in the South is to make eyes go there.

D. Well, when entities move through the parallel realities and then they reach a node and descend to Earth, they must physically change in some way? Their craft and their physical bodies must alter in some way?

B. Well, sometimes they do. And sometimes they just come as they are, depending on if there is a window.

D. Are most of the portals that they travel through natural? Does the Earth and the parallel reality create their own portal?

B. Well, the Earth creates the condition for a portal. It's like you (*the Earth needs to*) welcome. The parallel reality needs to find the correct position. There has to be a resonance between the two. It's an engineering that takes place between the Master Mind, and then the exchange takes place. So, on the North Pole there is actually a lot of—at the moment it doesn't seem to be that much—but like I said, in the past there were boxes left there. And now the entities

in the parallel reality don't need to go down, they can just monitor the boxes. Whereas on the South Pole, it's like bees down there.
D. Coming in and out?
B. It's not just from above, they are there, underneath. They're coming up.
D. Up from the Earth?
B. From like water caves. Up. They were left there. Whereas up here (*on the North Pole*) they left boxes. But they (*on the South Pole*) are there, so they are not in a parallel reality, in that sense. Because of the, Huhuh, malfunction in your eye, they can somewhat ride visible, or not.
D. So many topics.
B. Well, we talk about a lot, you and I. I'm gonna go, because Ophelia dragged away the chair. So I'm thinking that's a sign.
D. Does Ophelia have any thoughts she would like to pass over through you?
B. She says that you should just be happy, it's a happy time. Just breathe. And know that it's a joyful future.
D. That's really good advice, so thank you.
B. So, okay, I'll go. Chair has been removed. But I do feel like we should talk about a little bit about the Pole, at one point. Because it's right there! Every time I'm zooming in on things and learning, I see! Like in the corner of my mind, there it is. I think we should discuss the elephant in the room, which is the Center Pole, the Creator! Maybe we can bring back your friend?
D. Yes, he seemed to know a lot.
B. Ah. Mister O.
D. He said he would come back. But I'm glad you got to listen.
B. I got to listen. I didn't understand everything because sometimes what they do is take it back, like wipe it out. Gergen does that, and Ophelia. Like when you clean the counter, but it's my head.
D. That doesn't seem right.
B. Nay, one might say so. So I'm curious about the Pole because if it's there, it should be discussed. It's like the elephant in the room that everyone sees, but no one discuss.
D. It must be very important to the Fork and to the planet. (*I had missed that he was talking about the Creator.*)
B. Well, I'm not just talking about the pole on Earth.
D. Oh, you're talking about the Center Pole.

B. The Center Pole. The little pole, I'm pretty sure we're gonna talk about eventually, because there is communication going on here.

D. What do you observe about the Center Pole? Can you get any information about it, or is it just there?

B. Well, like I said, it's there. When we do all our cosmic research, you know, like, I see things. We zoom in and I see and I work and it's right there!

D. It's probably looking at you too!

B. Might look at me too, thinking, "Oh, what is that? Maybe I need to know more about that." And then I might say, "Well, I need to know more about you. Maybe we should exchange information. I tell you something about me, and you tell something about you." But the problem is, no one has really signed up to take me, and I have to go with someone. And it cannot be with the Moon People that don't communicate—I don't feel comfortable. Then it would be like me and the bubble. I need to go with someone familiar. But the center pole in the Earth, I can see there is activity. I can see like dots, deet–deet–deet–deet–deet, going mainly from North to South between those boxes, with those little bees (*aliens in UFOs*) that just come up. They receive information from those boxes. The way the Earth tilts also determine the general flow through the Fork. So sometimes when there is like a pause in the evolution, the Earth tilts a little bit.

D. People have conjectured that the Earth might change its axis, occasionally.

B. And that mirrors the flow through the little pole. But I'm talking about THE Pole.

D. I'm not so sure that anybody communicates directly with the Pole, do they? It's sort of a one–way street.

B. Ah. But let's begin with that. Let's begin with that street then, that I listen. And then, eventually, I can ask questions. But I'm fine just listening for now.

D. Well, the Eye, which is an extension of the Creator, it communicated with you. It heard your questions and then answered.

B. It did, indeed. So that one, I think the Eye comes from the Center Pole in some way, so I'm happy to begin there. So we'll see, but I've made my interest known to it. So maybe it's interested in me, too. But not TOO interested. I don't think it's a predator, but I don't want it to (*he makes a slurping sound*), and just snatch me, like,

"Oh, that one is done." So it's that love–hate relationship again. Well, not hate. Dislike, because I'm not comfortable.

D. Maybe that is fear.

B. Maybe that's the fear, maybe that's the friction. As long as I'm just sort of allowed to go there, maybe it's not gonna eat me, like take me.

D. Dissolved.

B. The problem is, once you are dissolved, can you manifest again?

D. Maybe that's the grand recycling program, where you go into hibernation inside the Center Pole, and then it spits you out again.

B. Oh, and who knows where you end up. That's why I said I'm fine with a documentary, before we take it on. But at the moment there has been no documentary, no one likes to talk about it, no one even…

D. Doesn't even come up in casual conversation?

B. It never comes up in passing, like, "Oh, you know when I went to the Center Pole," or "I heard this about the Center Pole." It never comes up. And believe me, I pay attention. But it never comes up. And you sort of give me a little pat on the back and you said, "There are certain things that are a treat and will come later on. From this point in your own evolution, it might appear as something it is not, because you don't understand." And then you said, "And then it's not genuine, it is not true. It's like an illusion, because you cannot comprehend the magnitude of what it is, at this time. Neither of us can. So even if we were to move closer, we would not understand, and it would be an illusion. Similar like Earth," you say, "certain things are illusions. So you want to blank your mind, your spiritual mind, in order for you to get to that level where you understand the level you are entering. And when you come that close," you said, "my feeling is that you have blanked your soul mind completely. So you are clean, because the Center Pole is clean. When a soul is born, we are born with certain filters in our soul–mind. And as we evolve, levels and layers are removed. And once we are closer to the Center Pole, we are completely blank. But if we were to see it—and it doesn't have to be the Center Pole, it can be anything—and that level or layer hasn't been removed, then we don't understand what we are looking at."

D. That is a truly fascinating description.

B. Ah. Well, you said that. You told me. Okay, I'm gonna go now, stool is gone. Did not come back, so I'm gonna go.

D. Well, thank you so much for sharing with us today. That was a really good talk.
B. We do a lot of things and we talk a lot. I talk more than you do but it's still a give and share. Alright, I'll go. Bye bye.

Bob: Soul Intention versus Karma (Sept 7, 2021)
This has to be one of the best descriptions they have given us about the difference between soul purpose and karma. It is short and, as Bob's talks often are, brilliant. This came at the end of a discussion about Pope Clement III and the teachings of Jesus, part of which is included in another section.

D. Any other thoughts today?
B. It's my school.
D. What are you studying?
B. Well, it's my school for my students.
D. Oh, so you're back to teaching?
B. I'm dividing my time. I'm being a teacher and I'm being a pupil. It's sort of a fifty–fifty thing here at the moment. I'm introducing into the karma program that I have to teach them—I'm talking about the spirit guides from the second. They have to fully understand that there are intentions coming down to Earth, but there is also a karma that needs to be addressed. So you have intention or soul purpose, and you have karma. And when those two are together in the experience, you would think that they would just go like this (*interlaces his fingers*). But as man grows, it shifts. It's like, "Okay, now I'm living and reliving the karma life," so then sometimes the soul purpose sort of disappears a little bit. Then you have to ignite and remember, and then the karma becomes a little bit on hold. What we see now, is that the karma that needs to be addressed versus intention, mission and also one's skill set, are not always aligned. A lot of times, what we see now is that karma repeats. Whereas purpose of solving and the mission is on halt. So mankind—I'm not talking about you, I'm talking about the group—is that they are repeating, like chewing over and over, the karma. And the purpose is just sitting on pause, on halt over here at the moment. Once man understands to break the cycle where they keep on repeating karma, they will understand and awaken the soul purpose. When that is acknowledged, then it can be a joined experience. At the moment it is limping.
D. Isn't the intent or purpose of life to resolve karma? Or are you saying the intent is always the spiritual intent?

B. No. The intent is like, if we talk about this one, karma has to do with the emotional journey that this one had to go through. That's not the purpose, that's not the intent. The intent was to come and to do this with you, to sort of help humanity, push them a little bit forward. Or, like he said, "Electrify them a little bit." And that is the purpose. That has nothing to do with this one's personal karma. So, when this one was trapped in the experience of emotional turmoil, the purpose was dropped. And we had to try to poke and make him remember. So, it's different.

D. I just wondered if karma was ever an issue of discussion prior to coming in?

B. Karma sometimes makes the soul trip. Because in the Coat of Karma, it feels like a straitjacket, and it (*the human*) forgets. It feels limited and not able to engage in the soul purpose. The soul purpose is not necessarily to address the Karma Coat. The Karma Coat is what you have accumulated. But the purpose is rarely to, you know, work on aggression. That is sort of happening automatically as you dress into body.

D. I think I might have misled people. I said that the soul plans to address certain karmic issues when it comes down.

B. No, no. It plans. Of course, it plans. Like this one was fully aware that emotional turmoil would come. So he planned on how to address it. You plan the Coat. Sometimes, if there is a life where you are not supposed to accomplish anything, there is a line in the Coat, and everything you are here to do is to look at that. When a struggle has gone on too long in the Coat, a purpose of coming is not always introduced.

D. Just let them work on that?

B. Just let the soul work on that, to not be divided. BUT as you evolve as a soul, you come in and you have a purpose—and that is also planned—but the Coat might be something that helps. Because it's not just to work on tricky stuff in the Coat. It can also be that, you know, in your Coat you will find that skill set in the pocket that will make this soul purpose come to fruition. So what I'm saying is that, a lot of times, hidden keys are sewed into the Coat that will help the purpose. But if the Coat is too heavy, the soul can feel like it's in a straitjacket, and it just keeps repeating—like bad behaviors.

D. As you were talking, I was thinking about Jeshua sewing together events. It implies the sheet would be adjusted based on decisions the individual makes, or what happens during a lifetime. So, is that sheet, in some way, related to the karmic events?

B. Indeed, a lot of times. But it's not like a uniform sheet, sometimes the purpose is also part of that sheet. So it all depends on what the journey is all about. But it's not very common that you just come down with a purpose and not a Coat. Even if you don't have a Coat, like you, for instance. You don't have a Coat, but you still need to find, in a Coat, the treats, the keys for you to become and to fulfill your purpose. So you still have little pockets in a human Coat, even if it doesn't relate to karma. But we sew in ways for you to be able to better fulfill your purpose as a human.

Bob: Epiphany (Sept 12, 2021)

This is nearly the entire September 12 session. We are leaving it intact because Bob gave beautiful insights about incarnation and soul destiny. In the early part, his description of a heavy Coat or winter clothing is another way of saying the human mind and emotions are overwhelming the soul responses. A person has the choice to respond in a human way or a soulful way to situations, and choosing the former makes the Coat feel heavier. Knowing and following the higher soul guidance will lighten the Coat, and life will feel more joyful.

He then recounts a conversation he had with Seth, who explained how souls may experience returning home to the Creator. Just like humans struggle to understand their purpose and reason for being on Earth, it seems souls also are in a state of forgetfulness until they have epiphanies along the way. The little cycle of incarnations on Earth is a mirror of the bigger cycle of individual soul existence. When a soul reaches a level of understanding why they were incarnating on Earth, the epiphany coincides with the folding of the Coat. Near the end of the session, he talks about angels, wings, and why humans should hug. Wonderful advice, as usual, from our Little Friend.

For humans, the gift of an epiphany is the clarity of your soul knowledge shining unfiltered into your emotional or mental centers. A small epiphany could be, for example, a realization which frees you from an anxiety or fear. A major epiphany is where a recipient is given knowledge that could be life-altering, if embraced. Some near-death experiences fall into this category. In my early 20s, I had an epiphany that permanently altered my emotional and mental states. I'm sure many people have had similar awakenings. In reading Bob's words, you may find it helpful to ponder how your current incarnation mirrors your soul purpose. Do you feel the human experience, the

Coat, steers your life? Or have you had an epiphany that expanded your understanding of your mission?

B. Huhuh. Ah, here we sit. Me and Seth. I've been with him a little bit because I made like a little essay—you made me do so—and there were certain things that I thought I could maybe get an expertise adjustment of words. So I went to Seth because I thought he knows what you know, but he said that I'm cheating. Huh. Ohh. He says, "What is this?" Then I said, "It's the essay on gravitational adjustments that will mirror life forms. I can't find Lasaray." Huhuh. And he said, "He's right there. He's in his study room. Why don't you go there?" Uhh. So, I did ask a little bit. Then he said I don't have to pass directly. I have more occasions to really get it right. Because I was concerned if I don't get this right, what will happen? It's one of those steps. But he said I shouldn't worry so much about passing. It's a little bit like humans, they're constantly worried about passing, fitting in. And sometimes that can sort of follow you into the spirit realm, like here, clearly, with me, that I want to pass. But I'm not saying that that is a human personality, I'm just saying that is more common in a dense environment. So he said, "The gravitational conditions actually mirror those sort of activities in life forms. Because if it's too much, it's heavy." So here, he said that you adjusted gravity over time. Meaning, it was easier before for individuals to access the fourth reality. Now it's more like you have those moon–boots on, like magnets, in some way. But before, you could bounce. At the moment, it's hard for man to understand that they have—it's like a memory that has been falling asleep gradually, he says, because higher councils have changed conditions. And as the gravity is so strong and concentrated as it is on Earth, it affects not only the ability for, huhuh, a rocket to go anywhere, but also, it's symbolizing like your inner rocket can't go that far, he says. So, it's harder when you incarnate to really be in contact and do inner travels, because the physical is highly affected from the environmental and gravitational conditions. So, I'm having a class now on the amount of gravity. He said that, currently, Earth is sort of sealed in this gravitational vacuum field. It responds only to the vacuum. It's a different outside, it's a different structure as it meets either the more spiritual realities, but also other physical parallel realities. That is why, from here (*Earth*), it's hard to go there (*beyond the Earth*). But an outside entity, belonging in a different gravitational reality, can easier find loopholes, he says, to come in. The trick, he said—and why you incarnate in the Elahim family—is to create loopholes, but from here. That's why you travel here in incarnation. It is to create loopholes for parallel friends to come in. That's what he says is your main purpose of being here. Because of the fact that there are councils who put Earth and this reality, this whole Solar System, in some way, but mainly Earth, as an encased experience. So, you incarnate in a physical body in order to create loopholes. Some of them are physical, occasionally, when you come here, he says. And some are like mental portals. So you create these openings for friends to come in. And that's what he said, "That's why we, as a family, go here. It is to maintain and open entrances and portals for our parallel friends."

D. Hmm. That's curious. Meaning, like when the Elahim used to come as the Anunnaki?

B. Came to open up portals for parallel friends to enter. Sometimes, he said, physically—and that's when we have this evidence about different things that occurred. And sometimes there are mental portals, or emotional portals, to outside realities. A lot of souls, he says, can do so—and I put that in my essay here, that you don't have to be an Elahim to create a portal, but then you are somewhat limited—but you open gateways, he says, for friends, parallel friends.

D. What about this lifetime?

B. This time you're not necessarily doing the same, but you're doing it under the radar. You're always doing it, more or less, but this time, you are here to ignite the mental capacity in the species. Because you want there to be a new way of relating to parallel realities. He said that, you are now on the threshold in your project. And that is to understand, also, parallel realities. Meaning, physical realities that one can come across. So in many ways, you are here to—I mean, you have sort of started the project by talking about us, he said, like the spirit realm, the Creator, and such. But, he said, the agenda is to also be aware and understand parallel friends. And that's what you did way back as well. It's to not create fear for the unknown. It's easier to not be afraid of God, he says. If you say God, most people feel kinda good about that. But when you say 'alien life forms', or when you start talking about entities from Mars, or when you start to mention Anunnaki, INSTANTLY, the little species sort of locks down and goes into the shell. So, in many ways, he says, we are here to bonk the shell on the turtle. "Bonk, bonk", he says. You don't use a hammer, you just knock. Huhuhuh You knock on the turtle, and eventually the turtle will come out. And when the turtle comes out, that indicates that they are ready. But there is a collective memory of the unknown not being as friendly, he says. So we also have to work on that. But the general idea when you come here is the engineering of gateways. I don't know if I should put that in my essay, but I said, "We never talked about this, really." And he said, "A lot of times, we work undercover, so the human life, the incarnation, sort of goes on in its own mundane routines. But on a subconscious level, we are always engineering openings for exchange of information and entities." But, he says, "It's on a subconscious level. A lot of times the human brain, the human awareness, are unaware about what my soul is doing there. It's similar with Lasaray. We are not fully aware. But occasionally there are those memory flashes, and that's when we remember certain things." Huhuh. I wouldn't have known this if I hadn't trespassed my boundaries in my essay and gone over to Seth and talked. I'm pretty sure you would have told me eventually, but you seem to have more of a schedule on what to tell me. I'm pretty sure you have a timeline in mind on how to proceed. Huhuh. And sometimes I'm not aware and I'm trying to bend those timelines a little bit.

D. At least Seth told you.

B. I asked, also, Seth, if he knew anything about the Creator, or if he had other friends, maybe, that know. I'm trying to be a little bit like, I'm asking but I'm using the method of, you know, "Maybe you want to share?" So I started my questions with him, asking, "What is your opinion about the Creator?" And he smiled.

D. Did he have an opinion?

B. He said, "It's the greatest friend you can ever have, and I'm happy, at one point, to be more of a close companion." And I said, "How do you think that friendship will look? Is it like a give–and–take? What sort of exchange do you expect from this new friend?" And he smiled, and he did like this on my back (*he made a patting gesture*), like that. He said, "I'm pretty sure, at one point, we will feel that tremendous belonging. And when you do so, it is simply like coming home, like you've been away on travels." He said I can think of when I have been on the sixth for a long time, and he said, "How do you feel when you come home to your old friends on the second?" And I said, "I'm really happy and I want to share. It's a sense of belonging and being with family." Then he said, "I think that's the same thing. When we eventually—," and he doesn't use the word dissolve, neither of you do, "once we join, it will be the same feeling that we will just remember coming home. For a human, it would be that fondness of a childhood memory." He said,

"In some way, when we are released from the Creator and we start our journey, we, like a human, forget a little bit about childhood. And rejoining with that is not like aging. It's actually like being a child again." That's what he said. And I think that I respond better to that, that I will just have my youth, rather than I would be like a cripple. He said, "Once you return, in my opinion, I think that is just like coming home. And you remember, 'Oh, this is what I remember!'. Like a human would remember the smell of the house, remember your mom's pies, remember Christmas." He said, "That's how I picture it. You meet everyone that you hold dear."

D. That's better than dissolving.

B. He said, "You don't dissolve. It's like gaining a new sight, another level of hearing, another level of understanding. It's like all your senses. When you are new, as a soul, you have to learn how to activate, and you learn, and you grow, and you travel, and you do certain things. But when you come back home, it's like an epiphany." So, I'm preferring to say that we are moving towards an epiphany, than I'm moving towards dissolving. So I'm taking that with me—that eventually, we will reach the viewpoint of a child and having an epiphany. He said, "Just think that you are heading towards that, and everything will be clear. It's like me getting another ear or a new set of eyes. Everything will just be clear."

D. I remember you said that when the soul is created, it has layers and levels in it that have to be removed.

B. To be removed. So he said, "At the moment, we will not have an epiphany. We will simply use the set of senses that we possess at this time in our evolution, and we will not be able to fully comprehend or have that epiphany. Because we do not have that extra level of senses activated."

D. Do you think that Ole, or Ole's mentor, have activated any of their senses?

B. I haven't seen Ole's mentor for a while, so I'm a little bit concerned. But now when I see it like this, then it's like, "Okay, Ole's gonna have like an epiphany in a bit!" And his mentor, who knows? It's not like I'm sitting with those councils, anyway. But Ole, he's very joyful at the moment. So I'm wondering, because Seth said, "Gradually, the closer you reach to your epiphany point, you will access another level of understanding, another level of feeling, another level of seeing. But you can't tell and you don't share, because it's an individual ascension. What I see might not be the same as he sees." And even the two of you, coming from the same place, you might not see the Creator the same. Even though you are created from the same source, you would think that when you come back, everything is just joined. He said, "In some way, that is true. But in another way, it is also that it mirrors your perception of the Creator. It's the sensation of belonging. Just think of a feeling of coming home. And my feeling of coming home and my experience of coming home is different than yours. It's just that part where you are fully aware."

D. I guess, from what you said last time, you have to be perfectly clean. I wonder if, at the very final stage, it is the same for everyone?

B. Well, he said that what he thinks is that you reach that point where you are completely clear about what you have achieved, what lessons that you accumulated. He said it is not just coming home, but it is to come home with the greatest gift to the one who created you. So you are, in some way, shot off to do things, but at the very end, you actually return with the intention that the Creator had with you. So you move away certain things, you access another set of eyes, and you accumulate experiences. You remove and clean yourself. He said on your own level it will be an epiphany. But when you completely join, it is like bringing home everything that the Creator intended with creating you. That's what he said. He said, in my case, for instance, if the Creator said, "I really want that coffee bean to come into fruition." And I made that! So, like when I come home, I'm gonna deliver that. It's a gratitude for someone creating you. I'm bringing back the gift of what the Creator really wanted me to do. And that's why it takes a little time, because I don't really know. If someone were to ask me, "What gifts would you return to the Creator with?" I wouldn't necessarily think of the coffee bean. Maybe I would think about my Individual. The Individual is really nice, but it's maybe not the general intent. You have to, level–by–level, remove certain things, so you come back to the Creator clean, with the intention it had with you from the beginning. And perhaps it only wanted me to create the coffee bean! Huhuh. When I reach that level that I can join, Seth said, I would understand that, "Oh, the only thing I was sent to do was to create the coffee bean." Once I reach there, when I'm not all over the place doing other things—which is important, that's soul evolution but it's not soul ascension, soul merging back home. The epiphany comes when I understand that the ONLY thing needed was the coffee bean. That is the final ascension, once you reach, on a soul level, the understanding of that intent. The thing is that the human karma program mirrors, a little bit, like that. So it's a....

D. A little cycle in the big one?

B. A little cycle in the big one. He said, "Once you completed your karma program, it's the same thing, you have the epiphany because each soul comes in with a soul intention for Earth," But then you have another soul intention in the big cycle when you move in the spiritual reality. But for those who take form or for those who travel—. I travel! I took a little form when I went to visit Siah (*on Etena*), for instance. I had a form, I bumped into things. You gave me a sneak–peak, a little bit, about how it is to be in a form. But Seth said the cycle is similar. Once you fold your Coat of Karma, you have completed and you understand that even if you were on sidetracks as a human—you have to face ignorance, you have to face arrogance, you have to face fear, you know, all these different experiences—when the Coat folds, the soul understands that coming to Earth, the only thing I had to do was create those portals for parallel realities, let's say, for you, since he said that is one of your main purposes. The other things are just sidetracks. But then again, that is on a subconscious level. So sometimes, the subconscious mission versus the human mission are not fully operating aligned. You have the Coat of Karma but you also have that other hidden agenda. "A lot of times," he said, "we did that before in not human form. At the moment, we are asked to do so in the human form. So even those who have no Coats," he said, "like my brother, he comes in and he continues the real project with Earth, but now we do it in a human body. And as we move into a human body, we also have to take on human assignments. And the human assignment this time around is that knocking."

D. I would think that what we are doing, together with you, is fairly important.

B. It's important, he says. But once you fold your Coat, then, let's say, for instance, maybe your main mission was to learn how to play the plunk guitar! Huhuh. Maybe that was it! The hidden mission was different. So, once you understand that your unique mission for coming to Earth, your Coat, had to do with happiness, or teaching, or agriculture, or whatever that might be, it's the same thing as coming to the Creator and understanding—it is that epiphany, once you understand why you were created, why you were sent off. When you can see, from a higher level with all your new senses, your path, and you can identify the intention and the mission that you have, and you bring home that coffee bean—then that is the ascension. And then I said, "Do you think it is the coffee bean?" Huhuh. He smiled and said, "No. I'm just giving you something to understand what I'm talking about. We don't know yet, because we're not that close. We don't have all those extra sets of eyes, and we are still dressed." (*Meaning dressed in the layers that give the spirit a sense of individuality or separation from Source.*)

D. Well, in the meantime, I appreciate the coffee bean.

B. Ah. Indeed. I'm gonna think about that, like, "What could my intention be?" He said you cannot have an epiphany about it because you don't know the master plan. Once I understand the master plan, and that doesn't just include me, but if I understood the master plan, let's say for you, to create portals and gateways between realities, then it's easier to begin to understand why you were created in the first place.

D. So in some way the pattern, the blueprint that the Creator gave you, is hidden from the soul?

B. Even so. Indeed.

D. I wonder if, in your case, Gergen, or in my case, Jeshua, sees the total pattern?

B. Not the total pattern, probably. But they know, as a mentor, they know your potential and they can—all spiritual friends you have in the spirit realm—assist you in some way to progress. But they see more. Like Jeshua for you, for instance, he has more layers removed. So he can identify and assist you better. But he's not the Creator, so he can only assist based on the information that is available to him.

D. That makes a lot of sense. And I suppose his mentor, whomever that might be, would see even more of my pattern, if he were to look?

B. Even more. And that's what I said, "Maybe I should be like a Wheel star and just go around." And then you say, "That might be just like a wish. You will not ascend just because of a wish." Well, I have a lot to think about here. But Seth said that I shouldn't stress too much because it's a long journey ahead. He said that it might even be that the real treat that you are bringing home to the Creator is yet to come. And I was like, "What have I been doing for all this time?" And he said, "Sometimes, along the way, before you reach that point where you come to your nut, you assist others in their progress." I think that my nut might probably be to cross boundaries and to travel. That's what I think.

D. It seems like your path is pointing that direction, based on everything you've been taught and all of our time together.
B. Ah. And again, you have the big cycle how you re-merge with the Creator, and then you have the karma program, which is a miniature version of that cycle program. He said a lot of times when you come across and meet humans—try to see soul versus the human—a lot of humans are so fully dressed in their Coat that it is really hard to detect a soul. It's disappointing, he said, but it serves a purpose for the general evolution. Don't be disappointed or discouraged just because you see the ignorance. Again, I was concerned about training all my beautiful sparkles—and then there is disappointment (*once they come to Earth*). He said, "Sometimes a soul comes in to create disappointment for others to detect that behavior, to detect that disappointment and to not want to be a part of it. What's going on right now is that a few are trying to penetrate all those heavy coats. When events take place, even those who, let's say, have a summer jacket on, can, by fear or being paralyzed, overdress." Currently, he said, it's like everyone are in winter clothes, even though, in general, there is summer and they should be in shorts and a T-shirt. BUT souls, due to the impact of the behavior of a few, are overdressing. And when you are overdressed, you overheat. Then you do not navigate correctly. You stand there in your ski overall and it's like 40 degrees (*Celsius*) and sunshine, and you understand nothing about what is going on, because there you stand in your ski outfit. He said the events that go on at the moment makes souls overdress. A good thing now is to be a cooling wind. Huhuh. He wanted to bring in big fans and just blow all the coats off, but Ophelia said no to that. Ophelia says, "Nope. No big fans." He showed me—if you think of those satellite disks that try to hear voices in space, huhuh, in the American country—he said if you were to bring in a fan like that, all coats will just fly off and all would be naked. Huh huh.
D. With the Coat, does it prevent them from hearing their soul?
B. Indeed. And not just prevent them from hearing their soul, but they become stiff, immobile in their ski overall. So, it's really hard, if you look around on people at the moment, it's really hard to see souls. He doesn't seem concerned about it. And you're off with your friends because there was some sort of loophole that didn't operate correctly. There was someone stuck. I don't know who's stuck, but I don't think it was here.
D. No one wants to be stuck.

B. No one likes to be stuck. Maybe someone's craft is stuck somewhere and you have to go—like a rescue truck if someone has flat tire on the highway, maybe that's sort of what you are doing at the moment. But someone is stuck, you say. So you left me here with Seth, and I have a great talk. Here we sit, he doesn't take me anywhere, we just sit. But it's nice to have a different opinion on things.

D. He might accidentally say things he's not supposed to.

B. Ah. I'm thinking that. He sometimes gives you that impression that he will, but he's no fool. He just says things in terms that I don't understand. And then I ask and then he says, "Oh, look at the time. Time to go." And I say, "There is no time, that's just an illusion." And he said, "Well, everything is an illusion, more or less. You just have to understand what is genuine. That even applies in the spiritual realm. That is why we have keycards, like passports, to move in between once we reach different understandings, new openings, and so forth."

D. That's an interesting perspective.

B. He said, at the moment, the only thing we can do at this time, because there is an abundance of—if you think of when it comes to elements, like astrology, he said, at the moment what is needed is the wind, which means air. But it has nothing to do with communication at this time, which air represents. He said, "It is to blow, to allow that sensation—even a storm sometimes wakes people up."

D. People are kind of trapped in their homes now. (*This was during the societal lockdowns imposed by many state governments.*)

B. It's similar like being stuck in the ski suit. It's the same thing, it operates in the same fashion, he says. Sometimes you have to open the door and blow people out. He said, "This is symbolic of what we are trying to do. Undress, open doors, and to understand that there are a lot of closed doors, a lot of heavy jackets. Sometimes, not all houses, all doors will open, and not everyone will step out of their ski suit and heavy jacket, even though they are sweating."

D. Their life is miserable because of the fear.

B. Because of the fear. But they still don't want to open and feel the breeze. He said, "We can use a storm, similar like bringing in something in a barrel. (*They often use the analogy of dumping a barrel of knowledge all at once, compared to bringing the knowledge in slowly, a cup at a time.*) Or, we can have like little puffs of wind. It's also to understand that not everyone will open the door. Not everyone will take off their heavy jackets, even though they are sweating inside. On a soul level, we know that. It's just as is. If they want to sweat inside, there is nothing that me, in incarnating form, can do. I cannot go and undress that person. I'm not allowed to kick in the door," he said. Ophelia told me that! Huhuh. You have to be willing to open the door, you have to be willing to undress. He said also, "A lot of times, in order to not be frustrated with your surroundings, you can try to look at the human, look at the Coat, look at the outfit it is wearing, and whatever word comes to mind—and it's only one word—so you can look at the person and just allow that word to come in. And that (*word*) will indicate where they are and if there is even, at that time at least, an opportunity or a window for that soul to respond. It could be like you see someone and the first word that comes to mind is, let's say, fear. Then you can address fear. You don't have to talk about spirit guides, you don't have to talk about all these different things. Address fear. If there is someone who is, let's say, happy. If you look at someone with your human eyes and identify the other human, and you hear the word 'happy', that is an ally. But also, to understand that," he said, "when we walk around as humans, we have like a big letter on display. And it can change," he says. Like me, for instance, I would have a big "H", because I'm happy. So I have a big "H". He says, "When I see you, Bob, I see "H", and then I have to see what H represents. Happy!"

D. He said that about you?

B. Ah.

D. I agree with that. You are very joyful.

B. Ah. So, you know. He said there are different things that we can use to navigate both in a soul reality, but also when we travel into incarnated form, to not drain our own energy, to direct our energy and efforts.

D. That's really good advice.

B. Here I've been sitting and talking. And now you come back and you said the rescue mission was successful. So apparently whatever got stuck—it almost feels like something got stuck in the net, like a fish—so you said that the rescue was successful.

D. Is this something traveling in a parallel reality?

B. Ah. It's not Earth, I see it's over there (*looking downward and gesturing to his right*), and we talk about Earth over here (*still looking down, but now to the left*) and you've been over there. There was something that was stuck, but is now rescued, you say, and no casualties. I don't know what that means. You said it was just a navigation error. Then you said, "This is why I don't talk about it with you because you are going to think, 'What if I have navigation errors with my bubble and get stuck?' And there will then be all these follow up questions. So, we don't talk about these things because I don't want you to think that that could happen to you. I'm monitoring you when you travel." So that's what I've been doing a little bit. I've been moving around and talking, you know. It's important to share.

D. What's the purpose of the paper you're writing? Is this for some advancement in your studies?

B. I've made my solar system, but in order for change, like evolution and so forth on my living planet, I have to also be aware of the gravitational adjustments. I don't want to lock him in; I want him to have free movement, in some way. But you also said it's not just related to free movement. It also encases the reality which also protects the reality. So, my essay is about balancing and understanding the occurrence, the cause and effect.

D. So as the gravity increases, the boundary gets harder to penetrate?

B. In some way, boundaries accelerate evolution. But there is also much more required to assist a reality which is encased, like Earth. So, I'm looking into this and I have my living planet as a prototype. But you said it sort of operates by itself, and it's not going to be touched so much. We already have the evolution and the intent in motion, you say. But I'm still learning how an encased reality operates. You say, "In a bigger way of seeing, it also relates to the fish tank." And maybe that is what happened, maybe someone got stuck between fish tanks.

D. Can entities travel through the barriers between fish tanks?

B. Well, we did. We traveled to the fourth. But we were in spirit form so we didn't come from fish tank five.

D. Someone that has taken on a form in, for example, fish tank seven, can they travel through the walls of the fish tank?

B. You never told me. What is your opinion about that?

D. I don't think it would happen. I think you can go as a spirit.

B. We haven't really talked about that. It became silent. Sometimes when that happens it indicates that you, Lasaray, don't want to talk about it, even though the human here asks questions. It became just silent.

D. Am I always present at the sessions?

B. Ah, you are indeed. You ask certain things sometimes. Well, okay, I briefly came in today and wanted to share about my visit to the sixth. Okay, I'm gonna go now but I'm happy that I get a little bit more than I came with.

D. Do you mean to the sessions?

B. Well, when I travel to the sixth. You were gone this time because there was some sort of haste with that poor individual that was stuck. A rescue mission was sent out.

D. Just the knowledge that everyone is observed and taken care of is comforting.

B. Ah. I feel much more comfortable now. I prefer the part of an epiphany than if I explode or implode. Who knows what dissolve means? Neither of you use that word anymore. But since I've heard it, I'm looking at it from another angle.

D. That's a little less stressful to think of it like that.

B. Ah. Now I'm gonna go back and go through my journals and maybe try to—it's probably not helpful—but to try to see what is the intention with me? What could the intention be to create me? Why did...

D. Maybe you are to spread joy and laughter, which you do.

B. An echo of laughter. So regardless of where you are, you can hear a little laughter. Maybe that's needed on certain places. I never have seen the Moon People laugh, for instance.

D. Maybe they do, you just can't tell. I laugh more since you have come around. Lasaray, I'm sure, is a lot happier with you around.

B. Ah, ah. Lasaray, you laugh, but you sort of bulk laugh, UHH HUH HUH, like that. So, we laugh a lot, of course, because of our history.

D. We have a long history together.

B. Long history. And I remind you of certain travels to Earth, you know, when this and this happened. Huhhhh. And we talk about that and analyze things and look at movies and see where I was present. And sometimes where I was not. Huhuh. Oh, and what happens when I'm not?

D. I'm glad you stay close.

B. Ah, ah. Sometimes it's needed. Okay, I'm gonna go now. Saving energy.

D. Alright, my friend. I'm really glad you came to our session today.

B. Ah, it was my time. I had certain things to talk about. Maybe I go to—I'm pretty sure that you and Seth have your classes together—

and I'm open to hear what you talk about, if you want to share. There are several places on the sixth that we haven't gone to. You do different things. You're very much like a rescue force with some of your friends. You say, "It's not rescue, it's maintaining. And sometimes we have to—" And it had nothing to do with a spiritual realm, it was in a fish tank. I don't know which fish tank this was, but it was a hole that created dysfunction for this poor entity. Someone was stuck. You just said it's similar like all these tunnels where cars and trains are going. You have to sometimes go in and shut the tunnel down so that no traffic goes through, so you can do maintenance. You said, "In this case, it was a car (*craft*) that was stuck that was not supposed to have gone through this tunnel. So we had to do a rescue operation before we could continue to maintain the tunnel." So you said, "Someone had gone in, not far in, but still enough in so that it couldn't come back out. And it could not move forward because the tunnel was not in operation." You had to remove the individual and the sphere in order for the continuation of maintenance to occur. It was just up here, you say, and Earth is here. So, it was just over there, and certain tunnels.

D. In the same galaxy?

B. Nah. It's not the Milky Way, the one here. Here is Milky Way, here is Andromeda, it is the one here. (*Based on his hand gestures, it is perhaps five times further away than Andromeda, and in a direction that is about perpendicular to the line between the centers of the Milky Way and Andromeda.*)

D. Okay. A ways off.

B. Nay, not so far away, you say. It's kinda close. When I see Andromeda over there, it's very red, it's very purple, red orange. When I look at the Milky Way, it's predominantly blue and green. It's different colors, and it represents different things, and we're gonna talk about that, you say. Andromeda, it's much more progressive there. It's generating prosperity—and you can see that because it's a more vibrant color. Whereas the green and blue indicates healing. It's a much slower vibration where the Milky Way is. You can see here that we have a lot to talk about.

D. Indeed we do. It's really fascinating.

B. Ah. Okay, Ophelia, she's saying I should go now. There's not gonna be more information, she says, about my galaxies that I see here. And no update on the poor fellow who got stuck. Just knowing that he was rescued, you say. His identity has not been revealed. Oh, okay, okay, I'll go now, but I'll be back.

D. Alright, my friend, thank you so much for coming and sharing with us. It makes for fascinating reading when I go through your notes.

B. Ah. We do lead a fascinating life, I must say.

D. We'll have lots of experiences to return to the Creator.

B. Ah. Okay, okay, I feel like I'm being pulled.

D. Well talk again soon. We'll try to get in a better rhythm with our sessions.

B. Rhythm is a dancer. (*He sang that as he swayed side to side. There was a brief comment about Christine's grandson, who was one year old at the time, before Bob gave a few opinions about hugging. Bob reveals that spirit guides wrap their energy around people for comfort, which is sensed as a hug.*)

B. [...] As a human, he should be hugged. He likes that. It makes him feel that he belongs. Maybe someone should have hugged you more. I did! I hugged you when you were sleeping because you did not get as many hugs as a human. So I wanted to provide that. You can tell that. When there are people who don't feel like they have hugs—and that is something that has been most unfortunate with this pan–demic (*he said it mockingly*), is that people don't hug. Because hugging unites and undress and open doors. When you are told not to hug, it creates a sadness and a stagnation in the evolution, regardless if it's a human evolution, or if it's a spiritual evolution in a human. So hugging is extremely important, you should say. If you are someone who does not have a person who hugs, then you should tell them that spirit guides hug them a lot. They just need to sit down, close their eyes and visualize that hug. Because visualization comes from somewhere. If they can't do that, they should just know that when they sleep, they are hugged.

D. That's really nice to know.

B. Hugging is extremely important when a soul goes into body. That's why we want you to hug each other, because once you hug each other, you relax and you can see things clearly. That is also why women who hug more in physical easier connect with soul purpose. Whereas, men just sort of do this (*gestures a pat on the back*), so it's harder. Men actually needs more hugging than women. You can also hug a tree, if you like.

D. I was thinking about the angel wings that people visualize. Is that in some way related to energy that surrounds them?

B. The angel?

D. When people think that angels have wings.

B. Well, the angels appear to have wings. But Ophelia is from the angelic realm, like it's called from here, but she doesn't have wings. She's not a butterfly. However, the vibration of them is wing-based. That is why humans visualize them as angels because it's sort of goes like this, their energy (*moved his hand back and forth, rapidly*), and that's why it appears as wings.

D. So it appears to flutter?

B. It flutters. Normally it is a fluttering behind the entity that is emerging, which creates the sensation of wings.

D. Ah. Okay. I was thinking about that this morning, because I couldn't remember if you had talked about it or not.

D. I never see wings when I go and talk to Josephine and Ophelia and so on. But on a higher reality, like up on the tenth, and so forth, who knows what sort of entities are there—we've never gone. But in general, from a human standpoint, when they see a being taking form, there is an energy behind it that goes like this (*moving his hand in a side-to-side wave motion*), and that creates the sensation of wings, for one. As a human, you are told before you leave that you will be hugged. When a person, a human, is not hugged, it creates a sadness. So you should hug.

D. Maybe that was why I was sad.

B. But I hugged you. Ophelia hugged you. But she didn't come with big mittens or wings like that around you. It was just the awareness of a hug. And as a spiritual helper, we can surround you, which a lot of people experience as wings holding them. But–but–but Ophelia comes in (*while he was talking*) and she says that there are those up on the eleventh—but they are bigger—and they seem to have a different form on the eleventh, she says. She must know them. I'll probably ask if we can go.

D. To the eleventh?

B. To the eleventh. She says that I would not be able to breathe there. It's a different condition there. She said I cannot come in. Ah! She did not say I cannot come in. She said I'm not gonna be able to breathe. Which means that I cannot get in. We breathe, even though we do not have lungs as a soul, but we absorb oxygen, spiritual oxygen, if you like, into our being. So we are breathing entities, even if we are in spiritual form. But certain places are not aligned with that—if you think of lungs. She said I'm not trained yet. I think it's probably similar like with my bubble versus my peanut suit—I still need somewhat of a training, probably. I asked you if you had gone, and you had not. I asked if maybe Ari had gone, and you said, "Eli. Eli has." I haven't seen Eli around for a while. Maybe he's up there.

D. I haven't heard from him either.

B. Maybe he's up there. We're not gonna go there, Ophelia says. Okay, okay, I'll go now.

D. Well, I'm glad we got that little extra talk in, so thank you for that. And thanks to Ophelia.

B. Okay. Thank you. Bye bye.

Council of Nine: Falling or Flying? (Sept 23, 2021)

This is a remarkably clear teaching on fear and trust. It needs no further introduction, as it is a brilliant summation of human behavior and soul potential. The Council of Nine uses a backpack as a symbol for human emotions and beliefs. Our backpacks begin to be filled when we are children by those around us. As we age, we are expected to sort through what has been pushed on us and get rid of what does not resonate with our soul. Those who simply follow the crowd and respond in accordance with groupthink will never soar above the earthly drama. However, it is never too late to choose to trust in your spirit. A beneficial practice is to pause and evaluate what drives the decisions you make. For example, do you believe a choice taken outside your comfort zone will make you fall or fly? Do you navigate by taking orders? Is your backpack filled with other people's beliefs? The freedom of flight is only given to those who have recapitulated their life and understood the difference between human and soul impulses, and have embraced the latter.

C9. This is the Council of Nine.

D. Hello, my friends.

C9. We are here as a unit, as your council. (*He cleared his throat.*) This one needs adjusting (*of the*) intake in the morning when we sit. Neglecting the rhythm, the flow, the ease for us to merge.

D. What advice do you suggest?

C9. Back to lemon water. We are here as your support system, the ones that know you from early times here, as well as elsewhere. We wish for you to grow in strength, to not be defeated by the energy and fear around you. You are here again together. It's not been that many times that you had the mission as of this time. We want you to rest assured that the support around you is intact, that the presence of higher councils are observing. Those who belong in higher frequencies, Council of Ten, even Council of Eleven. Ari operates as a mediator, connecting councils, not only spiritual, but those who are in form in other realities. It is a network. See it as a gigantic spiderweb, and you are simply the little spiders in the middle. You are not aware of the ripple effect and echo that your thoughts, your actions, are sending through this web, the web of knowledge. As the web of knowledge supports you, see it as a living entity, moving inwards, expanding. More layers, levels added as you progress. We are here to enlight. However, with enlightenment, one first encounters fear. You cannot reach the point of transformation or enlightenment unless you first dare to look at your shadow, dare to look at your path up 'til this point. Fully analyze and register the activities around you. How you respond to the flow of information, actions, energies, are crucial for change to occur. Once the individual feels like it's standing on top of a canyon, you have to dare to take the leap, even though you are not able to see below. At this time, we are forcing humanity closer to that threshold. We are forcing you to trust your path, trust your safety net. Man, at this point, are standing on the edge of a cliff. Below, the canyon, hidden in a mist, a fog. This is the divider. Once you know that you are safe, even though you do not know the end result of your choices, once you dare to fly, to trust your inner compass, to take that leap into the mist, the canyon, then you know that you are safe. We are pushing humanity to this edge. Some will, in fear, take that leap. Fall is different than fly. If you fall, you take the fear with you. As long as you are driven or acting upon fear, you will never fly. Those who let go, fly. And once you know the choice of falling or letting go, the end result mirrors your choice. We are here to let you know that humanity is standing on that edge. Some are already falling. Those who are ready to fly are silently observing. It's a choice that no one can place upon another. It is based on preexisting conditions, but also the navigation within. Just be aware that when you make a choice out of fear, you fall. When you make the choice upon trust, you fly. The end result, when you hit the new experience, the new foundation, mirrors the way you met that step.

D. Is that applicable to every decision one makes?

C9: In many ways, yes. But because we've seen humanity avoiding choices, avoiding the inner trust, simply acting upon human impulses, we have forced your race to this cliff where you are forced to make a decision. Some will fall. Some will fly.

D. Can you see the end result of what will happen?

C9: Yes. Across this canyon, a new era arises, a new land, a new environment. In order to reach this environment, the choice of the canyon needs to be met. Souls are being removed. New ones are on standby, already designed for the new field, for the new land. Some souls have a heavy backpack of experiences and lack of drive, lack of trust. You all have, in your backpack, a parachute. But some simply see it as a backpack, and the backpack is filled with bricks, rocks. Meaning, the individual, before taking action, already believes he will fall because the heavy backpack, thoughts, are not carrying you. You have to know that the backpack on your back is a parachute.

D. In some way, that relates to the lack of belief in the Creator, doesn't it?

C9: Yes. Yes. And belief in the ongoing cycles of life. When we say life, we don't necessarily mean human life. We mean the life of your system, life of your Solar System, life of your galaxy, life of souls, who will never be damaged. As long as one is focusing on the human life, you are trapped within that heavy backpack. When you see your backpack as a parachute, that indicates that you have grown in your awareness of the bigger cycle. We are aware that some will fall, and it is already preconditioned to why they came. Nothing is done to you as you travel out of lack of love. It is basically to ignite the consciousness in the body that you possess in the location. Here, we need the experience to mirror that choice. That is why you constantly encounter polarity, in order for us to be able to upgrade the species. In some way, we are not upgrading, we are returning to a prior prototype, who was more inclined to connect to their inner worlds, connect to their inner soul mind, the brain, the central, but also *(understood)* how to navigate through emotions, emotions that are trapped. As a soul, you simply are emotion, you ARE compassion. When you travel into form, compassion changes, becomes, suddenly, love—and we don't necessarily disagree with the word love. It is simply a lower form of the compassion that you are born with. It is like calling the Creator, "god". It just doesn't fully color. When you say "love", if you changed it to "compassion", which is the highest form of love, *(that is)* similar as if you call the energy that you worship the Creator. Then you are closer to understanding the bigger cycles. When you limit your mind by simply talking about love, light, god, then you are locked in the human way of looking at the divine. Again, we don't judge, we simply tell *(you)* to expand your vocabulary. Once you start to exchange the word "love" for "compassion", and you repeat it like a mantra, a new center within your heart, center point, opens up.

D. That shares some similarity to certain Buddhist philosophies.

C9. Hmm. Well, some are ahead.

D. What do you think of religions, in general, as it relates to the backpack?

C9. Religion is, in many ways, a backpack. Similar.

D. Does it make people believe in a parachute or a bag of rocks?

C9. A bag of rocks, because they have to do things in a certain way. When you believe that your backpack is a parachute, you don't have a manual of rules. You simply trust the backpack unfolding to a parachute. Those, unfortunately, with heavy backpacks, like religions offer, have a whole checklist before action. You can see that there is no trust. Simply an order. The soul doesn't navigate by orders, by a checklist. It navigates by trust. And by exchanging your vocabulary, you move more into the life of trust.

D. That's a really good teaching.

C9. So, what we ask is that you are aware that some will navigate by this heavy backpack, a checklist on how to behave. And they are locked in the human experience. The soul will see this as it returns, as it does what you refer to as a life review. When you do life reviews, you look at the karma, you look at the Coat, but you also look at the backpack. Did you fill your backpack up more this time, or did you remove obstacles in this checklist that you feel you have to have?

D. Is this in some way related to the belief system or the karma of the person?

C9. In many ways, the backpack mirrors the human. Because the human either fills it up or trusts. An empty backpack provides more, because you have the ability to fill it. But plenty (*of people*) are just carrying around backpacks that someone else filled—and that creates the checklist if you don't know what is, fully, in your backpack. Because someone filled it up for you, and you allowed it because you opened the zipper. When you keep your soul intact in your experience, the backpack is closed, empty, and ready for you to fill. But several are opening up their backpacks for others to fill. They give away the power to their life and existence. If you give away your power, don't complain if you fall. If you remain in your light, in your power, and feel connected to compassion, then you will fly. It's a balance that needs to be met, that needs to be addressed. What we see here, (*standing*) on the edge, are those who still refuse to investigate their backpack, to investigate their choices. They are simply balancing on the edge. I wanted to come and tell you that there are several councils that are not able to communicate, like the Council of Ten. When we reach higher on ten and eleven, you are closer to the creating force, and the entities are not in full form. They simply are a reflection of the Creator, the Center Pole. So, we are here on the behalf of everyone, those who care about the development here on Earth.

D. By having trust, we know that eventually things will resolve themselves?

C9. Sometimes trust is also taking a step back, to allow those balancing on the edge to make that choice. To not push, but also not reach out a hand. What we see now are plenty who try to do good by reaching out their hand. And indeed, they help the human, they help the backpack, but they do not help the soul inside, who needs to make that choice himself. We don't judge. Of course, we want you to help, but sometimes taking a step back, observing the game, observing the greater scenario, understanding that the reset, the soul reset, is to understand and to connect your soul mind with your center core. It's different than for a human. A human simply feels, it tries to avoid death. Whereas a soul welcomes death, because death indicates transformation. A human sees death as the end. A soul sees it as a gateway for growth. We are not saying that it's beyond our understanding—the concept of fear of death—we're simply asking (*humans*) to navigate differently. As you do, you will see that there is no death, that there are only beginnings. Death is the pickle of being trapped in time, because death indicates an end. Once you understand that there is no death—a simple beginning—your view of time will change. You simply see new thresholds of life. Nothing left behind, simply new steps. To understand the concept of time, you have to delete, first of all, (*the concept of*) death indicating an end. Once you see your experiences, regardless of where you are, as a beginning, then you rise above time.

D. That's also brilliant. Thank you.

C9. You are welcome. We have a friend. (*He was looking towards where Bob was standing.*) He has a different checklist. Not the same as the human checklist.

D. He has a lot of lists.

C9. He does. Until next time, simply be in the vibe, in the mindset—your soul mindset—that the words from within will fly like birds. See the hawk. Allow that to be a vision, an imagery of how your words fly effortlessly to humanity. Whether you speak or write, use this way of communicating. That is the advice I can give you.

D. Thank you so much for that. I will try.

C9. Sometimes it is easier to think that you talk from your center point than from your throat, from your mouth. When you visualize that you speak from your center, the mouth simply operates independently. So shift your focus on where you talk from. When you feel trapped on how to relay information, speak from your center point. You can see your mouth and head as a puppet working independently, but your words are coming from your center. And from there, see the eagles, see the hawks flying out. You simply shift the perception of speech and where information comes from. Speak from your center. The mouth is simply human, it just provides the sound needed. It has no function. If you don't speak correctly, you can see this and hear this if someone speaks. Is it mouth speaking? Then they are caught in the backpack. They are human. Sometimes when someone speaks, you feel a warmth; you feel a bridge between you and that person. Listen the same way as speaking. Do you listen with your ears, or do you listen with your center point? The illusion of man is that you speak and hear, (*that*) you have all your senses in your head, when they are actually in your center. You even smell from your center. The nose, ear, and mouth are an illusion, in some way, for the soul. It is a human invention and needed to connect with other humans, but not with other souls. So, all your senses are located in your center. Even your brain, your soul brain, is not in the head. You operated as an engineer to try to connect the strings between the soul mind in the center to the human mind in the top of the head. Remember that all senses are in your center, even your feelings, that some put in their heart. It is the first step to understand how to sense your surroundings. For those who are navigating by their heart, because it is closest, it has, in some way, less distance to the core of truth. Do you understand?

D. I do. That is, again, brilliant. I appreciate that.

C9. Once you understand that all your senses and experiences are in the same location. It is not ears, nose, mouth. The way you communicate is also from your center. There. Okay.

D. I will work with that idea and try to pass it on.

C9. Yes. Begin with yourself. Elaborate. Try, and you will see a difference.

D. Thank you so much for the guidance.

C9. You are much welcome. Elahim.

D. Elahim. (*Bob came in after the Council moved out, which is in the next section.*)

Bob: The Layer Cakes in the Wheel (Sept 23, 2021)

This part of the session is rather complex because of all the intertwining information. Bob was invited to a meeting of the Council of Nine, as an observer. He was shown the actual process of how the spiritual realities make evolutionary changes in the fish tanks. Within all creation, there are stages of development to reach the Creator's and councils intent. To take a simple example, if the intent of a designer is to build a new Parthenon, laying a foundation would be level 1. Cutting stones for the walls would be level 2, and so forth. Each level is a different type of knowledge, and as it is mastered, the building is one step closer to being a form–based manifestation of the original intent of the designer. In Bob's description, those levels are shown as steps on a pyramid (or layers in a cake). The closer to completion, the higher the pyramid. In an indirect way, he implies that the different levels are a reflection of the qualities of the related spiritual dimensions. In the area of our Solar System, the level is around 3 or 4. Andromeda is nearing completion at a level of 8, so it is much higher in the map he was shown. When Bob first entered the meeting, he was shown a flat map of the entire Wheel. It was then transformed into a three–dimensional map showing the actual levels of spiritual attainment throughout the fish tanks and spiritual dimensions. He was shown that the energy flowing into our region of the galaxy is changing, and is intended to lift the Earth and nearby solar systems up to a higher level.

This spiritual cake exists in different scales throughout all of creation. Even though we talk about the fish tanks being primarily the first through fourth dimensional vibrations, the spiritual layers are always present. And conversely, within the spiritual dimensions, the third and fourth vibrations are also present. The Library and the gardens on the fifth, for example, are permanent forms that may owe their stability to the slower vibration of the third dimension. Bob informs us that humans also have an inner pyramid or layer cake which they can elevate through spiritual practices and intent. The goal is to elevate the form to its highest potential.

B. Ah, you took me!

D. Oh? Where did I take you?

B. To meet the council. I did not talk.

D. The Elahim Council?

B. No. The Council of Nine. Well, they are kinda close. Some of the Council of Nine actually seem to belong with the Elahims. You said I can come, but I cannot ask and I cannot interfere, but I could absolutely come. So, I was sitting there, looking, and I could detect certain things. Ohh, they're mighty! And they have all sorts of things on their agenda. They roll out like a big star map and they kinda just look into where to go. It's not like, "Ohh, Earth." They have several locations, and I must say, it was a very friendly unit. I did see Ari, and I tried to wave. But you said he's not seeing me. But I did see Ari.

D. You were like a ghost?

B. Like a ghost. Talking about ghosts, behind Ari there were like big poles of energy in darker colors. Almost bordered to black, but it was like purple. They were standing behind. They had no form, but I could see they were individual flows of energies. And I saw them behind him from where I sat. The table isn't round, it's more like oval. And there is Ari. And behind, over there, there they were. There were seven of them and they had no form. They just stood there. It wasn't like I could see any features like a face or anything. And of course, I wanted to know, "Who are they?" But I was quiet because it didn't feel like this was the time to talk. I was quite amazed about this whole scenario that I observed.

D. How many were around the table?

B. Well, there was one here (*at the left head of the table*). This one seemed to be the oldest. Then there were (*quietly counting*) one, two, three... six is on the other side. It's actually eleven if you count them around, even though you think, 'Why do they call it the Council of Nine?' Ari is sitting there. Jeshua is here. Isaac is not here. Ophelia is not here. Ophelia comes sometimes.

D. Did I have a seat at the table?

B. You were here with me. But there's no empty chairs. But it seems like there are (*he counts again*) ten. Oh, there's a bigger gap here, that's why I'm thinking there might be eleven. Maybe that's your chair.

D. They said I was on the Council, and Zachariah is on the Council, so I think it is a larger group that rotates in, depending on the topics.

B. It's not the same actors, you say. But it's a bigger space there, so that's why I said eleven. Ari is here. (*He gestures towards one end of table.*)

D. So, did you hear and understand what they were discussing?

B. They were discussing about different actions that needs to be taken in different locations. That's why they rolled out this big map, it's like a big star map. It's not just the Milky Way. It's actually not stars, you say, "Look closer." And then I do, and it's actually the inner circle around the Pole, it's the spiritual dimensions. It's that web. I didn't see the Center Pole in it. Huhuh. No need to be the center of attention all the time, maybe. Huhuh. But the map is actually the spiritual realities around the Pole. And how you, from where you are, pop out to where you are supposed to be. So, they are looking at the general highways and how you travel around in the spiritual dimensions, but also outwards (*into the fish tanks*). It has to do with the spiritual reality around the Pole, the Center Pole. This is a map of the spiritual realities. But the Center Pole, the Creator, is such a teeny, tiny dot in the middle. Maybe it doesn't want to overshine the spiritual realities. So that is why I thought it was a map over a galaxy. And then you say, "Look closer. It's a map of the spirit realities hugging the Creator." And I said, "I don't see the Creator." And you said, "It doesn't want to overshine. That's the little crystal in the middle that you see." It almost looks like, you know, the Mayan temple, like steps. So, in some way, it looks like a cake. It's like the closer down (*the lower layers*) are closer to the fish tanks. It's like a 3–D version here I'm trying to give you. So, you have to see with something else than your physical eyes here. In the bottom is the connection to the fish tanks. And then the spirit realm is similar looking like the Mayan pyramid. And then there is the Pole. First it was just flat, when they rolled it out. But then they placed, in the middle, this crystal that is (*representing*) the Creator. And then suddenly it just rose up, like that, so it became like steps. It looks like steps in the Mayan temple, the pyramid.

D. Would the steps represent the dimensions?

B. Indeed. I was like, "Where am I, I wonder?" And I'm down here, because the second dimension is more dense, you say. You say I'm dense, so I'm closer to the fish tank realities. And then it becomes more fluffy, I would assume, as you go higher. I'm not saying that Ari is fluffy, or see through. But it actually is somewhat of a stairway. As this map transformed into a living map, it rose up and now the Center Pole is here again, and it sort of beams. And then in the back you have those seven darker entities that observe this. They seem to be, in some way... who can they be? They don't seem to engage.

D. How many steps can you see? Perhaps they represent the tenth or eleventh dimensions?

B. Yes, indeed! I see here the spiritual realities and there is actually a third step in the spiritual reality, because there is a kind of form. It's very different now, what I see here. I see the ring between the spiritual and the fish tanks. I see the fish tanks. I see one, two, three in the fish tanks. But in the spiritual reality it's not like we just skipped three and four. The three and four reality that we talk about here, these levels in the fish tanks are mirroring the same thing as the spirit realm. So, you see we have this big cake where me, I'm on the inside, and then the fish tanks looks so small! But they are like that circle around. But in the fish tank, around each galaxy or star family, it's similar because each galaxy has its own center pole, like a Creator. It's almost like you can drag it out, like that. (*He gestures as if he is pulling up the height of the layer–cake around the galaxy. The galaxies, planets and stars have a similar spiritual layering as exists within the spiritual dimensions.*) I'm quite amazed about this spiritual cake in the middle (*of the 3–D map*). Someone just put the crystal in the middle and then—I didn't see any hands, so I'm thinking that the people in the back are probably doing something, but there was not like someone came with a hand and just dragged it out like a tent—but it happened like that, it just rose. And then, when I look at the fish tank, I can see that it is similar. (*He shows how the flat map was changed to show height around the center point of each galaxy.*) The problem is that around Earth, it is a little bit flatter, so it hasn't been drawn out fully. But you can see it's the same structure (*like a pyramid*). But when I look at the fish tank here, I can see that there are different heights that indicate how long (*much progress*) they have reached in their understanding. When all the dimensions are compact, you would think that would indicate everything is aligned. But it's actually the beginning. I'm not sure if it's just the galaxies, but you say it is. You said, "Look at the Milky Way and see the center pole." And I see that it just needs to be stretched out a little bit, it needs to grow. It is becoming. I can see some over here in fish tank five that are higher. It's like looking at mountain ranges. They are different heights. The next one is higher, it has reached number 8 (*out of 10*). Whereas, the Milky Way, where Earth is, has only reached level 3 or 4. The Andromeda galaxy is actually higher. So someone, like these people in the back, whoever they are, has taken this tent and just (*Bob makes a slurping sound as he shows how the map over each galaxy was stretched up to indicate its spiritual attainment.*) But it all originates from the Center. We should probably go and talk with these guys because they are the ones that make the whole.... Ohh! I see what they are doing. They are the ones that are involved in evolution. I don't know if this is the Evolution Group, because they were more visible. I could see them. These, I'm not sure. But I can see here in fish tank five, standing up is the center pole. An invisible energy or hand has made it grow. Earth, you say, is on level 3 to 4, and it's about to rise, but there is still a ways left. Whereas Andromeda is an 8. There doesn't seem to be that many more than 8. You say that when all systems have risen to the level it is intended to be, then it moves on. You said, "Now raise your eyes, Bob, and look here in fish tank four. It doesn't have to do, necessarily, with where they are." I can see in fish tank four that all of them are on the same level. They are not as tall as Andromeda, which has risen to 8. But you said, "It has nothing to do with height. It has simply to do with that they reach the intention that they had. And some steps are smaller and more, and some steps are bigger and less. But it's still the same thing."

D. So fish tank five has a lot of different heights?

B. Heights. It's like looking down at all these different mountain tops. And here on the table is the spiritual map. They just rolled out this big map that I thought was about the stars. And then you said, "No. Look closer, Bob. Look at what is going to happen." And then suddenly someone put a crystal in the middle and you said, "That's the Creator." And I said, "Oh, that's small." And then, for some reason, from that point, it just grew. And here they sit and they look at it and they read it. I don't know about them. And you said, "It's not to be given right now. We don't communicate directly to them. But they are the ones in charge."

D. So, in fish tank five, the level of development isn't determined by where a galaxy is located within the fish tank? Those located closest to the spiritual dimensions are not more advanced?

B. Not what I can see here. All the fish tanks are on one level here on the bottom, and then here comes the cake, the spiritual dimensions. You know, like a squeeze box, but just up.

D. And is each layer smaller than the one below? If it is step-like, then the higher layers are closer to the Center Pole?

B. Ah.

D. What about the other fish tanks?

B. I can't see. I can see number four because you allowed me. But in four, all of them (*the galaxies*) are equally high, the mountains.
D. So that would imply that it is ready to move on into the next— (*Bob finished the sentence.*)
B. Into the next experiences of whatever that is. I don't know who flips the Wheel, if they do that. And we don't seem to be going somewhere to talk about it. But who knows what I will come to learn as I continue here. These entities in the back, I don't know if they are your friends. They don't seem to be that cozy–cozy. But they're doing something, and there are seven.
D. That's a really good description. I like that image.
B. It just (*makes sucking sound*) drags up. And everyone is reading this cake, and it seems like they are really analyzing it and looking into it. And then, when it goes back down, souls can go out where they are supposed to. In some way, it's a way to fill up the cake. It's very complex. But it's a living entity, of course. It's like you can do the adjustments in the spiritual cake here if you drag it out. And then, as you allow it to return down to the flat map, it is sort of set. And that is how new changes can take place.
D. If it is beyond your understanding, it is certainly beyond mine.
B. Well, we might want to talk to Ari about this. So I've been here, of course, looking at this and I'm quite fascinated about it. They are doing something with the spiritual realities. There are several disks around the Center Pole, the big ones.
D. You mean other Wheels?
B. We have twelve fish tanks in this disk. Other Wheels below and above.
D. I was thinking about this as you were talking, the Wheel of Creation.
B. It's just so teeny–tiny when I look into it here. You see this cake and then you know that there are several disks. The spiritual reality—I don't know if there is another spiritual cake in another disk. It doesn't seem like anyone knows about that. But it all comes together with the Creator. I can see that the disk above is smaller. You say that that disk has nine fish tanks. You say it goes in numbers of three, so the next disk above that has six fish tanks. And you said, "This I know. But I haven't gone. None of us go. We are where we are. But just understand that the number 3 is holy. It's the trinity, and it's part of all construction of matter, and matter is also the soul. From the middle (*Wheel*) we have 12 (*fish tanks*). Then there is 9, 6, and 3." Then I wanted to know if it goes

to 15, and you said, "No. It is polar opposites. We are the center, where we are now, and then there is 9 going the other way." (*Our Wheel is in the middle of the Ball of Creation. There are Wheels directly above and below our Wheel, and they each have 9 fish tanks. The Wheels above and below those each have 6. The two Wheels closest to the top and bottom of the Ball each have 3 fish tanks. The Creator is the Center Pole for all the Wheels.*)

D. You have to wonder what kind of realities exist above and below.

B. Above and below. I'm not sure who we can talk to about that. Huhuh. I haven't really gone that far in my Wheel, and now that I can see there are disks above and below. Before I saw like 3, but it is actually more.

D. How would you describe the holy trinity? You mentioned that, and I think it is really important. In matter, I think it is light, sound, and vacuum?

B. Well the holy trinity is to understand the divine geometry of creation. And that is, it has to have light. It has to have sound. And it then has to have intent. Everything stems from light and sound. You are born, in some way, from light. You become from sound, but your intent mirrors where you go in this cake, and also to the extension of where you are gonna go later on. Someone like me might not be configurated correctly to go to, let's say—if I were to go and fulfill my intent of my trinity—fish tank ten, for instance. Because we never talk about ten. So it doesn't seem like I'm heading that way. So, maybe that's not part of my trinity of being born, light; becoming, growing with sound; to understand intent, number 3. So, I just wanted to tell you that I've been seeing this show and I think I want to continue to look here. I do get overwhelmed, as it just keeps on growing. As you know by now, when things are growing, I want to grow with it. So I do have a lot of questions.

D. (*Laughing.*) I'm sure we will talk about it.

B. Ah. Well, we do talk in your study. And sometimes you say, "Today, we're going to go to a preview show." It doesn't mean we're going to do it. But just to humor my curiosity, we sometimes go to show me—it's like going to the movie. So sometimes you take me to places. The zooming device is a little bit like that, but we're still down here (*on the low parts of the map*). There we are, looking around at things (*in the fish tanks*). We didn't look at the cake, I did not see the cake until now. Ari and the Council of Nine, they just access the whole understanding and the whole purpose of creation. Because understanding that all spiritual realities are connected, that there is no separation, even when you shrink the cake, is something that you can bring when you travel into a form reality, like a fish tank, or whatever configuration that you take in another fish tank. You said, "When you feel like you are flat, like the map, and then you see that little center." And I said, "Is that the Creator?" You said, "It's similar like a human, because they are flat." You know that there is something inside of you, a heart or some sort of soul particle, but once you unfold this cake within— and you can do it in different ways. That's what the ancients knew. Those who were initiated in the understanding of being part of creation—they made that cake within and they grew. You say, "Now humanity is sort of bouncing a little bit over the map. They haven't the ability to expand to become that cake within." You have the ability to possess all this awareness and this feeling of belonging to ALL. But in order to do that, you have to expand that cake. And when you do that, you will see that you, being that little center, like I said, "Look at the Creator, how small," but then when we dragged this out, then it just blossomed and there it was with its big light. You said it's the same thing in a galaxy, it takes time to expand. In a human, one of the big tricks is to create that squeeze box and make it rise within you. It goes like this (*he shows it rising up*), depending on the experiencing factors of life, you say. But once you learn how to hold and to control this big pyramid within you, then you become your purpose. And that is what you said, you are looking into in new cycles to be able to not just bounce in the map like that, but to take it out. (*Expand it upwards.*)

D. Is that problem due, in part, to the design of the human body?

B. Ah. And that's why we said you should avoid wheat and sugar. It doesn't make you go. You can only be here, you're sort of locked. You can't build or access that, that's what you say. You say, "That's why we travel. It is to understand and learn how to measure what adjustments need to be done in the form that we are taking, in order for us to be able to expand within." So when you travel, you're trying to really focus on the mind. From the sixth, the highest level is to raise your pyramid to connect the human mind to the soul mind. So the pyramid within is very much related to sixth dimension knowledge, in your case. A fifth dimension soul has a different pyramid, but it still belongs in the same tree. So, there is no separation. It is just how you are designed in your trinity. You know, why were you born? How did you grow? What is your purpose? And then you try to take that purpose, regardless of where you are, if you are in spirit or if you are in form, and you try to expand that awareness into the form that you have taken. You become purpose. In this case, when you folded your Coat, you have understood and you have mastered the pyramid within you, your purpose, and to be a reflection of this big pyramid in the form that you took. That is when you fold the Coat.

D. That's really good. Thank you for that.

B. Ah, you told me. That's what you say.

D. How do you feel about your inner pyramid?

B. My inner pyramid? Oh, there's so many steps. You said I have to think of that it's not what I believe the steps to be, I have to identify my purpose steps. And that's when I will understand my trinity. I want to understand, and each soul wants to understand, "Why was I born? Why did I have this direction in my soul growth? What is the purpose of me?" Some are set to travel to collect data and to learn how to become the purpose in form. Me, not so much. I tried it. When I go to the fourth fish tank and I go to Siah, I'm somewhat a form. But it's not my purpose. Again, I'm just trying different dishes, like a buffet, and you humor me because I ask and I'm curious. And then you say, "Well, you can try it over here." So that's what I wanted to talk about today. But I think I want to go and talk to Ari. You can come because you tend to know my questions before I even have them. So it's helpful because you tell me certain things before I have to form my questions. I like that. It's a very productive friendship. It's not like we have to wait for others to understand. I kinda like when we do things, just us, and you tell me things.

D. And you tell me things too.

B. Well, I tell you what you tell me, in this case. But it's an amazing view. I'm gonna go now, but you wanted me to tell you this. Because you wanted to plant a seed, you said, about the endless opportunity that you possess inside, and that you wanted to expand your inner pyramid more. You said that I should just remind you of this concept.

D. I really like the imagery, so thank you for coming and sharing that with us.

B. I'm still not done with the show. Maybe there's more. But those in the back, I should tell you, do not engage. But I think that they are in charge of the show. I can see here in fish tank five, it's different. It's like little peaks, like cupcakes.

D. Like a map of the mountains.

B. A map of the mountains. Different cupcakes. Okay, I'll go now, but I'll be back.

D. Alright, my friend. It was a wonderful talk, so thank you so much for giving it. It's always a pleasure.

B. Ah. I'm not gonna tell this to my students, though. We're still trying to just go to, huh, fish tank five and experience things. If I were to add all this, we might drift far off our intended plan. I'm just trying to be a good teacher to them. But I'm not gonna tell about this. I might sneak in a word with Ole. He's probably seen this. He knows a little bit more, but he is more restricted with information. I'm pretty sure that Gergen knows exactly what I'm allowed to hear. When I say hear, it means what I'm allowed to absorb. Because as I absorb, knowledge becomes me. A human, they hear something and it goes out. When I hear, it stays.

D. I wish I could do that.

B. That's the pickle of being a human. You have to hear from your center and then it will stay. As soon as you try to hear and remember in the ball (*brain*), then it's lost, and it becomes colored and it goes the wrong way and it's just disorganized. The brain is disorganized by itself, you know, colored and mirrored by intake of food or electromagnetic waves. That's why you kinda have to lose your head, like a chicken. You have to experience and listen, then sense and smell and operate from your center. Just know that the ball, your head, simply executes signals, for good or bad. At the moment, you're stuck in there. That is why you want to be able to drop down to your core and experience from there. Okay, I'll go, but I'll be back.

D. Alright, my friend. That was wonderful.

B. Okay. Bye bye.

Ophelia, Bob: Becoming a Different Animal (Oct 4, 2021)

Ophelia gave an uplifting talk during the height of the worldwide folly connected to the flu–fear campaign. One of the biggest hurdles is that people have abandoned faith in a higher order, and in doing so, have lost the joy of living on Earth. She makes an interesting point that councils in the spiritual realms are never sure about their decisions. When facing the uncertainty of the unknown, they have trust and faith in the guidance from a higher order. If mistakes are made, they will learn something that will help them evolve and grow. On Earth, people who lack faith in the continuity of existence are easier to manipulate. When totalitarian regimes come into power, their first order of business is to exterminate religious organizations and silence people who question their authority. During the mass hysteria of the 2020 flu fiasco, those totalitarian methods were on full display as people were locked in their homes, churches were shuttered, and critics were censored and banned. The Cell, and those who control governments from the shadows, lead humanity into stockyards of submission by feeding them a steady diet of falsehoods and imaginary fears. There is a path to freedom, but it requires the seeker to become more in touch with their soul. A good place to start is by researching the afterlife. A majority of people who have had near-death experiences lose their fear of death, knowing that the soul survives and moves on to a greater reality. And many of them come back with a greater enthusiasm for living in a positive and compassionate way. Ophelia encourages us to use music to uplift the soul and become the emissaries who throw off the shackles of fear.

Bob followed Ophelia and played off her talk by using animals to represent the different responses to life. He humorously said society has gone from turtlehood to sloth-like, before giving examples of how different dimensions can best represent their home. The goal, he said, is for humans to go from being a domesticated pet to being more like wildlife. By becoming independent, humans are much more difficult for the establishments to control.

O. This is Ophelia.

D. Hello, Ophelia.

O. Good evening. Well, evening perhaps is not the right word. It does not matter. We are here together, Bob and myself, in order for you to feel relaxed in the female (*nurturing*) energy we surround you with at this time. We have talked about different ways of seeing the consciousness. We have talked about waves. We have talked about winds. And animals, such as lions and scorpions. At this time, what we are seeking is to increase the empathy, the compassion, and that relates to the female energy. It is not meant for the mental aspect to take a step away, but we need to balance. We have talked numerous times about the dilemma in a human reality between emotional and mental experiences. When the mental is collapsing, as we see in certain areas at this time—European Union being one—we see the fear, and fear is related to not understanding your surroundings. When you feel your surroundings, you will understand on a soul level what is going on. That is why, for a brief moment, we ask for the male energy, the mental aspect within your consciousness, to allow the higher senses to take flight. At this time, there are no flights, simply rotations, ground based. In order for higher consciousness to be brought in, you have to allow your wings to carry you. When we say wings, it means to trust that you can take flight. But when the consciousnesses are controlled—your mental aspects as well as emotional realities are controlled—we need to meet that with a wind of change. The wind of change, at this time, relates to taking a step back, absorbing the information from your center, not your mind. To clarify what is going on around you needs silence. Why do you think masks, higher voltage (*5G and EMFs*) also at the same time, surround your reality? It is for you to not be able to take flight. It is to make you grounded. Your planes, so to speak, have not been allowed to take flight. As we see the fear related to dying, know that that is part of this upgrade. Earlier civilizations had no fear of death. This is what we seek from the spirit realm at its highest form, is to not be afraid of change. Dying is the biggest change in a human experience, and what the human dreads the most. We are here to bring back the awareness of transition. To be joyful—not seek death—but to be joyful for life and knowing that life continues. In some way, it is easier at this time to reach religious groups than the scientific ones. Religious groups seek salvation. They seek eternity. Whereas the scientific communities do not. They are grounded. At this time, we put our efforts into those who believe, regardless of what belief they have. It is easier to change, to elevate your higher senses from that point, when you believe. Not when you are sure. When you are sure, like the scientific communities tend to be, regardless of if they believed the Earth was flat, or if (*they believe they*) have the right solution for your society, they are still sure. If you are sure, it indicates no elevation from that point. When you believe, you in some way stretch your awareness into the unknown. Therefore, the unknown is something that the scientific communities dread. So what we are asking of you is to move into a different way of communicating. Bring joy, bring music, allow the grounded planes to take flight. You cannot do anything about the boats rotating on the sea, lacking oars. Or even if they have oars, simply rotating in circles. Eventually, that will stop. But that is not your assignment. Your assignment is to lead others with your personalities, to see beyond the human veil. To lead with your higher consciousness is to activate your spiritual mind. Spiritual intelligence is never sure. No councils are sure in the spiritual realities. We constantly seek improvement. We are aware of other realities. We constantly seek to change, knowing that imperfection is the greatest asset to (*bring*) change. When you see that you are not perfect, for the lack of words that we have here, you seek change. You seek a higher consciousness. You seek improvement. You seek peace, and peace is different for each and every one. Someone might seek a peaceful work environment. Whereas others might seek the silence in nature. It's still the same goal, the same wish. Ignite in the people you meet, the desire to wish upon a star, if you like, like when they were children. Return to the basics. Don't get lost and never be sure.

D. That was a really brilliant talk. It's easy to feel somewhat oppressed and gloomy at this time.

B. Gloomy, gloomy, gloomy! Gloomy, gloomy, gloomy! Huhuh! Gloomy, gloomy, gloomy!

D. (*Laughing.*) Bob, did you just bump Ophelia?

B. No, we're joined. Gloomy, gloomy, gloomy! Huh huh. Okay. Bow out. I just wanted to make sure that I'm here so no one forgets. Ophelia never forgets. But she wanted to say goodbye, I would assume. She didn't say that, but I picked up on the waves that she was kinda done. That's why I came in. Okay, I'll let her have the final trumpet.

O. He's eager, as always.

D. Indeed. I was saying that it's easy to feel gloomy at this time, but I'm hoping that we can deliver messages in a way that you approve of and are uplifting.

O. The way that you can follow the guideline would be how you would be receiving information at the best. Talk to others the way that you would prefer to be talked to. So, I want you to know that you are taken care of. We observe, but we also take a step back. Due to the upgrades needed, we evaluate what the upgrades need to be, and also where humanity falters and where they rise, as a group. Music is something that will unify your consciousness and society. Listen to music that elevates you. We have told you that it will improve your writing, and we see that it does. It moves you into your soul mind, your soul compassion, your center core. When you listen to the music that makes your soul sing, you radiate that through the human experience. Find the music that resonates with you, and you will never be out of tune. Hmm.

D. That's a beautiful teaching. So, thank you.

O. You are much welcome. (*Bob came back in and then, very slowly, looked to the right and then the left.*)

D. That's rather sloth–like.

B. Trying to blend in. This is how I see humanity, like a giant sloth. Look, like this. (*He then made very slow gestures and turned his head very slowly.*) How do you think someone will take flight or move—even a turtle moves faster, a turtle has a direction—but the sloth, it just stops. Sometimes a turtle goes into hiding, but it's more curious, a turtle. But a sloth is more like this. (*He then turns ever so slowly and looks to the right.*) "Oh, what's happening over here? I'm hungry. Feed me." Like that.

D. I take it you didn't have a hand in designing that one?

B. Well. When it comes to a sloth, it wasn't like a mistake, at all. It was actually designed to monitor wildlife around it. That's why it wasn't supposed to move. Because the turtle came before, but the turtle tends to (*make sucking sound*) just hide. And we wanted like our eyes, the second dimension eyes, to be open. The difference between turtle and sloth is the sloth doesn't hide. It's just slow, but it still observes. A turtle tends to like, "Oh, better inside," and returns like that into its hidey-hole. Whereas a sloth is like, "Oh?" but it remains still. I didn't belong in that group. I haven't made that many animals. I did some. When I went to the 4-H Farm and I was in charge of a guinea pig, I did want to make a guinea pig because they were highly intelligent. But then Gergen said, "We will start with ants." And I felt like, "Uhh." I didn't see, but it is actually a higher percentage of intelligence in the ant than in my guinea pig, or even in the sloth. The sloth—I don't want to be mean—but it's not so intelligent. It's not designed to be intelligent. And that's why I'm comparing it to a human. At the moment, you are acting like a sloth, you are not acting very intelligent. But you have, actually, a brain; we gave you a brain. But a sloth was not designed to think, it was designed to observe. It was not designed to hide, like a turtle. So the turtle actually came first, but it tended to go into hiding. And what we see now, if we compare humans to animal life, then you've actually gone through the cycle of turtlehood, or turtleness. And at the moment we see sloth, to be like a little bit paralyzed, but eyes still wide open because you're afraid to fall asleep, you're afraid to die. So you have your eyes open. You don't just go into a hidey-hole and wait it out. But we also see the mentality of a flock, like the sheep. So we can sometimes, because there is so many different animal lives going on, we can use the human and just refer to it—when you go through your cycles—we can refer to it as different kinds of animal life. I would say that when you have had your peak of intelligence, you have either been close to the reptile family, or the bird family.

When you are closer to the birds, you are more connected to your higher SENSES. When you are connected to the reptile groups, you are more connected to the higher MIND. You have the ability to think your way through—you are not a sloth. A sloth simply observes because it is paralyzed. So, it's neither a bird or a reptile. It sits there in the middle, not knowing where to go. But it's cute. You care for it, you don't want to remove it. We don't want to remove the human, even though we kinda need to clean a little bit on certain places. And when we bring that information in, all sorts of turmoil goes on. And then you become paralyzed. I can relate to this being similar if someone were to say, "Okay, we're gonna have a group now who is gonna dissolve." And it would be like, "Oh, am I up? Who is gonna dissolve?" It would be commotion in the group.

D. We need some volunteers.

B. Volunteers. A sloth never volunteers. I'm not a sloth because I've never been paralyzed. As a spirit, you don't become paralyzed. I've had a taste of it, a little bit, when I was sort of manifested (*a form on Etena*) when I tended to Tess and Siah. I could relate to what humans are going through, a little bit. I was cautious, like a sloth, because it was new to me. I would say, when you see sloth behavior in your flock, just be aware that it's new to them. They don't know where to go. The next level, after sloth, you go into sheep. You want to be in a group. But you don't really want to be on the outside of the flock because if you are on the edge of that sheep flock, you are kinda *unsure*. You don't really know. But you start from within a flock of sheep and then you move outwards, gradually. Starting as a sloth when you come into human body. Change into different animal life as you progress as a soul in a human. The problem is that there are plenty of sloths down and there's also a lot of that sheep mentality. But those who are on the border can go either way. They are here to change into another animal. But changing fur, changing your clothes, like a sheep, like cutting it off, it's scary! You constantly, if you want to grow—and in this little story here, we're changing into a different animal—you also have to be okay with standing on that border. You (*Lasaray*) like to be like a giraffe. You like to be with your head above the trees, and not engage. So a lot of times, I can refer to you as a giraffe. Everything goes on, on ground level. And then I say, "If you just look down a little bit under the leaves, Lasaray, you will see that there is a lot of interesting things going on, on the savanna below you, meaning Earth life. But you're like, "It's okay, I have what I need up here. I have, within my reach, things to eat." (*He makes a chomping sound.*) "I have the sunlight. I'm all sorts of fine up here." The highest level—when we're talking about evolving through animals as a guideline—depends on what sort of soul type you are. The highest intelligence would be, if you are from Ophelia's realm, you are, in your blueprint, in your core, related to birds. You, on the sixth, are more related to the lizard as the higher intelligence. Those who are belonging in the fifth dimension have the ability of, like those animals on the savanna, the ones that can run and be organized in groups.

D. Jackals?

B. Nay, nay. They're (*the souls are*) not predators at all. They're friendly grass eaters. No one is a predator, really, by nature—on a soul level, that is—but you have to be on the other side. So, for the bird group, the highest level of evolution would be moving into the consciousness of a dolphin or a whale. So you have the different elements. Whereas the lizard group, they have to be moving into, because if you compare a lizard, they are cold-blooded, so we want to move you into more of a—not necessarily lions—lions, tigers... (*Bob looks towards Ophelia.*) Am I allowed to say all this? Are people going to be offended? Ophelia says it doesn't matter. So, on a higher level, the lizard family are actually moving—they pass through the level where this one is, of lions and predators. But it's not the final destination. I think that the giraffe is more of where you are when you fold your Coat, because you have the privilege to be here but still not be bothered. So you can see it from a higher level, whereas the lizard can never move in that sense. But you travel through different consciousness and behaviors. I would think that you, being the giraffe, you have earned those steps. This one is not a giraffe yet. When we think about those who run on the savanna, they actually are going from wildlife into farm life, but they're still in the animal level of likables (*comparables*). It's just whether they are wild or tame. So it's a transition of that. Like a ferret, you can have that—it's a wild thing—but you can have it as a pet.

D. So is it progressing as it moves towards tame?

B. No. Ophelia says it's the opposite. I got confused. You move from pet to wildlife.

D. And that's self-determination?

B. It's independence. So, you know, maybe I drifted off, but I wanted to give you like a picture of what we see here.

D. It gave us something to laugh about when we got home.

B. Something to laugh about—and we did! We still do. We still talk about fond memories, different things when we look back on the timeline of traveling. We do laugh and do look at things. I say, "Look there!" Huhuh. But you should know, in general, when life reviews go on with a soul in a human experience, spirit guides can use animals and animal life of different kinds to mirror how that life went, what the intention was. Normally this is done in the beginning, a little bit. It's like the 4–H Farm kinda thing, you know, a soul goes in and going to Earth is like going to the 4–H Farm. We use different animals to somewhat mirror what the intent was, how it went. What sort of animal did you wanna be, and what animal did you actually become? It's a way, similar like children, you learn about life in general depending on very easily accessed information, such as a different animal.

D. How would you describe the people running the fear show here on Earth now?

B. Uh, in some way, they are like bugs. But it's not like they are creating something, like the ant. It's more like they—I do like bugs. I don't want them to be any animal. But if they were, I would say they are more like the parasites.

D. There you go. Tapeworms.

B. Ah, they are like cockroaches and parasites. We all make mistakes. Parasites were not part of the big plan, perhaps. But again, we grow and we learn. Like Ophelia says, "If I was completely sure of everything, then I would leave no room for improvement." And the parasites, they are more like that. And that is something that a human can learn a little bit about. Whatever you say, whatever you do, what is the intent behind it? If you have no intent, maybe just retreat and be silent. Ah. Okay, I go now.

D. I appreciate you and Ophelia coming today.

B. Okay. See you home. Bye bye.

Gergen, Bob: Managing Expectations (Oct 20, 2021)

Gergen, a healing guide to Seth (Christine), came in first and gave some personal advice to her. He talked about how spirits will use roadblocks to change a course of action. The roadblocks can be personal ones, or they can affect the whole planet, such as the travel restrictions during the time of lockdowns. Bob then came in and described how he had to manage the expectations of the Elahim souls he is training to come to Earth. They want to come in and make great progress, but Bob had to show them that the incarnation program is a long grind. He ended the session by talking about one of his ideas to create a solar system that roams around and heals other solar systems. On more than one occasion, Bob has said that when he has ideas that cannot be implemented, or questions that cannot be answered at that time, Lasaray makes a note and puts them on the wall or in a glass box in his lab where they can be seen. Eventually, many of the questions will be answered, and his ideas, which are part of creation, may find an application in the future. Nothing is ever tossed aside or disregarded.

G. When one understands that roadblocks are not necessarily just there to hinder someone, they are actually helping the individual. Similar like it's helpful that you are not moving around across our planet. I say our planet, humanoids are not necessarily—it's a nice project, don't get me wrong—but, in some way, you are ahead of yourselves, and that is what we are trying to fix. Some are fixing the emotional aspects. I'm more concerned that you move around on landmass and wind and water in the same way, so we want there to be calm. And it has been for the last time (*few months*) here, and we are grateful. We have been able to HEAR the planet. And that is what I am saying, that we sit and observe and we LISTEN. But it's hard to listen when there is too much commotion. So we have collected data and we are content with the data that we have, and we do know the intent moving forward. So, in many ways, what I said to Seth we will also say to humanity—STOP! And if it is not behaving correctly, roadblocks will be put up.

D. What would you say if the governments try to force us to take what they are calling a vaccine?

G. They will not be able to. There are too strong forces against the whole play. I'm just talking here on the human level. On the spiritual reality, of course, you have all your support. So there is nothing to fear, in that regard.

D. The people that do take it are going to feel regretful, aren't they?

G. They will feel—and this is something that you should all be mindful of—no one likes to be the fool, and a lot of these people will start to feel like they are the fool. It's not so kind to poke them, even though I understand that it's a human urge. You always come to, at one point—regardless of what the topic is—out of the other end that you understand something that the previous group did not. Just think of the flat Earth, that suddenly someone understood, eventually, that it was round. Again, those groups are long gone, but it's the same thing. No one likes to be the fool that thought the

Earth was flat. Same here. So, the nice thing to do is to just allow that. Certain individuals are taking on this experiment so that we can study the behavior when one is put under the spell of rulers. No need to fear, nothing will happen. We have encased you from this, so there is no need to be too concerned about it.

D. I wasn't too concerned, but thank you.

G. There is no need to be, because it's not upcoming. Just know that this whole play will soon fall flat. Similar as the Earth once was flat. Huh huh huh.

D. (*Laughing.*) Very well. What about the weather manipulation that the governments are doing?

G. Well, that has somewhat ceased, due to the fact that there is less traffic. So, we have also manipulated the gadgets a little bit, huh huh huh huh, so they have not been operating as intended, one can say. That is a little bit of a trick that we, once in a while, are allowed to play. If you manipulate, huh huh huh huh huh, so can the spiritual realities! It's a game. If you play, you invite us to play with you. And it's quite easy for us to manipulate electronic devices.

D. The spirit realm always wins that game.

G. Always. Anyway, I'm gonna go, so Bob has his turn.

D. Alright, Gergen. It was wonderful to hear from you. Thank you for the information.

G. Okay. See you. (*Gergen moved out and Bob instantly came in.*)

D. Hello, Bob.

B. Huhuh. SO! We have actually continued our work with the little Elahims. My friends (*spirit guides from the second dimension*) are on standby to go. We are getting ready, in some cases—there are six, but not all three Elahims are gonna go. One is gonna go and two—there are three—but there is only one Elahim (*that will incarnate*) and then there is two (*from the sixth that are not Elahim*) that's gonna accompany him on a journey. And that journey will take place in North America.

D. Is that sometime in the next decade or two?

B. Indeed, indeed. Little Seth is still waiting. We had to, in some way, modify the personality a little bit. The hopes that he has are not realistic. I don't want to shut him down, but I want him to find that understanding himself. So he is working with his peer, trying to adjust expectations. Expectations should be long term when you start in your incarnation program. So he is aware of his long-term goals and how to fold the karmic Coat, but he has not dressed yet. So we want him to take it in cups, otherwise there will be disappointment. And it will take longer for him to reach the expected goal, if he is disappointed. We don't want him to come sulking back from Earth, like big Seth has done at times. Huh huh. So we are looking into that. We are gonna observe these three that are soon to come.

D. They are all going to be quite interested in how their pioneer does.

B. And I'm gonna listen, of course. So we've been with the tailors and looking into how to dress, and to also understand that not everything in each lifetime is about the purpose all the time. There are little things you are expected to take on, such as compassion and igniting others, and that has nothing to do with your program. So, sometimes you can accelerate your own path and your own Coat of Karma—might not say this out loud—but you could ignore, in some way, your Coat of Karma in a lifetime. Meaning, you missed everything in your Coat, but you were helping other Coats, so the overall experience and the overall journey was actually better.

D. So when you help people like that, doesn't that, in some way, reinforce lessons in your own Coat?

B Ah, it can. But when we see that someone steps outside their Coat, we're looking into what you're doing. Are you just being lazy and ignoring? Then that's not gonna go well. But if you, for some reason, started to operate not according to plan, but you were moving into and doing good for other Coats, or perhaps for another cause you were not here to take on, then, in some way, lessons that were later on in your travel itinerary is actually solved here, even though you didn't take care of it personally in your own experience.

D. It does benefit, perhaps, in the long run?

B. And even yourself, on a subconscious level, because you did not know. It might be like, "Okay, you went down and you were gonna kick-start the medical industry, but you did not. You dropped out of medical school and took the route of becoming a farmer, and you started to do agriculture and created a society of organic growth." Your mission did not fulfill, but because of the good that you did, you actually participated in progress. The Coat is, in some way, static, but it is also a living entity. So it can be that that lesson was shut down or put in the pocket and it was exchanged with a bigger lesson that was more aligned with progress than the intention from the beginning. So, it's not like when you come home they will say, "Oh, what happened? Why didn't you go to medical school?" It's not like that at all. Then the spirit guides and the ones who take your notes will look at the overall and feel like, "It was okay." So again, a Coat can be static, but it's also, in some way, a living entity and it can also be altered—but not by yourself. There are elders and the wise ones that will come in and maybe do a little bit of a talk. That's what we're doing with Little Seth at the moment. We're trying to tell him, "Your intention, as it is with all of you (*Elahims*), is to ignite the mind and to move into a higher science. BUT in order for you to get there, there are little steps that will be aligned with that intention, but it's not gonna be a full blown-up agenda."

D. A gradual process.

B. Gradual process. He also needs to learn—and you all do, because of the fact that you tend to like to work solo and you are quite independent as a group—and we work with that. One of the big things is to gather, to have friends, to have family, to do things in a group. You tend to not want to do group activity, those from the sixth. That's what I've been working on with you a little bit, you know, try to find yourself some friends. Join into a group project. And now you are saying to me, "Well, I have a group project. I have my little brother. I have you and I have Ophelia." And I can't argue that, because now you're doing what I told you, it's just that only one is human! So I say, "Okay, that's good enough. At least you engage in a group." Ah! Huhuh. Because now you know there is a group, but not all of them are humans. So, you know, we've been doing that, and we still have some of my notes to go through.

D. Did you have any that you brought with you?

B. Well, one of my notes are if we shouldn't really create another solar system.

D. You don't like the one you have?

B. I do indeed. But why settle with just one?

D. What's the purpose of the new one?

B. Well, I'm thinking that the purpose of the new one should be like, I would like to have a healing central and create a system that heals—I'm saying that because you constantly tell me, "Oh, there's haste. Got to patch up holes. Got to go, someone is stuck in a portal." It seems to be, to me, that the fish tanks are not operating properly. So I've been thinking, 'What I would like to create—since it seems like your work is not optimal since you're constantly off to haste—what if we were to create systems that are a living healing entity?' So, instead of something leading to haste, it detects it earlier, and it heals. I'm thinking, 'What could make it heal? What could make this hole that you were working on, at one point, heal?' And then I wanted to put in all that intention—because again, I have to have intention—and I'm gonna put all my intention on the sun. So in this system, it's gonna be a sun and then just a few smaller planets, if needed. I'm not at all sure about the details. I'm just giving you the intention here, because I do know that you are fond of intentions.

D. So it will be like a doctor sun that detects and analyzes the problems?

B. It's like a doctor sun. And as soon as a problem arises, it goes ling-ling-ling into my healing sun. And I'm thinking about that poor person that was stuck. We never heard what happened with him in his little craft. He was stuck somewhere and I thought, 'What if there were somewhat of like guarding systems that took care of that?' And then you say, "What if you put in this big spotlight and you're just blinding everyone?" Huh.

D. You'll have to fill it up with some twelfth dimension healing energy.

B. Ah. But you said, "The greatest healing is not coming from the light, it's actually coming from the darkness." So then I thought, 'The black holes?' And you nodded, "Yes, that's true. That's actually sometimes similar as a bright sun. It provides healing to the system." And then I said, "Maybe instead of making a sun, maybe we will dive into how to make more black holes, or maybe I do both?"

D. Black holes don't really exist, do they? It's a different type of celestial body?

B. Indeed, indeed. So, it's like a sun and it operates in some way similar, if you think of the wholeness. And sometimes you also say that it's not just what they appear to be, like a star. Like when I said, "That's a star." And you said, "No, it's not." Then you said, "Look, there's a black hole. Some are different, some are actually portals." So I said, "Maybe we should use the zooming device and just identify how many are what."

D. What do you think about the concept of electricity in the—

B. In my system?

D. Well, the electrical flow of energy from the Sun?

B. From the Sun? If man knew how to extract and work the Sun energy and the energy from nature, it would be less damaging to you as a species. It is when you try to manufacture energy and electricity, instead of using the natural resources, that it just becomes a failure.

D. Hopefully, in the next cycle, one of the Elahims will work on that.

B. They're gonna come down and they're gonna work on that. We have electric engineering coming in. But I wanted to just say that I'm signing up for the next cosmic program. And then I thought if I give you an idea on how certain things could maybe be solved with my healing system, but you countered and said, "You can't just bring in big spotlights because you will blind those who are supposed to be in darkness. It's that balance of light and dark." And here, light and dark has become like good and bad. But on your level, and mine as well, they complement each other. Sometimes the light has to be dimmed and the dark has to take over. To give you an example, it's like daytime and nighttime. What if you were to suddenly not sleep? What if there were suddenly just daytime? Then the humanoid, animal life and even plants will be confused. You said it's the same thing. And you say that that has also changed over time on different planets. If we have like your 24 hours, on certain places, it had been daylight for 20 hours.

D. It's a big project. I'm sure we'll come up with something.

B. We'll come up with something, and I just want to make sure that I'm part of it. I don't respond well to be excluded.

D. Pretty soon you'll be out patching holes.

B. Ah! We'll see. Okay, I'm gonna go now.

D. Alright, my friend. Thank you so much for coming. I always look forward to our talks and hearing your latest ideas.

B. Ah. Because I do have several. So I'm thinking that if I keep on bringing ideas—

D. One of them might stick.

B. Because you never toss my ideas away. Sometimes you say, "Okay, this is a little bit hard to manage." We have a box in the office. It's like a little glass box with no lid. That's where we put ideas that are a little bit ahead of its time. If it's a closed box, it's more likely that the energy dies, in some way. Like a person, you put it in a coffin and it dies. But my ideas, I don't want them to die. So you said, "Okay, let's create a little glass container," it's not a jar—it's a rectangle thing, "and here is where we put them." I said, "If we put it in a coffin, it feels like my ideas died, it feels like you killed them." And then you said, "I don't want you to feel like I killed your ideas. So let's do it like this instead." So we always see them.

They're right there. One idea was, for instance, I said, "If it's not possible for me to go everywhere, maybe we can invite some to come." And you said, "Who do you want to invite?" And I said, "Well, I don't know that much about the disk below, or the disk above. What is that all about?"

D. What kind of response did you get?

B. We put that in the box.

D. I think Ari said that no one travels to those.

B. Well, that's the easy reply. But it might be that they say that, so there are no questions. So you said, "At the moment, we will put that in the glass box here." Because I know exactly what's in this and I can also see that sometimes you have rearranged my notes. So, sometimes I can see that something has moved up, higher to my consciousness and my awareness. And then I wait because I know that it's probably due to be removed out into the open.

D. It's nice that all the thoughts and ideas you had eventually get answered.

B. Some, some. Ah. But some are quite dusty in the bottom. Sometimes you say, "No one knows," and then you put that with the dusty ones. And I'm not sure if I find that to be an adequate response. Just because you and I don't know, maybe we should just see if someone else might know someone that does. It might not be that Ari knows, but he might know someone who knows someone.

D. Alright, Bob. Thank you. I look forward to our next chat. We're going to try and do this more frequently. Get back in the rhythm.

B. Back into the rhythm. Huhuh. Rhythm is a dancer—and I like to dance. Okay, okay, I go. Ophelia says I'm just talking. Okay, bye bye.

D. Bye bye.

Klo: Hints on Free Energy Creation (Oct 31, 2021)
Just before this speaker left, he gave us the name, Klo. This talk is packed full of fascinating descriptions of ancient visitors, power plants, pyramids, ley lines and the Earth grid. Since this is the first time he communicated, his manner of speaking is not as smooth as those who speak frequently. By carefully studying exactly what he is reporting, it is obvious he is giving significant clues to a lost source of power. My interpretation, which is only a guess, is that electromagnetic radiation from the Sun was captured in some device outside the Earth's atmosphere and converted to light by visitors.

They beamed the light wave down to the ground onto very large disks made of gold or copper. The parabolic shape of the disk concentrated the light into a beam, and redirected the energy into pools of pure copper in containers of quartz on the surface. The heat from the light caused the copper to melt. Copper has a melting point around 1090 degrees Celsius. Quartz (SiO_2) is the crystallized form of silica (SiO_4) and melts around 1750 degrees Celsius. Molten Copper boils or vaporizes at 2570 degrees, at least in modern times. They have said, elsewhere, that the atmosphere was changed, and the critical properties of many elements have been altered.

It's not clear how the Anunnaki free energy system worked, but from various descriptions I can speculate that copper was heated until it vaporized. Then the pure copper gas or the molten copper and gas was transported by pipelines to plants where it was used to make electricity and fuel. Klo says that copper was not used in the fuel, but it clearly had a purpose. I can speculate again and say it might have been feeding a copper vapor laser that separated or created isotopes of other elements into a fuel, because we know that uranium, mercury, and gold were the primary fuel sources. The Moon was also used as a base for beaming light or high energy electromagnetic waves to the ground, after bouncing along a series of parabolic disks. He was quite specific about moonlight being a critical part of the process. Humans have always taken it for granted that moonlight is only light reflected from the Sun. However, NASA discovered high energy gamma rays are emitted continuously from the entire surface of the Moon, regardless of the lunar phase. The gamma rays are caused by the bombardment of the lunar surface by cosmic rays (protons). The possibility exists that the extraordinarily high energy gamma rays were converted into a continuous stream of lower energy microwaves, which were then sent to receiving stations on the ground. Whatever the process, it involved reflective disks made of gold or copper that directed beams of energy into material in or around the pyramids. We hope Klo gives more information on this process, as it could revolutionize how energy is manufactured.

Klo makes a couple of observations that might be challenging for the conventionally educated reader to follow. One is about the creation of energy, specifically oil and gas. Hydrocarbons are often referred to as fossil fuels, and there is no doubt that some are created from decomposing organic material. However, hydrocarbons are found throughout the Solar System. Saturn's largest moon, Titan, has vast oil and gas oceans that dwarf the reserves found on Earth. So hydrocarbons can obviously form from abiogenic processes involving the breakdown and recombination of water and carbon in the Earth's mantle. Oil and gas are the end result of their millions of years–long project. The beginning of the project was the construction of energy power stations and the placement of boxes around the Earth at strategic locations. The power plants beamed or transmitted energy along paths that became part of the Earth grid. The grid, in turn, caused changes to the flow of heat energy inside the Earth. Over time, that caused land masses to break apart and move in different directions. Where the tectonic plates move apart, large volumes of gases and liquids were (and still are) released into the atmosphere. The volcanoes and rift systems on the sea floor along expanding plate boundaries spew out tremendous volumes of different gases and liquids, including methane, ethane and heavier hydrocarbons. When the spirit realm introduced certain bacteria into the sea, oxygen was produced and eventually, plants and sea life flourished from the equator to the poles. The subsequent accumulation and burial of organic matter created the black shales and carboniferous rocks that became the source rocks for some of the hydrocarbons we use today. This summary is not as speculative as the reader might imagine, because it is based on explanations from multiple spirits who have communicated with me during the past 7 years. One cannot help but feel a sense of awe at the technical majesty and patience needed to execute projects that span eons of geologic time. Earlier, in the May 3, 2021 session, Bob was given a view into Earth's deep past during a meeting he had in a pyramid on Etena. He was shown how crystal energy was used to divide the crust of the Earth. The separate pieces of land were then free to be moved around through manipulation of the inner grid. He was told, "This was in the beginning of baby Earth. It was like in the beginning. We're talking billions (*of years*) back." Lasers and induced electrical and magnetic fields were used to alter the geology long before lifeforms were first introduced. And billions of years later, we now learn that these visitors are still managing the Earth project.

Klo. (*There was a long pause.*) Greetings, greetings. We adjust the energy gradually, as we progress into your circle with new information. Let's see what we can do with the level of flow. One moment, please. (*He was speaking rapidly at a high pitch. As he slowed down, his voice became deeper.*) We travel as a group, a group connected to your family, the Elahim. We met and operated in ancient times in northeast Africa. The memory within you will ignite. I ask of you to connect to the power that you possessed at one point. It is not meant to channel. You traveled here, not in human form. Neither of us ever had human form. You took the assignment. You, little brother, tried to influence the brain in a direct manner. We traveled differently, all of us, at one point. The collection of magnetic memory, the... (*He began to whisper.*) Ni–ni–nitrogen.... Bear in mind that we will begin a new chapter, where we unfold different keys hidden from that time when we traveled in a different form. The collection now hidden under sand. Yet, it can activate the understanding of how man operated with a simple connection through your memory. You do not need to lift it up from below in order for the ancient wisdom to emerge. How do you think the scientist, Tesla remembered (*the secrets*) of connecting free energy? (*Tesla was also an Elahim.*) How do you think that came to the surface? It wasn't a human mind that understood the electrons needed and the gravitation field supporting different energy waves, in order for malfunctions to be eliminated. Once you understand the holes, the engineering behind the malfunction of energy of free flow on resources that exist in air as well. Man now use oil, gas. But you have the free energy connected stronger in air (*the atmosphere*). Once you understand how to use and reuse the energetic field below your feet, there is no border between the elements. The scientific wisdom is to eliminate borders between water, fire, earth, mercury. You merge them and you can manipulate them in a way for purposes, such as energy, to become and travel. You are bound here by borders—time, space, elements, people, ocean, land—once you understand how you merge... Hmm. It might be too complex. Let's begin again. Let's reverse, let's begin slower. When you were here in a different form, you created, at one point, towers. The disks you made used sunlight, but used also at night to collect moonlight. You extracted the free energy available in your cosmos. The atmosphere (*was*) not so dense. At this (*present*) time, with the debris floating, it also creates a less open atmosphere for true signals. And most think we talk about signals to your soul, and that is true. However, we also mean the true power line that can be extracted here using cosmic energy in order for power plants to become. Strategically placed around, mainly, where there is a lot of quartz.

D. What type of energy was being collected? Was it solar, electrical, or some other form?

K. Solar energy transformed into electric energy, with the receivers being copper. Using copper disks, using platforms where there was a high level of quartz. This was to receive and use energy. When we use (*this energy*) for travel, we blend gold in the fuel as well as mercury. We do not use quartz, because quartz holds the power—it's like a magnet. Copper, quartz, take the power to its position. It boils it. It is not meant to travel on. It is meant to use as power. That's how a power plant operates. The moonlight was simply to... (*He didn't finish the sentence.*)

D. You're dealing with a pretty limited human mind.

K. It didn't cool it down, that's the wrong word, but it... we will leave it.

D. Changed it?

K. In some way, it made it usable. In that boiling point, it (*copper*) was not suitable to use here. Some of the craters that you see on earth are not from outside, asteroids or meteors, it is those boiling points. It became....

D. Too much?

K. Indeed. The craters, some exist—North America, predominantly. It's not meteor. High density of quartz, copper, iron, uranium can be found in those craters. It's where the plant was operating from. The moonlight simply was meant to direct the power from that point, in some way. We'll wait.

D. It would be helpful if you could describe the process?

K. Sunlight was used. Power plants were located where there were not that many disturbances of clouds. Very strong sunlight, long hours. The disks used, copper, collected the sunlight. It sank (*was directed*) into the ground; it became boiling.

D. How was the sunlight transferred to the ground?

K. HA!! HA!! Huhuhuh. Oh, you had help. Not just the disks. There were disks along the way. You had your disks down here, engineering it from the ground. But on the way down to it, there were helpers with disks that collected the beam down.

D. In the upper atmosphere?

K. Yes, yes. Some of them operated from the moon, engineering.

D. So the disks reflected light towards the copper or quartz? Or was it, in some way, connected?

K. The quartz simply made it possible to boil, to not explode. The copper was the receiver. In order for it to be met in a way that it didn't hit an explosive level, the sunlight, if you had had different disks such as just gold, for this purpose, the disk was big. The copper disk collected the sunlight and made it (*the copper in the ground*) melt. The quartz simply made it bubble, boil, without exploding. The copper and quartz operate in a way that you can increase temperature without explosion. If you had used other material, it would have been out of control. At one point, the crater expanded. The moonlight—we will talk about later—but this was used to open up a bigger source of energy to this planet. The craters you see on different places, strategically operating, some exist in Australia. They communicated, and here enters the wisdom and understanding of the moon. But the first level is to heat the....

D. Was the copper and quartz mixed together in some way?

K. It became. They were separate, but they became one. If you looked from above, you would see big, red dots, strategically on different places. One big one around Lake Michigan. Another one was central Africa. From central Africa, we placed some smaller ones—one, two, three—smaller ones, and it was a canal from the one in Africa. The main one that exploded, eventually, was in North America. The one that we took the most care of was the one in Africa. There is a crater in central Africa where we planted the—it's like a jet stream.

D. So, it transmitted through the atmosphere?

K. Eventually, but not at first. I'm giving you the up–start. From the one that was first, in North America, it collapsed due to size, pressure. It is a very advanced engineering. The one in Africa, different. We created canals, one, two, three, to smaller power plants in order for the energy, copper, melted, to flow. It was a network of energy. This was to stabilize the area in order for the later connection to the higher web as they merged. First, we wanted to strategically place different zones for higher entities to place their craft. The one in Africa, different. Three canals, like fingers. Once these were in place, crafts were placed on top. The one in North America, much bigger, collapsed. The system wobbled. The other ones still remained. The memory of this is explosions, big waves, tsunamis. The result, the aftermath, was that we used pyramids instead for open, red, boiling flow of copper. The memory on different places where you see pyramids are actually to stabilize where these boiling zones existed.

D. When the pyramid was on top, did the rock beneath still serve a purpose?

K. It served a purpose as a—it wasn't boiling anymore, but it was still in rotation and alive. It was to use it differently. When they are open, if you think of it as open wounds, you still have more power. The end result was that the power available was too much, and it wobbled. Even though you had friends strategically over each and every one, the end result is (*that*) you shut them down. Here enters moonlight. The moonlight damp (*dampens*). After this was changed, there were zones operating with different frequencies that were not—man did not know what to do. Certain shamans knew how to use these portals as a way to travel, to travel in spirit, but also to gather information from the fourth dimension. In order for those to be kept, pyramids were placed.

D. So that energy remained for quite a while after it was charged?

K. Still present.

D. How was the energy used? What was the purpose of storing the energy?

K. The beginning was to enhance, to kickstart the planet, to give resources such as gas, such as oil. To kickstart the planet, you had help from engineering, outside sourced (*aliens*). I hope you can see the work over time. The beginning was simply to give power to the planet, to enhance and increase resources; to be able to shift land mass and to stabilize spines, which also were helped by these craters. The one in Africa, unique. Did not have the sole purpose of providing energy. It was set up as a transmission central for travels, portal. The little ones, fingers, were resonating with the Orion Belt. One, two, three.

D. Is this in central Africa or North Africa?

K. The crater was not in the middle. North–central. Fingers went one, two, three. (*He held them up, indicating North. The easternmost was the one towards Egypt.*) Elahim operated this one, that headed towards Egypt. Those other ones were not operating similar, but they were connecting to the Orion Belt.

D. What was the approximate time frame that this occurred, in Earth years?

K. About 50 million years ago.

D. The pyramids were built much later then?

K. Yes, yes. Brand new. So, we will continue to discuss. But look for landmarks, understand craters. You will understand the complexity of power and how, once you overuse the resources, that these memories that we left are not as powerful and operating to the capacity they are intended. We do not want oil to be overused. Oil is one part that these (*energy*) plants gave. It was a gift to the planet. It was the blood, the veins started to pulsate.

D. So the power plants in some way helped to generate oil?

K. Yes.

D. How far into the Earth did the plants extend? Was it shallow?

K. Quite shallow, until they exploded. It created waves underneath.

D. Is there any evidence that can be seen from satellites which would show where these are located?

K. Yes. The one in North America. There are smaller ones, craters. You also find desert, American desert, craters. The park you talk about, the volcano.

D. Yellowstone?

K. Yes. Investigate the power that exists, the material, the minerals that exist around that area. Highly connected to this operation. There are smaller craters—I want to give you a picture when this one in central North America collapsed. Waves created—this is what some call ley lines. The time when you sat in the red mountains (*Garden of the Gods, near Colorado Springs*), and this one felt a highway, one of those came from that work.

D. So it left a permanent mark?

K. Permanent. Ley lines, as you call them. Veins. But it was intended, it was intended to give power but also to create the veins. Not the one in Africa. Those were different. The veins never stretched. They were only three, like fingers. But the other ones were to create power lines underneath your feet. You call them ley lines, some are grander.

D. What were the ley lines to be used for?

K. Power travels, similar as power can travel through satellites.

D. So the energy was used by inhabitants, or visitors?

K. Visitors, such as yourself, with friends. The ley lines are the same as when you send frequency and information through satellites. The difference is that you just phoof them up. We started with those power plants and when they sank, collapsed, different result. But the one here, (*in*) America, (*became a*) vein. You can use ley lines, if you understand. All ley lines reach to different zones strategically placed. That was the operation we did. If you learn how the ley lines, the web, operates, you don't need as much energy from your host.

D. Were they geographically set up so there was some geometric configuration?

K. Yes. We will continue to talk.

D. That's really fascinating. Thank you. Is there a name I should call you by?

K. Klo. K–L–O. Klo. (*It sounded like claw.*)
D. Thank you so much for that teaching.
K. Thank you. We will leave for now.
O. Okay. This is Ophelia.
D. Hello, Ophelia.
O. You met our friend, Klo. He is closely related to the sixth dimension but operates currently from the ninth. Friend to Jeshua, friend to you both. He operates predominantly in fish tank nine. Was here, at one point, with you. He never walked as man, but he is eager for you to remember who you are. Every time you have an interest in lives as a scientist, he is more or less nearby. The intention here is for you to find who you are. Your work will reach a higher dimension once you understand and write from your source. The next step is for you to become Lasaray in body, and we want you to enjoy this opening. It is a way for you to feel a part of the drama the human has played. There. Briefly, our friend will come in. He will have a separate session later. (*Bob's part of the session is in the next section.*)

An interesting side note, since he talks about heating quartz, is that pure molten silica can store more than 1000 kilowatt-hour of energy in a cubic meter. That is ten times more than can be stored by the commonly used molten salts. And molten silica has very strange properties of luminescence, where it glows like the Sun at high temperatures. In the last couple of years, the value of using molten silica for energy storage has been recognized. Researchers at the Massachusetts Institute of Technology (MIT), for example, are evaluating heating silica in two large storage vessels, one at about 2400 degrees C, the other around 2000 degrees. When energy is needed, some liquid from the high temperature tank is moved into the other one. As it cools, it released a tremendous amount of light, which is captured with photovoltaic cells.

Bob: Rearranging Notes (Oct 31, 2021)
In this brief talk, Bob gives a few intriguing observations about the effect of time and location on the energetic makeup of a baby that is being born. Both the date and geographic area are carefully selected for a soul coming into a specific body to fulfill its mission.
B. Ah. It became somewhat of a pause. I don't know. I was here on time, you know. Everyone said 'session'. I was here and then suddenly, someone came in, like in a fog.
D. Yes. That was one of our friends, and Jeshua's, as well.

B. Ah. Well. It's not like I don't need any more friends. I'm always open for new friends. We probably should go and talk to him. If he's gonna come in and disturb more, on my time, then I actually want to have somewhat of a talk. Because we have set up some sort of ground rules—oh, we... (*he looks to the left, towards Ophelia*). Ophelia says we have to share.

D. She also said that we're going to do a separate session.

B. Separate session! Separate session is gonna come here, maybe Friday. So, it will just be me then. But I also have been around and looked at things. I have talked to my students a little bit, but they are now on internship. We never did an internship. My friends are actually co-operating as spirit guides for others.

D. Oh, really?

B. Ya. The souls from the sixth have not traveled yet. But my spirit guides, my first and foremost responsibility, they are now co-assisting and helping (*as a spirit guide-in-training*). My spirit guides are on internship and it gives me a lot of free time. That's why I said I'm wide open to meet new friends. We've been going through my notes on the wall. We have rearranged certain orders of certain things, you know, when I'm gonna talk about this and that. What we are doing more, and what I want to talk about, is that we have actually gone to the Astrological Council again, to try to understand the coordination when souls come into body. To understand the dynamic of the Solar System combined with the inner system, the inner map.

D. That's very interesting.

B. It's quite interesting. So we've been there because I did complain a little bit. I said, "Now when I have all this free time, what should we do with me? Where should we go?" And then you said, "Well, would you like to go and learn more from the Astrological Council, so you understand the dynamic of when a soul is dropped?" Not just the suit, because the suit is resonating with the inner map and it's sort of shrunk to the soul as an entity, but how to make that little bundle of intention to kickstart and become a human that is intended. And here enters the when and where. It's not just about WHEN, it's also about WHERE. Because if I dropped you January 1st and placed you, let's say, in Asia, instead of where you were placed over there in that country, then it would not have been the same individual. So, geographically, it's quite interesting. And then enters also the different changes in what is upcoming in atmospheric and, let's say, global change, when it comes to climate change, and so forth. So the Astrological Council looks into that because the planet and the energy flow resonates with different dots placed on Earth, in order for the program of the Earth as well. The souls are just sort of dropping, but it's also about when and where different evolutions go on that resonate to the planet. So we're looking into that, also. We have planet and we have atmosphere. It's a cosmic dance, really, with all the players. Meaning the celestial bodies—not the stars so much. The stars sort of organizes this play. You say, "We can look at how, from an astrological point, when a soul is born. But if we extend that, you will learn and understand the Earth, and when the Earth runs through different cycles." It depends on how the planets are operating with these dots (*geographic zones*). So when it rotates, there are dots around the globe that resonates and it triggers, you say—similar as it triggers, like this one knows, it triggers different changes in a human evolution—it can also trigger the evolution of the planet.

D. Wow. That's really complicated because there are probably much longer cycles, I would assume.

B. Ah. Um. It runs longer. So I'm gonna go there and I'm gonna talk about that more. I'm having my separate session soon.

D. (*Laughing.*) Yes, you are.

B. You did see that I was a little bit gloomy, so you said, "Why don't we take these notes that are way down on the list and we move them up a little bit?" And that made me happy.

D. Which ones moved up?

B. This one moved up, the one of me going to the Astrological Council. It was further down. But you said, "Why don't we move it up here?"

D. So this is what you and I are doing. Is it also related to what we talk about in our sessions?

B. This is what we do. What do you mean, talk about?

D. Are all the notes things that you and I do together on the sixth, or are they things that we are going to talk about?

B. Nay. They are things we're gonna talk about, things I'm allowed to talk about. But this was because I had all this free time. I said, "I'm sort of in-between jobs because my spirit guides are on internship. And it's not like I'm designing a new solar system or a new Individual. So what should we do?" And then you said, "Why don't we take the Astrological Council and move that note up here?" So this wall is not just about what we do over there at home, this is also about what you said, "You can talk about this. You can share this in the next session."

D. Not too long ago, you said we were maybe a third of the way through the notes?

B. Well, maybe. But it's not like it's not coming in new notes. But again, certain notes get removed when we have covered a topic.

D. I guess we'll be doing this for another 10 or 20 years?

B. Ah. And I've also been with Zachariah in the Library (*on the fifth*). That was fun. I've been going through and looking at old notes. Not mine, but from the wise ones that have been—it's Earth related. There are aisles that relates to whole different realities.

D. Have you been allowed to wander the aisles and look around?

B. The Earth aisle. Not by myself. Zachariah has been with.

D. What have you been talking about?

B. I'll let you know later, but we've been there. Ophelia drags my arm. She says that, if I'm bored, to not just run around looking for new projects. She said that I should take a bath, because it cleanses my being. We do have liquid forms on the second. So it's a way to maintain the capsule and to somewhat—it's like a hibernation, kinda, that we use on the second. So Ophelia says maybe it's time for my bath, because I'm always on the move. It's like a tub. I don't know if you do the same on the sixth. I have never seen you in a bath as Lasaray, I've never seen you in a tub. But for us, we have somewhat of a tub and it's a liquid, it's not water, really. It's similar like water but there's more light in it. It sort of encases you, so it's a second light capsule, like a blankie.

D. Do you have to withdraw a lot of your energy from elsewhere when you do that?

B. Ah, ah. But don't worry, I'm not missing the opportunity to help you when you tumble around and trip on Earth. So it's not like, "Oh, sorry. Gotta go. You take care, I'm gonna go and take a bath," Ophelia says.

D. Okay. Well, thank you and thank Ophelia.

B. And the fog man. Whoever he is. He came in the fog and left in the fog.

D. Mysterious.

B. Mysterious. Okay, I go. Bye bye, bye bye.

Eli, Leon, Bob: What are we Looking at? (Nov 29, 2021)
Eli is an Elahim from the tenth dimension and a brother to Lasaray and Seth. He gave us some encouragement before describing the next wave of knowledge and some of the entities who will be speaking in the future. He said we are now entering the third phase of our work, out of the seven that are planned. So, *Wave 5* (upcoming publication in 2025), will mark the beginning of the third wave. The first two phases of knowledge are the sessions put forth in *the Spiritual Design, Wave 1* through *Wave 4*, and *Notes from the Second Dimension, Volume 1* and *Volume 2* books. Many of the future speakers will be visitors who have helped to create the greenhouse planet we now live on as guests. Eli allowed another entity to speak. He gave the name Leon, because he occupies a form on a planet behind the constellation of Leo. He said they are close friends to the aliens who occupy the Moon, which I assume are the Little Greys. He came to Earth once in manifested form to befriend a large animal during a previous epoch.

Bob later came in and recounted a story about an energetic cloud moving towards our Solar System that will affect Earth in the next 1000 years. Those on the sixth are aware of the cloud and will repair the structure so it does not cause too much disturbance to the planets. Bob said a similar event happened on Mars around 350,000 years ago which caused the Anunnaki and other aliens to abandon their outposts on that planet. The Anunnaki then moved their base of operations to Earth, where different types of primitive humans were already established in many areas.

E. This is Eli.

D. Hello, Eli.

E. Hello, baby brothers. Huh. You didn't think we would come back, did you?

D. I was hopeful.

E. Well, we're busy. So are you, just different busy. We applaud the work that you do. Especially at this time when there is turmoil within the consciousness. The physical simply execute what the brain and the heart sometimes signals. We are here to just give you the comfort to stay on your path. If needed, to simply shut down your cocoon, meaning your bubble, your self. We surround you always with a golden sphere, and we have guards protecting your energy. As you move forward into the next phase—and yes, this is considered the third phase, out of seven—we are introducing friends that might appear odd. From the human self. So, the friends that we are inviting, of course, belong in our tree. They are visitors from an ancient time and there are memories of them in the consciousness on this platform. We invite them because they have gateways to open. Gateways of locations where they operated, but also the hidden keys on how to maintain the layers within the atmosphere. When I say atmosphere, I'm not just talking about clouds and rains, and so forth. I'm talking about the invisible layers that exist within your lower atmosphere, which provides the meetings between parallel realities. Parallel realities is something that will be more eminent in your future work. We have visitors that will come, and I will introduce them as we go. There is a need to feel secure for Seth, as well as you. But to be sure, as we introduce them, Isaac, myself, and Tosh will be present. Simply to provide the familiar faces and presence, as we introduce those who, from a human standpoint, are unfamiliar.

D. Are these spiritual entities from home? Or are they occupying—

E. Occupying body. Occupying form. You might even have a sensation of smell in the room when they arrive. They communicate differently, and you will feel the need to compress, to adjust. The energy will feel different. You will know when they are here. But they are here to provide information about earlier encounters with parallel realities, and how they meet, and what occurred, and who came, and why they came, who are still here, where are they, why are they here, what is your role in this family tree of visitors, and so forth. When they come forward, as they have shown briefly now and then to little brother, there is a need to relax after. To be in your own bubble. To try to understand majestic (*experience*) of the encounter. Some will feel overwhelming, but in a good way. You are our eyes and ears for several parallel realities. And now it's their turn to have a say. (*The voice shifted, becoming more choppy and robotic. It seemed like Eli was allowing someone else to blend in.*)

L. (*Leon.*) We will move forward in this agenda with new entities. As they come forward, as we introduce them, this is one that is here today. We will allow different friends to communicate. Eli present. Isaac as well, as well as Tosh. We are friends and we wish no harm. We simply want to tell you our story.

D. Very good. What should I call you?

L. I am one of many. Will probably not get so much time. I am new in this group. You can call me Leon.

D. I've heard the name before.

L. Yes! Yes. We operate from the nearby constellation, or behind, the constellation of Leo. We are nearby in your system and we bring the energy of Leo. Maybe that is why I took that name, huh huh. It is not very familiar to me what exists on Earth that is referred to as humor. We observe and find it interesting. But I am, myself, not very humorous as an individual. We have seen your Little Friend. We have not yet met. However, there has been, to my awareness, hints that there is an interest from your Little Friend to visit friends in the Wheel. It has been given permission for him to visit us behind nearby constellations that are not, so to speak, in spiritual form. We are also close friends with the individuals that occupy your moon. Those friends we communicated closely with. They are now the ones that are present on your platform, so we are closely monitoring the Earth plane through their ears and eyes. They have more humor, I would say, probably, from a human standpoint. I am sorry if I appear somewhat boxy, it is not my intention. But the interest and the love and the care that we have just simply radiates differently. Don't judge the book by its cover, huh huh. Something like that, I've heard something like that. It's probably one little, maybe what you call a gimmick, of sorts. And–and–and–and I am new, and I have friends. But I want you to be aware that there are several in your nearby system that will make themselves known.

D. Have you ever occupied Earth in any form?

L. No, no. Well I-I-I-I went and I-I had, during different animal phases, I-I-I did become close friends, and I somewhat manifested myself as a form, in order to maintain the friendship of this animal creature. It was like a larger form of an armadillo. Not as small as the one you have now. They seem to have shrunk. The general population shrunk. Even your form is smaller, as I can see, my friend. But it was still somewhat of a mixture of an armadillo and—I'm not sure what you call those animals that have a long nose and eat ants?

D. An anteater?

L. A mix. A mix. Size-wise, height as a pony, length as an alligator. Big, bigger. Really intelligent. Good friends. I manifested myself to be near him. Close friendship. Similar like what you did with Siah. Same thing. Just took a form to be present with a friend. So, we will be back. But I'm just introducing that, from the constellation of Leo, we have been present here earlier than a lot of the other ones coming in.

D. What subjects will you be covering in the future? Discussing?

L. As of, for my group, we will discuss different events that took place in the area around Egypt and Israel. That is our base when it comes to Earth. That is where we have our strongest memory and imprint. Others will come and disclose information of other locations. Me, myself, briefly, like I said, had a friend. But it was in the same continent, just further west. Never traveled that much. We will give you information on different location.

D. Wonderful.

L. So, we will see. But your friend (*Bob*) will come, apparently. Studies inside the smaller wheel, you said, before we do the big one. Huh huh. So, I-I-I will be back. But I'm fascinated about the way you operate. And I will try to do better with my speaking ways, so I don't appear like the odd one in the group.

D. I think you speak remarkably well. (*He actually stuttered quite a bit, but I cleaned up the dialogue.*)

L. I-I-I do indeed but-but-but it-it could always be better. And then again, it is an adjustment, and I feel ready. Maybe I should just stay here for a while and-and-and just allow this to-to process. Because I can feel that only by my presence here.... Oh. Here comes Gergen! HUH.

D. Are you and Gergen friends?

L. I've seen him around. He was present with the animal life when I was here. Younger then, in his energy.

D. Not as bouncy now?

L. Less bouncy. Huh. This is like a big, happy reunion. It's probably not allowed to just stay in this, in the presence of Seth. I don't know if that is okay. But I can already feel the improvement of talking, even though it goes up and down a little bit.

D. You're much improved.

L. There we go, and we will return.

D. All right, my friend. Thank you for coming, Leon.

E. Yes. So, this is Eli again. Just wanted to let you know that there are friends incoming, and we will gradually build up your knowledge bank. We will begin with the group that Leon belongs to. And we will gradually build up, so that it's not rushed. Step-by-step, opening portals, opening information. Allow yourself to travel within yourself to investigate the portals that we open for you. You will find hidden keys and more that is resonating with your own travels.

D. Did you have any specific thoughts you'd like to share, since we hear from you so infrequently?

E. Just be present within your energy. Try to encase this energy that you process, so it's not scattered. Be selective in the engagements with others. Be selective in the information that fly around your heads, so to speak. Simply be joyful and protect your energy. Be mindful in the way you speak, and that is mainly for this one. What occurs around you right now is not your battle. You are here to ignite the consciousness. That is your only mission. Try to rest between. Don't get drawn into the war—the war of minds, the war of feelings. The physical simply execute. But it's a conflict within each individual and within groups. Don't get drawn into it. Maintain and stay focused on your goal. That is the only reason why you are here. You are not here to create war, in that sense. You are here to ask questions. Try to avoid any sort of turmoil that will mislead you from your path.

D. I'm assuming that there are certain things that we are told that we shouldn't release. I hope that—

E. We will let you know.

D. Okay. Thank you.

E. Okay. Simply be aware that there is a change after the new year coming in. There are new friends, new demands, new teachings. You will move into new territory, similar feeling like when you embarked on *Wave 1*. This is a new opening, and we want you to be aware that it's triggering a feeling of not knowing. We will help as much as possible.

D. I felt like an idiot sometimes, during *Wave 1*.

E. Maybe this will be idiot 2. But you are not an idiot, you simply need to adjust your mind. You need to move around things. Why do you think you're not working when this wave is coming in? If you had a split mind, you would not be able to comprehend and to select and move and understand the information that we will give. It will demand more of your human brain. It cannot be divided, as it was before.

D. I will do my best.

E. Briefly, there is someone here

D. Okay. Thank you, Eli, for that. It was really nice to hear from you again.

E. Oh, you are much welcome. And we are here, your friends, the Advisers.

D. Are the Advisers from home, or are these advisers for this project?

E. From home. Not necessarily for this project. Advisers from home, mentors. We always call them the Advisers. They help Elahim when we travel. Earth is simply one (*place the Elahim travel*). We're gonna disclose other locations that is neither Earth–based nor about human awareness. More travels, where you try to connect and understand different realities, and the evolution and what potentially can come if someone is not aware; or the triggers that a consciousness had to go through in order for it to evolve. Yes, so. Elahim. See you at home.

D. All right, my friend. Elahim.

B. (*Bob came in, but didn't say anything at first.*)

B. I had a problem with my assignment. (*He was working in our lab on the sixth, and Lasaray had left him alone.*) So, I went looking for you. I wandered around and I was like, "Where can he be?" And then I went into the sphere room, and you stood there by yourself, like this. (*He rested his right elbow in his left hand and held his chin with the free hand.*) Like you were pondering about something. And then I was like, "Whoa! What is this?" And then you looked at me and said, "Why are you not in the study?" And I said, "I had a problem with my assignment, and you didn't come. So I just came and looked for you. What are we looking at? What is this?" And you smiled and said, "Well, okay, since you are here." And the whole auditorium was filled of this big black hole. On the sides, it was like vibrating in green. And inside it was just like infinite space. And I said, "Well is this like a black hole, like something that has collapsed?" And you said, "No, I'm working here now to understand how to fix the borders." And I said, "Is this a dilemma?" And you said, "Well, it's a prototype. I'm observing. It's like if you have a sweater and it starts to rip. The circle, the border, it's extremely important. It can either continue to rip or you fix it. And when you fix it, it can either stay and heal itself in the same size, or it shrinks and it merges in, like that," you said. (*He cupped his hands towards each other, like he was holding a ball, and then shrank the size.*)

D. Okay. Is this—

B. This is not here. You said, "Since you're here, this actually doesn't belong in fish tank four or five. This is actually belonging in fish tank seven." It's an example, a prototype from fish tank seven, and that you need to introduce it (*somewhere else*). But you have to fix it, you said. And you're learning from a prototype, a mistake that was made in fish tank seven, in order to fix something that has occurred in fish tank five.

D. Huh. That's fascinating. Is this something larger than a galaxy?

B. It seems like it's the size of the Earth's Solar System. You said it seems to be somewhat incoming. And you said, "It's not like it's going to eat the Solar System, but it might change the rhythm in it. And because this is incoming," you said, "I'm looking at an earlier prototype that occurred in a different location, fish tank seven, in order for us to make sure that the Solar System is continuing its path of predestined evolution." So it's something that is incoming. And you said, "Come over here, Bob." And we looked in like a big table, bigger than a kitchen table. (*Bob explained how the table projected a 3D image of the Milky way and nearby galaxies. Withing the Milky Way, an energetic fog was shown, heading towards our Solar System.*) It looks like a big cloud. It's gonna go underneath. You said, "We have to make sure that it stays intact and perhaps even shrinks. If it expands, it will change the Solar System too much. I'm looking at it, first of all, so it doesn't rip and become bigger. I'm learning here from the example in fish tanks seven, so we can make it shrink. We cannot necessarily, in this case," you said, "change its direction. It will go there. But we can change how it eventually encounters and meets (*our Solar System*)." And you said, "This is what happens. Like on the planet Mars, people (*visitors*) had to move because there was an encounter that made it not suitable to live on. There were disturbances and it became too hot." So entities, such as yourself and Seth, moved from Mars to Earth at that time. "And now," you said, "this happens all the time. But we're faster, so we make sure that it doesn't disturb. Because this is incoming, we can see that if it's just left alone, it might not be as good. It's not like it will wipe out the Solar System," you say, "but it will change the conditions. It will probably lead to another ice age that will last much longer when it comes to Earth. So, we simply need to work on it a little bit." You said, "We cannot change the directory (*direction or trajectory*) where it is going, but it needs to be shrunk a little bit and we must make sure it does not rip more. So," you said, "that's what I'm doing here. Why are you here?" I said, "I struggle with my assignment." And you said, "What was that assignment?" And I said, "It was the soil that you gave me from the store. It doesn't seem to match the roots and my seed." And when I said that, I had my jar. And when I saw your project and I looked at my project, I was like, "Uugghh." (*He sounded disappointed.*)

D. It's all the same.
B. You said, "It's all about creation and life, and maintaining life."
D. If it wasn't for you, there wouldn't be any life to protect.
B. That's what you said. "If it wasn't for you, Bob, there wouldn't be a plant. If it wasn't for you, the Individual wouldn't be relaunched." So, you said I'm also a creator. But when I see my jar with my little seed here, you know. (*He was looking down at his hand, and then up towards the huge wall display Lasaray was pondering.*) I mean, I'm not sure. You said it's all about creating the right foundation for prosperity. And when prosperity is not in the mix, when destruction is a bigger risk or chance than prosperity, then do it over. So that's what you say.
D. Well, the cloud that is coming in between Andromeda and the Solar System, does it contain stars and planets and material like that? Or is it energetic?
B. Ah, a little bit. But it doesn't look like a regular galaxy. It looks like what I see here on the big screen. It's like a big empty space that travels like a silent cloud. It's flat.
D. In Earth-years, roughly what are we talking before it starts interacting?
B. You say it's like within a thousand years. And that's also why the spiritual counsels are so eager to raise consciousness when it comes to how to help the environment. "Because," you say, "we can only do so much. We engineer here, but the foundation where these two are merging—and the thing is, it's not going to fly over—it seems like it will merge. So we're looking into some sort of rearrangement in the system." You said, "It happens all the time. That's why we are so eager to help the planet. Here we're talking about Earth, but there is equal assistance and interest to maintain the original structure in ALL the planets in the system."
D. Is this incoming cloud directed towards our Earth system or galaxy specifically, or is it just randomly roaming through?
B. It's in the galaxy. It has come in. It is in the Milky Way Galaxy, it's just continuing its path.
D. Will it pass through and keep moving on?
B. It will continue to move on. And that is what you said, "We want it to move on. We don't want it to get stuck."
D. Is this incoming cloud directed by the Creator or other councils to do a specific task?

B. You said, "Sometimes it can be like a side effect that occurs. Mainly, it is like dust if a system has collapsed." It sort of docks off and it starts to travel, a piece of it. You said it's similar like that.

D. Huh. That's very interesting.

B. It just travels. I said, "Is this what you do with your friends, the haste group?" And you said, "Yeah. We call them the Advisers. But this is what we work on. We want to make sure, because every time a star, or especially like a solar system, runs its circle through (*its life cycle*), it collapses, in some way. It compresses, or it splits up and things start to change into different forms. And some dedock. When they do that, we have to monitor that one."

D. Hmm. That's really interesting work. But then again, so is the seed.

B. Ah. Well, I just wanted to say that I'll probably go back to the study now. But I don't really want to. I think this is quite interesting. And you said, "I just need a silent moment to ponder." Then I said, "When you say that, does it mean, like, alone?" And you said, "If you go back to the study, Bob, I'll be right behind you. I'll be right there. I just need to study this." And I said, "Are you gonna solve this today, or are you gonna be standing here a lot?" And you said, "No, this is not something that you resolve in a day." Huhuh.

D. It's kind of like all these waves of information coming in to us. It takes a long time to figure out.

B. You said, "First, you have to you know what needs to be fixed, and then sometimes we can we can redirect. But," you said, "this one is too big. So this one WILL fly over or it will encounter. It is already in the Milky Way Galaxy. We just need to make sure that when the Solar System meets this silent cloud—. It's pretty flat, like a pancake. It's like a flying pancake, one could say."

D. Does it have a lot of dust in it?

B. Ah. It looks dark. It doesn't look like a light pancake.

D. Hmm. Is that what would cause the ice age?

B. "Indeed," you say, "it could." So you say that's also why you want to make sure that Earth is in its best shape and form as well, when these two meet. You said it's like you want the Earth to go to the gym, one could say. "We want it to be more healthy. We want it to build up its muscle and save energy, and just be well." You said before, about around 300,000 human years ago, you said that it was a similar interaction, and then Mars was in that phase of change. And you said, "We had to leave really fast."

D. Did Mars at one time have an atmosphere and water?

B. Yes, indeed. And you were there, and it changed. And you said, "That's what we don't want to be repeated." So you were there for a long time. But something happened, you said, around 350,000 to 370,000 years ago. You said it started a bit earlier, but it wasn't like a big thing. At first it was a gradual decline, and then something happened that made you have to go fast, around 300,000 years ago.

D. Did it affect the Earth at the same time?

B. It became a little bit of a cough. It changed the atmosphere because of the distress that Mars was in. But you left and you came here. But it affected a lot of the cycles of the Moon around that time, because of the atmospheric changes around Earth. Because of the layer, it also affected the Moon cycle a little bit. And that's also why the Earth tilted, at one point, a little bit. You know, it's simply like an adjustment. But you say, "That's what we looked into." And it's been (*happening over*) a longer period of time. I was here, of course, around that time, and I remember that the moon looked a little bit different. It was like it had more of those eclipses, suddenly.

D. Huh. That's really fascinating. I guess the Earth and the Moon are gradually drifting apart, so they must have, at one time, been closer together?

B. Ah. It appeared differently. But something happened around 300,000, you say, but it also happened earlier, like, way earlier. You say we don't need to put numbers on everything because there isn't really numbers. But you say, "Way earlier." And I say, "Was it pre–me?" And you said, "No, it wasn't pre–you. But it was like baby–me."

D. Early you?

B. Early me. It wasn't pre–me, but early–me. Okay, I'm gonna go now. But I'll go back to my room and leave you alone in your moment of silence. And probably you'll solve it, so this doesn't become like a habit that you just leave and stand here like this all the time. If you do, you know, like I'm happy to maybe help.

D. Well, it sounds like fun.

B. Okay, so I'll go back to the study and then you come when this silent minute is over.

D. Alright, my friend. Thank you so much for coming today. It was really interesting. It was a good talk.

B. Okay. So I'll go. Bye bye.

Ari, Ophelia, Bob: Blindfolds and Snowflakes (Dec 12, 2021)
This is another excerpt from a public Séance. It is rare that Ari communicates during public talks, but it pleased us that he joined for this one. He began by talking about the ongoing and upcoming changes humans can expect. Even though there appears to be a lot of turmoil, the spirit realm is always in control of life on Earth. If one accepts that premise, then it is much easier to relax and find joy in day-to-day activities. Ophelia and Bob followed Ari with their own direct and caring messages for us all to reflect upon.

A. This is Ari. Greetings to you all. There you are my friend, and all the other friends participating. We are here as a group, the Council of Nine and those friends of yours on the sixth. Some in this group are aware of adjustments needing to be maintained and addressed in order for an ultimate journey to continue. Some in this group are pioneers in that field of revolution. Revolution is what you are observing around you at this time. There are parallel realities embracing you, cheering you on, if you like, that have been through different phases harder than this one. The turmoil that mankind experience at this time is an illusion. Some of you are already aware of the illusion. Some are needing to be removed of blindfolds. Some will have their blindfolds on for their journey to come. It is not up to you to remove all blindfolds. In some way, it is an upgrade. It is an upgrade of the human body, for new incarnations to be able to proceed in the cycles to come. Each time a new cycle is upcoming, there is a sensation of division. The old versus the new, if you like. We are aware that mankind seem to cling on to the old. But this is a phase to be welcomed. It is to be rejoiced and to be in the mindset of spirit, your spirit. If you address the world with your human mind, you will feel defeat. If you see the world through your center point, through your soul mind, you see solutions. You see the upcoming incarnations that are possible for you and others. Man tend to say, "Embrace and look at the children." See the children, the child, that you are going to become in a future life. Send respect and love to the future self, making choices and adjustment in your present self. Who do you want to be? What family members do you wish to have with you? Some will be left behind. Friends and families, human ones. See the difference, see the opportunity that lies before you, once you see the world through your solar plexus instead of your human mind. I also want to let you all know that there are parallel realities embracing you. For those who are actively seeking proof, it is simply a thought away. The parallel realities belong in this fish tank, your universe, but they are further along communication-wise, (*and in their*) technology. The technology that we see man engaging in at this time creates traps. It is not a solution, as they are not made from the soul mind. It is a human invention trying to copy alien, parallel realities.

D. Are the aliens attempting to assist us, in some way?

A. Yes, yes. They are assisting some with technology, science. The result will not come in this cycle. That's why we are saying (*to*) look for your future lives, look for future incarnations. What you do now (*will*) set the tone and color for your future. Some things will not be solved this lifetime, for some. And again, there are blindfolds that will not be removed. The intention of what is going on is to understand polarity and the power of choice. To also navigate differently than through your human mind. To navigate by your inner compass provides openings where others simply see doors. This is why we address you, as a group, here tonight, due to the fact that you are open. You will see the difference in those that you come across if they are acting from their human mind or soul experience. Some are not ready to understand. And that is not your burden to carry. You have responsibilities, but first and foremost to yourself. As you ground yourself and heal yourself, love yourself, love the place that you are at, you are already far ahead. There are plenty at this time, who do not care about themselves, who spin around. See that snow bowl, the little gadget that you play with around Christmas—the one with glass. You shake it and snowflakes fly around. That is similar to what we see. We shake you a little bit and all the snowflakes are just flying around in this captive environment that you are in. If you were to see the beauty of the snowflake, instead of turmoil. It is not a storm. It is controlled by spirit, but you simply experienced that we're shaking it. You can choose to be a snowflake flying uncontrolled in the wind, in this glass bowl. Or you can join the other snowflakes and see the power that you possess as a group. Stupid, really. If one only knew that the whole fish tank is shaking a little bit.

D. When you say the turmoil is directed by spirit, does that suggest that the spirits have something to do with the current dilemma on Earth?

A. The dilemma is caused by humans. BUT the events and the outcome and the opportunities that come are spirit-made. We simply shake humanity a little bit. The way the snowflakes are directing and flying are human made. The intention might, from a human standpoint, be a little bit questioning, one might say.

However, we are upgrading your species, and in order to see where the snowflakes fly, go, how they respond to a little bit of a shake, we need to see the community, the group consciousness, and where you are at. At this time, man feels divided. Many feel like they are alone, when you're not. You can merge together and become a snowball, instead of a snow flake. And believe me, this snowball can roll and create an avalanche. That is the option that lies before you. Become that avalanche, or be a snowflake flying uncontrolled, based on some other winds that you did not create. Huh huh!

D. If humans, if the bulk of people don't make snowballs and an avalanche, do the spirits—

A. They will be removed. Can be removed. I'm sorry to say, but can be removed as malfunctioning. Humans tend to be offended by things. From the spiritual realm, we see the greater cycles. And it's simply the bottle, the vehicle itself, the body, that is removed. The soul comes back in a better, more upgraded version. Like we talked about before, (*you are now*) moving around in the propeller plane, but your soul is designed to maneuver a rocket, or a NASA (*spacecraft*). You might feel like, "Okay, an upgrade is needed. Change is needed." But as long as those cling to the old, who are afraid of the new, they will be, in some way, removed. Then we are removing and adjusting the mind, so that they are more clear in connection to heart and the center point. The tendency of fear and lack of choice is a dilemma that we are observing, and have been, for a long period of cycles—here you call it time. We shake the ball now and then, to see where mankind is at, to see what adjustments need to be made. Why do you think there was a peak in ancient Greek, for instance? There had been a shake in the snow ball prior to that peak. If one knew that a new peak of heightened intelligence—and yes, Bob, I see that you are present. But we are discussing here and you will have to wait your turn. What I was saying, is that if one knew that this is simply that shake before a new peak. You are in a canyon in your development. Several canyons have been before you, where you had to be shaken or climbing up, changed or transformed into a new version of incarnation. So.

D. That's very good. Thank you.

A. Huh. Bob is here. Well, okay. I will step aside, for this time. But I want to leave you all, with a sensation of hope. A sensation of strength. You are the revolution that we want to see. You are the snowflakes that have the opportunity, possibility, to become the snowball. Joined, you will create the avalanche.

D. There's a lot of people in our world that are ruled by fear. That seems to be a majority of the population.

A. It is a problem with the way man, at this time, solves problems. Put a pill in it. Put two pills in it. And the lack of compassion for another individual's experience—you do not listen. You simply put a pill in someone who is under distress. In the spirit realm, you are embraced by your friends, sometimes even by the healing power of angelic beings. There are those who need to be heard, not just be given a pill. As the mind goes numb due to its faltering under the unnecessary treatment, it makes decisions that are irrational. The only thing we can say is that blindfolds are equal with the amount of easy solutions, like a pill. (*People are not addressing and solving their personal problems.*) It also sometimes needs to be addressed what you eat. So it's not just a pill, but it's also to not be too lazy in the way you prepare your food; to take pleasure in preparing what you are then later putting into your body. It's not just to ease hunger, that's not just why you eat. It is an art form to create a meal, similar as you create a painting, or the way you sing. We want you to sing, we want you to open up your vocals and let everyone hear the beauty that comes from within you. You don't like to sing, I know. You don't have the voice for it. (*He had turned in my direction.*)

D. No one would think that was beautiful.

A. Well, it is a beauty. And again, humans tend to think that what they do, what they cook, what they say, is not beautiful. When your thoughts, what you say, when it comes from your center point, it is always filled with colors, filled with compassion. Nothing bad can travel from your center point. Nothing bad can travel on colors, as we have said. So there.

D. That's lovely, thank you.

A. We'll see you at home.

D. Alright. Thank you.

A. Elahim.

D. Elahim.

O. Hmm. Just briefly, this is Ophelia.

D. Hello, Ophelia.

O. We are so happy to be able to share this light and this energy frequency with more than just the two of you tonight. The power that the group possesses is bigger and more profound than you think. We would love to send healing to those in need of that at this time. There are sadnesses that you, as a human, might encounter. I want to provide you that comfort (*of knowing*) that everything is as it should (*be*), that you and your loved ones, here and in spirit, are protected and cared for, that you have the ability to merge all realities within your experience here on Earth. Simply close your eyes, allowing all dimensions to merge with you. For those who feel sadness, we will provide that light and compassion and embrace you. Everything is as it should (*be*). Nothing is malfunctioning, as I heard. It is simply a change. You are protected, and we observe you from the highest levels. And yes, Bob. Bob is here.

Bob came in and made some introductory remarks, and then delivered this encouraging message about the gifts from your spirit guides that are waiting in your future. He also talks about the difference between being a snowflake blown around in the wind and a snowball.

B. What I would like to say now is that in this sensation and spirit of Christmas and holiday, in the sensation of magic. I'm quite a little bit of a magical kinda being, I would say, perhaps. Ophelia says I blow my horn, and that is true, sometimes. But I want to provide a little bit of that curiosity that comes around this time of year. You know, like, "Ohh, what's under the Christmas tree? Is that gift for me?" Just know that all gifts under your Christmas tree are for you. And your soul prepares gifts under the Christmas tree, in some way, for you to find. And if you do not necessarily put up the Christmas tree, you can simply, in your mind, visualize this tree, and see for yourself now. If everyone here were to close their eyes and picture their own Christmas tree. You know, one, two, three—do. There. Close your eyes, see your Christmas tree. And now see, under your Christmas tree, how many gifts do you see? It might be one big one. It might be several little ones. Might be like square, round, soft, hard, but they are your gifts. And each of these gifts are for you to open in the next year. It is like little guidance or treats along the way. And some would probably see like one big one. But you should be curious about the treats that are yours to reveal. And again, even if you don't have a Christmas tree in your home, you always have it within you. And you can always close your eyes, see the Christmas tree, and then, boom, how many Christmas gifts do you see? And when you open them, one-by-one, they all are from your higher self or your spirit guides. And don't be like greedy, like I have ten and I'm gonna open them all. Don't be like that. See which one resonates with you at that time. And it might be that these are gifts that are not ready to be opened in January. One gift might say, "No, wait, wait. I'm not until June or July." Then you have to respect the gift, because it's something that's gonna come to you that is a treat. If you are in the mindset that you will be given treats moving forward, then I'm just saying, life will be quite more magical and joyful to experience. What I don't like now, what I see now, is that they try to take away people's magic. (*Via social distancing and lockdowns.*) They try to take away the sensation of joy. And we do not approve. I do not approve. And I whined and complained to Ophelia, and I said, "Let's do a reboot. I don't think this is good." And Ophelia said, "It serves a bigger purpose. We are shaking the crystal ball, but we also want to see how man, the snowflakes, how they are solving the shake." And I say, "Well, why don't we just tilt it and begin new? But she said, "Nope. That's not what we're going to do this time. This is not a reboot. This is what we want, for people to do the change. The incarnation should do the change. Not just the spirit realm coming in like, boom, making everything change. Because what is the lesson? There is so many treats and lessons that are provided now for humanity. But they simply see it as punishment and turmoil. They simply see the shake. They don't see the order in the shake. The order of the snowflakes that they are. There is a divine order in this glass ball."

D. Yes. The soul might be asking for certain challenges to see how it performs?

B. Ah. Exactly. And some will be like, "Oh. I'm just gonna be the snowflake. I'm just gonna do what everyone else does. I'm just gonna fly here in the wind. Oh, scary! Scary! I'm just waiting for my turn to be told what to do." And then some are like, "No, no. I don't want to be told. I'm not just a small snowflake. I have the possibility to become a snowball. Then, if I expand my consciousness and if I join others, I can create an avalanche." And then you have those who are like, "Ohh, I'm not sure we are supposed to create an avalanche. I think we should just be snowflakes." So those are the three categories. But there is an order here. It's a system, and just know that you can, if you start to see the world in those categories, you also see those who are already creating the avalanche. And your snowball can just merge with that. And then the other ones, flying around in the wind, let them fly there. It is what it's supposed to be, apparently, because we're not supposed to tilt the ball. We're not supposed to do a reboot either. But what I want to say, anyway, is to kinda be a little bit upset if someone tries to take your magic. Your magic can be like your singing voice. If someone says, "Shush. Don't sing. Shush. Don't go there. Shush. Don't be like that. You have to be like this or that. You can't be a snowball. You're only a snowflake." Then it creates a sadness, a human sadness. But inside, the soul is really trying to make itself heard, making sure that the human self understands that there is a lesson and a gift to be poked like that. Because you are being poked. Snowflakes are poking each other because they don't really know where to fly in this wind. So there is a beauty and a divine order here. But for many, it appears to not be.

D. That's a really nice analogy. I like the way you present that idea. So thank you very much, my friend.

Bob, Ophelia: Dreaming (Dec 24, 2021)
Christine and I held a 'separate session' to see if Bob wanted to share any ideas for Christmas. If he knows he is going to be the first speaker, he will often merge with Christine before she has finished her preparatory meditation. So, on this day, I could see that Bob had already joined and was just sitting quietly, waiting for me to begin the final lead-in. I did our normal ascent up the mountain, but I joked about him helping to create the birds and butterflies. Once it was his turn to speak, he pointed out that I missed a few things he helped to create. He then gave a very interesting talk on dinosaurs.

B. I also created like the trees—you forgot to say that as we passed—I also helped. And the grass. I didn't like that much to create grass. I didn't really see the purpose. I can see that the lawn somewhat has a purpose, because everything has a purpose. If I didn't know it before meeting you, I knew that after meeting you, that everything has an intention. And I have to have an intention—and there is an intention with me. I'm still figuring that one out, you know, what is my main intention? What does the Creator want me to fetch and bring back home?

D. Maybe you're supposed to drag Lasaray back home after each life.

B. Maybe he doesn't know how to get back, so maybe I'm like a rescue team, of sorts. Maybe that's what it is, like I'm the fetcher. Who knows what else I'm gonna fetch, like a rescuer. You know, like those dogs that comes out in the winter and they have like whiskey to help people come alive if they're frozen. I'm not saying that you're frozen, but you don't necessarily like cold. But we have picked lives in cold because it's part of the training, that you also have to learn how to survive in different environmental shifts. So, we have done that as well. Part of the incarnation program is to also not just pick different bodies—you know, like, now I'm going to be yellow; now I'm going to be a little bit round; now I'm going to be whatnot; and you pick all these different attributes for your personality. But it's also advised that you not just go to a beach. You can kind of see that, based on where people vacay, you know, how far they've been in their journey. If they are just really adamant about going only to the beach, they might come across like a relationship of sorts where that person will guide them to go skiing, for instance, just so you learn how to navigate in the vehicle in different environments as well.

D. Hmm.

B. It's advised to do that. We had like winter program kinda early on, like when you were the Yeti. So we did the winter program early. And also, we've been in the Russian area as well. And I think maybe it was that it became too much, and that's why you don't like that, necessarily, right now.

D. But yet, here we are in Sweden.

B. And here we are in Sweden. But there are different lessons and different treats, based on where we put you.

D. Well, we have electric heating now, so that's helpful

B. Well, I'm just saying that you said that there was electric heating that was much more advanced pre– our program, when you were here in blue dot lives (*manifested*). So you set up like a network. You say that there was a much more advanced energetic plant for the planet itself, when you were here in a form that more looks like you do at home.

D. You should help me remember.

B. I said that the current civilizations are stumbling a little bit in their technological advancement, so maybe you can just sort of do like a repeat. But you said that there were different conditions then. There were actually, at that time—and this specific time occurred BEFORE, you say, almost before and simultaneously as the dinosaurs. It wasn't among the dinosaurs. You said it was on a different location, so they didn't disturb. You said that there were, at that time, more looking not like they do now. Not just dinosaurs. Because dinosaurs, you said, was a project from another star system, and they (*the visitors*) were sort of taking care of them. You know how you manage those drones?

D. Yes.
B. It was similar like that, you said. There were several outsiders that (*were involved*). It was like a big playground for some. So, some of the dinosaurs were like the drone, but they didn't fly. It was just like they were remotely steered, you said, but not from here. You said that they were up there, like somewhere around Orion's belt. And there was some that thought it was really fun. They steered (*the dinosaurs*) and it was like a playground. But then you said, "I did not play." And I get that. You're not the most playful individual. You said that you were here for an assignment, and the assignment had to do with accessing some sort of energetic web. You established it, and it was wide apart. It was like saying one tower was in Texas, and the other tower was down in Australia. and then the one from Australia went across, and so it became like a network. It was operated by you and some others. Seth did not come. Seth was still in school, you said. Huh huh. But Eli did, a little bit. It's like a spark. As soon as the spark is ignited, it just travels freely in this connection, in these lines. It wasn't like a solid line, it's simply a transmitter and a receiver. And they create, using the grid that exists, an abundance of energy, you said.
D. What was the energy used for?
B. Maybe for the drones! Huh huh. Nay. That was just for play. You say that it was used for landing, coming in and going. I did not see that. But you said that you did that a little bit. This was before everything came into the incarnation program.
D. That started a long time after the dinosaurs.
B. Ah. Maybe Sniffer was there. He must have seen some sort of strange activities, I'm thinking.
D. Was that a note you brought in to talk about, or were you just pondering?
B. I was pondering that out loud. I do that. And in my pondering, new questions and new notes come up. That's sort of the way I operate.
D. That was a curious time in Earth history.
B. Ah. What I wanted to say, with that story, huh huh, was that there was an easier way to access energy before, than the way energy is used now.
D. Was something changed in the atmosphere, or was the Earth altered in some way?
B. There were changes in the grid, so it's not possible in the same way, you say. The grid, the Earth grid and the magnetic field, it's not functioning the same. So, once you start to modify the

magnetic field underneath your feet, it changes not just the way that one can operate and use different resource, but it also changes the mammals, itself. That's what you say

D. How many civilizations have there been? I sometimes get confused. I know there was one between like 50,000 BC to 20,000 BC. Going further back, there was one of like 500,000?

B. About 300,000 BC, when this one came.

D. Was it a human type of civilization?

B. Nay, he did not look like a human, he said. Nay. Well, this you should maybe shush–shush on, Ophelia says. There were humans here, but they were more like pets, and they were used as workers. They didn't have a leading role in a society. But they were quite good in collecting things, they were like samplers. So, they collected samples and stuff. You know, like you have those dogs that go sniff out truffles? That's what they used the early humans for.

D. So there were visitors here that—

B. Like Seth came as a visitor the first time. He did not take a human form, did not sign up for it, he said. This was before both of you took on human form and you were here doing different assignments. Like I said with you, it had to do a lot with communication—and him as well. All Elahims are about communication. It's just that you have different fields and angles to that same topic.

D. Hmm. I was trying to piece together the timeline. I think you said I was down in the Yeti form about 450,000 years ago—the one that wouldn't die. (*See earlier July 7, 2021 session.*) It was a cross between a mammal and a manifestation.

B. Ahh, well, it was earlier than Seth coming down 300,000 (*years ago*). It was before that. But then again, it wasn't like you came down and then you just kept on coming. It was a huge gap before you came again. I mean, you kinda encouraged your little brother (*Seth*) to come. You promoted it as something good. It probably is, but you sort of launched that idea and said that you were going to do that. But this one didn't have that same interest. He said, "Why can't we just come like we do?" And you said that there's gonna be changes in the way you can travel here and that you were gonna shut down his space programs. I don't know how that flew within the group and in the family. It's like having an airport, you know, and then you just shut down the runways. It's similar like that. So, I'm not sure how that came about. But then you said, "We can still go, but we have to go differently." And that's what you did. So, it came to a halt in what you normally were doing here. Then suddenly, you started to go more into that humanoid software. Meaning like, "Okay, what is a feeling? What is a lower kind of thought? What is the muscle tone, that you kinda operate differently, that is not fully functioning?" You kinda did it as a favor to some of the councils, but you wanted to study the mind. (*The Elahim normally manifested a form on Earth, but when changes were made to the atmosphere, incarnating was unavoidable.*)

D. Okay. That's what I thought you said earlier.

Bob continued to talk about looking into fish tank three, which is currently in a dream state during its hibernation. He had been given a helmet that allowed him to see what took place. What he saw, looked like bubbles of new intentions, coming in, replacing old experiences and galaxies. Later, he drew the parallel to the human sleep, where the soul accesses information about past lives within the fourth dimension. The soul is often trying to influence the human mind during sleep, so it is worthwhile to examine the feelings behind remembered dreams.

B. I can see them coming and they're brand new and they're going to become something.

D. What are they going to become?

B. A galaxy. Not all, you say. (*Lasaray is always communicating with Bob during our sessions.*) Some are just gonna be solar systems. Some are... huh? (*He was looking to the left, listening.*) Some are just gonna be observatoriums, you say.

D. I know the Creator Disk sits below fish tank three. Is it interacting in any way during this time?

B. Well, they are the ones that sort of, you know, do things. They're quite mysterious, or maybe they're shy. Because they don't come forward, so maybe they're shy. I can't see them, but it's an activity that goes on. But, like I said, it comes in new bubbles.

D. Is it on the side of the fish tank?

B. It's on the border to fish tank two.

D. I always get confused about this, but do the fish tanks rotate above the Creator Disk clockwise, or anticlockwise?

B. The Creator Disk underneath goes anticlockwise. The solid fish tank disk goes clockwise.

D. So they turn in opposite directions?

B. Ah. It's a whole system going on here, as you can understand. And we're just in the beginning of exploring this. But if I explore and try to look into the dream, I'm seeing that the big part has to do with the understanding of the experience. And those new bubbles coming in are just brand-new and fresh, and they are taking the place of certain things that were sort of tired, you say. It's like, you know, an old person dies and a new one comes in.

D. What happens to the old galaxies?

B. They shrink, become a raisin. And from that they become like—I mean, the whole galaxy takes a little time to shrink. It's a whole system going on here. I can see those new ones popping in, you know, brand-new, ready to do something. They're much clearer in the way they look.

D. Clear intentions?

B. Clear intention. And the old one might just want to be a raisin.

D. I would assume that the sixth dimension has some involvement?

B. You're involved with it, with those coming in. "With popping them in," you say. And then I say, "Is it like when Ia gets an egg?" And you said it's similar. So, instead of taking care of sparkles, like Ia (*does*), and listening to the intention and singing, you say, "We also have our similar process. But we toss our intentions into the fish tanks."

D. Everything kind of has a similar cycle then?

B. Everything is the same. But I don't see you singing to the bubbles here that come in. But you don't like to sing. You laughed and said, "We sang before we set them off." Maybe that's like singing for them to go on a happy field trip.

D. You remember when you were baking your solar system, and other things happened to it? Did you implant any music into it before you sent it off? (*In 'Notes, Volume 1', Bob's model of his solar system was converted into an energetic pattern that was later placed in fish tank five.*)

B. No. But I did send care and compassion and happiness. I wanted it to have a happy excursion and a happy journey. That's what you said, "Ia sings. We do the same, but we might not sing." So you have your own way. There are different ways, but it's the same thing. You said, "We also have those who, like Ia, tends to the little ones, the sparkles. We also have those who tend to and send off galaxy sparkles who are about to start their journey in different fish tanks. And because fish tank three has been asleep, there's a lot of new ones coming in." And what I see here, those who become raisins are kinda done. (*Bob often refers to older spirits as being like a raisin, a bit more weathered.*)

D. It sounds like a big step on the ladder of learning.

B. Ah. But with fish tank three, you should know that there's a big, big science behind the hibernation. And it's the same big mystery and science behind when a person dreams. When you dream, it's a miniature version what I saw here in fish tank three. You gather puzzle pieces and information and events that you have collected over time. And sometimes that "time" indicates other lifetimes. And that is why certain dreams doesn't make sense, because it belongs in either a parallel reality where you, as a soul, are occupying some sort of a space and body as well, or (*a destination*) that you are traveling between. But it's a way to proceed. So dreaming is a way to learn how to use and collect the data that you have and move it. And certain things that you dream should be moved to a future lifetime. So, you have certain ideas that occurred on a subconscious level as you walk around in your daily life. But as you dream, it might come up, and it might not make sense, because that specific event or idea or person is belonging in a future life. So, you're constantly creating as you sleep.

D. That does bring up the complex question of future lives. Time here is linear, so is it like you're putting it in a little cup to use later, or is it actually influencing the future?

B. It's paused. When you dream, you can analyze certain things because you access the fourth reality. And in the fourth reality, you access all of your past lives as well. The problem is that sometimes, if the physical is stressed, then it's accessing, also, other people's dreams. And that's what you have to be mindful of. And you will know the difference, if it's a dream that is not just yours. You will feel it in your center point if you access another dream than your own. But you're constantly creating, and you can move certain things that comes into your dream, into a future life.

D. Hmm. So it's something that's a potential or possibility for something that will happen in the future?

B. Indeed. Certain dreams are like that, that you dream of something that is beyond what is available to you at this time. And then, it's your soul that is actually pre-planning future incoming journeys. So, you can make a little note about that. Your current person will not know if this is happening. But just know that certain things that you dream of, that might seem futuristic or not belonging in the current time, it can actually be that your soul is pre-planning another visit. [...]

D. If your work as a spirit guide is sort of coming to an end, how do you feel about that?

B. It's not coming to an end! Well, I'm still a spirit friend.

D. Of course, you are still my spirit friend. But I mean, as far as coming to Earth.

B. It's actually quite nice if I don't just have to, you know, pamper you and tend to you all the time. Because you are quite clumsy. In the future life, 2178, you're not going to be clumsy. I didn't design you as clumsy, and we're not gonna do like random boring things. I mean, you're gonna go to school, but we have a mission. It's not like this time, that I had to wait for you because you were elsewhere. You're not gonna be elsewhere. I said, "I don't want there to be, like this time, that you were doing other haste elsewhere. And then I have to wait." We couldn't do what I said before (*our project started in this life*). I had all sorts of ideas that we could do, but ohh, no one listened to me. If you're gonna come back, it's gonna be more like high-end mission. And I also want you to come back as a father, at one point. Seth was denied to become a father to Little Seth, so I volunteered you as that for Little Seth. Because I overheard a conversation that Little Seth had about some lives around 3000 AD. It's gonna be more scientific and there was a talk about that, you know, and I overheard it. Like I said, I hear things as I move around. That's the beauty with me, that I'm mobile. So, I'm catching up certain things, and then I put it in my memory bank. And then I thought, "Huh. Little Seth is out without a father. Who can that be?" Ohh, hmm. Then I thought about Seth. But it was like "Oh, nay, nay. That's not gonna fly." And Ophelia, she was like, "No. No." And Gergen said, "No. Seth is gonna go elsewhere. He's going to do other things." And then I said, "Ohh. Lasaray might go." And then I have to think of, "How can I get Lasaray to do this?"

D. Well, you're going to be guiding the spirit guides that you send with the ones from the sixth, aren't you?

B. I'm gonna monitor, like Gergen does. But it's like having drones, in some way. Because I have to let them fly. I have given them wings, as spirit guides. I've given them all the training needed in my school. Now I have to let them fly. But what I don't tell them is when they fly, they're drones. And I'm sitting there guiding them, a little bit. Then I thought, "Hmm. Is that what Gergen did with

me?" Maybe I thought that I was freestyling and doing everything by myself, but maybe I also was a little bit steered, like with a wind.
D. Maybe you should ask him?
B. I ask him a lot. He's busy, he runs around a lot.
D. What do you think he's working on?
B. There is something with the magnetic field, over with the spine, that needs to move. (*The Andes Mountain range is being moved.*) He's a lot with the geologists, at the moment. And I'm not gonna ask. Because if I ask, I'm gonna be sucked into the spine work, and it's not really what I want to do. And then it's gonna be, "Oh, let's listen to the songs." And then it's gonna take all sorts of time, and I'm elsewhere.
D. Do you know if there's any geologic activity planned in the near future?
B. Iceland. Iceland and Japan will have activity.
D. Is it going to upset the delicate financial systems that are in place?
B. It's gonna continue to be a pause in your flying around, and that's what we want. That is part of certain things that occur. It is to minimize the general moving around so much (*of people*).
D. What do you see with the population of the Earth in the next few years, like during the rest of my lifetime?
B. Well, there's gonna be a little bit of a coughing. Earlier civilizations did better physically. It has to do with an awareness of what you digest, what you eat, and what you inhale to maintain your vehicle better. So, the greater idea, behind everything that goes on, is an awakening on how to be more clean. Eat clean, live clean, move around clean—more like that. And with that, those who resist those kind of thoughts and upgrades, if you still just want to continue to go to McDonald's, then you're gonna cough.
D. Cough your way right out of a body.
B. Like I said, we're looking into the engine. Not me personally, because I left that assignment. But there is a big ongoing project to modify the intestines and the engine and how certain things just flow. Well, I'm gonna go back and sit in my helmet and wait for signals.
D. That sounds like fun. I'm interested to hear more about fish tank three.
B. Well, it's fascinating with someone who sleeps, even a person who sleeps. Some people get scared if they think they're supervised or observed, in that sense, but when you breathe in and out when

you dream, you, yourself, remove and shift and analyze certain events, like we talked about. But there is also someone that puts in fresh thoughts into your being. So it's like a recycling that goes on as someone—person, fish tank, galaxy—sleeps.

D. Is that someone like you? I mean, do you ever do that for me?

B. Do what?

D. Put in fresh ideas?

B. I'm trying to. But it has to go through Jeshua.

D. So Jeshua would be the one that helps to modify ideas?

B. I'm talking with Jeshua sometimes. And then he said to me, "Puff this in." And then I do. Like when you didn't die. (*My first life as half–manifested, half–Yeti individual.*) I had to talk about it with Jeshua. I said, "I need to puff something in him so that he feels like he's hungry or he needs to eat the berries," so I talked to Jeshua about it.

D. I suddenly developed a taste for poison berries.

B. Ah. It's better than to be like hit with a tree in a storm or something. Because then you would have blamed me, saying like, "Why didn't you help me to move aside?" So it's better to say, "Well, you seemed hungry. Oopsie." Okay, so I'm gonna go now.

D. Before you leave, does Ophelia have any thoughts she would like to pass along?

B. Just be in your own space, she says. Because you, yourself, can create the mindset that you want to be in. Don't be influenced by like neighbors or people in passing. To create your own reality is crucial, she says. To not just be like a sponge—for good or bad. Sometimes, when you're a sponge and you just sort of take in influences, even if they are like–minded as you, it's not you. You need to create your own mind, your own mindset, your own willpower, your own reality within you. It's like you need to protect what is you, a little bit.

D. She's saying that to...?

B. Everyone. To be aware that, even if you are next to someone that is on the same level and of the same mind as you, it's not you. You need to be aware of creating your own space and your own reality within you. And it's important to shield your higher mind, your higher senses, and not be influenced so much by neighbors. Even if the neighbor is, you know, exactly like you. But it's not you. You need to start identifying who you are. And once you really understand who you are, then the shifts and the weather phenomenon, the winds around you, it's going to be much easier to just let them pass.

D. That's probably particularly appropriate at this time, since everyone seems to be all stirred up.

B. Indeed. And it's easy to be stirred up, even within your own group. But in order for you to do a change, to do good, you have to be in your own space. So it's crucial to sit and just listen. Sit in silence and just listen to what you find and what you feel within you. And to also, in that space, you will be able to detect if a thought or a feeling, even if it resonates with you, is not yours. So as long as you don't recognize who you are, then you just become like a collective thought. And it's important to try to break away from the collective at this point, in order for you to later join the collective. But if you just fly around like a leaf, you will not understand, fully, the power that you carry within you. It's a way to know how to maneuver.

D. That's really good advice

B. Ah. Okay, I'm gonna go now.

D. Thank you. And thank you, Ophelia.

B. You gave me a backpack. Another backpack. It was like filled with rocks, I thought. But it was not. It was actually filled with different crystals—rocks or stones—crystal stones from all fish tanks. It's a gift!

D. Oh, that's a nice gift.

B. Ah. And when I said, "What is this? It's just so heavy." And you said, "Open it." Inside here there is a rock and a crystal, or a meteor thing, a small thing. But like a sample from all fish tanks, even fish tank one.

D. Do they look similar?

B. Nay, they don't look similar.

D. So, there are distinct differences?

B. Distinct differences. One looked like a selenite ball. I have here now twelve. And you said that it's a gift and I'm gonna try to identify which one comes from where. But you have collected, from each fish tank, a sample. I put it in my backpack.

D. That's a nice present.

B. That's a nice present, isn't it?

D. Merry Christmas!

B. Merry Christmas to me.

B. Okay. I'm gonna go now. Toodeley–doo. Bye bye.

Willaby, Bob: The Library of Life Records (Mar 23, 2022)
We decided to include a session from 2022 where Willaby introduces himself. He has become a delightful contributor since this first talk, and has filled in our gaps of knowledge about life records and the incarnation program. He is a senior member of the Circle of Elders, which is the fifth dimension council that manages all life forms on our greenhouse planet, so they know more than anyone about the karma program and evolution. Willaby is the council member who approves the missions of the Elahim when they come to Earth. His mannerisms and way of speaking are so disarming that sometimes I miss the seriousness of what he is saying until I transcribe the recordings. Willaby long predates life on Earth and has not had to undergo the karma program. He did incarnate once, having a solitary existence as a shepherd, simply to experience nature and be with animals. When you read Willaby's ideas, it may be helpful to remember that his perspective of the human drama is both spiritual and timeless.

Years ago, Christine had a vision about a meeting where she (Seth) and Lasaray were going over final details prior to this lifetime. In addition to Bob, Ophelia, Jeshua, Isaac, and Gergen, there was a male entity in a white robe with a white beard standing alone on the opposite side of the table, listening to the discussion. She didn't know who it was, but Willaby mentioned the meeting and said that it was he who was listening and making recommendations. (This was revealed in another talk.)

In this session, Willaby tells us that a lot of souls are preparing to fold their Coats, which includes a final exam. They will be tested to maintain their spiritual composure when facing adversarial conditions. The graduates are handicapped with less soul percentage, while at the same time being challenged to respond and interact with the deluge of new Coats entering the program. One unusual statement he makes is that when the human was dumbed down around 10,000 years ago, the animals were also modified so that they would not be more spiritual and aware than the humans.

When Bob came in, he gave a truly fascinating description of the staging area where souls prepare for an upcoming incarnation. It is also where they return to document the experiences in their personal book of life. Bob paints a beautiful picture with his words of a place that all of us are very familiar with.

W. Excuse me. We will try to regulate the information in the vehicle. This is new friends. New friends. We have met. You can refer to us as the Circle of Elders. The Circle of Elders reside on the area of study in, on, in, on—what to use—the fifth dimension. We are eleven in numbers and we are the final councils allowing information to transpire and transform into the Earth plane. I am a close friend to you both. I am indeed involved in the meeting of the two, in human form, that is. You can call me Willaby. The intent of you both meeting in such a dramatic way was first rejected from your little brother. The importance, of course, is to also learn how to navigate through human emotions. And it's important for you to understand that the people around you are also human related in their capacity and feelings and thoughts, and so forth. In order for you to be able to understand fully, it was asked from your higher counsels, and friend such as Ophelia, Jeshua, and Isaac. Isaac, of course, wanted this to occur. Huh huh huh. It was, of course, an adjustment, as this little brother wanted to dive in directly into the project, coming in more in like an adult form. (*Meaning, a walk–in.*) But we said no no no no no. You have a memory of doing so, huh huh, but it is not possible at this time. The Circle of Elders, with me included, are eleven in numbers. We do not know if everyone will transpire in this way. You are mostly familiar with me, so I will take the microphone, as I have heard you call it. We are very much connected to the Earth's events and humanity, needing to balance humanity activity with the wellbeing and activity of the Earth plane, the environment and planet as a whole. Both having, you should know, all have—how can one put it—it's not karma when it comes to the planet and seas, but it's an understanding and growth, similar to the Coat of Karma that souls experience on a personal level. We have the collective coat, and we have the individual Coat. At the moment, we have allowed a lot of the emotional aspects in the Coats to be activated. But you should also know that the planet has its own progress and evolution to work through. It's mainly to adjust to changes in atmosphere and so forth. So, as you can see, we have two programs in place. There is the (*human*) activity and so forth, which is secondary. Man tend to think that they are the primary focus—that's fine, of course—however, the Council of Elders have different capacity and interest. And me, myself, work a lot with the balance of the two programs, the evolution versus the karma program, and how they interact. We were asked to wait until certain times were right for the two of you to be in this location where you are at currently. Feel the greatness of the land that you are on. It is clean, it is healed from old wounds. When you were in the area of the lakes and the Michigan area, that location has not been healed. That is why you did not feel happiness and connection to the land. That doesn't necessarily mean it's bad. It has simply not progressed. So, to answer your question, no no, it would not have been possible to do this kind of work and feel inviting for the higher healing capacity and be content if you have been physically located in that area. Huh huh. So there is a reason why we have waited for this moment when you are both physically located here (*in Sweden*). So, indeed, here we are.

D. It's nice to hear from you, finally.

W. It was, when we planned, it was also because of your friendships. There were several interested in communicating. Of course, Bob is a lovely spiritual friend and we allowed him more time, more platform. We have actually waited a little bit extra. And I'm not saying that it's not all good and all well to have him having more time, because it's absolutely deserved. But it was, in some way, intended for the fifth dimension (*to communicate*), which, if you think of it, has been somewhat sleeping—wouldn't you agree?

D. I totally agree. We know very little about what you do.

W. It was intended for us to come in at a later time. We are indeed more connected to the activity on the Earth plane, and we will be glad to assist you with questions when it comes to the Earth plane, as well as, I must say, to the activities in the fourth reality. Willaby is the name.

D. Have you ever participated in the Earth drama?

W. Huh, I–I–I must say, it was in an early stage. I came down tending to sheep, a shepherd. I wanted to observe the activity. This took place in the region which is northern France, Fraunce, depending on how you like to talk. I was a shepherd and it was mainly to... I wanted it to be... It was not karma. It was simply the experience of the land and the connection to animals. It was a while ago, but it was not to work on any specifics, like the karma program. I'm afraid to give you that information that I did not attend to that whole program. However, it was a joy, indeed, to simply allow oneself to travel as a vacation, if one can say. So, it was merely to experience a calmer side of life. To be in the center of my flock, even though they were not humans. It was a great connection in the group and I took great pride to tend to them. It wasn't to solve anything or to make something happen. And man should also be proud of those encounters, when lives come and go in a fashion of not necessarily inventing something. You have no idea of the soul contract and the soul intention. In my case, it was simply to be in the middle among the sheep. It was disturbing times of predators and I took care of them. I surrounded them with not only my light circle, but I also created like a fence. So, indeed, I did create those fences that you now see and that this one finds endearing—the ones that are a puzzle. I'm not saying that I invented them, but that is how I built the circle around my sheep. And it was a great joy to tend to them. (*He is describing the traditional Swedish stick fence, a style from ancient times. Long slender poles or saplings were cut and positioned so that one end was on the ground and angled at 25 to 30 degrees from horizontal, then tied to fence posts. The advantage is that the poles do not have to be cut into short pieces, which is hard work with a stone ax.*)

D. Wonderful.

W. So, I did do something, in that sense, because I did something for others. It was not necessarily others when it came to a human karma program. It was my flock of sheep.

D. Well, that's probably good experience, being on the council. Are you the one that kind of oversee what happens on Earth?

W. We are similar in level and order and status and development, but since I am the one that you have communicated the most with, me, Willaby, would be the one that might deliver certain messages. There are others. They are all here, of course. And you should know that Ophelia, Isaac, and Jeshua (*which he pronounced Jeh-shooo-WAH*) have all come in and allowed us now to speak. It is time, it is absolutely time. It is also to understand that when two programs collide, like they do at the current time—we have the human karma program, as you know, the volume has in some way increased. Meaning that a lot of Coats are about to fold. We are in a graduation cycle. Meaning, when certain Coats are about to fold, it also comes in challenges for those who are about to graduate. Meaning, we also invite those with new Coats. So, when we are in the cycle of graduation where certain Coats will be folded, and some will also deport, will not come back in a while. See it as somewhat of an exam for those in the end of their karma program. So, we invite a certain amount of events. So, what I can give you as information is that when there have been certain turmoils and peaks, it's actually the graduation systems that are in place. Meaning that there are certain Coats that are ready to graduate and depart. And when that happens, we invite new Coats, who will challenge the older one. And also, events will challenge the older ones. So it's a graduation program in this corner. At the same time, we also have a request from the higher councils. Some will not communicate, I'm sorry to say. But they will give information through me, Willaby, and I will try my best to tell you what is going on. There is some changes and adjustment in certain ocean beds. And also, spines need to be adjusted, as I'm pretty sure you have already heard of from Gergen and the others—also very connected, of course, to us. So, it's not a graduation program over here, but there are adjustments. As you can see, you are in that phase on the Earth plane where there are two rotations, two programs. One, where there's graduation. It's simply that there are more Coats graduating right now than, let's say, 1850, when there were less Coats graduating. But in order for them to graduate, how can one know which one is ready to graduate if there is not that extra touch of turmoil?

D. So, is it like the final exam?

W. Finally exam for graduation, indeed. And the final exam is: How do you handle the new Coats coming in with a lack of connection and, in some way, also displaying ignorance and lack of judgment? Also be aware that when a soul is about to fold the Coat, you come in with less soul energy then you have done in your earlier travels. So, from this little pool of knowledge that you have accumulated over your program and journeys, once it is time for graduation—you call it final exam—the soul energy coming in with a lower percentage, meaning it's harder to navigate and find your source, but there are also more challenges coming your way. How would you otherwise be allowed and understand the final exam? Do you understand the picture?

D. I do.

W. There you go. So, there is a time when there is a final exam for several—and it's not geographically just in certain locations. There are, it almost looks like a mountain range, it's a line. So we have a big line going from the Nordic countries, all the way down a little bit here to the to the east, going down through Poland, Hungary, down to Greece. There is a lot of exams going on, final exams. Meaning on the other side, there are more ignorant—maybe we should rephrase—more less–developed Coats. So, if we talk about Europe, we have (*put new souls*) in certain locations, hubs, let's say. We have London, we have Frankfurt, we have Brussels, we have Paris, in this beautiful countryside where I once went. It's actually a sadness to see the land of France, how it has changed. Once given such great strength and power but also been given so much in their own agriculture and land—and how that did not transpire into a greatness of giving. That is one of the lessons as a collective karma. Once you are given the opportunity to expand your knowledge or your agriculture, how do you channel that gift? Do you give, or do you conquer? And in the English region, we have seen a trend where one travels to conquer. Huh huh. That backfired, and it came back. So, we see and we observe. But there are Coats folding in the east block, from the Scandinavian countries, a little bit east, through a line down to Greece. Greece being, of course, a center of higher wisdom, at one point. I sense that I have taken up too much of your time, and I do apologize. It's a pleasure to finally come through, me, Willaby with my friends, with all of us.

D. I'm glad you come in. I've always been wondering what exactly happens on the fifth.

W. We will, indeed, discuss more about the intention of the karma program and the intention of evolution on Earth as a whole. It might be of interest to the Coats—to your readers—to understand and feel a sense of calm when it comes to certain events. Some, indeed, are in that final exam. But again, how do you meet challenges? So, it's not just a trumpet and a graduation festivity, it's also to encounter certain, more tricky, Coats and events.

D. This is slightly off topic, but I've always wondered, approximately how many lives do souls have before graduation? I know it varies a lot.

W. It varies and it has to do with the intention. It can also come to a pause, a long pause, between incarnation cycles. The general soul coming from the fifth reality has a tendency to, in a human form, to be around 548 lives. That is somewhat of a format. However, it also depends on their design. There are also those who are up to 2300. I would say that that would be the limit. So from 548 up to 2300 is a general outline of lives, normally. But it depends. When I say 548, that specific soul might have a different set-up, a blueprint, in the beginning. So it depends on the total intent. Also know that the karma program has changed over time. Now you bring in a different kind and amount of soul energy that you did not (*bring*) before. Also, do you there (*Lasaray*), do you count like the mole lives as a life? So, some of these lives are also, could be later on, as a mole. And it can actually happen before a Coat has been folded. Normally, it's to pay back, if someone has not fulfilled its mission, it offers oneself the opportunity to be passive. So it can actually sometimes happen that a soul pays tribute to the spirit realm by offering 2 percent and being somewhat numb. But do you

count that as a life? Because then it's not part of the karma program.
D. I see the point there. When did the karma program begin in earnest?
W. The true karma program, as it is designed as of now, started about 7000 BC. 7000 to 10,000 BC. There was a gradual change, an upgrade, around 10,000 BC area. Before it was incarnation, as you like to call it, but it was in a different capacity. And it had nothing to do with the amount of soul energy—it hasn't really changed that much over the timeline. However, the design in the brain, predominantly, was different. Meaning, even if you had a 30 percent now versus 30 percent then, it was a different experience before 10,000 BC, because the filters in the brain were different. It was a higher connection to the soul mind.
D. So the karma program is somewhat related to the type of vehicle?
W. Type of vehicle, indeed. So, the amount of soul energy is somewhat similar in the way we talk about 2 percent. Not to be confused about traveling here in manifested form. We do not necessarily work with that. That is other of your friends. But when it comes to incarnation and when it comes to traveling in with parts of your soul energy, it's been somewhat similar over eons. It's just basically changed, depending on the design and manufacturing in the bottles.
D. I completely understand.
W. The karma program you asked about, as of right now, it started somewhat around 10,000 BC. It was a cooling that went down in the general area where there was a lot of snow and ice and cooling, and that is when it was a new cycle. (*Willaby precisely identified the beginning of the Younger Dryas, which was a 1000–year period of cooling in the northern hemisphere. The spirit realm triggered volcanic activity to coincide with modifications to the atmosphere and lifeforms.*) As we went into the cooling program, the brain and the modification in the bottle adjusted. Not just in humans, you should know. Also, in animal lives. It's a balance. You cannot necessarily have the leading mammal with less brain capacity than like an animal who understands, because there has to be a balance, in that sense. So, we very much adjust in all species. It is to create a sense of harmony within the animals. At this current time, for instance, there is a lot of consciousness in the elephants. They understand more of what is going on, and there is a sadness in the group. So we are working progressively to somewhat

minimize the understanding of what is happening around them as a group. So, there is a great sense of warmth around (*them*) that we send a circle—similar like I did with my sheep—we surround the group of elephants. There is a sadness in this great mammal, and they understand more than one maybe hope for. So we try to surround them and help them, gradually modifying, together with the second dimension, just modifying the direction towards understanding. It's so there's no sadness, in that sense. You can see the dilemma. If someone doesn't have the power to lead and control—maybe control is a bad word—to set the pace of others, if you do not have that capacity because your physical form is different, but you understand more than those who do (*are in control*), there is an imbalance. And, of course, you can see that there will be a need to put a pause. That's what we also did when there was this winter that came in, with the greater mammals. We're not making them fall asleep, the capsule, we simply want to modify their understanding. And sometimes we do it directly in the physical, but we can also—shh, do not say to the Little One—but we can also send in a wind and put somewhat of a blankie. It feels almost like someone has taken that (*he makes motion like smoking a joint of marijuana*), so they become a little bit numb. So, we do have tricks.

D. It seems like if you're taking a lot of the graduating students off and leaving the young ones behind—

W. Ah! But you do not know who is coming in, do you?

D. (*Laughing.*) No. An improved version?

W. An improved version. It's not a V-8 engine it's a V-10. Huh huh huh. Humor, it's important. So, I think I made my point by showing myself here for you, my friends. And I must say that I am proud of you and little brother (*Seth*). I knew—this one told you about a scene in the memory of having an outline of when to come down. Do you remember?

D. Yes. I do.

W. Pointed where on the plan. I was on the other side of that table. Tell this one that I'm here now. So, from that scene it was him, it was you, it was also Isaac standing on that side of the table. And we put out a scroll to show where the two of you should meet, and so forth. On the other side, observing this whole plan taking form, there was me, in white. To just give you a picture, we kinda portray ourself, a little bit, in human form. It's also because there are plenty of souls related to Earth. So you can see myself in white. I show myself with white hair and a little bit of a white beard. Not long as a Merlin, huh huh. I'm a little bit rounder in my figure and I'm not as tall, not as grand. Huh huh. But some have a need for something grand, and they see a Merlin. (*He changes how he appears, based on the observer.*) I'm smaller and rounder in my shape. But yes, indeed, it was me observing the final touch of the three of you coming in. (*Seth, Lasaray, and Bob.*) Okay, I'll probably leave at this time, but you will hear more from us.

D. Good! I hope so. I really enjoyed speaking with you today.

W. Yah, yah. So, if there is no more questions at this time, I think that I will allow another friend to come through.

D. I always have questions.

B. (*Bob came in and said nothing, but was making faces which cannot be misidentified. So I said goodbye to Willaby.*)

D. Goodbye, Willaby.

B. (*Bob turned to the left and mimicked me, rather loudly.*) GOODBYE, Willaby. Goodbye, Willaby.

D. (*Laughing.*) You know him, don't you? He spoke highly of you.

B. We've met. Well, I speak highly of him, too, because he always gives me like extra assignments. He's actually sometimes the one that— and it doesn't just have to do with you, or the two of you—he actually gives me like notes to pop down into both of you. Like where to go, or what to do. So, he is, in some way, a puppet master. A silent one. Silent until today! Huh huh. I like him. I'm not allowed to come to their council meetings; but there's no need. He's a little bit like Ole, just not so small. He somewhat has the same role.

D. It sounded like he was pretty well involved with what is going on here.

B. Ah. In different ways than me. But there is a big group, and they sit in like a big temple. It's similar like that temple I saw on Etena, it's quite similar. Maybe they have like a general design when they build things. Huh huh. I don't know.

D. Everyone likes the pyramids.

B. Ah. But this is not a pyramid. It almost looks like the Pantheon. It has really tall pillars, and it's an area of study. Zachariah is somewhere around here in all his classes. But this is an area of study when it comes to the Earth plane. It looks like the Pantheon but it's bigger, it runs longer. There are places where they study. There's also like really nice gardens outside. I've been here, you know, wandered a little bit with Zachariah. Sometimes with

Zachariah, I just sort of tag along. I said, "It's fine if you just want to sort of ponder out loud. If you have an issue or something, sometimes the answer comes just by saying it out loud." Huhuh! And he said, "I say it out loud." I said, "I don't think you do." And he said, "I muffle the barriers of sound to you." But I've been walking here with Zachariah a lot. It's a wonderful energy of knowledge. And you can see all this preparation for Earth, and all those coming back having life reviews. And there's an area also with libraries in here. It's a lot of activity! It's not AT ALL like your lab, not at all. It's like a lot. And everyone wears white, including me. Zachariah has a little bit of—and the other teachers—has a little bit of a different color on. They aren't pure white. Maybe it's just to show....

D. Their status? (*The teachers wear white robes but have colors, crystals, or emblems on their upper body to signify who they are and where they are from.*)

B. Status.

D. Is this Pantheon anywhere near the main Library?

B. Ah. You know how they built, we saw—you saw—that documentary about Alexandria? Similar like that. It's like a city almost, if I give you human terms. So it's like the Pantheon and then there are similar Pantheons, but they are libraries. It's very similar to Alexandria, the way it was built, the way it was intended. And it was also because some of the (*ancient Greek*) engineers actually had a direct contact, and in some way tried to mirror this spiritual reality on the fifth. So all the Earth journals are stored here somewhere, and it's also where you go to class when you prepare for a life. To give you a picture here, you know, you come from the sixth but every time you travel (*to Earth*), you come and you prepare (*here*). And before the final departure from the spirit realm, you actually all stay and gather information and collect data on this area on the fifth, before you transfer through the fourth down into a human body. It's like a....

D. A staging area?

B. Ah. And you read up and you get in contact with your Earth books, if you like, and your Earth journals. Because when you come back from an Earth life and you leave a report, it's predominantly done in this area. You can do it visually, or inside your being in different ways, but it's all stored here. BUT the soul experience—because this is the human experience—the soul experiences is a different journal, and that is brought home to where you originally belong.

D. So the difference between what the soul records and what the records of the human experience is—

B. Different.

D. So the soul records are the spiritual essence of what things meant? The lessons specific to the soul?

B. Ah. So it's important also to know that certain things are stored within you like an inner journal, and that is just traveling with you. It's like you eat and you just grow as you eat. You don't want to be fat, but you want to be spiritually fat, if you get my meaning here. Your Coat is folded, but you look like you do, but the inner soul energy is fat. Huh huh. It has expanded based on eating, based on accumulating and getting information. It's like being full, like you have eaten what is available on the table, and that's when you fold. So, the soul experience is brought home but it's not necessarily left like in a book, or in a storage unit, or on records. It stays within you.

D. Part of your knowledge?

B. Part of your knowledge. And I'm just giving you a way to see it. It's like you just expand.

D. So your spiritual being becomes larger and brighter?

B. Larger and brighter. But the way you look doesn't change. It's just that—it's like the lemonade—you start with like a lot of watery lemonade in your soul. But as more and more knowledge is accumulated and filled, it's like it just becomes more and more of a concentrated lemonade. And finally, there's no water. Do you see what I'm saying?

D. I do. That's a great description.

B. So, that is the soul journey. But the human journey is stored on record in this great area of study and libraries, and so forth. I like to go here because this is where Gergen took me. He didn't take me in here first, we went into the gardens. A lot of times, you see cluster groups walking around, either two–and–two (*a pair*), then you know that there is like some sort of consultation going on between them. And sometimes when there's a group of four and six that travels, then they are normally headed to class. And sometimes I'm trying to ask those groups that are passing—I don't interfere when there is a two group because it feels like you should not—but when I see a group heading for study, I'm always curious. You know, like, "What are you going to study?" Sometimes, I see like a group of four or six, normally, never more than six. One actually talked to me, and I said, "What are you doing? Where are you going?" And she said, "We are a soul family and we're going to be a soul family on Earth. We're just getting the last information," as they were walking. And I walked next to them. But what I also detected then was that behind me, further back, about five meters behind me, there was Zachariah. Ah, huh huh. But at least they shared. So, they were a group of souls heading to get their final briefing because they were going to be soul family. Some were gonna be cousins and some were gonna be siblings—they were like six that walked (*in the group*). So when I see that, I know that there is like preparation and briefing going on for Earth, in this area of study.

D. What's the general attitude like among souls that are headed to Earth? Are they happy, or—

B. Happy! Happy. Those who walk around here, I've only seen happy. But there are chambers where there are certain transformations or adjustments in the energetic sense of self that take place. It's mainly to try to clean certain old behaviors that are not beneficial for the journey. It's not like they are removed, they are simply—it's like a healing chamber, similar looking like my bubble. And there are workers surrounding this sphere where this soul is in. And it has to do with certain past behaviors that will make the soul a little bit hesitant to go. It is a somewhat of an encouraging, healing sphere. But they don't do it by themselves. That's why I said it looked almost like my bubble, because I can see that they are round. It modifies and encourages a soul who knows that it has a tendency to fall into old behaviors. But this group that came, this group of six, they were just happy. They didn't go to a transformation sphere or an encouraging bubble.

D. There must be a lot of souls around, if everyone who goes to Earth is running through there?

B. Indeed. In some way. But like when the two of you came here, a lot of times you just come and have a look-see in your book, and then you go. It's not necessarily like you sit and stay for a long time—especially not you, because you don't have the Coat. So you are not briefed about what to encounter, you are just briefed about the mission. You're not briefed about, "Okay, I'm going to face this and this. I'm going meet this and this individual to work on the emotional or mental stress. And I'm going to do this and this." You are basically just sort of getting an outline, and that's all you need. In your case, when you looked briefly, glanced into your book on the way down, you were like, "Okay, I'm going to be born there. I'm going to go to school—check, check, check—and there she is. Meet my brother there." And then you left. Everything else was secondary, you know, like the details were secondary. You just saw it like a big "Z". Born. Study. Work. Meet. It looked like a big Z pattern".

D. And here we are.

B. And here we are. But this one had a memory of meeting the soul that is now her mother. And they have been sitting and learning things in a classroom, when this one started some of the journeys way back. So the two of them met. So, it's also to meet souls that you travel to Earth with, and that normally take place in this area. So, the daughter and the mother in this life, they tend to meet here. It's a calming place. It's a lot of gardens—I will have this one draw it for you. It's in an L shape here. Here is the Pantheon, the long one, and it goes in like an L shape. And here is like gardens. And over there it's a different Pantheon temple, and that's more of a library, it seems. (*Bob was gesturing towards where everything was, from his inner perspective.*)

D. What about the ones that are returning? Do they come back to the same place, or is there a different area for them?

B. Well, the records are stored here. Preparation classrooms and returning classrooms are not necessarily the same, because when you return you have to reflect. You can't just go hide among your friends, because then it's not a true reporting, is it? So, when you come back, you don't go into a bubble unless you all are in need of a cleansing experience when you return. If it's basically to record life events, when you return—I mean, I can only talk about you. I don't know what the others are doing. But with you, when you come from the sixth, you come to a place and then there's a little pedestal, and there is your book. Then you come in, and in this life, you were like, "That's the Z". (*Bob made a Z shaped motion with his finger, which was the pattern of the life-path written in Lasaray's book. It goes sequentially from birth to death. The main goals and intentions include education, work locations, people, and footprints.*). And then you left. This book is always open for you to return to, like in meditation and dreams. And you can return here and look through to get information. And you do, because you need more information (*during life*). You did that a lot when you were the important scientist. You did return to find different inventions and how you could upgrade certain things when you dreamt, and so forth. But when you die, when you return, you look and you come back and you fill in the Z. Did you go as the Z (*follow the original plan*) as a human? That's what you're gonna do when you return.

And if you come back and you see, "Uh–oh, I did not do the Z, I did a circle." Then the reporting is different. I'm not saying that it's a letter, but it's a pattern. And when you come back as a soul, you are supposed to fill in (*in your life book*) did the pattern actually become. So, in your case, we have the Z. You went (*to Earth*) and you were born there (*he points to the top left corner of the Z*) in West Virginia, studied engineering over there (*moves finger*), you worked there in Michigan, studied (*spiritual research*), work over there, and then here we met. But if you did not do that, then you might come back and write in your book the letter O, or the letter B. Then the journey wasn't complete. It might not have been wrong, you might have taken a different shortcut, but what we want to see is that you come to the end result. So when a soul comes back and reports, this first reporting, it's supposed to fill in the form, or the image, that was the last imprint they saw, and just see if it matches. And then you continue.

D. So how did we do?

B. Well, you are here, so it's all fine. I don't see this one's book. But, let's say, that you did NOT fulfill. So when you returned, based on your choices, then you might have just gone to Michigan and stayed there. You might not have gone traveling and worked in other places, and you might not have met this one. So when you came back, you only drew that first line, because that was the only thing that transpired by the journey.

D. I see what you are saying.

B. And it's a little bit different when you don't have a Coat. You don't have to, you know, "Uh–oh. Do over." But still, due to the power of choice, you want to also, when you come back, you want to color that image that the outline was. There's no words in this (*book*), simply symbols. So when the soul comes back, it reflects and it fills in (*stores life review in the book*). And then, "Did it actually become the intended pattern?" Let's say that the image is like little stars, like five stars, five area of development. And when the soul came back it saw like, "Oh, I think I did that one, and that one, and that one. But those two, I did not." And they have to be honest, and sometimes a light being is assisting here. All events come with a color. So, let's say that these five stars that the soul sees coming down, let's say that they are like green, blue, red, yellow, orange. And the first one that was supposed to be green, meaning, that specific event and teaching in that area, and the soul comes back and it instantly and directly paints it blue. Then it didn't really become the intended plan for that specific knowledge. Do you see what I'm saying? I'm not gonna, you know, exhaust the topic, but you kinda understand the outline here?

D. Yes. I do follow the concept.

B. So, (*as it leaves for Earth*) a soul looks in its book, it has patterns, it has an image, it has colors. And when a soul comes back, it fills in the colors of the actual events and happenings. And then, that is how it is stored and understood.

D. So for each life, as you flip through the pages, you see all these patterns that represent what you learned and what you did?

B. Ah. And it's your main spirit guide that organizes the specific image. And they are different. So, if I flip in your book, it's not like we have Zs all through. Some are maybe like with circles and different things, and other kinds of symbols—and you have to color them. And as you do, it will either match or not match. So, let's say that you came down to learn about compassion and love. And then you come home and directly you feel, "Oh, I loved myself." Huh huh. "Oh, but did you love others?" So those two colors will not match. So that's how reporting takes place. So, you see?

D. (*Laughing.*) Yes. I do. That's interesting because we don't get a whole lot of information on the fifth.

B. More is gonna come. And I'm also maybe allowed to talk. But maybe not. Today the important thing was to understand the reporting. So, I'm not gonna be too long in the tooth—I might have a separate session.

D. That's good. We're trying to get back into the swing of things and start accumulating more sessions.

B. And it's gonna come more like, huh huh, easy topics, some of them. And I have new adventures planned for me, you said. We're gonna go places.

D. By easy topics, do you mean things that humans will understand?

B. Could relate to. Like in this case, we talked about the area of preparation, and the area of return and recovery. And also how the whole reporting of the incarnation program is established. It's basically—a lot of it has to do with—sometimes it's colors and sometimes it could be (*symbols*). Let's say we have a star and you can come back and you're supposed to put the star in, like a puzzle piece. Let's take the topic again of you coming down to be a good leader. So you were given certain personality benefits to be that. And then you come back (*after life*) and you really put in the puzzle piece on how you solved that. And if it doesn't match, then there's also a teaching in that. But a lot of times it has to do with colors.

So you come down and you look through and it's like, "Okay, here we have all those colors representing certain aspects of the journey, and also where that specific event or lesson should take place and in what field—mental, emotional, and so forth." And then you come back (*and are asked*), "How did you solve that assignment?" And then you color, authentically and organically, on how that really happened. And then there is a match, more or less. And that is how it is stored and read.

D. It does make me wonder, though. If you have all this pre-planning that goes into all these lives, it suggests everything is very highly choreographed?

B. Ah!

D. It's almost like the future is somewhat predetermined, in a general way. Is that true?

B. Ah. I would think so. But they don't tell me, because if they tell me, I might tell. A lot of this is Willaby and his friends, because they are the great planners for outcomes and the general evolution. But they are connected to the Evolution Group and are on different councils. Again, it's like a cone. Everything sort of comes down and it follows through this grand Circle of Elders. They don't share—I mean, I'm friends with Willaby—but he doesn't always share. He's very much, you know, he puts his arms around me—he's not as strict as Zachariah. He's like Ole, but he takes his time and we wander a little bit here and he allows me to communicate and meet—meet and greet, and so forth. But I'm not participating.

D. You're not helping with the decision making?

B. Not as of yet.

D. Does Ole ever assist?

B. Ole and Gergen. But they don't have a permanent chair. With the Circle of Elders, it's not like Ophelia and Gergen have a permanent chair. But there are two guest chairs on the other side of where Willaby sits. Those (*guests*) are always changing, depending on the topic at hand, I would assume. So if I ever get in, I'm gonna be over there at 9 o'clock on the guest chair. But I'm not there yet. I don't even know where they gather. I've asked, "Where do you have your meetings?" And it's silence about the topic. So I don't know, I haven't seen where they sit. But there are two guest chairs. Sometimes Ophelia comes, and Isaac and Jeshua come. So when there was this meeting about certain things with the two of you, then Isaac and Ophelia came. Jeshua, I don't know if he also came by.

D. There's a lot of coordination that has to occur.

B. Ah, mmm. Planning. So, I'm going to go now but I'm gonna come back.

D. I hope so. Thank you for all that wonderful information.

B. It's just a little detour of where I've been.

D. I think people will be really interested to read about that.

B. Ah. It's not just about me and my travels, it's also for the greater good. And Willaby said that, "Sometimes, you have to take a step back and give information that is more beneficial for someone else." So, okay, that will be it. But I'm not gonna say that I'm gonna be with them, because I'm not invited yet.

D. Go wander in the garden by yourself.

B. Huh huh. I mean, there are friends here that you can talk to. But I'm not disturbing if there's a couple, because I'm thinking that there's some sort of consultation going on. Sometimes I see them sitting on benches in the garden.

D. Like when you and Isaac walked through the gardens there?

B. Exactly. That was a consultation. It was like coaching and pampering and taking care of my concerns. Okay, so I'm gonna go now. It's important, though, to talk about these levels because there are a lot of people who have recollections of this area. So it is important to talk about that. Not everyone will understand, you know, about creating a galaxy or traveling in my peanut-suit and everything that you do, you know, like when galaxies rip. It might be confusing for some. So we also want to take it down a notch, and that's what Willaby said. We have to also think of the greater good for the general interests. It's important to know the whole design of how things are operating.

D. We can't ignore an entire dimension.

B. Nay. And they're gonna come through more frequently. Well, okay, so off I go.

D. Alright, my friend.

B. Okay. bye bye.

Christine and I made the final changes and corrections to this book from our summer cottage, which is located on a beautiful island in the Swedish archipelago. Surrounded by nature, with few distractions, we deliberated on how best to balance the messages from our spirit friends. It should be understood that "we" means Christine, myself, and Bob. He is ever-present and always within earshot of our conversations. There is seldom a day that goes by when he doesn't make himself known, always eager to share his insight or wit. When we are unsure about something, I will just ask Bob a question and he will tell Christine or step in and speak directly to me, as he did in June of 2024, when he gave us this final message for the book. Christine and I were sitting on the porch, reflecting on something Bob had previously articulated, when he stepped in and said, "I want people to be excited about evolution and to understand that they are participating in evolution. Evolution is not something just placed upon them, it's for everyone to create. You have to create the garden around you. If you don't plant the flowers, the garden you seek will not exist. It's not like hard science, really. It's not so tricky. But you have to be willing to participate." This beautiful message captures the very essence of the spiritual design as it relates to humans. As we close *Wave 4*, we hope you found a few seeds to plant in your own life. When we meet again in *Wave 5*, we will present material delivered by our spirit friends in 2022 and 2023.

Acknowledgments

It is with deep gratitude that we acknowledge the indispensable contributions of our editors to this *Wave 4*. If you came to this page after reading the preceding ones, you are aware that the content is highly esoteric in places, and the sentence structure often drifts towards the unconventional. To thoroughly edit this 173,000-word manuscript demanded monumental patience as well as a deep familiarity with the subject matter, which very few people have. It is our great fortune that both Susanne and Kari possess those credentials and have dedicated themselves as partners in this project with the spirit realm.

Kari Beckstrand has been part of this work since 2018, and contributed her editing skills to improve our last three books. She attended our first-ever public talk at the Full Moon bookstore in Lakewood, Colorado, and has participated in most of the spiritual development classes and public séances that we have hosted since then. Kari works in the field of human healing as a licensed Professional Counselor. We hope the children and families whom she counsels appreciate her gentle spiritual nature as much as we do. Kari, being in a younger generation, has agreed to be one of those who conserve the library of our work and radiate it into the future.

Susanne Kromm has helped to edit every book we have published. She is also the one who does the bulk of the translations into Swedish. Susanne studied to be a teacher and is fluent in Swedish, German, and English. So, when translating from English to Swedish, she sometimes translates into German first, to find better matches with Swedish words. For that reason, the Swedish translations are incredibly accurate versions of the English. Susanne has listened to many of the sessions and will make corrections based on her understanding of the material. And finally, she offers kind guidance when the tone of my commentary wanders away from the spiritual purpose of our work. In the summer months, Susanne nurtures a wonderful garden where many second dimension spirits are welcomed and present.

About the Authors

Christine Kromm Henrie is a spiritual channel, a certified past life and between lives soul regression therapist, psychic, and karmic astrologer. She was born and lived in Stockholm, Sweden until 2014, when she moved to the US and married David Henrie, with whom she now shares her work.

She had an intense spiritual awakening in 2009, during a past life regression, which became the starting point for her practice with the higher realms. She began to receive messages and visions from her spirit guides about her soul assignment to develop the skills needed for them to speak through her. Accepting their advice, she studied different modalities of mediumship, psychic development and astrology in Sweden and England during the next five years. This intensive training enabled her to perfect the link and the ability to maintain this altered state for extended periods of time.

After moving to the US, her formal training continued in soul regression and hypnotherapy, becoming a licensed regression therapist. Christine has three offices in Stockholm, Sweden, where she offers private soul regressions and progressions, assisting people to recall lessons from past lifetimes and memories from their spiritual home. Past life regression and astrological consultations are also available online.

A near-death experience at age eleven, and a transcendental epiphany in his early twenties, led **David Henrie** to lifelong inquiry into the nature of the spirit. His studies focused on NDE's, reincarnation, spiritualism, and the theological beliefs within Buddhism and other pre-Christian religions. After a lengthy career as a petroleum engineer and executive in the US, he now lives in Sweden, where his time is dedicated to writing and research. David conducts the trance sessions and converses with the spirits Christine channels. He transcribes the recorded dialogues and assembles the teachings into their co-authored books.

Christine and David give lectures about the channeled material and the regression work, helping people to remember their soul mission and purpose. Their practice and publishing imprint is through **Access Soul Knowledge**, a Swedish company.

For further information, please visit:
www.AccesSoulKnowledge.com.

www.ingramcontent.com/pod-product-compliance
Lightning Source LLC
Chambersburg PA
CBHW030509080526
44586CB00011B/123